© 2018 BlackStone Tutors Ltd
Published by BlackStone Tutors Ltd
www.blackstonetutors.co.uk
Email: info@blackstonetutors.co.uk
Tel: +44 (0)20 3393 8934

ISBN: 978-1-9996701-1-5

TABLE OF CONTENTS

BMAT SECTION 1 WORKED SOLUTIONS

BMAT Section 1 - 2003

1)   The correct answer is E

From the calibration graph, it can be deduced that the water fills the tank slowly at the bottom, becoming faster in the middle and once again slowing down as it reaches near the top. This means that the tank is wider at the bottom and the top than it is in the middle.

Only the vertical cross-sectional shape of the tank given in option E can have this effect on the increase in the height of water in the tank.

2)   The correct answer is C (People who buy ready meals are unaware of their healthy properties)

The passage talks about "Ready meals" and the undesirable effects they can have on our health. Sale of these ready meals is significantly increasing, and due to the risk they pose to our long-term health, the argument says that they should be labelled with health warnings in the same way as cigarettes are.

Statement C would strengthen the argument by stating that people buy and use ready meals because they are not aware of their unhealthy properties. This adds to the reasoning of the argument and strengthens the necessity of labelling prepared meals with health warnings.

Statements A and B would weaken the argument because it would mean that people may be aware of the unhealthy properties of ready meals, but they still buy them because they have no other choice. So, the conclusion of the argument would be invalid.

Statement D only addresses the dangers of ready meals for our health and does not consider other unhealthy lifestyles and habits. So, this statement is irrelevant to the reasoning or conclusion of the passage and thus cannot be considered as either strengthening or weakening the argument.

Statement E is a generalised stereotype, and one cannot accurately predict how each consumer would respond to a health warning on one of these meals.

3)   The correct answer is B (33)

The best way to identify the incorrect entry is to check each one against the total figures in their corresponding rows or columns. If the sum from adding the numbers in a particular row or column does not match with the total given in that row or column, the entry is therefore incorrect.

The first option gives 14, which, in the table can be found in the second row (Bus) of the first column (Year 7). Adding 14 with the other numbers row-wise or column-wise, the total figures, 76 row-wise and 150 column-wise, are correct. So, 14 is not the answer.

By doing this for each option, the number 33, given in option B, is the answer because it is the only number given in the options which, when added to the other numbers in its row and column, gives a different figure than the given total in the table. 33 is in the first row (Car) of the second column (Year 8)

The total with the other numbers in that row will come to 30 + 33 + 16 + 18 + 10 = 107, but the given total in the table is 102. Likewise, the total with the other numbers in that column will come to 33 + 16 + 12 + 89 = 150, but the given total in the table is 145.

4)   The correct answer is C (The government's action is likely to deter poorer students from going to university more than richer).

The passage says that the government has changed the way in which it provides financial support for students and provides loans that the student must repay when he or she enters employment. It also says that research has shown that students from more impoverished families are more likely to be deterred from going to university by the prospect of debt. Therefore, it can be inferred that students from poorer families are more likely to be discouraged from going to university due to the government's action (option C).

Option A can be excluded due to the prospect of debt being the deterrent, not a lack of interest in further study.

Statement B is irrelevant to the passage.

Statement D is not correct because the passage states that students from poorer families are more likely to be deterred by the prospect of debt.

Statement E is irrelevant as the reading does not suggest any reason for the government's decision to change the way in which it provides financial support for students.

5)   The correct answer is 109

Since the cabbages were laid in a square grid, the number of cabbages in a grid will always be a square of a number, for example, 5^2. The number of cabbages left or missing when he tried two square grids was 9 + 12 = 21. Therefore the two numbers have squares with a difference of 21. $10^2 = 100$ and $11^2 = 121$, and the difference between them is 21. So, the square grids he tried were of 10 and 11. The first grid with 100 cabbages, had nine left therefore he had 109 cabbages in total. The answer can be verified with the second grid in which he needed 12 more cabbages to complete the grid of 121. So, the number of cabbages he had was $121 - 12 = 109$.

6)   The correct answer is D (Internet voting would unfairly discriminate against some sections of society).

The passage examines the practical issues involved in introducing the option of voting via the Internet. It also states that it may be undemocratic because it would give an unfair advantage to those parties whose voters tend to be young and better educated.

The core message of the argument, or its conclusion, is that internet voting would unfairly discriminate against some sections of society who are not comfortable with computers and internet. Thus, statement D is the correct choice.

The other statements given in the options cannot be considered as they do not reflect the fundamental reason for the author to write the passage or the main message the author intends to convey.

7)   The correct answer is A (14)

The average length of a surgery session in 1995 was 140 minutes.

Consultation appointments are made 10 minutes apart

So, number of patients seen = 140/10 = 14

8)   The correct answer is 27

For 1995:

Average number of surgery sessions a week = 8.5

Average length of a surgery session = 140 minutes

Time spent on surgery in a week= 8.5 x 140 minutes = 1190 minutes

Average time spent on home visits a week = 408 minutes

Total time spent on surgery and home visits in a week = 1190 + 408 = 1598 minutes or 26.63 hours

Therefore, to the nearest hour, the average family doctor spends 27 hours on surgery and home visits in 1995.

9)   The correct answer is C (4)

For 2000:

Average number of patients seen per week = 155

If the doctors work for 50 weeks per year, number of patients seen in a year:

$$= 155 \times 50 = 7750$$

There are 5000 family doctors, so total number of patients seen in a year:

$$= 7750 \times 5000 = 38750000$$

Population of Santesia   = 10000000

So, number of times the average patient sees their family doctor is:

$$= 38750000 \div 10000000$$

$$= 3.875 \text{ or approximately 4 times.}$$

10)   The correct answer is D (183 minutes)

If the number of family doctors was cut to 4500, but the total number of consultations and surgery sessions remained the same, then the total working time by the lower number of doctors must still equal that by the 5000 doctors.

This can be represented by the equation: *5000 X 165 = 4500 X t,* where *t* is the working times the 4500 doctors will have to put in.

$$t = \frac{5000 \times 165}{4500}$$

$$t = 183.33$$

Therefore, an average surgery session has to be at least 183 minutes.

11)   The correct answer is A (average length of a surgery session)

The number of patients seen per week increased from 1995 to 2000 by 15.

Considering the options provided and their corresponding values in the table, options B, C and D remain more or less the same for 1995 and 2000. There is a significant change only in the average length of a surgery session which increased by 25 minutes. This is the factor that contributed most to the rise in numbers of patients seen per week between 1995 and 2000.

12)   The correct answer is A

To find the right answer, the average numbers of patients seen per week in home and surgery consultations during the two years must be known.

The total average number of patients per week is 135 in 1995 and 155 in 2000.

The charts from the options show that all of them with the exception of A have the total numbers of these two years higher than the actual numbers. So, only A can be the correct answer.

This can be verified by these figures as follows:

The average length of a consultation in 1995 is 9:59 minutes, rounded up it to 10 minutes.

The average length of a surgery session is 140 minutes

So, the average number of patients seen in a session = 140 ÷ 10 = 14

The average number of surgery sessions a week = 8.5

Total average of patients seen in consultations per week = 14 X 8.5 = 119

The average time spent on home visits a week = 408 minutes

The average length of a home visit = 25.5

The average number of patients seen in-home visits in a week = 408 ÷ 25.5 = 16

The average length of a consultation in 2000 is 10 minutes.

The average length of a surgery session is 165 minutes.

Therefore, the average number of patients seen in a session = 165 ÷ 10 = 16.5

The average number of surgery sessions a week = 8.4

The total average of patients seen in consultations per week = 16.5 X 8.4 = 138.6 OR 139

The average time spent on home visits a week = 412 minutes

The average length of a home visit = 25

The average number of patients seen in-home visits in a week = 412 ÷ 25 = 16.48 OR 16

This means that for 1995, the ratio of patients seen in consultation versus the number that was seen in in-home visits = 119: 16

Moreover, for 2000, the ratio of patients seen in consultation versus the number that was seen in in-home visits = 139: 16

13)   The correct answer is B (27)

To find the right answer, consider each option and reduce each number by 1/3 three times, there should be eight left after the third.

By doing this, or option B (27), is the correct answer.

1/3 of 27, 9 people get off at the first stop leaving 18.

1/3 of 18, 6 people get off at the second stop, 12 remain.

1/3 of 12, 4 people get off at the third stop, and finally, 8 remain who get off at the fourth stop.

14)   The correct answer is E (It assumes that excessive Internet use causes isolation and obesity).
The passage points out the serious and undesirable effects of excessive use of the internet. It states that some teenagers are spending as much as eight hours a day using the Internet and that both isolation and obesity are increasing amongst children. It urges parents to enforce stricter controls to make sure that the Internet is not causing their children to have long-term physical and emotional ill health.
The main flaw in the argument is that it assumes excessive Internet use causes isolation and obesity. While the internet and isolation and obesity may be correlated, excessive internet usage does not necessarily lead to isolation and obesity.
Statement A is not true, as the aim of the passage is to point out the ill effects of the excessive use of the internet, not its benefits. Statement B only mentions teenagers who spend eight hours per day using the Internet as an example to show excessive usage; hence this can also be excluded.
Both statements C and D are not flaws in the argument.

15)   The correct answer is C (97)
First, calculate how many matches there are for each of the teams in one group:
Teams have been assigned the names A, B, C, D, E and F.
Team A has two matches each against B, C, D, E and F = 22 X 5 = 10
Team B's matches against A have already been included, so B has two matches each against C, D, E and F = 2 X 4 = 8
Team C's matches against A and B have been included previously, so C has two matches each against D, E and F = 2 X 3 = 6
Team D's matches against A, B and C have already been included, so D has two matches each against E and F = 2 X 2 = 4
Team E's matches against A, B, C, and D have already been included, so E has two matches against F = 2 X 1 = 2
F's matches against A, B, C, D and E have already been included.
Therefore the total number of matches played within one pool = 10 + 8 + 6 + 4 + 2 = 30
Total number of in-pool matches played in two pools = 60
Six teams in a pool have to play the other six teams in the other pool one time each
Total number of inter-pool matches = 6 X 6 = 36
The total number of matches now adds up to 60 + 36 = 96
With the final match, this number becomes 97, option C.

16)   The correct answer is C
From the graphs, the only ones that show proper areas defined by the intersection of *x* and *y* are A, C and D.
In option A, the shaded area is outside the defined area, while the graph in option D does not correctly represent the condition: y>2, since according to this graph, *x>y*
Option C has the correct area shaded to represent the equations given in the question.

17)   The correct answer is B (The number of nematode worms per cubic metre of soil is negatively correlated with the concentration of fertiliser residues).

The finding that the number of nematode worms per cubic metre in the soil is higher when there is a lower concentration of fertiliser residues in the soil proves the claim given in option B, as the two statements are essentially saying the same thing. Statement A implies that the concentration of fertiliser residues in the soil does not affect the number of nematode worms. The claim that the worms process fertiliser residues cannot be justified by the finding that says that the population of nematode worms is less in areas with higher concentration of fertiliser residues.

Statement C is incorrect as the finding does not disclose if the reason for lower numbers of nematode worms is purely due to the fertiliser residues or if other factors are involved. Hence, the claim that removing fertiliser residues from the soil alone would encourage the growth of nematode worm populations is not justified by the finding.

Statement D is wrong as the finding does not state if the reason for the reduced numbers of nematode worms is due to fertiliser residues interfering with the reproduction of nematode worms or due to other factors involved. So, the claim that fertiliser residues interfere with the reproduction of nematode worms is not justified by the finding.

18)   The correct answer is 5

The question states that 15 students take chemistry, and 13 students take biology. So, there are only two students who take three subjects who can take both mathematics and physics.

The question asks for the largest number of boys taking these two subjects. Therefore, considering that these two students and the three students who take all four subjects are boys, this means that a maximum of 5 boys that could be taking both mathematics and physics.

19)   The correct answer is D (Julie arrives one hour before Clare)

Both Julie's and Clare's clocks are keeping the same time, and neither of them corrects their clocks.

If Julie puts her clock forward one hour and Clare completely forgets about it and leaves her clock unchanged, then Julie's clock is faster than Clare's by one hour. Therefore, when they meet at 11 a.m. the following day, Julie will arrive 1 hour before Clare.

20)   The correct answer is B (Early consultation for minor symptoms incurs high costs in doctors' time).

The passage says that men are much less likely to use preventive medical care than women: men tend to seek help only when their conditions have worsened, whereas women often consult a doctor when they have minor symptoms. The effect of this is that men usually go to doctors only when they already have advanced conditions which are more difficult and expensive to treat. The argument concludes that spending time and money on persuading men to seek advice at an earlier stage would be worthwhile, considering the savings on treating advanced conditions.

Statement A is a plausible reason for why, as stated in the argument, men do not seek advice on minor problems, which strengthens the reasoning of the argument.

If statement B were true, there seems to be no reason why consulting a doctor at an earlier stage would save money. In fact, the expense may be much higher the earlier consultations start. So, this statement weakens the argument. Statement C suggests the reason why, as stated in the argument, women are quick to consult their

10

doctor whenever they are worried or have minor symptoms. Therefore this statement also strengthens the reasoning of the argument.

Statement D is irrelevant to the conclusion of the argument that seeking advice at an earlier time would save money on treatment of men.

Statement E also strengthens the argument's reasoning that treating advanced conditions are more difficult and expensive.

21) The correct answer is 7.2 seconds

This question requires the use of the relationship speed = distance divided by time

The distance is 100 m or 0.1 km

For this problem, relative speed needs to be considered because the target is also a moving object. The 110km/hr speed of a cheetah is negated by the 60km/hr speed of the zebra. So, the speed at which the cheetah will gain on the zebra is:

$$110 – 60 = 50km/hr$$

$$Time = 0.1/50 = 0.002\ hrs$$

$$OR\ 7.2\ seconds\ (0.002 \times 3600)$$

22) The correct answer is E (It was abandoned in or later than 157 AD).

To answer this question, the dates on the coins must be considered to represent when each coin was made. Currency made in a year is used for, in most cases, years and decades. Therefore, it would be wrong to consider that since the first coin was of 88 AD, the Roman occupation of the site began before or in that year. The Romans might have started their occupation much later than 88 AD, and brought coins with them made in 88 AD.

Likewise, it would be wrong to assume that since the third coin was of 157 AD, the Roman occupation ended in 157 AD.

Taking these into consideration, the only statement that can definitely be true regarding the dates of occupation of the site is option E. The Roman occupation could not have ended before 157 AD since that would mean that a coin made in 157 AD had to be brought by the Romans before it was manufactured. The occupation ended in or later than 157 AD.

Option A is wrong as a coin made in 157 AD could have been used for any number of years by the Romans, while they continued to occupy the site.

Options B, C, and D may or may not be true; however, there is insufficient evidence to be certain one way or the other.

23) The correct answer is B (Gardeners will ignore encouragement to use alternatives to peat).

The argument says that peat harvesting endangers the wetland habitats of wading birds, and due to this reason, gardeners are being encouraged to use alternatives to peat. However, at the same time, gardening has become the most popular hobby in the UK, which means that demand for peat-based compost will also remain high. The argument thus concludes that habitats of wading birds will inevitably decline if gardening continues to be so popular.

The passage states that there is a way to lessen the undesirable effect of peat, which is by using peat alternatives. However, since the argument still concludes that habitats of wading birds will inevitably decline if gardening continues to be so popular, B must be assumed by the author.

Statement A is incorrect as it makes its conclusion on the condition that *if gardening continues to be a popular hobby*, it only states what will happen under this condition. This means that even if gardening does not continue to be the *most popular hobby* in the UK, the conclusion will remain the same. So, this is not necessarily the assumption.

Statement C is not correct. In fact, the passage states that gardeners are being encouraged to use alternatives to peat which can be safely assumed to be an action by environmentalists.

Statement D is not necessarily true nor cannot it be assumed as the argument does not mention whether the use of peat-based compost is due to unavailability of cheap peat alternatives at garden centres.

Statement E only points out the dangers faced by habitats of wading birds in relation to the use of peat by gardeners. Therefore this is not an assumption and can therefore be excluded.

24)   The correct answer is C

From the information provided, only the statement given in option C can be reliably justified. This is because despite the Finance Minister's tax and benefit measures, the Fair-E coefficient, which shows income inequality in Ruritania, has not been reduced.

Statements A, B and D may be true or false, but there is no adequate information given to justify these reliably, hence they can be excluded.

Chart one portrays the percentage change in the household income from tax and benefit measures only, which shows that the wealthiest people fell by 4%. However, there is no other information to justify that the real wealth of the rich class drops by over 4% thus statement E can also be ruled out.

25)   The correct answer is D

The information provided reveals that tax and benefit measures introduced by the Finance Minister have resulted in the redistribution of income from the better off to the less well off. This should result in a reduced Fair-E coefficient; however, this is not the case, and the income inequality is still increasing. This can only happen when the above-average income of the better off people rises at a faster rate than those that are below-average, so much so, in fact, that the redistribution of tax and benefit in favour of people on below-average incomes has no significant effect on the Fair-E coefficient.

From this fact, it can be concluded that even after tax, above-average incomes in Ruritania have continued to rise more rapidly than those that are below the average.

Statement A may not necessarily be true. The rise of inequality in Ruritania may not be caused by the government's fiscal policy alone. In fact, it was the aim of the government's fiscal policy since 1997 to get rid of inequality in Ruritania.

There is no evidence to support statements B and C in the given information. So, these are not reliable conclusions.

Statement E may not be necessarily correct. It is highly possible that poverty has been reduced, but the above-average income rises so rapidly that income inequality has been increasing as a result.

26)   The correct answer is E (1, 2 and 3)

All three statements are compatible with the given data and could all contribute to the rise in the Fair-E coefficient in Ruritania.

Statement one claims that many of the new benefits are means-tested and complicated, with the result that $4.5 billion-worth are going unclaimed. This may be one of the reasons the income of the poor is not improving as much when compared to the rich because large amounts of money allocated to them do not reach these people.

Statement two states that "according to the Ruritanian Ministry of Finance, the number of people paying top-rate income tax rose from 2.1 million to 3.2 million." This rise in number paying top-rate income tax could be one factor contributing to the increase in the Fair-E coefficient.

Statement three says that "since 1996-97 there has been a surge in the number of high earners." This rise in the number of high earners could be one factor which is contributing to the increased Fair-E coefficient.

27)   The correct answer is C (Poland, Ruritania, USA, Panama)

Consider the degree of inequality between the rich and poor in these countries based on their Fair-E coefficient:

Poland - 0.2

Ruritania - 0.35

Panama - 0.6

USA - 0.4

Therefore the order as listed in option C is the correct one.

28)   The correct answer is B

The argument says that at 11 years old, children of parents who smoke are shorter than those of who do not smoke. It concludes that smoking reduces the growth rate of children up to 11 years of age.

The main flaw in the argument is that it wholly attributes the reduced growth rate in children to smoking by parents, an assumption for which it does not give any evidence-supported reasoning. Option B correctly points out this flaw in the argument by stating that lower average heights in 11-year-olds may be associated with parental smoking, but not caused by it.

The statements A, C and D, do not identify the flaw in the argument since there is nothing in the given passage that assumes otherwise.

29)   The correct answer is E (30)

The probability of Amanda choosing a red sweet is 30%. Thus, the probability of choosing either blue or yellow is 70%.

Let the probability of choosing a yellow sweet be x and that of selecting a blue one be $2x$ (since the likelihood of her choosing a blue one is twice the probability of her choosing a yellow one) which can be expressed as:

$$x + 2x = \frac{70}{100} \qquad \text{or: } 3x = 0.7 \qquad \text{or: } x = \frac{0.7}{3}$$

To make the numerator a whole number, multiply both the numerator and denominator by 10, which gives:

$$x = \frac{7}{30}$$

Therefore, the probability of choosing a yellow sweet is 7 out of 30. The probability of selecting a blue sweet is *2x,* which is 14 out of 30 sweets.

This gives the total number of sweets which must be at least 30.

The findings can be confirmed by calculating the number of red sweets, which is 30% of 30

$$30/100 \times 30 = 9$$

If there are nine red sweets, the total of the three colours of sweets now becomes:

$$9 + 7 + 14 = 30$$

This then confirms that the total number of sweets is 30.

30)   The correct answer is C (1 and 2 only)
Doctors in Great Britain can work for the public health service, a commercial service, or both. 30% of doctors in Great Britain work, at least some of the time, for the commercial sector.

From this passage, it is clear that doctors who work for the commercial sector full-time or part-time make up 30% of the total number of doctors in Great Britain. Therefore, 70% of doctors work for the public health service.

Statement one, which says that some doctors work only in the public health service, is correct.

Statement two, which says that more doctors work in the public health service than the commercial sector, is true because 70% of doctors work for the public health service.

Statement three may be true, but it cannot be deduced from the current information.

Therefore, only statements one and two can be deduced solely using the information provided.

31)   The correct answer is A and C
When considering the statements, only options A and C can be equivalent. To say that Anne is not older than Susan is the same as saying that Susan is at least as old as Anne. Because if Anne is not older than Susan, she may either be younger than Susan or Susan may be older than Anne; however, the only thing is known from the statements, without a chance of being proven wrong, is that Susan has to be at least as old as Anne.

32)   The correct answer is E (The change in holiday patterns will be more than a short-term phenomenon.)
The underlying assumption or the unwritten link between the reasoning and the conclusion of the argument is that the change in holiday patterns will be more than a short-term phenomenon (statement E). That is why the argument calls for government action. If this was not the assumption or if this were not true, the conclusion of the argument would be rendered invalid.

There is nothing in the passage which suggests that bargain offers may tempt people, thus statement A can be excluded.

Statement B is not the assumption of the argument since it is calling for the government to take action on the changes in holiday pattern. If the argument assumes that the government is unwilling to respond to the situation, there would be no point in making the case.

The passage only talks about air travel, which people fear due to terrorism threats. Therefore statement C can also be excluded.

The author does not consider the people's response to the threats of terrorism as an over-reaction. Instead, the article calls for the government to take actions to better facilitate the changed travel pattern due to this response instead. Therefore, the argument does not assume that there has been an over-reaction to threats of terrorism, making statement D also incorrect.

33) The correct answer is D

Based on the available information, the position of the horses from the first to the last position at the first turn is Crackdown, Bistro, Drumbeat and Arctic Ape. The information reveals that Drumbeat cannot be in last place since it has to have another horse behind it to drop back by one place later on. Similarly, Bistro cannot be in first place since there has to be another horse in front of it for Bistro to move up one place later on.

Therefore, if Bistro moves up one place, Drumbeat drops back one place, and that is how they finish the race, their final position would be Bistro 1st, Crackdown 2nd and Arctic Ape 3rd with Drumbeat at the last place.

34) The correct answer is C (15cm³ concentrate)

40 cm³ concentrate should be diluted by adding 320 cm³ water (40:320 = 1:8)

Since Jean added 400 cm³ water to 40 cm³ concentrate, the mixture is over-diluted by 80 cm³ of water.

To obtain the correct concentration of the resulting mix, more concentrate must be added so that it has 1:8 concentration with the 80 cm³ water.

Therefore, Jean must add 10 cm³ concentrate. (10:80 = 1:8)

35) The correct answer is C

Looking at the information in figure one, the death rate is much higher than the birth rate in the first two years. This should be shown by a sharp decline in population. The difference between the death rate and the birth rate gradually lessened till the fifth year; this should be shown by a progressively lower rate of population decline.

The rate of birth and death is reversed in the second half of the ten-year period. So, its effect on population should also show the reverse of that in the first five years and gradually increase and reach a high rate of increase towards the final period.

This decline and rise of the population are shown correctly in option C.

36) The correct answer is B (518 AD)

The number of years in between year 9 and year 72 is 63

If year 9 = 455 AD, then year 72 = 455 AD + 63 = 518 AD

37) The correct answer is C (The birth date of Gildas)

If the birth date of Gildas was known, this would provide the date for when the battle of Badon was fought. It is mentioned in the passage that records indicate that Gildas was born in the same year as the battle of Badon.

38) The correct answer is B (511 AD)

If the Welsh Annals were late by 28 years, the battle of Camlann, which they recorded as fought in year 93, would have been fought in year 65. The information reveals that "year 9" in the Welsh Annals coincides with 455 AD in the modern dating system

So, the year 65 would be 511 AD.

39) The correct answer is 506 AD

If King Maelgwn died at year 103, and Gildas was 43 years old then, the latest possible date for the Battle of Badon would have been the year 60, or 506 AD.

40) The correct answer is C

The Welsh Annals and records give the Battle of Badon as year 72 or 518 AD, and Gildas birth in the same year. They also indicate that Gildas wrote his book when he was 43, which should have been year 115 or 561 AD, after Maelgwn's death.

This leaves option C which shows that Gildas wrote his book after Maelgwn's death.

BMAT Section 1 - 2004

1)   The correct answer is C

An isosceles right-angled triangle is a triangle that has a 90-degree angle for one of its angles, and the remaining two angles are equal. Two of its sides are also equal in length.

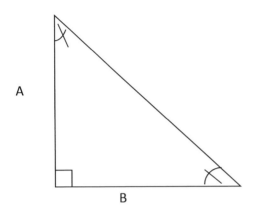

A

B

2)   The correct answer is C

By visualising whether the shapes given in the options can be made up by four of these tables, it can be seen that there are not enough tables to make up the square shape of the desired size for the middle part of option C:

A -

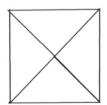

B -

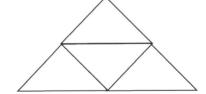

C -

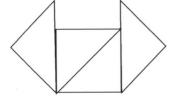

D -

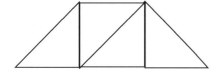

E -

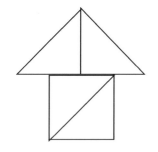

3) **The correct answer is C (Levels of smoking have reduced in response to higher prices).**

Statement A would weaken the argument because it would show that people consume fatty foods not because of their relatively lower price, but because they like it. If so, even a significant increase in the cost of fatty foods may not lower consumption.

Both statements B and D are irrelevant to the reasoning or conclusion of the passage and thus cannot be considered as either strengthening or weakening the argument.

If the statement in option C were true, it would strengthen the argument because it could be used as evidence proving that increase in the price of a commodity reduces consumption. Likewise, taxing fatty foods will increase the price, reducing its consumption by the people, and also lower the comparative price of fruit and vegetables. Statement E is irrelevant, and if the government takes measures as per the suggestion of the passage, the results will not be a short-term one.

4) **The correct answer is B (10)**

The question asks about the *minimum* number of cross-headed, 3 mm diameter, 50 mm long screws that there could be in the box. Therefore the best place to start is by considering the opposite, the maximum number of screws other than the ones following this particular specification.

40 screws can be of slot heads

20 screws can be of 4mm diameter

10 screws can be of 5mm diameter

5 screws can be of 35mm length

15 screws can be of 20mm length

So, out of a total of 100 screws, there can be a maximum of 90 (40+20+10+5+15) screws other than those following the exact specifications.

Therefore, this means that there can be, at a *minimum*, 10 cross-headed, 3 mm diameter, 50 mm long screws in the box.

5)   The correct answer is A (It assumes that the teaching method is the cause of the improved standards.)

The passage says that the standards in literacy and numeracy have increased in primary schools. It attributes this to the government's insistence on all primary schools spending at least one hour per day on literacy and numeracy work, and its stipulation that a substantial part of the time should be spent in whole class teaching. Thus, the argument concludes that whole class teaching is more beneficial than small group or individual work.

The flaw in the argument is that it assumes the improved standards to be the result of the change in the teaching method alone, disregarding other factors leading to this improvement. Hence, statement A best expresses the flaw in this argument.

Statement B is incorrect, as the argument only talks about the improvements seen in the standards of the pupils. So, the fact that teachers have more or less work to bring about this improvement is irrelevant in this context. Moreover, it is not necessarily true that teachers would have to take on additional work due to this change in method.

Statement C is not necessarily correct. The passage only says that there have been improvements in standards; these improvements may be from an already high standard.

Statement D is incorrect as there is nothing in the passage from which one can assume that the improvements are short-term in nature.

The argument does not overlook the benefits of small group and individual work; however, since there have been improvements in the standards, which it attributes to whole class teaching, the argument concludes that whole class teaching is more beneficial than small group or individual work. Therefore statement E can also be excluded.

6)   The correct answer is C (1 km)

If Suki was half a kilometre from home when Tom leaves 10 minutes after her, then that would mean that Suki walks half a kilometre in 10 minutes. Since Tom's speed is four times that of Suki's, he will cycle half a kilometre in 2.5 minutes.

In this case, Suki needs 40 minutes to reach school, and Tom requires 10 minutes.

If Tom leaves home when Suki still has 30 minutes to walk, he cannot have reached the school only 5 minutes before Suki. Instead, he will arrive 20 minutes before Suki.

The other options can be considered using the same method; revealing that only option C is correct:

If Suki was one kilometre from home when Tom leaves 10 minutes after her, then that would mean that Suki walks one kilometre in 10 minutes. Since Tom's speed is four times that of Suki's, he will cycle one kilometre in 2.5 minutes.

In this case, Suki needs 20 minutes to reach school while Tom needs five minutes.

Therefore, if Tom leaves home when Suki still has 10 minutes to walk, and he reaches the school in five minutes, which is five minutes before Suki.

7)   The correct answer is E (Everyone should try to live longer).

The passage examines a result shown by recent research that people who keep pets tend to live longer than those who do not. It considers as the explanation that dog or horse owners exercise more, owners enjoy the soothing properties of stroking a furry animal and the emotional benefits of affectionate relationships, which all combine to benefit human longevity. It concludes that everyone who can own a pet should do so. However, it also points out that owning a pet may not be suitable for people allergic to animals.

The argument concludes that everyone should own a pet if he or she can do so. The reasoning for this finding is that people who keep pets tend to live longer than those who do not. The assumption, or the unwritten link between the argument in the passage and the conclusion, is that everyone should try to live longer.

Statements A and D have no relevance to the conclusion of the passage. So, neither of these can be considered to be the assumption of the passage.

Statement B can be excluded as the passage only states the benefits of keeping a pet or pets, there is nothing in the passage to assume that the degree of benefits is proportional to the number of pets.

Statement C can be excluded because the argument uses these animals as examples. The conclusion shows that the argument is about animals in general, not about any specific animal or animals.

8)   The correct answer is D

Since they share the profits equally, it can be assumed that they also share the cost of buying materials. So, Bill owes half the cost of the materials to Alf, which is £120.

The client paid £780 to Bill, half of which Bill has to give to Alf, which is £390

Therefore, the total amount Bill has to pay Alf is £ (390+120) = £510

9)   The correct answer is 13.0

Note that the question requires the answer be rounded to the nearest 0.5 million. Therefore, approximations of the number of episodes of care for each cause are as follows:

Diagnosis	Number of episodes
Disease of circulatory systems	1.2 million
Diabetes	0.1 million
Cancer	1.4 million
Disease of nervous systems	0.3 million
Disease of respiratory systems	0.8 million
Disease of digestive systems	1.4 million
Disease of genitourinary systems	0.8 million
Complications of pregnancy and childbirth	1.2 million
Injury and poisoning	0.8 million
All other diagnoses	5.0 million

Therefore, the approximate total number of episodes of care in hospital for all causes is 13.0 million.

10)   The correct answer is A (3.1 days)

Number of days spent in hospital for cancer = 4,343,199

Number of episodes of care for cancer = 1,400,000

Therefore the average number of days in hospital for cancer

= 4,343,199 ÷ 1,400,000 = 3.1023

Or, approximately 3.1 days

11)   The correct answer is A (120,000)
Number of all episodes of care for cancer = 1,400,000
1/7 of number of episodes of care for cancer

$$= 1,400,000 \div 7 = 200,000$$

Therefore, total episodes of care for lung cancer   = 200,000
Let the number of episodes of care for lung cancer in women be x
Since the number of episodes in men is 50% more than that in women, the number of episodes of care for lung cancer in men:

$$= x + 50\% \text{ of } x \text{ or } x/2$$

Therefore:

$$x + x + x/2 = 200,000$$

$$\text{OR } 5x/2 = 200,000$$

$$\text{OR } 5x = 400,000$$

$$\text{OR } x = 80,000$$

x or number of episodes of care for lung cancer in women = 80,000
Number of episodes of care for lung cancer in men

$$= 80,000 + 50\% \text{ of } 80,000 = 80,000 + 40,000$$
$$= 120,000$$

12)   The correct answer is A & C
The number of episodes of care for cancer and diseases of the circulatory system is 1.4 million and 1.2 million respectively. The average stay for cancer, having more number of episodes of care, is half that for diseases of the circulatory system. The only reasonable explanation for this can be either statement A or C.
Option A states that many cancer treatments only require a short stay in the hospital. If this is the case, then the total number of days in the hospital would be much lower than the other, even though the number of cases is higher.
Option C states that the distribution of stay times for circulatory diseases is more heavily weighted toward more extended stays in the hospital. In simpler terms, circulatory diseases in general require a longer stay in hospital than cancer-related hospital stays. If so, the total number of days in hospital could be much higher than for cancer, even though the number of cases is fewer.

Statement B is not correct as it is not supported by the statistics.

Statement D can be excluded as this is irrelevant to the question.

13) The correct answer is B & C (6 and 7)

Using the information on how points are awarded and by calculating the points that can be won and the points that can be deducted, it can be seen that both options B and C can be the correct answers.

For option A – If John gave five correct answers; he would have got only 15 points, so this cannot be the answer.

For option B – If John gave six correct answers; he would have got 18 points, so this can be the answer.

For option C –For seven correct answers and three incorrect answers, John would have got 18 points (21 - 3), so this can be the answer.

For option D – Eight correct answers would have given John 24 points; even if he gave wrong answers for the remaining four, he would still have got 20 points (24 - 4), so this cannot be the answer.

For option E – If John gave nine correct answers, he would have got 27 points; even if he gave incorrect answers for the remaining 3, he would still have got 24 points (27 - 3), so this cannot be the answer.

14) The correct answer is B (A necessary, but not a sufficient condition for life as we know it).

The passage says that the unusual molecular structure of water ice is responsible for forming a layer of insulation on the surface, and without this protection, the seas would freeze and life as we know it would not exist.

The passage demonstrates that without this unusual structure of water in its solid form, life would not be possible. Therefore, it is a necessary condition for life to form. The passage also suggests that the condition itself cannot form life, so it is not a sufficient condition. Option B correctly states this fact.

15) The correct answer is B

By visualising the outer flaps of the cardboard (having one, two and four dots on their faces) being folded up so that the tip is pointing straight out, the two dots will be aligned on the right side of its face closer to the face having one dot. There is no positioning of the die which can cause the two dots be aligned as shown in option B.

Therefore, the diagram given in option B cannot be a view of this die when viewed from above a vertex.

16) The correct answer is D (Only those animal experiments that benefit animals, as well as humans, are acceptable).

The passage examines the criticism by animal rights campaigners of using animals for medical research experiments as morally wrong. It argues that some campaigners ignore the many benefits which medical advances have had for animals themselves as well as humans. The passage suggests that if the animal population, as well as human population, benefit from experiments on only a small minority of animals, those experiments are morally acceptable.

Statement A is incorrect as the passage does in no way undermine the importance of animal rights.

Even though statement B can be found in the passage, it is only one of the reasons given by the author in supporting its conclusion; therefore it does not adequately express the conclusion.

The passage sets a condition for animal experiments to have moral justification and does not support or justify all animal experiments. Therefore the generalised nature of statement C makes it incorrect. It does, however, clearly state a condition for such experiments to be acceptable, which is, that they should benefit animals as well as humans. Therefore, the statement that expresses the conclusion of the above passage is as stated in option D. The passage does neither consider animal experiments in non-medical research nor is this the main message it tries to convey. So, statement E cannot be the conclusion.

17) The correct answer is A (ABCD)

Barbara, weighing 80 kilograms initially, cannot weigh less than Colin, who initially weighed 75 kilograms and lost more weight than Barbara at the end of the year.

Option A, which gives the increasing order of their weights at the end of the year as ABCD, is therefore not possible.

18) The correct answer is A

The core message that the author intends to convey with this passage, or the conclusion of the passage, is that the worst aspect of the Exxon Valdez oil spill is that its consequences have not yet played out.

Statements B, C, D and E give supporting evidence which can be found in the passage all of which lead to the conclusion (statement A).

19) The correct answer is C (594 cm^2)

A block of 1 cm^3 marble only has its surface area exposed, but when crushed into powder, 0.1 mm^3 cubes, the surface that is exposed to the acid will increase. The existing surface area first needs to be calculated as well as the potential surface area which can be created by crushing the marble. The difference in surface area is the correct answer. The surface area of 1 cm^3 marble=

$$1cm \times 1cm \times 6 \quad = 6cm^2$$

Since 1cm^2 = 100 mm^2, a 1 cm^3 marble can be made into 10000 x 0.1 mm^3 marble
Surface area of 0.1 mm^3 marble =

$$0.1mm \times 0.1mm \times 6 = 0.6mm^2$$

Surface area of 10000 X 0.1 mm^3 marble =

$$0.6mm^2 \times 10000 = 6000 \ mm^2 = 600 \ cm^2$$

So, difference in surface area between a 1 cm^3 marble and 10000 X 0.1 mm^3 marble =

$$(600-6) \ cm^2$$
$$= 594 \ cm^2$$

20) The correct answer is D (Lifelong exercise is associated with maintaining good health).

The passage states two facts that show the relationship between exercise and health. Firstly, it says that old people in underdeveloped countries generally do not have high blood pressure problems because they maintain a high level of physical activity. By contrast, elderly people in developed countries are affected by problems of increasing blood pressure. Secondly, obesity and diabetes are more prevalent among young people in developed countries because of their lack of exercise.

Both of these statements are given in the passage as supporting evidence to come to the conclusion that lifelong exercise is associated with maintaining good health, making statement D correct.

Statement A may be an assumption, but not the conclusion because the passage does not mention or suggest changes in lifestyle.

Statement B can be excluded because while the passage talks about the effects of the lack of exercise in general, it is not the intention of the argument to point out specific illnesses.

The passage points out the undesirable effects of the lack of physical activity in younger age groups, which shows that the benefits of physical activity are enjoyed at a young age too. Therefore statement C is incorrect.

The passage gives an example each of the effects of lack of exercise in both young and old people without giving more importance to one or the other. So, statement E cannot be taken as the conclusion

21)   The correct answer is D (85)

The last column in the table for men gives the percentage of all the men who take 6 grams or less as 15 percent. This means that 15% of a total of 567 men take the maximum recommended daily salt intake or less.

$$15\% \text{ of } 567 = 85.05$$

22)   The correct answer is 7.6g

Interpolation is the process of finding a value between two points on a line or curve. If the increase or decrease of the values is linear, it is easy to find a specific value anywhere on that line. However, in many cases, such as in the statistics of salt intake, this increase or decrease forms a curve, in such instances, interpolation can be used to find the value.

The median can be calculated by considering the amount of salt taken by 50% or less of those in the survey.

This 50% value lies in between the 9 and 6-gram group, as this group contains between 66% and 31% of those in the survey.

Let m be the median salt intake

By using interpolation:

$$\frac{m-6}{9-6} = \frac{(50-31)}{(66-31)}$$

$$\frac{m-6}{3} = \frac{(19)}{(35)}$$

$$m-6 = \frac{(57)}{(35)}$$

24

$$m - 6 = 1.6$$

$$m = 1.6 + 6$$

$$m = 7.6$$

Therefore, the median salt intake for women in the survey is 7.6g

23) **The correct answer is A**

To answer this question, the information given in the last column for men needs to be considered. However, since these are cumulative percentages, to get the correct percentage for each group, the previous number from the number given in each group must be deducted. The table provides percentages only for men who take up to 18 grams; the remaining 9% can be safely assumed as taking more than 18 grams of salt per day.

Percentage of men who take 0 – 3 grams of salt per day = 4
Percentage of men who take 3 – 6 grams of salt per day

$$= 15 - 4 = 11$$

Percentage of men who take 6 – 9 grams of salt per day

$$= 39 - 15 = 24$$

Percentage of men who take 9 – 12 grams of salt per day

$$= 60 - 39 = 21$$

Percentage of men who take 12 – 15 grams of salt per day

$$= 79 - 60 = 19$$

Percentage of men who take 15 – 18 grams of salt per day

$$= 91 - 79 = 12$$

Percentage of men who take above 18 grams of salt per day

$$= 100 - 91 = 9$$

This is correctly represented by bar chart A.

24)   The correct answer is B (The numbers in the survey are not evenly distributed across the age range).
Looking at the statistics in the table, the number of people surveyed in each age group differs and is not evenly distributed across the age range. It is therefore possible that the intake of salt depends on the age of a person. So, a higher number of people surveyed in an age group in which salt intake per day is high or vice versa may cause bias or misrepresentation in the figures.

25)   The correct answer is 10
Number of patients = 20 -2 = 18
Total time taken by the doctor for her appointments and others = 12 minutes for one patient + 5 minutes each X remaining 17 patients + 8 minutes urgent phone call + 5 minutes emergency appointment = 110 minutes
Therefore, the doctor was late by 10 minutes.

26)   The correct answer is B (Gardeners will ignore encouragement to use alternatives to peat).
The argument says that peat harvesting endangers the wetland habitats of wading birds, and due to this reason, gardeners are being encouraged to use alternatives to peat. However, at the same time, gardening has become the most popular hobby in the UK, which means that demand for peat-based compost remains high. The argument thus concludes that habitats of wading birds will inevitably decline if gardening continues to be so popular.
The passage states that there is a way to lessen the undesirable effect of peat, by using peat alternatives. However, since the argument still concludes that habitats of wading birds will inevitably decline if gardening continues to be so popular, statement B must be assumed by the author.
The argument makes its conclusion on the condition that *if gardening continues to be a popular hobby*, it only states what will happen under this condition. This means that even if gardening does not continue to be the *most popular hobby* in the UK, the conclusion will remain the same. So statement A is not necessarily the assumption.
Statement C is not true. In fact, the passage states that gardeners are being encouraged to use alternatives to peat most probably by environmentalists
The argument does not mention whether the use of peat-based compost is due to unavailability of cheap peat alternatives at garden centres. So, statement D is not necessarily true nor is it assumed by the argument.
Statement E is not the assumption of the argument. It only points out the dangers faced by habitats of wading birds in relation to the use of peat by gardeners.

27)   The correct answer is A (32)
By counting the time taken by each light and noting when they share the same time again, it can be seen that this happens after 47 seconds.
First light: 3 + 8 + 3 + 8 + 3 + 8 + 3 + 8 + 3 = 47
Second light: 2 + 7 + 2 + 7 + 2 + 7 + 2 + 7 + 2 + 7 + 2 = 47
This means that from the time they became visible at the same time, it takes 47 seconds for them to become switched off at the same time.
Since the lights became visible at the same time 15 seconds ago, the time taken by them to disappear from view at the same time is 32 seconds (47 - 15).

28)   The correct answer is B (121.6kg)

The mass given in the question is the combined mass of the metal sheet and weight of water. The total mass of the container double the diameter and height can be found by calculating how much the mass of each will increase under these conditions. The equation for this is:

$Surface\ area\ of\ a\ cylinder = \pi\ x\ diameter\ x\ height$

When the diameter and the height double, the surface area will become:

$(\pi\ x\ 2\ diameter\ x\ 2\ height)\ or\ 4(\pi\ x\ diameter\ x\ height)$

Therefore:

$(\pi\ x\ diameter\ x\ height) = 800g\ (0.8\ kg)$

This means that:

$4(\pi\ x\ diameter\ x\ height) = 4\ (0.8kg) = 3.2kg$

The volume of water in the original cylinder was:

14.8 kg (15.6 kg – 0.8 kg)

Volume of a cylinder:

$= \pi\ x\ radius^2\ x\ height$

If the diameter (the *radius* is quadrupled) and height doubles, then the volume =

$(\pi\ x\ radius^2\ x\ 2\ height)\ or\ 8(\pi\ x\ radius^2\ x\ height)$

If $(\pi\ x\ radius^2\ x\ height) = 14.8kg$

This means that:

$8(\pi\ x\ radius^2\ x\ height) = 8\ x\ 14.8kg$

OR 114.8 kg

Therefore, the total weight will become (3.2 + 118.4) kg = 121.6 kg

29)   The correct answer is C (1 and 2 only)

Doctors in Great Britain can work for the public health service, a commercial service, or both. The passage states that 30% of doctors in Great Britain work, at least some of the time, for the commercial sector.

From this passage, it is clear that doctors who work for the commercial sector full-time or part-time make up 30% of the total number of doctors in Great Britain. Therefore, 70% of doctors work for the public health service.

Statement one, which says that some doctors work only in the public health service, is therefore correct.

Statement two, which says that more doctors work in the public health service than the commercial sector, is also true because 70% of doctors work for the public health service.

Statement three may be true, but it cannot be deduced from the information provided.

30)   The correct answer is E (28 g/l)

In the 250ml bottle, there is 200ml of 30g/l and 50ml of 20g/l.

If one solution is of 30g/l, this means one litre of solution has 30 grams of sodium chloride

Therefore, 200ml will have 6 grams of sodium chloride

The other solution has a concentration of 20g/l, which means that one litre of solution has 20 grams of sodium chloride. So, 50ml will have 1 gram of sodium chloride.

When these two separate solutions were mixed, there is now 7 grams of sodium chloride in a volume of 250ml.

Therefore, in one litre (4 x 250ml), there will be 4 x 7 = 28 grams

This can be expressed as a concentration of 28g/l.

31)   The correct answer is B

First, consider who leads in each section and by how much time:

In the flat section (1 km), the runner's speed is 6km/hr; he completes this section in 10 minutes. The cyclist's speed is 30km/hr; he completes this section in 2 minutes. Therefore the cyclist leads this section by 8 minutes.

In the mud section (1.5 km), the runner's speed is 4km/hr; he completes this section in 22.5 minutes. The cyclist's speed is 3km/hr; he completes this section in 30 minutes. Thus the cyclist's lead has considerably decreased, with his 8-minute lead from the first section negated by the 7.5 minutes the runner has gained.

However, the cyclist still leads by 0.5 minutes.

In the uphill section (0.5 km), the runner's speed is 3km/hr; he completes this section in 10 minutes. The cyclist's speed is 2km/hr; he completes this section in 15 minutes.

The runner now leads by 4.5 minutes.

In the downhill section (1 km), the runner's speed is 8km/hr; he will complete this section in 7.5 minutes. The cyclist's speed is 40km/hr; he will complete this section in 1.5 minutes.

The runner's lead of 4.5 minutes is negated by the 6 minutes gained by the cyclist.

The cyclist leads by 1.5 minutes until he reaches the finish line.

These changes of leads are shown by options B and E only.

In option E, the change of time of lead is after the muddy section is shown to take place at 2 km, while this takes place at 2.5 km, so this option is wrong. Option B correctly displays the time and distance.

32)   The correct answer is A & C

When considering the statements, it becomes apparent that only options A and C can be equivalent. To say that Anne is not older than Susan is the same as saying that Susan is at least as old as Anne. Because if Anne is not older than Susan, she may either be younger than Susan or Susan may be older than Anne; however, the only thing known from the statements provided, without a chance of being proven wrong, is that Susan has to be at least as old as Anne.

33)   The correct answer is 14%

The peak of fatalities in Japan was at 4900 in 1993 and declined to just over 4200 by 1997. The decrease in number of fatalities from 1993 to 1997 is 700 (4900 - 4200)

Percentage of fatalities = 700/4900 X 100 = 14.286

Therefore, the answer is 14%

34)   The correct answer is B

Paragraph three states that from 1987 to 1992, claims in the US for sprains and strains increased in proportion compared to other injuries. In 1987, 75 percent of BI claims were for sprains and strains, and 45 percent for "all other injuries." By 1992, sprains and strains had risen to 83 percent, and all other injuries had fallen to 40 percent. This is correctly explained by the statement in option B. If some of the claims were for sprains and strains along with other injuries, it is possible that injuries that could have been recorded as other types of injury were recorded as sprains and strains. Thus, sprains and strains alone would not have necessarily increased to such a puzzling proportion.

The passage states that for insurance statistics, whiplash is recorded as "sprains and strains," and that it is reasonable to equate these two terms. However, since this had been followed in 1987 as well, it does not explain the increase. Therefore statement A can be excluded.

Statement C can also be ruled out as it does not explain the proportions of different BI claims in paragraph three. Even if this statement were true, it is still puzzling as to why such a large proportion of *false claims* are for sprains and strains.

Statement D is irrelevant to the question and does not explain the proportions of different BI claims in paragraph three.

35)   The correct answer is 22

Let the number of BI claims per 100 insured vehicles in 1980 be x

Between 1980 and 1993, the number of BI claims per 100 insured vehicles rose 33 percent to 29.3

This means that:

$$x + (33\% \text{ of } x) = 29.3$$

$$x + (0.33\,x) = 29.3$$

$$1.33\,X = 29.3$$

29

$$x = 29.3 \div 1.33$$

$$x = 22.03$$

Taken to nearest whole number, the answer is 22

36)   The correct answer is B & C

The anomaly stated in the question is that the likelihood of a BI claim being filed in an accident that involved a property damage claim rose 64 percent between 1980 and 1993.

Statement A is irrelevant and does not explain the anomaly.

Statement B offers some explanation for the apparent anomaly. If lawyers introduce a no-win-no-fee service to claimants seeking compensation for personal injury, and the same does not apply to property damage cases, people would be more willing to claim insurance for BI. This is because they have no risk of losing money as fees to lawyers if they lose the case.   Statement C also offers some explanation for the apparent anomaly. The statement means that there is less possibility of being denied insurance for BI.

BMAT Section 1 - 2005

1)   The correct answer is C (1 large, 1 medium, 2 small)

The quickest way to identify the correct answer to this question is to count up the number of black, white and grey squares and find the simplest ratio.

There are 9 black, 9 white and 20 grey squares.

This simplifies to 1:1:2, which is option C.

2)   The correct answer is D (School sports should prepare children for adult life).

An assumption is an unwritten link between the reasoning and the conclusion. Thus, the first step to identifying the assumption is to determine the conclusion. In this case, this is that "Schools should recognise [that competition is unavoidable] and revert to traditional sports days." In considering each of the options, immediately A and B can be discarded as these are not assumptions, nor are they relevant. Option C can be ruled out, as this is not an assumption but anecdotal evidence. This leaves option D which is implied by the statements in the last two lines which states that 'competition for jobs...is unavoidable" and that "schools should recognise this", suggesting that it is their responsibility to prepare children for life outside of school.

3)   The correct answer is B (5)

Assign the letter b for birds and s for sheep.

Julia counted 13 animals therefore:

$$b + s = 13 \text{ (or } b = 13\text{-}s)$$

Given that birds have two legs and sheep have four and Tim saw a total of 36 legs, the equation can be represented as:

$$2b + 4s = 36 \text{ (or } b + 2s = 18 \text{ simplified)}$$

From here the equations need to be integrated, so that equation one is in equation two:

$$(13\text{-}s) + 2s = 18$$

From here, solve for s:

$$13 + s = 18$$
$$=s = 5$$

Put s =5 into the original equation:

$$b + 5 = 13$$

b= 8

So they saw five sheep and eight birds, making the correct answer B

4)   The correct answer is A (Local movement is independent of overall expansion).

The question requires a reason for why the universe is expanding but galaxies collide, or, in other words, there is movement both towards and away from each other. The best answer here is one that is general and gives an appropriate reason for both expansion and collision. Thus the correct answer is A as it fulfils both aspects. Option B is very specific as the passage is talking about galaxies in general. Option C does not explain the collision of galaxies. Thus it can be discarded. Option D does not explain either the expansion or collision and therefore it too can be excluded. Finally, option E can also be discarded as this too is irrelevant to the collision and expansion.

5)   The correct answer is 30 to 49

The answer to this question can be found relatively quickly when comparing the final columns for both males and females. Only the age groups 30-34, 35-39, 40-44 and 45-49 show the cancer deaths for females exceeding those for males. Therefore the correct answer is 30-49.

6)   The correct answer is B (Humans have evolved to tolerate natural pesticides in food crops).

With these types of questions, the best place to start is by determining the conclusion. The conclusion is that "since our consumption of natural pesticides vastly outweighs that of synthetic pesticides, our health is at greater risk from natural pesticides than from synthetic ones." To weaken this argument, the correct answer should provide a reason for why this conclusion may not be valid. Looking at the options, both A and C strengthen the argument, while option D, is not relevant for the comparison between natural and synthetic pesticides. Hence, option A is the only statement which effectively weakens the argument.

7)   The correct answer is £10500

Using the table, the stamp duty for a house bought for £350000 will be 3%. Therefore, 3% of 350000 is £10500.

8)   The correct answer is C

There must be almost vertical parts to the graph, as for a £1 increase between the different bands, for example, £119999 (0%) and £120000 (1%) there will be a considerable increase in tax, and so graph B is incorrect as it shows an almost constant incline. Graph D is also incorrect, as the tax paid will not be constant within a band – it will be relative to how much the house is within the band. Finally, option C is correct, and A is not, as the vertical parts of the graph should become steeper as the percentage tax paid increases for each band.

9)   The correct answer is B (£2800)

The first £120000 is free; the next £130000 is taxed at 1% which is £1300. This leaves £50000 (since 120000 + 130000 = 250000) which falls into the next band of 3%. Thus 3% of £50000 = £1500.

This gives the total tax of £1300 +£1500 = £2800

10) The correct answer is £3300

The usual price for the purchase will be £260000 x 3% = £7800 tax.

By cheating, the price will be £249000 x 1% = 2490 (rounded to £2500) plus the £2000 for the 'fittings and furnishings' gives the total price of 2500+2000 = 4500

So the amount saved is: 7800-4500 = £3300

11) The correct answer is A (Those who study German and French but not Spanish).

The quickest way to answer this is to annotate the Venn diagram. Based on the information provided, the small circle is Spanish. The circle to the left is French as all students who study Spanish also study French. This leaves the circle on the right assigned to those students who study German. Therefore, the shaded region is those students who study both French and German but not Spanish.

12) The correct answer is E (The use of cannabis by those aged under 15 is a recent development).

The first step in identifying a point which will weaken the argument is to determine the conclusion that the passage is trying to draw. In this case, this is that "it cannot be true that smoking cannabis causes schizophrenia". From here, each statement can be analysed:

Statement A supports the argument and thus cannot be the correct answer. Whether or not there are cancer-causing substances in cannabis smoke is irrelevant to the topic. Therefore, statement B can also be excluded. Statement C is very general as it has no link to cannabis or schizophrenia. Thus it can also be eliminated. Statement D is also irrelevant as the argument is considering the psychological effects of smoking cannabis, not the physiological effects it might have on other organs or systems. Thus, by the process of elimination, statement E is the correct answer.

13) The correct answer is B (65%)

The first ray of light must pass through two layers of glass, each of which allows 80% of the light to pass through. Therefore:

$$0.8 \times 0.8 = 0.64$$

Not all of the light passes through the glass. The information states that 15% (or 0.15 as a proportion) is reflected back by either the first or second layer of glass, so, in other words, this means that the light can either pass through the first sheet (0.8) or be reflected by the first sheet (0.15). Of the light that successfully passes the first sheet, it can either pass through the second sheet as well (0.8) or be reflected by the second sheet (0.15), so probability then becomes:

$$0.15 \times 0.8 \times 0.15 \times 0.8 = 0.0144$$

Therefore the amount of incident light can pass into the room is:

0.0144 + 0.64 = 0.6544 or 65%

14)   The correct answer is E (1 & 3)

This passage concludes that "although nuclear power is seen as problematic because it produces dangerous waste, it will have to continue to be used in 2050." The evidence for this is that energy consumption will reach this point and that renewable energy sources such as wind, tidal and solar power will be "unable to meet the shortfall in supply". Thus, the correct answer will need to contradict this in some way. Statement one achieves this as this may mean that government's goal of 2% economic growth may not be achieved and so the energy consumption may also not reach this level. Therefore statement one can be considered correct. Statement two is irrelevant to the conclusion as the passage is concerned with the use of nuclear energy not whether the government can facilitate the storage of its waste products. Statement three is correct as speeding up the development of other energy sources, could mean that nuclear power does not have to remain a viable option.

15)   The correct answer is D (60%)

Assign the letter p to represent packets of biscuits. The shopkeeper purchases four packets (4p) and sells them for the price of 3 packets (termed 3y). From this sale, she gains 20% profit (or 1.2). This can be represented by the equation:

$$3y/4p = 1.2$$

This equation can then be rearranged to get:

$$y = 1.6p$$

1.6p is the equivalent of 60% increase (or profit). Therefore the answer is D.

16)   The correct answer is D (0.6m)

This question can be solved merely by reading the graph. When the dipstick measures 0.15 metres, he has 400 litres of oil. Thus if he orders another 500 litres, there will be 900 litres in total, meaning that the dipstick should read 0.6m.

17)   The correct answer is E (human activity has changed the British countryside over the last 800 years).

The general theme of this argument is that people should not say that the natural beauty of the countryside is being ruined by wind farms as there are many other factors which have also altered the British countryside since the 12th century. When considering the options, the best statement will be one which encompasses this idea: Statement A, therefore, is too general and does not directly relate to the countryside, so it can be discarded. Statements B, C and D, are all irrelevant to the theme of the argument, thus leaving option E which is the best answer.

18)   The correct answer is C (Banning players who protest aggressively would reduce the incidence of such behaviours on the pitch).

The main argument in this passage is that "we should not tolerate such aggressive behaviour in a civilised society" and that "players acting in this way should be automatically banned." Therefore, when considering the assumption, it must be the missing link between these two ideas. Statement A cannot be inferred from the information provided. Thus it can be discarded. The passage does not state if a civilised appeals process exists in football. Thus this information cannot be inferred either, making option B incorrect. Option C provides a link between the two ideas as one must assume that by banning players it would mean that there would be a reduction in the amount of aggressive behaviour seen. Therefore option C is the best answer. Option D, while possibly true, cannot be assumed from the information given. Option E is incorrect as children can imitate any behaviour, regardless of its nature. Therefore this statement too, can be discarded.

19)   The correct answer is 3200

To answer this question the column with the heading "Division annual rate" should be used. The overall crime is 37838. To get a monthly rate, this number needs to be divided by 12 which mean that the correct answer is 3153, which can be rounded to 3200 (or 3100, which is also accepted.)

20)   The correct answer is F (1, 2, & 3)

Confounding factors are those which cause a person to question the validity of the data. All of the statements in this question are confounding factors. There is a negative correlation between CCTV installation in the target area and overall crime in the area, which however, may not be a causal link. There were other factors which may have influenced the data, such as the improvements in lighting (statement one), an anti-burglary initiative operating in the target area (statement two) and the change in parking regulations (statement three). Each of these improvements may have influenced the data. Thus it cannot be said that the CCTV installation alone is responsible for the fall in crime rates.

21)   The correct answer is 9%

The target areas percentage change for burglary can be calculated using the "start" and "end" columns for burglary:

$$((\text{End rate} - \text{Start rate})/\text{Start rate}) \times 100$$

$$(131-161)/161 \text{ or } (30/160)$$
$$\times 100$$

$$= 18.75\%$$

To find the division percentage change for burglary, the division annual rate "start" and "end" columns must be used in the same formula as above:

$$(6442-7164)/71654 \text{ or } (700/7000)$$
$$\times 100$$

= 10%

The difference between the two values is 18.75-10 = 8.75% (or 9% rounded)

22)   The correct answer is 22%

By removing the vehicle crime figures from the overall crime row, the new start rate will be:

1526-279 = 1247

Since the vehicle crimes have been removed from the start, they must also be removed from the end rate as well:

1098-126 =972

From here the percentage change formula can be used:

((End rate –Start rate)/Start rate) x 100

((972 -1247)/1247) or (275/1250)
x 100

= 22% change

23)   The correct answer is E (1 & 3)

The buffer area is an area which surrounds the target area. Data from the buffer area reveals if the crime has relocated from the target area to an adjacent area, making statement one correct. It also helps determine whether the CCTV installation has actually caused a drop in the crime rates or if this is a general trend for the area as a whole, making statement three correct. Statement two can be excluded as it is not relevant to the idea of a buffer area.

24)   The correct answer is A & C

When considering the scores on the graph, it should become very apparent that there are a large number of students gaining exceptionally high marks (even as high as 100%). It should also be evident that even fewer students are earning very low scores, with no one earning less than 25%. This means that the students are doing better than expected so the easy questions must be very easy and the difficult (hard) questions must also be too easy. Thus the correct answers are options A and C.

25)   The correct answer is C (E to G)

The path plan shows the route to travel without meeting any other letters. Each option can be ruled out very quickly as each path is traced. Option A, moving from C to X can be excluded since the letter I is encountered. Options B can also be excluded as letter C will be encountered. There is a direct route from letters E to G. Thus option C is the correct answer. Option D which is route F to G can be excluded as the letter E blocks the route. Travelling from J to X can only be completed via the letter I, thus option E can also be excluded.

26) The correct answer is A (A necessary but not a sufficient condition).

The structure in the passage can only be found in female birds, the complete absence of it is necessary to determine if a fossil is male. However, it cannot always be found in a female fossil either as the passage states that the medullary bone is depleted as a part of the female's reproductive cycle. Therefore, if the bone is present it is defiantly not male, but if it is absent it may be male, or it could be a female fossil in a particular part of the reproductive cycle. Therefore, the absence of the medullary bone is not a sufficient indicator of a male skeleton, as other evidence would also be required. Hence the correct answer is A.

27) The correct answer is B (1 & 2)

Statement one is correct, 1/6 x 30 = 5% which means that even if the entire group of 17-34 years were responsible for the 15% who used public transport and the 10% who walked or cycled, this still leaves 5% (which is 1/6) who travel by car.

Statement two is also correct as half of the 30% who are 16 or younger (so in other words 15%) could travel by public transport.

Statement three could or could not be correct. 85% of the sample is under the age of 60, meaning that all of them could travel by car and public transport and none by walking or cycling. However, there is insufficient information to determine if this is the case.

28) The correct answer is B (2)

The first piece of information that is important here is that there are groups of four numbers which add up to 14. Looking at the numbers, the following combinations (in order add up to 14):

4 4 2 4
1 5 6 2
4 2 5 3

The last two numbers are 5 and 5 which totals ten. This means that the next two numbers must equal four so that the total of 14 can be reached for this set of four numbers. Since there must be two numbers, this immediately rules out number four on its own. To solve this, the last piece of information must be used which states that "it never generates more than five consecutive odd or even numbers. Since there have already been four consecutive odd numbers, the combination must be an odd number plus an even number. This also rules out numbers one and three as options, leaving two, which is the correct answer.

29) The correct answer is F (1, 2 & 3)

The first step in solving this problem is to identify the conclusion, which is "global travel helps to immunise the population". From here, each of the three reasons can be analysed to find which ones could cause the conclusion to be considered unsafe. Statement one is correct because a lack of frequent travel, means that these individuals are not exposed to the pathogens in question. Which means that they cannot develop an immunity to them, thus if the disease does reach Great Britain, it is likely that these individuals will be affected. Thus bird flu is still concerning. Statement two is also correct because it is a true statement. Just because someone is immune to a vast number of infectious diseases, it does not necessarily mean that he or she is immune to bird flu. Statement three is also correct as the quality of nutrition is influenced by a strong economy as well as other factors, such as the environment in which they are raised, for example exposure to chemical, pesticides, contaminated water.

30)   The correct answer is D (11 in 24)
The fastest way to work out the chance of getting the best of the four cars is through the following:
If the best car is viewed first, it will not be bought, so the probability is zero. If car number two is better than car number one, then the probability of him buying it is 1. If number three is the best car, then the chance of buying it is ½ since he could have picked car number two. If car number four is best, the probability is 1/3 since he could have purchased cars two or three. From here, total the probabilities and divide by four since there are four vehicles to choose from:

$$(0 + 1 + 1/2 + 1/3) / 4$$

The probability is, therefore: 11/24

31)   The correct answer is A (1 only)
The theme of this passage is the benefits and risks of taking aspirin. Thus the statements must reflect this. Statement one talks about the balance of risks and benefits – a direct link to the theme of the passage. Thus it can be deemed correct. Statement two is very general and does not take into account a person's history or lifestyle. Certainly a sedentary occupation can increase the risk of clots. However individuals who play a sport or incorporate physical activity into their lifestyle, outside of their sedentary work, would not necessarily require aspirin. Thus statement two can be excluded. Statement three is not found anywhere in the information provided. Thus it can also be excluded.

32)   The correct answer is D (266)
The sequence reads 2 5 5 5 3 5 1
To ascertain the number, the rule that "elements are multiplied together until a smaller number is encountered" can be used, so the number reads:

$$(2 \times 5 \times 5 \times 5) + (3 \times 5) + 1$$

$$250 + 15 + 1$$

$$= 266$$
(option D)

33) **The correct answer is B (5)**

There is a lot of information in this passage, and it will take time to identify the relevant pieces for this problem. The second paragraph states that one in three individuals visited an alternative therapist, out of a total population of 247 million.

$$247 / 3 = 82 \text{ million people}$$

Line three in the same paragraph quotes 425 million visits to alternative health practitioners. This means that the number of visits per person was:

$$425/82 = 5 \text{ visits per person}$$
(Option B)

34) **The correct answer is C (Time pressure on the medical practitioners has contributed to the increased popularity of alternatives therapies).**

The main issue here is the "time it takes to get to know their patients, to listen, counsel and reassure is – unfortunately – at a premium." This is where alternative medicine has stepped in to fill the void, which means that statement A is not necessarily true given that the passage suggests that they are listening, reassuring and so on. Statement B is not necessarily true either since the author talks about the different definitions of alternative medicine, some of which claim to cure diseases. Statement C is correct as it directly paraphrases the main issue or pressures placed on conventional doctors. Statement D is incorrect - the passage states that the cornerstone of alternative medicine is "the belief in the body's ability to heal itself"; it does not say that some conventional doctors do not share this belief. Statement E is also not necessarily correct as some treatments have side effects, some of which may be worse than the symptoms of the disease.

35) **The correct answer is D (Doctors' behaviour has influenced the change of attitude towards alternative therapies).**

Statement A cannot be implied as the side effects of the treatment may be a sign that the therapy is working and the disease is being cured. Statement B is incorrect given that the passage states that "the best doctors are frustrated that the combined art of healing with the science of medicine is getting harder and harder to do". Statement C also cannot be implied as this passage has nothing to do with pharmaceutical companies or their interests. Statement D is correct as it reflects the void that is being filled by alternative therapists, which is that "doctors have less time for patients".

BMAT Section 1 - 2006

1) The correct answer is C (250:1)

If the seabird population has fallen by 60%, then it used to be 80/0.4 = 200:1.

However, the original human population must also be factored in, which has increased by 25%.

Dividing 1 by 1.25 gives a ratio of 200:0.8. Divide both sides by 0.8 to get a final ratio of 250:1.

2) The correct answer is E (Freedom of speech in a democracy cannot be unrestrained).

The passage is not stating that freedom of speech and tolerance cannot co-exist; only that freedom of speech must have limits placed on it. Therefore statement A can be excluded. It also does not state that inciting hatred should be banned or illegal, thus ruling out statement B.

It does state that freedom of speech is 'generally considered a key feature' of democracy. However, this is only inferred not confirmed. Thus statement C can be ruled out. While the passage does state that limits have to be placed on freedom of speech, it does not say that this is more important than tolerance of minority groups – there should be a compromise, making statement D also incorrect. The passage does specifically state that 'freedom of speech must have limits put upon it if democracy is to be sustained', therefore statement E is correct.

3) The correct answer is B (1 and 3 only)

Shape one can be made by placing the bottom half on the left-hand side of the top half.

Shape two cannot be made as the smaller tables do not provide the obtuse angle shown in the top right or bottom left corner.

Shape three could be made by rotating the shorter sides to the centre.

Shape four could not be made as this would require flipping of the smaller tables.

4) The correct answer is C (It is the job of political journalists to inform voters about the political issues).

Although political journalists may not focus on the right issues, the passage does not imply that they are distorting the truth, thus statement A can be ruled out. Furthermore, the passage does not mention or suggest that voters believe everything they read in the media (as is the case less and less nowadays), thus ruling out option B. Democracy is not explicitly linked to the requirement that voters know about ministers' mistakes. Although it may have the effect of doing so, the passage does not state that political journalists are aiming to destroy the careers of politicians, only that they focus on their mistakes. Thus options D and E can also be excluded.

However, the text does explicitly state that 'the media have an important role to play in a democracy, [to keep] voters well informed about the political issues', making statement C the correct option.

5) The correct answer is 62 seconds

The first train has a total of 615 + 80 = 695 metres to travel. As 45km/h = 12.5m/s this would take 55.6 seconds.

The second train has a total of 615 + 120 + 40 = 775 metres to travel. 775m divided by 12.5m/s = 62 seconds.

6) **The correct answer is C (The print media are inconsistent in their approach to this issue).**

Statement A is an inference that could be made. However, the passage is not about which is more influential, as the data to support this is missing, it states that the two show conflicting views. Thus statement A is not a conclusion.

The fact that the media publishes articles about the dangers of anorexia indicates that they are aware of the effects of the published photos, making statement B false.

The fact that they print both articles about anorexia and images of thin women supports the statement that they are inconsistent in their approach. Thus statement C is the correct option.

As the passage does not mention the opinion of the public on fashion models but does imply it through the required demand, statement D is thereby incorrect.

The passage does not go into detail about the level of understanding of anorexia and bulimia, only stating that articles are published (on current knowledge), thus statement E can also be ruled out.

7) **The correct answer is B (4%)**

It can be seen from the table that 58.7% of the total Asian population achieved 5 A* to C, while only 55.1% of white students achieved the same grade. 58.7 – 55.1 = 3.6% difference. 3.6% rounds up to 4%.

8) **The correct answer is E (Chinese)**

Of the ethnic groups that do not have English as a first language:

White had a VA measure of 1019.3

Mixed had 1005.8

Asian had 1021.9

Black had 1018.7

Chinese had 1036.0

9) **The correct answer is D (Pupils from only one ethnic group with English as a second language perform better at GCSE than their equivalents with English as their first language).**

The total VA measure of all male pupils was 977.5 while the total of all girls was 997.3. Therefore statement A is incorrect.

The proportion is calculated by total eligible pupils/eligible pupils under other than English as a first language:

White = 0.013

Mixed = 0.100

Asian = 0.861

Black = 7053/20391 = 0.346

Chinese = 0.771

Other = 0.677

Therefore, statement B is incorrect.

The difference is calculated by (total % A* - C for boys) – (total % A* - C for girls):

White = 9.9

Mixed = 10.9

Asian = 10.9

Black = 13.7

Chinese = 8.0

Other = 9.8

Therefore, this statement is also incorrect as Chinese has the smallest difference in performance.

Statement D is calculated by comparing the total % A* to C for 'other than English as a first language' with total % A* to C for 'English as a first language:

White = less by 2.7

Mixed = more by 0.3

Asian = less by 12.2

Black = less by 3.2

Chinese = less by 4.3

Other = less by 7.4

Therefore, this statement is correct.

10)   The correct answer is D (The bigger improvement in Asian girls biases the averages).

Answers A, B and C cannot be disproved by the data, while option D can –the considerable improvements in the scores of Asian girls (1026.5 – 1033.3) is not enough to bias the averages significantly.

11)   The correct answer is E (1, 2 and 3)

The results of the study provide a clear link between the length of cannabis smoking and the ability to recall words. Therefore statement one is correct. The research also suggests that cannabis can affect the brain activity for more than 24 hours after smoking it, as all groups had not smoked cannabis 24 hours before the experiment, but the heavier smokers could recall fewer words. Thus statement two is also correct.

It is not known what the IQs of each group were before the experiment, but this could be a possible explanation by chance. Hence statement 3 can also be considered correct.

12)   The correct answer is A (30c)

The new price per unit would be 2/3 x $1.50 = $1/unit.

If the supermarket is still making a gross margin of 40%, this would mean that the supplier receives 60c.

The supplier would have originally received ($1.50 x 0.6 =) 90c

90c – 60c = 30 c

13)   The correct answer is 68p

23p = 23p

32p = 32p

37p = 37p

49p = 49p

50p = 50p

62p = 42p + 20p
68p = 49p + 10p + 9p (Requires three stamps)

14)   The correct answer is C (The opinion of experts does not guarantee the reliability of their method).

Statement A is incorrect as it is the reliability, not the usage of the technique that is in question. Statement B does not identify a weakness as it states that no one, including scientists, knows whether it is reliable because its accuracy has not been measured. Statement C is correct as opinions do not always correlate with fact. Statement D is correct in that it does not prove reliability, but this is not the main reason for not doubting reliability focussed on in the passage.

15)   The correct answer is C (Windyhill)

This question will require some trial and error.

There are only two pairs that are due north and due south of each other (Rheindown/Clashandarran and Aultviach/Ruilick).

The fact Clashandarran is south, and east of Aultviach means that Aultviach must be location A, Ruilick must be location E, and Clashandarran must be location B and Rheindown D.

Wellbank is due east of E. Therefore Wellbank is F.

The only two left are G and C, and as Beauly is southwest of Windyhill, by elimination, Windyhill must be location C.

16)   The correct answer is B (4 only)

Statement one is incorrect because the passage says that developed countries have set targets, but that does not mean that less developed countries have; only that it is unrealistic to expect them to do so.

The opinion of developed countries on the importance of alleviating poverty and reducing global warming is also not discussed; only that developed countries are setting targets to reduce greenhouse emissions. Thus statement two can also be ruled out.

The passage has not discussed whether prosperity in less developing countries is improving, only that this is a focus of the government, which means that statement three cannot be assumed.

Statement four's 'it is considered unrealistic to expect such restraint by the less developed countries as they attempt to improve their economies and thus reduce poverty' can lead the reader to assume that developing countries can only improve their economies by activities which generate greenhouse gases. Hence this is the correct assumption.

17)   The correct answer is B (3)

Two chose to go on Apocalypse which means they also went on the Carousel.
The total cost:

$$= 2 \times (\text{£}9 + \text{£}3.50) = \text{£}25$$

This leaves £100 remaining.
The ten packets of bubble gum at 25p each would then leave £97.50.

The remaining children must have gone on the Armageddon =

$$£7.50 \times 8 = £60$$

This leaves £37.50 left to divide between eight children to go on either the Helter Skelter or Dodgems.
The Dodgems = £5
The Helter Skelter = £4.50

$$8 \times £5 = £40 \ (£2.50 \ over)$$

Helter Skelter is 50p less than Dodgem. Therefore, to remove this £2.50 excess, £2.50/50p = 5 children must have gone on the Helter Skelter, leaving three children to go on the Dodgems.

18)   The correct answer is C (It assumes that the use of pesticides is the only way to avoid making a loss).
The method of use is not discussed in detail, so statement A is incorrect.
Damage to the environment and yield do not always correlate but often work in tandem. Therefore statement B is not the flaw.
No other method is stated as available for avoiding a loss, so it is fair to conclude that the passage assumes this is the only method. Thus C can be considered the flaw in the argument.
The effect of farmers is not mentioned and is likely to be insignificant; therefore statement D can be ruled out.
The passage does not confirm that people who live near farms have been affected 'it is alleged, on people who live near farms…'therefore statement E can be excluded.

19)   The correct answer is E (Wednesday 24th May)
Ayesha misses six sessions while on holiday, thus, it will take her 18 sessions to recover. There are 12 sessions before she hurts her shoulder, meaning she requires six more. Her sore shoulder causes her to miss four more lessons, adding a total of 12 more required sessions to get back to peak physical condition. Assuming she can restart training on the 4th (Thursday), she will be fit again after 18 sessions, which means she will be fully fit on the 24th of May.

20)   The correct answer is B (36% is the closest answer)
There were approximately 31,500 practitioners, 12,500 of whom were female.

$$12,500/31,500 = 39.6\%$$

21)   The correct answer is C (6,000)
48% of female GPs were practising part time, meaning:

$$0.48 \times 12,500 = 6,000$$

22)   The correct answer is D (a rise of 10%)

In 1994, 32% of practitioners were part-time, this number increased to 48% in 2004. In 1994, there were 27,000 GPs, compared to 31,500 in 2004.

In 1994, 32% of GPs were part-time = 8,640 GPs. These worked the equivalent of 4,320 full-time GPs, meaning there was the equivalent of 22,680 full-time GPs.

In 2004, 48% of GPs were part-time = 15,120. This meant there was the equivalent of 23,940 GPs.

This represents an increase of 5.6%, which is closest to the answer of 10%.

23)   The correct answer is B (21)

The average = 22.5

If Suzie's guess is closer, this means the weight must be <22.5.

As the mean value is the closest, the value must be 21.

24)   The correct answer is C (Unless H5N1 mutates, a worldwide epidemic amongst humans of this strain of bird flu is unlikely).

Statement A is incorrect because a lack of prevention is not necessarily correlated with the number of people who will catch the disease.

Statement B is also incorrect because a high level of mutations does not mean there will be an epidemic. Like the mutation itself, the effects of a mutation are highly unpredictable.

Currently, the flu cannot be transmitted easily between people. For this to become possible, a mutation would have to enable this. Therefore statement C is the correct conclusion.

Birds are not the only source of the flu – other humans are, thus statement D can also be excluded.

25)   The correct answer is B (64:3)

If one hour passes:

The area of the minute hand will be pi x 8.4^2 = 221.67

The area of the hour hand will be (pi x 6.3^2)/12 = 10.39

This is a ratio of 21.33:1 = 63.99:3 or 64:3

26)   The correct answer is D (1 and 2 only)

It is possible that demand may have increased such that green technologies cannot cope and nuclear energy is needed. It is not known, only predicted, how much of an effect green technology will continue to have.

Therefore statement three provides a reason why the above conclusion may be safe, not unsafe.

27)   The correct answer is 5 hours

Assuming that the total flat = 10km, the climb = 5km and the descent = 5km:

The flat will take 2.5 hours to walk,

The rise will take 1.67 hours to walk,

Moreover, the descent will take 5/6 = 0.83 hours to walk

Total = 5 hours

28) **The correct answer is B (When there is enough food to go round the snaffers can breed freely when the population is large, there is high mortality due to starvation).**

Statement A is false as the graph shows that there is a change in the population each year. Otherwise, the graph would be a straight line.

Statement B explains the shape of the graph well – when the population is low, there is an increase (due to food for example). Likewise, when the population is high, the trend line starts to decrease (due to starvation)

Statement C is inconclusive. Exact numbers cannot be attributed based on the population trend as the graph is not accurate enough to do so.

Statement D is inconclusive because the population peaked when the gradient = 1, not 0, as this would mean there is no change in population growth (is the same next year).

Statement E is inconclusive as this would show a line oscillating about the current line.

29) **The correct answer is D (1 and 3 only)**

Statement one does not confirm that ingesting acrylamide is less dangerous for humans than for animals. It only suggests that the increased fat intake and bacterial populations must also be taken into account. Therefore this can be concluded from the passage.

It is unknown whether ingesting acrylamide is less dangerous for humans than for animals. Therefore, it cannot be determined whether cooking above or below 120 degrees is healthier, so statement two is inconclusive.

Statement three is correct because eating roasted or fried potatoes do inevitably pose some risks – acrylamide presence at temperatures over 120 degrees and an increased fat and bacterial intake under 120 degrees.

30) **The correct answer is A (19)**

The volume of the shape produced by the 2cm cubes is going to be 3 x 4 = 12 for the vertical sections, 3 for the core region and then 4 for each of the four horizontal corners 4 x 4 x 12 = 152cm^3.

The volume of one 2cm cube = 8cm^3.

152/8 = 19

31) **The correct answer is B (The former giants of IT no longer look down on Google).**

The last paragraphs state that Microsoft does not want anyone repeating on the internet what it achieved in computer systems, meaning Google has not yet achieved this. Therefore statement A is incorrect.

It also states that the three recently looked down on Google and that they do not anymore, thus statement B is correct.

The solution to merge with Google's rivals is implied in the passage but is not indicated to be the only possible method, thus statement C is not necessarily correct.

It is stated in the last line that consumers will lose out if the players gang up against them – not if they merge, which could prove beneficial as long as they are not against the consumer, thus making statement D incorrect.

32)   The correct answer is (must have been at least £660 million)

Revenue is now 180% of what it was in the first quarter of 2006, equalling over £1.2 billion.

£1.2 billion/1.8 = £667 million. Therefore, the revenue in the first quarter must have been at least £660 million.

33)   The correct answer is C (That the danger facing Google is the prospect of an alliance)

It is unknown whether the dragon (Microsoft, e-Bay and Yahoo) or the knight (Google) will win or the feelings of either, thus statements A, B, D and E can be ruled out.

The only thing that can be determined with certainty is that the three heads of the dragon form one body, inferring that the threat to Google consists of Microsoft, e-Bay and Yahoo, i.e. an alliance.

34)   The correct answer is C (1 and 2 only)

Statement one indicates that Google is gaining pace in comparison to Microsoft due to its corporate link with AOL.

Statement two indicates that is also gaining pace in comparison to the other companies as it is getting a more significant share of the market.

Statement three is inconclusive as it does not reveal the relative proportion of the internet's potential that Google is grasping and so it cannot be said whether it is gaining pace in comparison to the other companies.

35)   The correct answer is A (Competition is generally good for consumers).

Generally speaking, competition is indicated to be good for consumers due to 'rich entertainment and opportunities, as long as the players do not gang up on them'. Therefore statement A is implied.

Nowhere in the text does it mention that the big companies must merge with one another, only that they have the option to merge, thus statement B can be ruled out.

Statement C can be disproved by the history of Google – rising against the 'giants'.

Although it is implied that the three giant companies will team up against Google, the notion that any of them could merge with Google has not been discredited. Thus statement D can also be ruled out.

Likewise, the threat of Google is highlighted, but the threat of the other companies has not been discredited. Thus statement E can be excluded.

BMAT Section 1 - 2007

1)   The correct answer is B (6.5m)

The following formula describes the growth of the tree:

$$h = 30 - (29 \times 0.9^{\,t-1})$$

Where h is the height of the tree and t is the number of years.

This equation considers the height of the tree at the end of the first year, the theoretical maximum height of the tree and the increase of 10% of the difference per year.

After three years of growth, this equation would be:

$$h = 30 - (29 \times 0.9^{\,3-1})$$

Therefore h = 6.51

2)   The correct answer is C (uniquely dangerous)

It is clear from the information that WMD's are indeed a serious threat when the number and method of deaths caused by nukes in World War Two are described. The passage also puts forward an argument for the use of WMDs, suggesting that they are necessarily devastating and morally unacceptable by describing the damage and horrible ways in which they were used to kill people during World War Two.

The text does, however, explain that WMDs are not uniquely dangerous when it compares the number of deaths caused by WMDs to the number of deaths caused by 'conventional' bombing. This explains that although on a different magnitude to WMDs, conventional bombing is still dangerous and so WMDs are not unique.

3)   The correct answer is C

The total increase in sales is 300,000.

60,000 of this is due to Asquith.

40,000 is due to Burton.

50,000 is due to Coleridge.

100,000 is due to Darwin.

And 50,000 is due to Elgar.

It is clear the largest contribution to the increase is from Darwin, therefore only A, B and C are viable charts based on this information.

Of these, the pie chart that shows an equal contribution from both Coleridge and Elgar needs to be selected. The only pie chart that displays this is C, which is, therefore, the correct answer.

4)   The correct answer is A (1 only)

Statement one would weaken the argument of the passage if correct as it implies that the high number of fatalities is not due to the lack of skill or mastery of young first-attempt-pass drivers.

Statement two would strengthen the above argument, as young passengers are unlikely to hold a licence and therefore be present in a supervisory capacity.

Having 100 hours of driving experience would mean that drivers are more likely to pass their first test with a 'much higher level of mastery of driving skills', strengthening that argument of the passage.

5)   The correct answer is B (geriatric)

The percentage occupancy is calculated by (the number of occupied beds divided by the number of available beds) x 100

The acute sector has 84.8% occupancy

Geriatric has 91.3%

Mental illness has 87.9%

Learning disabilities have 84.4%

Maternity has 63.1%

6)   The correct answer is B (It ignores the possible effects on the crime rate of other leisure activities).

The statement does not assume that boxers are never aggressive; it states that boxing is not primarily about aggression.

The passage does not mention the effect of any other leisure activities that may or may not be set up at the same time as the boxing club.

Again, the statement does not state that most young men lack discipline and self-restraint, only that boxing can help to increase these features due to its focus on them.

The passage implies that this is the exact reason young men take up boxing 'the way to reverse the trend towards inversing violence amongst the young is to encourage more young men to take up boxing.'

7)   The correct answer is E (1/10)

There is a 3/5 chance the second flower will be different from the first, then a 2/4 chance the third will be different from the second, a 2/3 chance the fourth will be different to the third and a ½ chance the 5th will be different to the 4th. Multiplying these probabilities together provides the total probability of 1/10.

8)   The correct answer is C (The lack of a simple explanation does not make an occurrence paranormal).

The passage does not state that paranormal phenomena are impossible (which is the same as saying everything that occurs has an explanation). Instead, it suggests that a lack of explanation does not make the occurrence paranormal – this is the case with the fire-walking: most people are unaware of the methodology, but this does not mean it is a paranormal occurrence. The passage also does not state that spoon bending and telepathy do not occur, only that they are often considered to be paranormal.

9)   The correct answer is E (14.6g)

A 2kg cat would require (30 x 2 + 70) = 130 kcal per day. Factor in the sepsis condition and this would increase the kcal/day requirement to (1.6 x 130) = 208 kcal/day.

As the cat only requires protein for maintenance since it is not in hepatic or renal failure, thus, the requirement would be 208/100 x 7 = 14.56g of protein.

10)   The correct answer is C (0.9g too little)

The energy intake required would be $(70 \times 1^{0.75}) = 70$.

Factor in the post-trauma condition and that would increase the required energy to $(1.3 \times 70) = 91$ kcal/day.

This means the kitten would have to receive 91ml of CCFR per day to match its energy requirements. Thus providing $(91 \times 0.06) = 5.46$g of protein per day.

The kitten would require 7g/100kcal meaning as she is taking in 91kcal per day it would require $(91/100 \times 7) = 6.37$g of protein.

$5.46 - 6.37 = -0.91$g

11)   The correct answer is C (ES)

A cat suffering renal failure would require 4g/100kcal of protein per day. This would require energy content to protein ratio of 1:0.04 in the feed formula – ES has this exact ratio.

12)   The correct answer is C (150 ml)

100ml of CCF would provide a ratio of energy to protein of 1:0.09. The required ratio is 1:0.06 to match that of CCFR. ES has a ratio of 1:0.04.

This means that 3 parts ES for every 2 parts CCF would be needed $(2 \times 0.09 + 3 \times 0.04)/5 = 0.06$.

Therefore for 100ml of CCF, 3/2 of ES this would be needed = 150ml of ES.

13)   The correct answer is C (5)

Considering one group value on the bar chart, for example, 9% of the 16-24 year group drank on x days or more.

The total number of 16-24-year-olds is 99 (taken from the table).

9% of 99 = 9

The data shows that 9 (3 + 2 + 4 = 9) 16-24 year olds drank for five days or more, therefore x = 5.

14)   The correct answer is A (Many dogs that had a hearing impairment did not show an increase in anxiety on 27 February 2001).

Statement B would not offer support as it states seismic waves are detectable up to 100m while the city is 240km away.

Whoever observed the dog's behaviour is unlikely to have a significant result on the findings (although it might make it less precise and accurate), and insignificant when compared to the percentage of anxious behaviour observed and the chances of this happening. Thus statement C can be ruled out.

Statement D provides an argument against the passage and the method of detection by dogs; it does not support it.

Statement A does support the passage as it implies that dogs with poor hearing were unable to hear and therefore respond to the impending earthquake.

15)   The correct answer is C (Paul by 29 votes)
P = 116
E = 58
A = (116+58)/2 = 87 = one third of the total votes.
Therefore Paul won, and by (116-87=) 29 votes.

16)   The correct answer is A (It assumes that what is true for a group is true for each individual).
The passage is only talking about the relationship between education and longevity for people in Sweden, and so statement C is invalid. Likewise, it does not mention the health of the individuals at the time of educational attainment or the lifestyle of the individuals. Thus statement D is incorrect. It does, however, generalise the findings of the study to individuals 'so it is clear that someone who is awarded a PhD in Sweden will live longer than they would have done if they had not studied for a higher degree.

17)   The correct answer is B (2 only)
The number of puffs does not affect the total nicotine of the cigarette and therefore its addictiveness, thus statement one is irrelevant. Likewise, statement three mentions drugs blocking nicotine are being tested – these are not yet released to the public and so would not have any effect on the level of addictiveness. However, if statement two were correct, this would mean that the typical smoker may take in the same amount of nicotine as the higher nicotine content is offset by, the fewer number of cigarettes smoked, therefore presenting a flaw in the argument.

18)   The correct answer is B (1.5m)
Bob can buy 140/2.8 = 50 slabs maximum. This means that the area laid must be five slabs wide and ten long = 3.5m wide and 7m long. As the patio garden is 5m wide, the paving slabs would leave 1.5m width for the flower bed.

19)   The correct answer is B (19 minutes 15 seconds)
The time gap is 4 seconds between the two drivers.
1 minute 10 seconds = 70 seconds.
70/4 = 17.5 laps.
If each lap takes the faster driver 1 minute 6 seconds, then 17.5 laps would take 66 x 17.5/60 = 19.25 minutes = 19 minutes 15 seconds.

20)   The correct answer is D (10.6%)
The number of men screened positive would equal the number of false positives + the number of true positives = 85 + 21 = 106 per 1000 = 10.6%

21)   The correct answer is C (3.3%)

Study one is PSA. 0.1 x 0.26 = 2.6% true positives and 0.9 x 0.8 = 0.72% false negatives, therefore the total rate of confirmed prostate cancer is 3.32%

22) The correct answer is A (P and Q)

The percentage of true positives in DRE is 8.5% while the percentage of false negatives is 2.1%. Therefore PSA gives fewer false negatives and fewer true positives.

23) The correct answer is B (6)

0.1 x 74% = 7.4% of men get false positives from the PSA test whilst 8.5% of men get false positives from the DRE test therefore 0.074 x 0.085 = 0.00629%.
Multiply this by 1000 = 6 people.

24) The correct answer is D (neither a necessary nor a sufficient condition for globalisation).

The passage states that the internet is not essential for globalisation. It does however state that to move goods and people around the world easily affordable transport is necessary.
It also states that the internet is not a sufficient condition for globalisation as it allows the exchange of ideas but not the movement of goods and people, which is the definition of globalisation.

25) The correct answer is B (4.9 billion gallons)

If (334,000+54,000) would produce 35 billion gallons of ethanol then every billion gallons of fuel requires 388,000/35 = 11,085 square km of land. 54,000/11085 = 4.87 billion gallons of ethanol currently being produced.

26) The correct answer is C (1/2)

The possible seating arrangements are:
OxP MNx
OxP NMx
OxP xNM
ONM Pxx
OMN Pxx
Oxx PNM
Therefore the number of situations where Q and R can sit in adjacent seats is 3/6 = ½.

27) The correct answer is C (417)

6/50 = 12% of the chicken population has had rings on their legs.
12% of the chicken population = 50
Therefore 100/12 x 50 = 416.7 chickens.

28)   The correct answer is A (A later study showed that myopic parents are more likely to leave children's lights on than those without myopia).

Children with myopic parents are more likely to develop myopia, since this condition can be inherited, not because their parents have left on the light. If myopic parents leave the light on, this indicates that either the parent or the child struggles to see at night time.

Statement B does not indicate a flaw as the study only concerns the development of myopia in children. American children may also be exposed to different trends with regards to sleeping with the lights on than the rest of the world. Finally, just because a child does not wear glasses does not mean that they do not have myopia.

29)   The correct answer is C (Sales of diamonds are an important source of revenue for the 'recognised governments' of war-torn countries).

The fact that it may never be possible to trace the origin of a diamond means that one can never be sure it is a 'clean' diamond, meaning it will always be morally unjustifiable.

Military intervention may have a more significant effect than the money generated from the sale of conflict diamonds, but this does not mean that conflict diamonds do not still have a considerable impact on war-torn countries and the purchase of diamonds is therefore still morally unjustifiable.

If the sale of diamonds also supports the recognised government, one could argue that by purchasing the diamonds they are funding the fight against rebel groups and so the purchase is morally justifiable.

The last statement has nothing to do with the moral justification of diamond purchase, and may even imply it is more morally unjust.

30)   The correct answer is E (Q and S)

R will have no right-hand side face as viewed vertically.

P will have no 'north' side face when assembled as viewed vertically.

31)   The correct answer is B (156 bpm)

$$217 - (0.85 \times 60)$$

$$= 166 + 4$$

$$= 170 - 14$$

$$= 156 \text{ bpm}$$

32)   The correct answer is D (Education beyond the age of 21 or 22 on average does not enhance women's wages).

The wages are proportional to those leaving school at each age, for each sex when compared to the wage earned by people who left school at 15 for that gender. This means the absolute value of the wages is unknown and so one cannot say whether men or women earned more, only who increased their wage by a more significant percentage by leaving at ages up to 19. Therefore statement A can be ruled out.

Statement C is proved wrong by the various flat lines shown. For example; between ages 18 and 19 for men the wage did not increase.

Statement D is correct as the wage peaks at 21 years and decreases as the leaving age increases.

33)   The correct answer is C (That higher wages are due mainly to the extra education).

Graduates with extremely high wages create valid data, not bias so statement A is incorrect.

The data does not reveal the wages people earn at different ages, only the wages they earn on average following leaving education at certain ages, thus statement B is irrelevant.

They would have to assume that other factors play a minimal role in increasing these wages to place a link on the school leaving age and wages; otherwise the relationship would be invalid. Thus statement C is correct.

Statement D would completely invalidate the link they generated from their findings, and statement E is not relevant as the investigation is into the earning potential of school leavers, not their earnings in the first year.

34)   The correct answer is B (Graduates in low paying jobs in the public sector are more likely to be trade union members).

Trade Unions were created to protect the lower skilled workers from exploitation. If financial returns are less for the trade union members, this suggests that the graduates that are members of the trade unions are likely to be in lower paying jobs. Therefore, graduates in lower paid jobs are more likely to be trade union members than their peers in higher paid jobs.

35)   The correct answer is D (The average gradient is lower than it would have been otherwise).

The graph that considered older people would have had a negative gradient – the later they left education, the less they would earn. When combined with the younger generation, this would offset the steeper trend and reduce the slope.

BMAT Section 1 - 2008

1)   The correct answer is D (Some Malgons are Tvints).

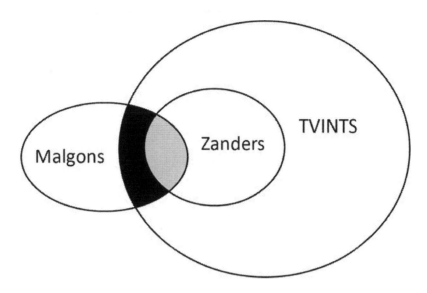

It is essential to draw a Venn diagram when answering this question.

'All Zanders are Tvints'; Based on this statement, therefore the circle representing 'Zanders' can be drawn within the circle of the TVINTs

'Some Malgons are Zanders'; To capture this idea of '*Some,*' the circles must be drawn overlapping, this area of overlap is shown in grey.

There is also a second region of overlap in Black which reveals that: 'Some Malgons are Tvints'; thus, the answer is D.

2)   The correct answer is C (Reciprocal altruism is compatible with traditional evolutionary theory).

First, begin by eliminating all of the conclusions which don't relate strongly enough to the argument presented: A; B; D. This leaves options C and E. In normal circumstances, E would be correct. However, it fails to recognise what separates 'reciprocal altruism' from true 'altruism'. This is that the former is an investment made by the bird to secure their future which means that they are still pursuing personal survival. Therefore, E cannot be correct, and the only true conclusion is C.

3)   The correct answer is B (15%)

The giveaway is the use of the operative 'or' which hints that the sum of 2 probabilities needs to be found.

Total number of screws = 250

Chances of selecting a 4mm screw 35mm long = 20/ 250 = 0.08

Chances of selecting a 4mm screw 45mm long = 18/250 = 0.072

$$0.08+0.072 = 0.152$$

$$0.152 \times 100 = 15.2$$

Rounded to nearest 1% = 15%

4)   The correct answer is A (whether they have been involved in major drug discoveries).
With respect to the nature of the argument, answer A is most applicable. This is because the author is attempting to explain to the reader that the mere fact that animal testing was part of the process of finding a significant drug is irrelevant; what truly matters is how that animal was used in the process. Answer A, therefore, is the only argument which reflects the general theme of the argument and completes the gap.

5)   The correct answer is E (Six)
The first step is to work out which die is 'conventional' and which is 'unconventional.'
The grey die must be conventional. The reason for this is that in image one of the grey die, the number 6 is on top, and the number 3 is on the adjacent face to 5. In image two, the die has been rotated so that the number five is still on the left side, while 6 has replaced the number 3 on the adjacent face: meaning the number 3 is now on the bottom of the die. In this second Image, the number 4 is on top
Based on the conventional die principle, where opposite faces make a total of 7: 3+4 = 7, the grey die is conventional and the white is unconventional

To work out what number is opposite 2 on the unconventional die, consider what remains constant in both images: the number 6. Use this as a point of reference to determine the solution

In Image one of the white die: 6 is on top; the numbers 3 and 5 are also visible. Thus: 3 and 5 cannot be opposite 6; only options left are 1, 4 and 2.

In Image two of the white die: 6 is visible once more, but this time 1 and 4 are visible. Thus 1 and 4 cannot be opposite 6, leaving 2. Therefore, the number on the opposite face to 2 must be 6.

6)   The correct answer is D (1 and 2)
The title conflates the idea of all digital interactions with just social networking, which is an incorrect assertion. The digital landscape is much larger than just social networking, and it is plausible that men between the ages of 45-54 are using other sites: their social media presence does not reflect the entirety of their digital use. Also, the data sample used to justify the headline is too small.

7)   The correct answer is D (19.6%)

$$60cm \times 60cm = 0.6m \times 0.6m = 0.36m^2 \text{ (large squares)}$$

56

60 x 40cm = 0.6m x 0.4m = 0.24m^2 (rectangles)

40 x 40cm = 0.16m^2 (small squares)

Area of the patio = 5x4 = 20m^2

Number of large black squares = 6

Number of rectangles = 6

Number of small black squares = 2

Sum of black area in patio = (6x0.36) + (6x0.24) + (2x0.16) = 3.92m^2

Percentage of Patio which is black = 3.92/20 = 0.196 = 19.6%

8)   The correct answer is 39%

Identify the relative risk column (left-handed over non-left-handed)

Perform the sum: 1.39-1 = 0.39 = 39%

9)   The correct answer is B (2.5)

361+65 = 426 (total cases)

153422 + 19119 = 172541 total (estimated) person-years lived

426/172541 ~ 4.25/170

= 2.5%

10)   The correct answer is A (2.5)

144 + 20 = 164 (total cases)

65245 total person-years lived

164/65245 ~ 1.65/65

= 2.5%

11) **The correct answer is D (The same hormonal changes in the mother cause the foetus to have a tendency to be left-handed and to have a susceptibility to breast cancer).**

Assessing each of the options, statement B is irrelevant to being left-handed. Statement C fails to provide an appropriate causal link. Statement E is negligible because the 'relative risk' value takes into account the number of people in the group, so it does not matter the number of people involved. Only statement D gives a potential causal reason for the positive correlation seen.

12) **The correct answer is A (£1,638)**

No. of adults = **z**; Ticket Price = **y**

Last week's profits = **zy** = £1560

A 40% increase in adult attendance = 1.4z

A 25% drop in price = 0.75y

1.4z multiplied by 0.75y = 1.05zy = 1.05 multiplied by 1560 = £1,638

13) **The correct answer is E (2 and 3)**

With regards to statement one, one cannot be sure that pressure groups have not manipulated people's opinions, thus it can be omitted. Statement two is correct because if 34% of those questioned think cars contribute more to climate change and 40% think planes do, and then at least some of these people are wrong. Statement three is also correct, because if 47% think air travel should be limited, but only 15% are willing to fly less often, there must be some who think air travel should be restricted but are unwilling to fly less often (say all 15% that are willing to fly less frequently also want to limit air travel, there are still 32% who match this criterion).

14) **The correct answer is A (3)**

Steve Cram set his WR (world record) time in July 1985
The next WR was set in August 1985
The next WR was set in July 1995
The final new WR was set in 1998 by HEG
So there have been 3 in total

15) **The correct answer is D (The human body reacts to low-level radiation from mobile phones).**

Only D can be correct as the passage says that cells respond to low-level radiation from phones.

16) **The correct answer is D**

For the initial part of the tank, for every increase in measurement along the dipstick, there is an even greater volume of liquid. Therefore, there is an accelerating curve, suggesting options D or E.

The line on the graph then becomes flat/straight because the measurement along the dipstick is constant with respect to the volume of the liquid; this still leaves D or E as possible options.

What separates D as the correct answer, is that when the tank narrows, an increase in the measurement along the dipstick precipitates a lower increase in volume – creating a decelerating curve.

17)   The correct answer is A (1 only)
 Only statement one is correct – the argument asserts that pop stars and celebrities should not be promoting environmental awareness for a variety of reasons, but if they have a vast sphere of influence, perhaps they should.

18)   The correct answer is A (2)
The resulting solution must contain 1% or less of the chemical.
The volume of each droplet could be as high as $0.025cm^3$ based on rounding and the water volume as low as $5cm^3$
To ensure that the limit of 1% is not exceeded, 1% of $5cm^3 = 0.05cm^3$ which is the maximum volume of chemical that can be used. This equates to $0.05/0.025 = 2$ which means that a maximum this solution can have is two drops.

19)   The correct answer is 79
Adding to the average lifespan 3.6 years with 30 minutes of running a day =

$$75 + 3.6 = 78.6 \text{ or } 79 \text{ years}$$

20)   The correct answer is C
3.6 years additional lifespan years added for 30mins running and 1.4 years gained for walking
Percentage Increase:

$$= (3.6-1.4) \times (100/1.4) = 157\%$$

21)   The correct answer is C (It infers more than is supported by the evidence in the passage).
This observation is not stated in the passage; however, if the study has used information from the Framingham Heart Study, one could assume that some of these individuals would have been middle-aged and the benefits could have been observed in this study. Therefore the inference could be drawn from this information in the passage.

22)   The correct answer is D (It is the exercising rather than other factors which increases longevity).
The conclusion from the passage is that: 'people who exercise regularly really do live longer'. This statement proposes a causal link between exercising and living longer. However, there may be additional unseen factors which

contribute towards the extension of life of which the readers have not been made aware. Option A does not need to be assumed for the conclusion to make sense. The intensity of the walking/running is not an idea explored in the passage either; one can be overweight and still exercise a lot, countering the assumptions outlined in C and E.

23)   The correct answer is D (107 seconds)
One flash for each of A and B; 2 flashes for C, D, E and F; 3 flashes for letters G to N and four flashes for the rest

$$(2x1) + (4x2) + (8x3) + (12x4) \text{ flashes}$$

$$= 82 \text{ seconds}$$

Add 25 seconds for each gap:

$$82+25 = 107 \text{ seconds}$$

24)   The correct answer is D (Nowadays, players can make more money from appearances and outside commitments than they do from winning competitions).
The first line of the second paragraph suggests they used to have to win many times just to make a living, whereas now they can make millions only from appearances, and it can be assumed that making that much money from appearances is more than one needs to live.

25)   The correct answer is 245
Before the election, Party B had 'x' seats; Party R has 2.5 times more seats as B thus party R = 2.5x seats
After the election, Party R's lead was reduced by 56.
This means B gained 28 seats and R lost 28 therefore:

$$B = x +28$$

$$R = 2.5x - 28$$

R now has 1.5times more seats B translating into the following equation:

$$R = 2.5x - 28 = 1.5(x+28)$$

$$x = 70$$

So the total number of seats:

$$2.5 x + x$$

$$= (2.5 \times 70) + 70 = 245$$

26) **The correct answer is D (1 and 2)**

Statement one is correct; the argument insinuates that only those who have been convicted should have their DNA stored because it is these people who will re-offend in the future. However, they could be first-time offenders, who may not be convicted.

Statement two is also correct; as those who are not found guilty of certain crimes may in fact have genuinely committed them and are not first time offenders, meaning their DNA sample should be kept according to the author's logic. Statement three suggests that DNA evidence may not be necessary to solve these crimes, which would strengthen the argument against DNA storage, rather than weakening it.

27) **The correct answer is C (70 km/hr)**

The convoy's speed can be termed x and the courier's speed termed y. Using distance = speed x time, the time to get from the front to the back = 1/120 hours, and add the speeds of the convoy and courier to get the net speed of the courier travelling backwards.

$$1km = (1/120) (x+y), so x + y = 120$$

The time to get from the back to the front = 1/20 hours, and to get there, find the difference between the speed of the courier and the convoy to get the net speed of him travelling forwards.

$$1km = (1/20) (y-x), so y - x = 20.$$

Solve simultaneous equations x+y=120 and y-x=20 and y = 70.

28) **The correct answer is E (None of the above)**

All answers are correct. The third sentence assumes statement one - that increased climate change will cause increased flooding. The last sentence assumes statement two - that there will be limited geographic mobility due to flooding, which implies there will be no action taken to prevent this flooding. Statement three is correct because the argument suggests that people in flooded areas will find it even more difficult to sell their houses.

29) **The correct answer is C (37)**

There are ten numbers in the sequence rather than 12 which means that two of these numbers need to have single digits, to make up the six lottery numbers.

Test the combination of numbers it could be - there is only one correct combination. For example, since the maximum number is 49, the 7s must either be the second digit of a number or just be a 7. Furthermore, numbers cannot be repeated; so there will only be one 7 and one 37. Thus the combination is 34 37 4 27 33 7, with the highest number being 37.

30) **The correct answer is E (1 and 3 only)**

Statement one is correct - because there is another more common cause of accidents,however, it does not mean that these speed traps are not of use. Statement two is incorrect - the fact remains that drivers under 25 cause more accidents than drivers who speed, a fact that the writer clearly states in the passage (hence it has not been ignored). Statement three is correct - the last sentence suggests safe, and responsible driving does not include obeying the speed limit.

31)   The correct answer is B
One way to do this is by visualisation; draw a 3D grid that is 3 x 2 x 2, to see which parts of the grid that piece F and G would cover, this reveals that the only piece to fit in is B.

32)   The correct answer is E (27)
An average of 14 cycle trips per person per year equals 1% of their trips. Thus, there are 1400 trips per person per year, which is roughly 1400/50 = 27 per week.

33)   The correct answer is D (8% of the population cycle between 1 and 11 times per year).
Statement A is not correct - 85% cycle less than once a week, the distance is unknown. Statements B and C cannot be inferred as there is not enough information. Statement D can be inferred - 15% cycle at least once a week, 8% at least once a month, and 69% less than once a year. This leaves 100 - 8 - 15 - 69 = 8% that cycle between 1 and 11 times a year.

34)   The correct answer is C (A significant number of people with average or above average incomes do not own cars).
The graph suggests that having higher levels of car ownership decreases the cycling frequency. The text indicates that having more income means that a person cycles more. Statement C provides the reason to explain the inverse relationship between income and cars.

35)   The correct answer is B (2 but not 1)
Statement one is not correct. Males between the ages of 21 and 29 cycle 78 miles a year, making 27 trips, so 78/27 = 2.6 miles per trip. Males between the ages of 11 and 16 cycle 74 miles a year, making 46 trips, so 74/46 = 1.5 miles per trip. The first result is less than double the second. Statement two is correct, males between the ages of 11 and 16 cycle 46 times a year and males between 17 to 20 cycle 29 times a year, so the younger cohort cycle more often. However, they average less per trip (74/46 ~ 1.5 miles, compared to 59/29 ~ 2 miles per trip).

BMAT Section 1 - 2009

1) The correct answer is 15

The key to this question is to understand that this is a cumulative frequency graph. Hence, to establish the number of monarchs who reigned between 20 and 40 years, subtract the cumulative number of monarchs who have reigned up to 20 years from the cumulative number of monarchs who have reigned up to 40 years.

$$35 - 20 = 15 \text{ Monarchs}$$

2) The correct answer is B (The highest levels of pain relief and medical intervention are not possible away from a labour ward).

A statement that is 'implied' is one that is strongly suggested, without adding additional substance or any direct mention. Statement A is not mentioned and the passage does not suggest that the health secretary is wrong or right regarding this issue thus it can be ruled out.

The final paragraph states 'the labour ward...surrounded with as much pain relief and medical intervention as possible' implies that to have high levels of pain relief, this must be in the hospital setting. Hence, option B is the correct answer

There is no mention or suggestion that there is a cost-cutting motive to the plan change, nor that home births are more cost-effective, therefore statement C can be excluded.

The final paragraph refers to the debate amongst feminists and how this issue has 'divided women for decades'. Hence statement D is inaccurate and can also be excluded.

There is no mention or reference to any clinical outcomes for mother's or babies, therefore, making statement E unfounded.

3) The correct answer is D

This question is best answered by tabulating the information provided:

		Option				
		A	B	C	D	E
Heights	A	6	6	6	6	5*
	B	4 *	4*	3	3	3
	C	3*	4	5*	4	4
	D	2	2	2	2	3*
	E	3	2*	2*	3	3

For height A, four out of five answers state a height of 6 boxes, hence it can be established that option E is incorrect as it states a height of 5 boxes (this has been starred in the table). For height B, three out of five answers state a height of 3 boxes, hence options A and B are incorrect (these are also starred in the table). For height C, three out of five answers state a height of 4 boxes, hence options A and C are incorrect. As the process is repeated for heights D and E, option D becomes the only option which does not have any incorrect heights, making this the correct answer.

4)   The correct answer is B (The Government was right not to spend heavily on precautions against prolonged snowfall).

The main conclusion of an argument is one which can be supported by reasons given in the passage and can often be deduced using the 'therefore rule'.

While statement A may be true, this statement is relatively vague and does not represent the main reason as to why this article was written.

Statement B is the correct answer as the second half of the passage is biased toward this side of the argument, stating that the recent severe weather is 'one such case' of preventative measures costing too much compared to the likelihood of the event happening.

Statement C is not a conclusion as pandemics and asteroids are only an example given to support the main conclusion.

Statement D opposes the conclusion given the "likelihood of a prolonged period of heavy snow" quoted in the passage and hence is inaccurate.

Statement E is entirely irrelevant to the passage and is neither stated nor implied.

5)   The correct answer is E (21)

This question is best answered through the use of a tally chart as shown below. The information in the question gives the following information:

There is at least one grandchild born in each month (therefore tally one in each month)

There are three pairs of twins born in April (therefore the total for April is six; or possibly seven, eight, nine etc. however the question asks for the minimum, and hence six is the absolute minimum number of grandchildren born in April).

There are a further two pairs of twins (to have the minimum number of grandchildren, these twins would be allocated to separate months. They could be allocated to any months without impact on the calculations, and for reference, they have been placed in May and June).

There are double as many granddaughters as grandsons (therefore the total number of grandchildren must be divisible by three)

Jan	Feb	Mar	April	May	June	July	Aug	Sep	Oct	Nov	Dec
I	I	I	IIIIII	II	II	I	I	I	I	I	I

When the number of children in the tally chart is totalled, it reaches 19. The minimum number above 19 which is divisible by three is 21, hence making 'E' the correct answer.

6)   The correct answer is G (1,2 and 3)

In this question, each of the statements requires assessment regarding whether they will weaken the argument being made. Note, unlike other questions, there may be more than one weakness or assumption and hence any statements that may weaken the arguments being made are being asked for.

Statement one weakens the intermediate conclusion that campaigns are not necessary; it thus weakens the main conclusion that ecstasy is not as dangerous as people believe.

Statement two weakens the comparison made between horse-riding and taking ecstasy. If horse riding were considered an unsafe activity, there would be no benefit of comparing ecstasy to it.

Statement three weakens the evidence supporting the reason provided in the passage. If fewer young people use ecstasy than engage in horse-riding, then the comparison is not appropriate and lacks weight.

7) The correct answer is C (£70)

Given that the cost of gold or silver membership would be the same, the following equation can be used to calculate the number of visits:

$$80 + 1x = 100 + 0.5x$$

$$0.5x = 20$$

$$x \text{ (number of visits)} = 40$$

Using the number of visits, the total cost with the bronze membership is:

$$70 + (3 \times 40) = £190$$

The total cost with the gold or silver membership would be:

$$80 + (1 \times 40) = £120$$

Hence, the total saving of changing membership is £190 - £120 = £70.

8) The correct answer is B (Greater than 0.25 but less than 0.33).

The second and fourth bullet points respectively contain the key information to answer this question. Firstly, the total number of people who did not report a crime to the police is 421; while the number of people who said that this was because they did not believe the crime was sufficiently important was 133. Some long division will produce the following:

$$133/421 = 0.3159$$

9) The correct answer is G (None of the above)

Statement one is incorrect, as not only does the information provided relate to past information (rather than predicting the future), it also states that the percentage of not reporting was 38% which is less than the 'at least 50%' in this statement.

By adding those who lacked confidence in the police (215), to those who were not satisfied with the speed of response (224), to those who were not satisfied with the work of the police (324) this provides a total of 763, which is less than half which is required to regard something as a majority. Therefore statement two is incorrect.

A total of 698 people reported a crime last year (1119 – 421 = 698). The number of people who were dissatisfied was 548 (224+324 = 548). Given that there is no overlap in these numbers and there is no additional information to suggest otherwise, it cannot be concluded that 120 people gave more than one reason for saying they were dissatisfied. Thus statement three is incorrect.

10)   The correct answer is A (failure by the police to deal with many crimes reported in previous years).
There is no reference to options B, C, D, or E in the information provided, thus making these unlikely. The number of people dissatisfied with how crimes were dealt with previously suggests that they most probably had previous bad experiences, making 'A' the most likely explanation.

11)   The correct answer is D
The key to this question is to identify that the end product will be a right angle triangle. Options 'A' and 'C' can be excluded as when they are folded in half they produce acute angles rather than right angles. Option 'B' does not adequately fold into the desired shape making option 'D' the correct answer.

12)   The correct answer is B (The government is introducing legislation for slimming pills to carry clear warning labels).
Statement A is unrelated to the conclusion or the arguments proposed, therefore it can be excluded.
Statement B directly targets the conclusion of 'The government should do more to combat the harmful effects of slimming pills'. If the government is introducing legislation for these products to carry warning labels, they are directly addressing the concluding issue hence weakening its validity.
Statement C, if anything, would strengthen the conclusion, as an increase in the demand for these pills would, in turn, require an increased need for government intervention.
Statement D is arguably a valid point, the cost to the taxpayer is unrelated the arguments being proposed.
Statement E makes a point similar to 'C' which strengthens the conclusion, suggesting that slimming pills lead to avoidance of the underlying cause of their excess weight, hence supporting the need for government intervention.

13)   The correct answer is E (2 and 4)
For the right-hand bag to have half the marbles of one colour and half of another colour, the total number of marbles must be an even number.
By combining this knowledge with statement two, it can be concluded that the minimum number of marbles in the right-hand bag would have to be four, six or an alternative larger even number.
Given these two pieces of information, it is impossible for statement four to also be correct. If all the colours in the right-hand bag started off as the same colour (for example four green marbles) it would take a minimum of four transfers (two greens out, two reds in) to result in an even number at the end. However, only two transfers take place, and the end number of reds and green marbles are even, making statements two and four incompatible.

14)   The correct answer is A (That people will be more likely to reveal the truth in interrogation if they feel more at ease)
An assumption is an unstated reason, and in this question, rather than asking for the assumption in the argument, it asks for the assumption in the 'decision to use this colour scheme'. The respective colours are chosen because they

have a 'calming effect' and 'enhance communication'. The end goal of an interrogation is to obtain the truth, and it is an unstated and important link that if suspects are calmer, then they will be more likely to reveal the truth, hence making option 'A' the most suitable assumption.

15) The correct answer is D (18)

This question first requires the identification of how many potential options of individual squares there are (that do not have any horizontal, vertical or diagonal neighbours). As shown in the diagram below, this number is 7.

CP			BM		VH	LE	JS		MD
	WS	PL			TD				
	CE			1			DW		2
		SP				DS			3
	EK	AD		JS	FR		TB		4
					SP		BM		
BM		5	6						OA
						7		AD	
	RJ	NT		GT				LE	
CP	Fr				MH		RJ		

As in the question, two squares are bought, which requires the total number of combinations as option one can be bought with option two, three, four five, six or seven and so forth to be calculated. It must also be considered that some of the options cannot be bought with others, as they would be vertically, horizontally or diagonally connecting:

Option (1) can be bought with any of the other six options = 6

Option (2) can be bought with either option four, five, six or seven (as it is already counted with option one and with option three, there would be two adjacent squares = 4

Option (3) can be bought with either options five, six or seven (in addition to those already counted) = 3

Option (4) can be bought with either options five, six or seven (in addition to those already counted) = 3

Option (5) can be bought with option seven (in addition to those already counted) = 1

Option (6) can be bought with option seven (in addition to those already counted) = 1

Option (7) has already been counted

Hence, the total number of options is 6 + 4 + 3 + 3 + 1 + 1 = 18

16) The correct answer is Silver: 38; Bronze 36

Figure two states that the total number of medals won by the United States was 110, with figure one stating that 36 of these were gold medals. Hence, the number of silver and bronze medals was 74 (110 – 74).

Using figure three, one can establish that:

$$(36 \times 3) + (\text{Silver} \times 2) + (\text{Bronze}) = 220$$

$$(\text{Silver} \times 2) + \text{Bronze} = 112$$

Given that 'Silver + Bronze = 74, simultaneous equations can be used to calculate the number of silver medals to be 38, and hence the number of bronze medals is 36.

17) The correct answer is 13

Australia won a total of 46 medals, with an unspecified number of gold, silver and bronze medals. The information provided allows the following two equations to be formulated:

$$G + S + B = 46$$

$$3G + 2S + B = 89$$

Subtracting the top equation from the bottom equation produces the following:

$$2G + S = 43$$

For Australia to have the minimum number of silver medals, they must have the maximum possible number of gold and bronze medals (as the total number of medals remains constant). Australia must have won less than 16 gold medals (which is the number that Germany obtained) since it has not been recorded in Figure 1. Hence, the maximum number of gold medals that Australia could have obtained is 15. Subtracting this number into the formula results in the number of silver medals:

$$13 [((2 \times 15) + S = 43); S=13]$$

18) The correct answer is D (15)

This question is more straightforward than the phrasing may suggest. Although exact division can be performed, a simple comparison of the different ratios should be sufficient to obtain the correct answer.

China ratio: 51:100 = 1:1.96
United States ratio: 36:110 = 1:3.05
Russian Federation ratio: 23: 72 = 1:3.13
Great Britain ratio: 19:47 = 1:2.47

Hence, Great Britain would rank second.

19) The correct answer is F (1 and 3 only)

Assessing each of the statements in turn:
Norway's weighted medal total is 4.5 multiplied by 4.6, which is approximately 21, so achieving three gold and five silver medals [9 +10 = 19] is possible and suggests they won two bronze medals
Iceland's weighted medal total is 0.3x6.8 = 2. Hence it could not have gained three medals.

Slovenia's weighted medal total is 2x4.5 = 9, hence if it gained one gold, one silver and four bronze medals, this statement might also be correct.

20) The correct answer is C (Both 1 and 2)

To determine the answer, calculate/approximate the values for Great Britain, Russia and the United States:

Great Britain = 98 / 62 = Just over 1.5

Russia = 139/142 = Just under 1

The United States = 220/306 = Just over two-thirds

Using this information, it can be concluded that both statements one and two would be correct.

21) The correct answer is 50g

Maria's total energy requirement is 4.0 Joules. The 'leftover drink' contains 1.5 Joules and if the nurse uses 300 ml of the total 400 ml of the second drink, she is using three-quarters of the total energy value of 2.0 Joules (and thus she is using 1.5 Joules)

Adding the energy obtained from these two sources makes a total energy intake of 3.0 Joules (1.5 + 1.5), meaning that a further 1.0 Joule is required as supplement powder. The supplement powder contains 2.0 Joules per 100g, and therefore 50g is needed to supplement 1.0 Joule.

22) The correct answer is A (1 and 2 only)

Statement one is assumed in the phrase from the passage 'the most valuable praise is that which the recipient regards as appropriate'. This is suggesting that people can evaluate how much praise they deserve, or 'know to be appropriate', hence statement one is correct.

The final statement assumes that people can assess how much praise others deserve, which therefore assumes statement two.

Statement three is an opinion that may be held by the author and is not necessarily an assumption for the conclusion or reasoning provided. Thus it can be excluded.

There is no mention of the consequences of self-esteem, and hence statement four is an unfounded conclusion and can also be excluded.

23) The correct answer is E (29431434)

To answer this question, the key rules from the information must be examined and then applied to each option: The sum of the eight digits must be a multiple of ten. Therefore the only digits to vary between the six options are the second and eighth digits. As the second digit increases by one, the eighth digit decreases by one, hence making all of the respective totals the same (30). Therefore, all of the options are divisible by ten and adhere to this rule. Additionally, the first three digits represent the month that the samples were taken in, and the subsequent two digits are the date the sample was taken. With all options stating that the sample was taken on the 31st of the respective month, it is possible that one of the months may not have 31 days hence making this option impossible. The information also states that 124 months after the clinic first opened is the month of September. Thus 254 months (130 months/ 10 years, 10 months) after the clinic opened would be July, which correctly has 31 days. As one reviews each of the options (by adding ten months, or subtracting two months), it becomes apparent that 'E' is incorrect as November only contains 30 days.

24)   The correct answer is E (None of the above)

Assessing each of the statements in turn:

As the data relates to only those young girls who became pregnant, the results cannot be generalised to encompass all young people and their association between alcohol and sexual activity. Therefore statement one cannot be inferred.

There are no statistics or evidence to suggest that stricter controls would result in fewer teenage pregnancies, neither is this suggested, thus statement two cannot be inferred either.

As per statement one, the data provided relates to only those young girls who became pregnant and hence cannot be generalised to encompass all young people. Thus statement three cannot be inferred.

25)   The correct answer is A

This question is best answered by drawing a rough graph of each of the options in turn. Option A reveals, that the graph drawn matches the graph in the question, hence making this the correct answer.

26)   The correct answer is E (The role of sounds in an ant colony could aid the survival of some species).

While statement A is a possibility, this conclusion is not directly suggested or stated in the passage. Thus it can be excluded.

Although the 'Rebel's large blue butterfly' does exploit ant colonies, the passage does not say if this is the only species to do so, or if it is the most notable species to do so. Hence, it cannot be deduced as to whether this statement is factually accurate, let alone whether it is the main conclusion. Therefore statement B can be ruled out.

Similarly, statement C is unfounded, and may be classified as an assumption or inference; however, it is most definitely not the conclusion of the passage.

The passage does not state the cause of the evolution of ant's abilities to communicate and hence it cannot be concluded that statement D is accurate given the limited information provided.

Statement E can be reliably concluded as the 'Rebel's large blue butterfly' is described as an 'endangered species' that is benefitting from taking advantage of ants communication methods, thus aiding the survival of their endangered species.

27)   The correct answer is B (Tuesday)

The key to this question is to establish how many tokens are required for a free lunch each day. Using appropriate judgment, as well as trial and error, this can be calculated as follows.

Tim receives seven tokens each day, and if Tim is to run out of tokens after eight lunches, then each lunch must require more than seven tokens (as otherwise Tim would never run out, and instead accumulate tokens on a daily basis).

Hence, assuming that lunch cost eight tokens, after six lunches Tim would be left with 14 tokens (as he would use one additional token each day). Alternatively, if lunch cost nine tokens, Tim would be left with eight tokens after six lunches, which is insufficient for lunch that day. The list below shows when Tim cannot get a free meal:

Tuesday 9th – 8 tokens (cannot get a free meal)
Wednesday 10th – 15 tokens (can get a free meal) → 6 tokens remain following lunch
Thursday 11th – 13 tokens (can get a free meal) → 4 tokens remain following lunch
Friday 12th – 11 tokens (can get a free meal) → 2 tokens remain following lunch
Monday 15th – 9 tokens (can get a free meal) → 0 tokens remain following lunch
Tuesday 16th – 7 tokens (cannot get a free meal)

28)   The correct answer is B (It assumes that the existence of Earth-sized planets in the 'habitable zone' is sufficient for life to exist).

In a question like this, it is often useful to consider what one believes is the flaw in the passage before reviewing the options. The passage makes a significant leap between the ability to find planets which have similarities to Earth and the fact that finding such planets will lead us to find a life away from Earth. With no evidence, that these similar planets will have 'life', such a conclusion cannot be drawn. This flaw is almost paraphrased in statement B making it the most appropriate option. Statement A is incorrect as it focuses on the similarity of the 'life forms' between these newly found planets and life forms on earth, rather than the general flaw of there being no evidence of life in any form on other planets.

29)   The correct answer is D (7)

Working from the top left square (square one) it can be seen that this is not repeated. Square two (second from the top left) is repeated in a rotated version of squares six and eight. Square three is repeated in squares five and seven. Squares nine and ten are also repeats of each other. The remaining squares are unique making a total of seven different patterns.

30)   The correct answer is D (Common sense explanations are less likely to be valid than those based on scientific enquiry).

As previously mentioned, the 'therefore' rule is a useful method for determining the conclusion of a passage. Statements B, C and E, are not stated or inferred by the passage making them incorrect. The passage does not directly criticise 'common sense explanations' instead it minimises their validity in relation to scientific explanations thus making option A unlikely and supporting option D.

31)   The correct answer is D (5)

Using the rules provided, the lift will initially stop at floor ten (this is equally as close as floor four, but has a greater number of higher floors requesting lifts)
The second stop will be at floor seven, as it is the nearest floor; the third stop will be floor four; the fourth stop will be floor zero with the fifth stop being floor 14, and finally, floor 16 will be the sixth stop. Thus, five stops will have been made before it reaches floor 16.

32)   The correct answer is C (Potatoes)

This question requires the use of one's well-practiced percentage change formula:

$$\% \text{ change} = \frac{(\text{final} - \text{initial})}{\text{Initial}} \times 100$$

Additionally, through a quick analysis of the options, a significant change between 1997 and 1998 of almost 50% increase can be seen, compared with the much smaller changes in other items

33) The correct answer is C (Livestock)

This question requires relatively straightforward trend analysis. There is an initial increase, followed by a levelling and subsequent decrease after 1996. By comparing this pattern with the options in the table, a very similar pattern for the 'Livestock total', data can be seen.

34) The correct answer is D (If volumes of production have not changed a higher percentage of farm crops than horticulture must be sold overseas).

Statement A is incorrect as vegetable output increased after 1997, even more so than flowers.

There is insufficient information to conclude statement B, as the information provided relates directly to output rather than pricing.

While statement C may be true, the low Scottish incomes of 1980 may be equally attributable to other factors.

Statement D is supported by the data with an evident decline in farm crops and not in horticulture. Thus this is the correct answer.

There is insufficient information to conclude statement E. Therefore it can be ruled out.

35) The correct answer is E (63%)

The 'Commentary on 1998 figures' states that prices were lower due to farmers having to drop their prices for commodities being exported from the UK. If the pound fell by 5% in 1998, and the drop in the value of sheep was due entirely to that, it would be expected that the value of sheep would be 5% less than the 1997 value.

$$0.95 \times 245 = 232.75$$

Hence, if all of the sheep were being exported, the value would be 232.75. However, their value is actually 237.4, which means some of the sheep are not being exported.

To calculate the proportion of sheep that are being exported, one must calculate the difference between the 1997 and expected 1998 value

$$245 - 233 = 12$$

$$(12 - 4.5)/ 12 =$$

$$7.5/12 = 62.5\%$$

BMAT Section 1 - 2010

1)   The correct answer is A (25)

To work out Alex's BMI, his height and weight and must be known. His height is given in the question as 162cm; his weight must be calculated from the information in the text. Using the table, if Jay has a BMI of 22 and a height of 150cm, his weight must be 49kg (3rd row). Similarly, Charlie's weight can be deduced as 58kg (5th row). If Charlie, Jay and Alex's weights total to 172, then Alex's weight must be 172-58-49=65kg. Using the table, a height of 162cm and weight of 65kg gives us Alex's BMI at 25. Therefore the answer is A.

2)   The correct answer is C (A strong economy may be a precondition of a flourishing arts sector).

This argument assumes that because successful societies have a flourishing arts sector, the flourishing arts sector must have caused the success of that society, and so increasing the provision of the arts would make a society more successful. This is not necessarily the case and hence represents a flaw in the argument. In fact, the success of the society may have caused the arts sector to flourish, which is highlighted in option C making it the correct answer as it draws upon the flaw above. All of the other options may provide a case against subsidising the arts, but do not directly refute the basic reasoning of the argument and so cannot be deemed correct.

3)   The correct answer is C (Erin)

The white diamond is the 8th diamond along the x-axis and so represents the 8thlowest (or 5th highest) score in test one. The white diamond is also the 8th diamond along the y-axis and thus represents the 8th lowest (or 5th highest) score in test two. The 5th highest score in test one is Erin's and to double check this, her score is also the 5th highest in test one, so she is represented by the white diamond making the answer C.

4)   The correct answer is C (Action to deal with global warming should include tackling spam as one of the strategies).

Statement A is too general a conclusion to draw from the argument, as the argument relates specifically to spam and not all problems.

Statement B is incorrect as the argument makes no indication towards the relative priorities of tackling spam as opposed to congestion.

Statement C is the correct answer as there are claims in the passage that spam contributes to global warming and that tackling spam can reduce CO_2 production, so the text directly supports this conclusion.

Statement D is incorrect at the passage states that merely filtering spam does little to reduce the energy cost of sending out spam emails in the first place.

Statement E is incorrect as no comment about this is made in the text.

5)   The correct answer is D (5:55 pm)

72 cakes will require six batches (72/12=6). Each batch takes 70 minutes to make (40 minutes preparing + 25 minutes in the oven + 5 minutes cooling). Assuming one cannot cool and prepare cakes simultaneously; 25 minutes are saved on each, as preparation can begin while the previous batch is in the oven. This time is not saved on batch

one as there is no earlier batch in the oven. Therefore, the total cooking time for six batches is 420 minutes (6 x 70) minus 125 minutes saved during the baking of the last five batches (5 x 25), which totals 295 minutes, or 4 hours 55 minutes. This gives answer D which is 4 hours 55 minutes from 1 pm.

6) The correct answer is B (2 only)

Statement one does not represent a weakness. The argument is constructed using the reasoning that if we stopped burning all fossil fuels, then climate change would still not be averted. Therefore, even if we did not stop burning all fossil fuels, climate change would again, still not be avoided.

Statement two represents a weakness in the argument. If we could reduce CO_2 levels in ways other than stopping the burning of fossil fuels and relying on the absorption of CO_2 by oceans, then this may 'avoid the disastrous consequences of climate change' thus disproving the conclusion even though all the calculations in the model may still be correct.

Statement three does not represent a weakness in the argument as past predictions do not necessarily influence the rigidity of this particular model.

7) The correct answer is B (2)

The darts scores are only between 002 and 501, therefore, the first digit can only ever be a 0, 1,2,3,4 or 5, but cannot be a 5 in this case as then the score would be 505 which is higher than 501. Three of the lights in the first digit are permanently on; therefore the digits 0-4 must be examined to determine whether they can be made from the digit 8 using up to 3 lights less than the digit 8 does. The digit zero is 8 without the centre light, so the first digit could have been zero. The digit 1 requires a light in the second row, second column, which is not present in the digit 8, so 1 could not have been the true first digit. Digit 2 is similar to the digit 8, but without the use of two lights in the 2nd and 4th row, so the true first digit may have been 2. Digit 3 requires more than 3 lights to be converted into an 8, so cannot have been the true first digit since 4 lights are required. Digit 4 has a light in the 2nd row, 2nd column which is not present in the digit 8 and so the true first digit cannot be 4. Therefore the first digit can only be 0 or 2, so the true score is either 005 or 205, and there are only these two possibilities. Hence the answer is B.

8) The correct answer is A (That toy preference in humans is the result of socialising).

Options B and C are supported, not challenged by the first paragraph, and so cannot be correct. Option D is challenged to an extent, but option A is challenged more clearly and directly by the text, as toy preference is indicated to have a biological, as opposed to social, origin. Option D is an over-interpretation of this challenge as toy preference cannot be extended to all animal behaviour.

9) The correct answer is A (The more aggressive sex monopolised the toys that were the most attractive to the monkeys).

Option A is the correct answer as it indicates that toy preferences may be sex-independent. Instead, most attractive toys happened to be those considered most traditionally to be masculine and therefore were monopolised by the more aggressive males.

Option B is incorrect as it makes no challenge to the idea that male monkeys might choose certain toys that females would not, regardless of how long those monkeys spent with the toys once chosen.

Option C is incorrect as it supports rather than challenges the inference of sex-dependent preferences.

Option D is incorrect as the inference relates specifically to vervet monkeys and this option does not directly challenge this monkey-specific inference.

Option E is incorrect as it has no relevance to the inference at hand.

10)   The correct answer is A (Spending time with an object is a reliable indicator of interest).

An assumption is an unstated fact that must be true for a claim to be correct:

Statement A is the correct answer; as it must be true to accept that monkeys which spent longer with a toy preferred that toy more.

Statement B is incorrect as the claim that vervet monkeys exhibited sex-dependent preference may still be true regardless of the nature of the human toy preference.

Statement C is incorrect as the claim that female vervet monkeys preferred pots and dolls may still be true regardless of the wider implications that pots and dolls have in society.

Statement D is incorrect - if it was assumed, the claim in paragraph two would have had to have been rejected as opposed to accepted.

Statement E is incorrect as it is not an assumption and, if true, would have contradicted the claim in paragraph two.

11)   The correct answer is D (neither 1 nor 2)

It cannot be assumed from the photograph alone that all or even most, monkeys respond in the same ways as humans would to a toy car, without being coerced,. The vervet monkeys may have been 'gently encouraged' or possibly even forced to interact in a certain way with the toys pictured. Therefore both statements one and two cannot reliably be inferred, and thus, the answer is D.

12)   The correct answer is C

The following table outlines the numbers of each type of square in each type of tile.

Type of Square	Tile				
	A	B	C	D	E
Black	2	1	3	4	5
Grey	4	2	2	2	4
White	3	6	4	3	0

Four out of these five tile options must be selected for the floor pattern, and the total number of grey, black and white squares respectively must be the same when adding the figures in the table for these four tiles. Option C cannot be part of the pattern as adding the figures for black, grey and white for tiles A, B, D and E gives a total of 12 for each colour. The totals obtained when adding up the number for any other combination of four tiles are not equal therefore the answer must be C.

13)   The correct answer is E (The fact that a negative story is inevitable does not mean that it should be ignored).

An argumentative flaw, if present, is one that challenges the reasoning of the passage such that even if all the claims in the passage are true, the conclusion would still not necessarily follow on from these claims. Statement B does not satisfy these criteria and hence, is incorrect. Statement A is incorrect, as even if the third option of 'neutral' exam results were included, the reasoning would still be flawed. Statements C and D may be true but again, even if these predictions were supported by evidence, or if exams were becoming easier, the reasoning would still be flawed and therefore C or D are not the best answer. Statement E is the correct answer as it highlights a problem with the reasoning of the argument as opposed to merely one of the claims in the argument.

14) The correct answer is D (6)

This question must be answered by working through the potential answer choices from the bottom upwards. There are seven elements in the display so, for the answer to be seven, all seven elements must change from one number to another. This is impossible as all ten digits share a common element (bottom right) meaning this element must be kept constant, except for the digit two, as this does not require more than seven element changes to transform into any of the other digits. The next potential answer is six - changing from digit one to digit six requires changing six of the seven elements (all but the bottom right) and hence the answer is D.

15) The correct answer is D (Boys are more than twice as likely as girls to be killed or seriously injured as pedestrians or cyclists).

Statement A cannot reliably be inferred from the passage as boys may simply be more accident prone as cyclists; equally statement C cannot be reliably inferred either for the same reason. Statement B cannot be reliably inferred, as there may be more boy pedestrians than girls. Statement E cannot be inferred as no information pertaining to the likely success rates of road safety lessons has been provided. Therefore, statement D is the only option that can be objectively justified using only the data in the passage and no additional information.

16) The correct answer is D

The die could be rotated 90 degrees anticlockwise in the vertical plane (so that 3 now occupies the top face of the die) leaving the remaining faces as 5 (in the same position) and 1 (where 3 previously was). A subsequent 90-degree rotation to the left (anticlockwise) would move the 1 to the left face (where the 5 previously was), keep 3 on the top face, and move a 2 to the right face (where the 1 previously was) as illustrated in option D.

17) The correct answer is C (Because one museum overseas is looted it does not mean that others will be).

An argumentative flaw, if present, must challenge the reasoning of the passage such that even if all the claims in the passage are true, the conclusion would still not necessarily follow on from these claims. Of all the possible options, only statements C and E challenge the reasoning of the passage, the remaining options challenge claims or make assertions. Statement C challenges the central idea that protecting an artefact from looting is not necessarily of primary interest for the world and so represents a flaw in the entire argument. Statement E challenges the safety of the British Museum while statement C is a more complete flaw as even if all the artefacts were safe, this statement would still be valid.

18) The correct answer is D (15)

This question requires the visualisation of the tessellation of the letter H as indicated in the diagram below. In this diagram, each small rectangle has dimensions 2cm by 4cm. A maximum of 2-3 H's can fit horizontally on each row of the 24cm card, and 6 rows can fit on a column of the 33cm card. Therefore there are a total of 15 shapes, making the answer D.

19) The correct answer is 217 million

According to the text, in 2005, 'the total number of passengers at UK airports' was 228 million. Additionally, '9 in 10 air passengers at UK airports in 2005 were travelling internationally.' Since the remaining 1 in 10 passengers are domestic and have hence been counted twice, to answer the question the figures must be amended to only count these domestic passengers once. 10% of 228 million is 22.8 million (this is the number of domestic passengers counted in 2005). Half of this figure represents the actual number of domestic passengers (11.4 million). Taking this away from 228 million gives a total of 216.6 million, or to the nearest million, 217 million.

20) The correct answer is C (9 million)

There were 34 million passenger movements in the UK and Spain in 2005. Each of these 'movements' would encompass one passenger counted at a UK airport.

228 million passengers were counted at UK airports in 2005, most of whom would each represent a single passenger movement.

15% of 228 is approximately 34. The graph shows that in 1980, there were roughly 60 million passengers. 15% of this is 9 million; therefore C is the correct answer.

21) **The correct answer is F (1,2 and 3)**
Between 1980 and 2005 (which is 25 years) the number of passengers increased by roughly 160 million (from approximately 60 million to 228 million) giving an increase of approximately 6.5 million per year. Between 1955 and 1980 (also over 25 years) the number of passengers increased by 55 million from 5 million to 60 million, giving an increase of just over 2 million per year, which is less than one-third of 6.5 million per year. Therefore statement one is correct. Heathrow and Gatwick account for a total of 101 million (68+33) passengers out of the 228 million in the UK. This represents a proportion of over 40% of UK passengers at Heathrow/Gatwick. Therefore statement two is also correct. There were 228 million passengers in 2005, and 500 million are predicted for 2030, suggesting an increase of roughly 270 million passengers over 25 years, which is over 10 million passengers per year. Therefore statement three is also correct, and since all three statements are correct the answer is F.

22) **The correct answer is D (The data have been correctly interpreted and do support the conclusion).**
The data has been correctly interpreted as on analysis; it is apparent that both dips in passenger numbers in the 1990's and 2001 were more than recovered as current passenger numbers exceed these troughs. This suggests that future dips may also recover, making the answer D. Although the previous data is no guarantee of the future, the text states that the 2009 dip will 'not necessarily' prevent a strong recovery. This statement can thus be justified as it allows for uncertainty.

23) **The correct answer is E (12/35)**

	1	2	3	4	5	6	7	8	9	10	11	12	13	14	15
1	1,1	1,2	1,3	1,4	1,5	1,6	1,7	1,8	1,9	1,10	1,11	1,12	1,13	1,14	1,15
2	2,1	2,2	2,3	2,4	2,5	2,6	2,7	2,8	2,9	**2,10**	2,11	2,12	**2,13**	**2,14**	**2,15**
3	3,1	3,2	3,3	3,4	3,5	3,6	3,7	3,8	3,9	**3,10**	3,11	**3,12**	3,13	**3,14**	**3,15**
4	4,1	4,2	4,3	4,4	4,5	4,6	4,7	4,8	4,9	**4,10**	4,11	**4,12**	**4,13**	4,14	**4,15**
5	5,1	5,2	5,3	5,4	5,5	5,6	5,7	5,8	5,9	**5,10**	5,11	**5,12**	**5,13**	**5,14**	5,15
6	6,1	6,2	6,3	6,4	6,5	6,6	6,7	6,8	6,9	**6,10**	6,11	**6,12**	**6,13**	**6,14**	**6,15**
7	7,1	7,2	7,3	7,4	7,5	7,6	7,7	7,8	7,9	**7,10**	7,11	**7,12**	**7,13**	**7,14**	**7,15**
8	8,1	8,2	8,3	8,4	8,5	8,6	8,7	8,8	8,9	**8,10**	8,11	**8,12**	**8,13**	**8,14**	**8,15**
9	9,1	9,2	9,3	9,4	9,5	9,6	9,7	9,8	9,9	**9,10**	9,11	**9,12**	**9,13**	**9,14**	**9,15**
10	10,1	**10,2**	**10,3**	**10,4**	**10,5**	**10,6**	**10,7**	**10,8**	**10,9**	10,10	10,11	10,12	10,13	10,14	10,15
11	11,1	11,2	11,3	11,4	11,5	11,6	11,7	11,8	11,9	1110,	11,11	11,12	11,13	11,14	11,15
12	12,1	12,2	**12,3**	**12,4**	**12,5**	**12,6**	**12,7**	**12,8**	**12,9**	12,10	12,11	12,12	12,13	12,14	12,15
13	13,1	**13,2**	13,3	**13,4**	**13,5**	**13,6**	**13,7**	**13,8**	**13,9**	13,10	13,11	13,12	13,13	13,14	13,15
14	14,1	**14,2**	**14,3**	14,4	**14,5**	**14,6**	**14,7**	**14,8**	**14,9**	14,10	14,11	14,12	14,13	14,14	14,15
15	15,1	**15,2**	**15,3**	**15,4**	15,5	**15,6**	**15,7**	**15,8**	**15,9**	15,10	15,11	15,12	15,13	15,14	15,15

The table above illustrates the potential draw combinations with the first drawn number represented by the left-hand column options and the second drawn number represented by the top row options. The combinations which satisfy the criteria outlined in the question are highlighted in bold, with some notable exceptions as shown. The total number of possible combinations is 210 (15x15-15) as the same number cannot be chosen twice, of which 72 are acceptable. 72/210 = 12/35, therefore option E is the correct choice.

24)   The correct answer is C (There are no other possible explanations for the extinction of the dinosaurs).

An assumption is an unstated fact that must be true for the conclusion to be justified.

Assumption A is incorrect as for whether volcanic activity caused additional fires or not would make no difference to the argument at hand as acid rain was not observed regardless.

Assumptions B and D are also incorrect as the cooling of the atmosphere is stated to have been caused by volcanic activity and so volcanic activity would indirectly be the cause of any atmospheric cooling related extinction. Both of the options above do not have a significant influence on the conclusion and thus can be excluded.

Assumption C is the correct answer if C was not assumed the underlying argument would be invalid.

Assumption E is incorrect as this is not indicated in any way – the word 'always' is too prescriptive.

25)   The correct answer is A (14)

The current score is 9, which places the person in last place behind the scores of 22, 13 and 11. They could switch their 7 of hearts for an 8 of spades, giving them a total score of 20 (as it is doubled because they are of the same suit) but this would only move them to second place. Instead, if they exchange the 2 of spades for a 7 of diamonds, they will have a score of 14 and be in first place, as the previous first placeholder will now only have a score of 6. Therefore the answer is A.

26)   The correct answer is A (The problem of providing out of hours medical care is partly of the public's making).

Statement A is the correct answer as it is indicated by the fourth and fifth lines of the passage. Statements B and E are both incorrect as nowhere in the passage is there an indication that the burden of the solution should fall specifically on 'doctors'. Statement C is incorrect as although true, it is merely an intermediate conclusion that supports the main conclusion which is A, making statement A a better choice than C. Statement D is also incorrect is it represents a reason which supports the main conclusion of A.

27)   The correct answer is C (9)

If Phil hits the same number twice, he cannot win. Therefore he cannot aim at 3,12,1,10,8 and 2 as there is a risk of scoring the same number twice. Considering the worst case scenario for the remaining options, if he were to hit 1 with his third dart, he would need a minimum score of 9 with his last dart to total at least 30. There is no target that guarantees a score of at least nine, so he cannot aim for 4 as there is a risk of hitting 1. Similarly, he cannot aim at 11 as there is a risk of hitting 2, in which case he could not guarantee a score of at least 8 with his last dart. Aiming at 7 means he might hit 3, and would thus need a minimum of 7 on his last dart, which can also not be guaranteed. Therefore, by process of elimination, if he were to aim at 9 he could hit 4 by mistake but would need a minimum of 6 on his last dart which is guaranteed by aiming for 6 and so can be confident of winning a prize. Therefore the answer is C.

28)   The correct answer is A (1 only)

Statement one would strengthen the conclusion of the argument which states that 'the name alone had influenced public opinion' and that this influence was not guided merely by false reporting of the case. Statement two would weaken the argument as it would indicate that the media influence was not due solely to the name alone but also due to the recommendation for the harshest possible punishment to readers and that this unduly influenced their thoughts. Statement three would also weaken the argument for similar reasons –in that the influence was not due to the name alone but also due to subjective language.

29)   The correct answer is C (188g)

The average apple mass in a pack needs to be close to 200g. Taking 200g away from all the apples provides easier figures to work with, which results in masses of -27, -18, -12, -3, 7, 19 and 24 grams respectively. This makes it easier to see the appropriate combinations of 24, -3 and -18 (summing 3) and -27, 19 and 7 (summing -1) which are both within the allowance of + or – 3 from the total. Therefore the apple which is -12g away from 200 is left, which is option C.

30)   The correct answer is B (Expensive schemes aimed at improving education cannot be justified).

The passage expresses the importance of good teachers and highlights that this would be contraindicated by hiring candidates with lower qualifications, thus assuming statement A necessary. Statement B is not assumed as the passage only indicates that the expensive teaching scheme was unjustified because the results were poor, not unjustified by virtue of its cost alone. Statement C needs to be assumed to indicate that the poor improvement of California from 49th to 48th in the rank was due to a lack of improvement in absolute and not just relative quality. Statement D is also assumed as the final sentence indicates a causal relationship between bright teachers and doing 'well at school' which can be taken as an improvement of 'pupil's performance'. Therefore the correct answer is B.

31)   The correct answer is D

Figure One:

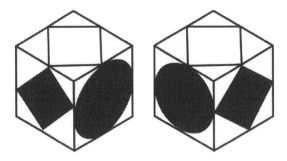

Figure Two:

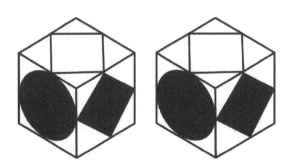

Figure Three:

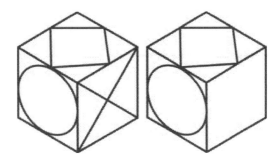

The 3D assembly of the cube nets pictured in the passage has been illustrated above. Figure one shows the net provided at the start of the question on the right and a representation of net A on the left. The positions of the black square and black circle have been switched for net A so this cannot be the correct net. The same issue is also present for nets C and E and so they too are not the correct nets. Figure two shows a representation of net B on the left and the desired net on the right. Here, the position of the white circle and the X shape have been switched, so net B is not the correct net either. Figure three shows net D and the desired net which assemble to form identical cubes.

32)   The correct answer is C (6:1)
Initially, it is necessary to add up the average incomes of the top two 10% blocks and compare them to the bottom two. This means finding the ratio between roughly 212,600 (162,029+50,656) and 33,500 (16,203+17,338) which is close to 6:1, making the answer C. A quick way to see this is approximating the figures to 210,000 and 30,000 which is 7:1. Option C, therefore, is closest to this ratio.

33)   The correct answer is C (40%)
This question requires some long division and approximation: 162/400 = 40%

34)   The correct answer is C ($21,500)
Suppose the population consisted of merely ten people, so each person represented an 'average' 10% bracket in totality. Taxing the top two people would yield 20% of $212,685, or $42,537. This figure would then be distributed amongst the remaining eight people so that they each get 42,537/8, or $5,317 each. Thus the bottom earner would earn 16,203 +5,317, or $21,520, making the correct answer C.

35)   Correct answer is B (2 only)
The graphs show data points for separate countries. Therefore no comparison can be made as to the situation within any given country, only between countries. Therefore statement one cannot be concluded. The first graph shows a strong negative correlation between income inequality and health, such that less inequality (which is reflected in 'variability') corresponds with increased health.

BMAT Section 1 - 2011

1)   The correct answer is D

By sketching the pattern for each of the columns over the five day period, it is easy to arrive at a pattern for each chart.

Chart A represents cloud cover (%) as there is an increase between two bars of equal height, followed by a drop, then an increase up to the highest point for the last bar. Following this same method, chart B represents the chance of rain (%); chart C represents average wind speed (mph), and chart E represents maximum temperature (^{0}C). Hence, the answer is D, as it does not represent any of the rows in the table.

2)   The correct answer is E (None of the above)

Statement A cannot be drawn as a conclusion, as there is mention of whales trying to adapt and no mention of extinction. Statement B might be true, but it is not the point that the passage is trying to convey. Statement C is not correct, as the whales are trying but they may not succeed. Statement D is linking two different sentences in the text, and there may be no correlation between these two ideas. Therefore option E (none of the above) is correct.

3)   The correct answer is C ($425)

$$80 - 15 = 65 \text{ (cost for deluxe room/night without meals)}$$

$$65 \times 6 = 390 \text{ (room price for six nights)}$$

$$5 + (6 \times 5) = 425 \text{ (room price + car hire)}$$

4)   The correct answer is E (It does not establish that children who play computer games no longer interact with each other).

Statement A can be ruled out immediately as this passage focuses on the gaming aspect of the internet, not the benefits of the internet as a vast source of information. Statement B can be ruled out as the argument is not focused on 'the other skills' children need to learn but those of a social nature. Statement C can also be ruled out as the article is purely about children's gaming habits, not adult's gaming habits. Although the passage states many children play most of their games on computers, it does not indicate that the only way children learn to interact with each other is through games. Hence, the children may interact with each other in other ways, which will not hamper them socially thus statement E is the correct option.

5)   The correct answer is F (3 and 4)

Options three and four are 90^{0} rotations of one another, and one and two are 90^{0} rotations of each other. However, looking at one, it cannot be placed in x to form a viable reflection; hence this means that option two is also wrong. Thus, three and four must be right, which can be checked by visually rotating them.

6) **The correct answer is C (Brain scans on the same group before they became taxi drivers would not have shown the same results).**

Assumption A is not linked to the conclusion that learning the city's road network increases memory power. Assumptions B and D are also not related to the conclusion, thus the best answer is assumption C.

7) **The correct answer is A**

The question states that the plane must be able to carry between 163 and 177 passengers. Thus, F is not suitable. Once F has been excluded, only two options remain which fit the passenger capacity, these are options A and H. The fuel consumption per mile (gallons) for an empty plane is 3.0 for both A and H. However, H has a higher fuel consumption per mile with each additional passenger (0.07 to A's 0.01).

8) **The correct answer is D (On average, a woman in her 40s or 50s earns less than £0.80 for every £1 earned by a man in that age range).**

Statements A and B are not mentioned or inferred anywhere in the text, and thus, can be ruled out. Statement C could be correct if the text said between the ages of 22 to 39, but since it limits itself to 30, it is unknown if the pay difference is 11.2% at 30. Statement D is correct as between the ages of 40 to 59; the pay difference is always higher than 20%.

9) **The correct answer is C (£20,700)**

22.8% is approximately 23%.

$19,700 - (0.23 \times 19,700) = 15,169$

$20,300 - (0.23 \times 20,300) = 15,931$

$20,700 - (0.23 \times 20,700) = 15,939$

$21,300 - (0.23 \times 21,300) = 16,401$

The answer is C, as 15,939 is closest to 16,000.

10) **The correct answer is C (Mothers would choose to take up higher positions for which they are qualified after they have started a family).**

Statement A is not related to mothers not wanting the long hours and intensity associated with senior positions thus it can be excluded. Statement B is contradictory to the text, as it says the mothers are qualified for these jobs. The use of 'only' in statement D makes it incorrect, as the text clearly states that the pay discrimination is partly due to it.

11) **The correct answer is D (If the average part-time pay for men in their 40s is £15 per hour, women of the same age, on average, will earn £8.82 per hour).**

Paragraph four compares women and men who are both 30 with those who are both 40. Since statement D is the only statement that refers to this, D is the correct answer.

12) **The correct answer is D (6)**

The six different tiles are top left, below top left, right of the previous tile, below the previous tile, the right of the previous tile, and below the previous tile.

13) **The correct answer is B (A human genetic disorder (of specific language impairment) is found to be caused by a mutation in HAR1).**

For the hypothesis to be strengthened, it must be shown that either the gene is not found in other organisms, or it is found in regions of the brain associated with communication, or defects in the gene cause language impairments. The only statement which fulfils this criterion is statement B.

14) **The correct answer is C (10)**

It can be deduced that:

Central – has 2 draws and 3 losses

Western – has 1 draw and 4 losses

Central and Western must have drawn one match. All other teams must have won against Western. One of the other teams drew against Central. Hence:

Northern – has 2 wins and 2 draws

Southern – has 1 win and 2 draws

Eastern – has 3 wins and 1 draw $((3 \times 3) + 1 = 10)$

Hence, the answer is C.

15) **The correct answer is B (2 only)**

The only weakness is statement two, as statement number one is contradictory to the content in the paragraph (ECB defines those rights) and statement number three is not relevant to the argument. Hence, the answer is B.

16) **The correct answer is D (Tanganyika)**

The greatest average depth is given by the smallest ratio of area^2 km: volume^3 km. The smallest ratio is 31, 500: 23, 600; hence the answer is D.

17)   The correct answer is C (3 only)

Statement number one does not need to be assumed, as the last statement mentions that the outbreaks will occur in only those who have consumed the infected beef. Statement number two is incorrect, as inheriting the V variant is unlikely to prevent infection, but instead, increase the incubation period. The fact that the passage said there would be two further outbreaks suggesting that those with the V-V combination will suffer from vCJD, and that the M variant is not necessary for susceptibility. Hence, the answer is C.

18)   The correct answer is B (4 years)

(43-21) x 5 = 110

6 x 20 = 120

Hence Ruby earns 240 + 110 +120 + 40

Thus, 110 + 120 +40 = (R x 20) + (14 x 5)

Hence, R = 10

So, Ruby has been employed for four more years (Hence, the answer is B)

19)   The correct answer is A (Drilling represents a more favourable option than not drilling).

Drill:
Drill and small strike: -72, 000 (loss)
Drill and medium strike: 320, 000
Drill and big strike: 380, 000
Total: 628, 000 profit

Don't Drill:
Don't drill and big sale: 200, 000
Don't drill and small sale: 300, 000
Don't drill and no sale: 0
Total: 500, 000

Hence, the answer is A

20)   The correct answer is D (The probability of a 'medium' strike is the same as the probability of selling the drilling rights at $500,000 or more).

Inference A is incorrect, as a medium strike makes a profit. Inference B is incorrect, as the total profit from a medium strike is 400, 000, which is lower than both a small sale and a big sale. Inference C is incorrect, as the profit x chance gives a total profit of 628,000 for drilling. Inference D is correct, as both probabilities are 0.8.

21) **The correct answer is F (1,2 and 3)**

The total costs are 800, 000 + 500, 000= 1, 300, 000, which is greater than 1,200,000. If drilling costs were reduced by 25% to 600, 000, the total costs would be 1, 100, 000 and profit could be achieved. However, currently, the chance of making a profit is 10%. Hence, all three statements are true, and the answer is F.

22) **The correct answer is E (3 1 2)**

$$0.03 \times 10, 000, 000 = 300, 000$$

$$628, 000 - 300\ 000 = 328, 000$$
(Potential profit that can be had by proceeding to drill without insurance)

$$628\ 000 - 200, 000 = 428, 000$$
(Potential profit that can be had by paying the insurance and proceeding with the drilling)

500, 000 is the potential profit that can be had by deciding against drilling

23) **The correct answer is D (7)**

6	9	4	2
5			10
7			1
3			8

Each row must total 21, therefore, the missing number on the left vertical, must be added

$$21-3-5 =13$$

The numbers left to choose from are 2, 4, 6, 7, and 8. Immediately 2 can be ruled out as there is no 11, to total 21. Likewise, the number 9 has already been used in the horizontal line, therefore, the only options left on this side are 6 and 7. This narrows the options down to C and d. For the horizontal line the numbers must total:

$$21-9 =12$$

However, this time there are numbers to complete. Thus the numbers must be an average of 4 (with one higher and one lower to compensate for the fact that there is only one 4. Therefore 4 will be used which means that the other two spaces must total:

$$21-9-4=8$$

From the options left the only combination which gives 8 is 6 and 2 which confirms the position of the 6 and 7 from the vertical left-hand side. Thus the answer is D, which is 7.

24)   The correct answer is A (Jed only)
In the law of logic: 'If A then B = If not B then not A'. A in this case is 'Petermass will be playing', and B is 'Fredericks isn't fit'. Hence, if Fredericks is fit, Petermass will not be playing. So, only Jed was right.

25)   The correct answer is C (One mix has 100ml oil, the other has 110ml oil).

$$(2/3 + ½)/2) = 7/12 \text{ oil (105 ml)}$$

$$(1/3 + ½)/2 = 5/12 \text{ vinegar}$$

$$(½ + 7/12)/2) = 13/24 \text{ oil (97.5 ml)}$$

$$(½ + 5/12) /2) = 11/24 \text{ vinegar}$$

105 is roughly 110 ml, and 97.5 is approximately 100ml

26)   The correct answer is C (Planets with the potential to support human life are really common).
The conclusion is the 6th line of the paragraph: 'The fact that we were able...like this must be really common'. Hence, the answer is C.

27)   The correct answer is A (0)
A is the correct answer as it is not possible to arrange any of the other pieces to form either of the two suggested shapes.

28)   The correct answer is C (1,3 and 4 only)
The amount of CO_2 emitted when existing buses use one tonne of their current fuel needs to be considered. In addition to this, the distance that a bus can travel using each fuel also requires consideration. These two facts are taken into account alongside the amount of CO_2 emitted in transporting the fuel. Hence, the answer is C.

29)   The correct answer is D (18 km/hr)

Since Claire walks at 6km/ hr, it would have taken her 30 minutes to get from the swimming pool to the library.

$$20= 10 \text{ minutes} = 1/6 \text{ hour}$$

$$3km/ (1/6 \text{ hr}) = 18 \text{ km/hr}$$

30)   The correct answer is B (The phenomenon of pulsars travelling at high speed through the universe could be caused by the existence of sterile neutrinos).

Statement B is correct as the conclusion is that the pulsars whizzing through the universe at speeds of thousands of kilometres per second is evidence for the existence of sterile neutrinos.

31)   The correct answer is C

There must be two cylinders in the first row, one in the second row, two in the fifth row, and one in the sixth row. The 14 cylinders left are in the third and fourth rows. Two columns in the third and fourth rows contain three cylinders. Hence, there are four stacks left that must contain eight cylinders. The most any of these four stacks can have is three cylinders. Consequently, all options are okay for the first and third column, as they all have more than two cylinders in both columns. If the second column has one cylinder in both the third and fourth row, then the six cylinders remaining must be divided into two lots of three. This does not occur in C, as the third column has two cylinders when it should be three. Hence, the answer is C.

32)   The correct answer is C (32)

$$1500 \text{ patients x } 5.26 = 7890$$

$$7890/250 \text{ days} = 31.56 = 32$$

33)   The correct answer is D (67%)

The equation to calculate the rate is Nurse Consultation rate for a given year/ mean consultation rate for the same year.
Followed by: (rate for year 1 – rate for year 2)/ rate for year 1, and then multiplied by 100 to give a percentage.

For 1995 this equals:

$$0.8 /3.90 = 0.205$$

For 2006 this equals:

$$1.8 /5.26 = 0.342$$

$$(0.342 - 0.205)/ 0.342 = 0.67$$

$$0.67 \times 100 = 67$$

34) **The correct answer is C**

The answer is C as it shows the ratio that can be observed in the first graph the best.

35) **The correct answer is C (All the people surveyed have become 11 years older).**

Reason A would mean that more people would seek consultations, so this could be a potential explanation. If reason B were true, there would also be more consultations. C is not very satisfactory as age is not necessarily an indicator of health. Statement D would also lead to more consultations to allow the GPs to increase the amount of preventive medicine they do. Hence, the answer is C.

BMAT Section 1 - 2012

1)   The correct answer is D (Dalton)
The basis for answering this question efficiently is to approximate the percentages required. 10% of the population is roughly 860,000; this rules out all options apart from A and D. 20% of the land area is approximately 5200 (10% being around 2,600); this leaves 'D' as the correct option.

2)   The correct answer is C (Pale-skinned people should be recommended to take Vitamin D supplements).
Taking each option in turn:
The word 'need' in statement A indicates that the option may be incorrect. The other options should be assessed first before deciding if this is the best option.
Statement B is a reason which supports the conclusion, rather than a conclusion in itself. Thus, this option can be ruled out.
Statement C is the correct option. The test of whether a statement is a conclusion is if it still makes sense when 'therefore' is put in front of it. Based on the direction of the passage, this most suitably fits as the conclusion.
Statement D is irrelevant thus can be ruled out.
There is nothing in the passage which compares pale to dark-skinned people. Statement E is quite sweeping and generalised in any case (whereas conclusions should be quite narrow in focus), which should suggest that it is not likely to be the conclusion.

3)   The correct answer is F
The question itself is a little confusing; in essence, it requires the elimination of one of the six options given to end up with the same number of each pattern of tile (and same area) with the remaining five options shown. The best way to do this is to take each option and see if it fits the criteria. Therefore:
If A is eliminated, the result is six black tiles and four white tiles which does not meet the required criteria.
Eliminating B gives five black tiles and six white tiles which does not fit the criteria either.
Eliminating C leaves three black tiles and five white tiles which does not fit the criteria.
Eliminating D results in six black tiles and five white tiles which does not fit the criteria.
Eliminating D gives an equal number of black and white tiles, as well as three spotted tiles and six checked tiles, thus not fitting the criteria.
Eliminating E will result in equal numbers of black, white, striped, spotted and checked tiles, which fits the criteria and is thus the correct answer.

4)   The correct answer is B (Electric cars cannot yet be fuelled without increasing emissions of CO_2 from electricity production).
The key here is to eliminate incorrect options before narrowing down on the correct answer.
Option A may be true, but it is not the main message being conveyed in the passage.
Option B relates to the passage more closely than 'A', and if the word 'therefore' is placed in front of it, it makes sense as a concluding statement.

Option C uses 'never', a sweeping, exclusive term that makes the given statement incorrect. We do not need to envisage new technologies that can utilise wind power more effectively etc., just that we cannot conclude that wind power never can provide more electricity than it does now.

D – There is a subtle difference between options D, and B. Option D is a definitive statement about the limitations of fuelling electric cars, while B acknowledges that this limitation is the situation at present, allowing for the fact that the situation may be improved in future.

5)   The correct answer is E (440)

This question is potentially time-consuming because of the number of arithmetic calculations required. Improving the speed of these calculations (through practising) will undoubtedly save time in the BMAT:

$$\underline{Total\ area} = 18 \times 12 = 216$$

Shrubs: consider the length of the garden (18) and calculate what is already known:

$$3\ (lawn) + 1 + 1 + 1 + 0.5 = 6.5$$

$$18 - 6.5 = 11.5$$

11.5 is the total length of the two shrubs, so area

$$= 11.5 \times 4 = 46$$

Lawn and pond: use the width of the garden (12) and the same method as for shrubs:

$$1 + 1 + 1 = 3$$

$$12 - 3 = 9$$

$$9 \times 3 = 27$$

Vegetables:

$$1 + 3\ (pond) + 1 + 0.5 + 0.5 + 1 = 7,$$

$$18 - 7 = 11$$

$$11 \times 3 = 33$$

Thus, $46 + 27 + 33 = 106\ m^2$

$216m^2$ (total area) - $106\ m^2$ (occupied area) = $110\ m^2$ (paved area)

As 1m² requires 4 paving slabs (0.5 x 0.5 = 0.25 m², 0.25 x 4 = 1 m²)

110 x 4= 440

6)   The correct answer is E (It suggests a causal relationship between discussion and reading).

The way to answer questions relating to 'flaws' is to determine the 'conclusion' of the argument first. For this passage, this is: 'if parents spend time discussing these issues with their children, they will help their children read well'.

The most effective way to figure out a conclusion is to put 'therefore' in front of the sentence, and if it fits and is consistent with the line of argument of the passage, it is the conclusion. Taking each option in turn:

Statement A has nothing to do with the conclusion, thus it can be ruled out.

Statement B is not the best flaw that could be given, and in any case sounds like an assumption.

Statement C is somewhat true. But not an inherent flaw in the argument, as it has little to do with the conclusion. If the question was asking about statements that weaken the argument, then perhaps this might be reasonable.

Statement D, while arguably a valid point, it does not relate to the conclusion.

Statement E provides the perfect answer. The conclusion does indeed suggest a causal relationship between discussion and reading, based on the statistics (i.e. correlation). Correlation does not necessarily imply causation, and this is the flaw.

7)   The correct answer is A (1 hexagon, 2 triangles and 3 squares)

The way to work out questions about patterns such as this is to work out what the repeating unit of the pattern is. The image given is misleading as there is overlap between the shapes. Instead, the best way is to look at the non-overlapping part, which is the area of the image below with the tick. The part of the image to the left with the cross next to it may also appear to be a repeating unit because it seems non-overlapping, but upon further consideration, it has four squares in it, whereas the overall shape formed by one hexagon has 6 squares (combining two 4 square areas would create too large a shape), so it would not fit the pattern.

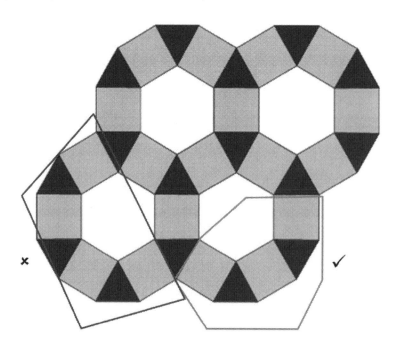

8)   The correct answer is C (7.15)

Start by using the following formula:

$$\frac{total\ number\ of\ cases\ in\ 2009\ and\ 2010}{total\ number\ of\ patients\ days\ in\ 2009\ and\ 2010}$$

There are relatively large numbers provided, so the best way is to estimate the amounts and consequently obtain an approximate answer. The total number of cases is 3, and the total number of patient days is 11,549 + 30,432 ≈ 42,000. Thus 3/42,000, but to get a rate out of 100,000, the value of 42,000 must be multiplied by around 2.5 to get around 100,000; repeating this for 3, gives the total of 7.5; the nearest answer is 7.15.

9)   The correct answer is D (38%)

Looking at the cases for 2009, it can be seen that the total number of cases for that year is 69, and Organisation 3 had the most cases at 26. Therefore the answer is 26/69. However, the answer needs to be in percentages. Just by looking at the fraction, all options can be ruled out apart from 'D' and 'E'. By approximation, this should reveal that the fraction is closer to 38% than 44%; it can be confirmed by doing a simple short division calculation:

$$69\overline{)26 \cdot {}^{26}0\,{}^{53}0\,0} = \cdot 37$$

10)   The correct answer is B (5.67)

Organisation two had 16,163 patient days for 11 months of the year. This roughly gives 1,500 patient days per month (16,000/11), so roughly 17,500 patient days in the year (16,000 + 1,500). There is one case in these 17,500 days. 17,500 which roughly go into 100,000 over 5 times, but this is definitely less than 6 times. Thus options C, D and E can be ruled out. To decide between A and B, 17.5 x 5 = 87.5, leaving 12.5 remaining; 12.5 is more than half of 17.5, so the answer must be more than 5.5. Thus the answer is 'B'.

11)   The correct answer is E (None of the above statements)

Avoid the trap of calculating extensive amounts of data to see if the statements are true or not.

One cannot really make a valid comparison between large hospitals and other organisations with the data given, as the amount of data given from organisations other than large hospitals is insufficient. Thus, statement A can be ruled out.

There is only one organisation with just a small hospital: Organisation two. This is not enough information to be able to draw conclusions, and in any case, that hospital has 0 cases of infections. Therefore statement B can also be ruled out.

One cannot reliably conclude statement C to be true as there are many organisations with both large and small hospitals within them. The breakdown of how many cases were attributable to either type of hospital within these organisations is also unknown. Moreover, there are several organisations with just a large hospital, but only one with a small hospital, so they cannot be reliably compared. Thus statement C can be omitted.

For statement D there are no organisations with just TCs or DCs to be able to say Cdl did specifically occur within both of these hospital types. Moreover, Organisation 2's solitary small hospital had no cases, so this is untrue (remember, there is no other way to prove any other Cdl cases occurred in a small hospital in all other organisations).

As one cannot reliably conclude from the options given, option E is considered the most appropriate.

12)   The correct answer is B (5 hours 15 minutes)

There is a lot of irrelevant information given here, which needs to be filtered through.

Nicola needs to take the first bus from the airport on Thursday, which would be the 09:15. It takes 50 minutes to get to town, so she arrives at 10:05. As she wants to be back at the airport by 17:00, she needs to take a bus at or earlier than 16:10. The latest suitable bus is the 15:20.

Therefore, if she got to town at 10:05 and left at 15:20, she has had 5 hours 15 minutes, leading to option B.

13)   The correct answer is D (The unusual weather in the UK could have been caused by the melting of the Arctic ice).

The conclusion does not always have to be explicitly stated in the passage. Options A and C can be quickly eliminated because they use definitive phrases such as 'only' and 'must'. This is too restrictive for a conclusion and must be discarded. Option B is not as definitive but still states that the UK 'would not have' experienced such weather if the Arctic ice was not melting, but this is not necessarily true, and indeed, not what the passage is saying ('is what one would expect').

Option D stands out as a better option as it makes sense if 'therefore' is put in front of it, relates to the thrust of the argument and does not use definitive or sweeping phrases like those seen in options A and C thus; this is the correct option.

14)   The correct answer is D

Visualising what the correct shape would look like is probably the best way to solve problems of this nature.

The orientation of the stripe in option A does not correlate with the orientation of the 'X' and triangle. Hence this option is incorrect.

If there was a horizontal stripe instead of a vertical stripe in option B, this could be correct. (Refer to orientation at far right of unfolded diagram)

Due to the folding arrangement in option C, the three shapes would not be together in the pattern shown. Instead, it could work if the black line was from 'side to side' rather than 'top to bottom'.

Option D fits the net correctly and is, therefore, the correct answer.

The white circle and the horizontal line are incorrectly positioned in option E. Therefore this option can be ruled out.

15) **The correct answer is C (The amount of oxytocin in the sprays sold online is too low to have any effect on children).**

The first step in identifying a point that weakens an argument is to determine the conclusion of the passage, and from there deciding which statement would undermine the idea of the main conclusion. The conclusion of this argument can be found in the last two lines of the passage and usually begin with words such as "so"- 'so parents of children with autism are damaging their children's health by using the sprays'.

Envy is a negative emotion, and so if anything, this would strengthen the argument that parents are damaging their children's health by using the spray. This means that statement A can be ruled out.

Statement B again strengthens the argument. If studies confirming the benefits of oxytocin have never used children as subjects, parents' use of it again seems potentially harmful.

Statement C is the correct answer. If the amount of oxytocin in these sprays is too low, the claim that parents are damaging their children's health with these sprays becomes less valid.

Statement D may have some relevance to the argument, but it is ambiguous whether the 'effects' would be positive or not, so this is not the best option.

Statement E once again further strengthens the point that oxytocin is not beneficial, thus bringing its use into question.

16) **The correct answer is C (44%)**

The entire conservatory does not need to be counted here, instead just the single repeating unit, as each unit has the same proportion of black tiles. By counting the number of each tile, and then approximating the amount that is black within them:

The number of white tiles: 5

¼ black tiles: 4 = 1 full black tile

½ black tiles: 12 = 6 full black tiles

Total number of full black tiles: 4

Therefore there are 11 'full' black tiles in total, out of 25 in the repeating unit, giving the final answer of 44%.

17) **The correct answer is G (None of the above statements)**

Statement one includes 'would', which suggests a causal relationship between improved staffing levels at weekends and death rates. The passage is not as conclusive on causality, as it merely states that 'this [as well as lower availability of specialist services] may be contributing to the increase in mortality'. Therefore this statement can be discarded.

Statement two may seem to be a reasonable conclusion. However, the passage talks about the weekend provision of community services as a reason for the increased mortality rate. Patients are dying in hospitals instead of at home (thus implying that they will die regardless); because of this increase in dying at hospitals, the mortality rate has increased for hospitals. Enhanced weekend provision of community and primary care services would not make a difference but just lower the mortality statistics. This means that this statement can also be discarded.

The word 'should' used in statement three, assumes that low staffing levels cause patient deaths, which is not proved in the passage. Therefore, this can also be discarded.

18) **The correct answer is A (between 10% and 30%)**

Using the data given, the number of people with both appliances can be termed 'x'.

The number of people, who own a dishwasher but do not own a dryer, is:

$$(75\text{-}85) - x$$

Similarly for people with dryers but not dishwashers:

$$(35\text{-}40) - x$$

There are also the people who have neither – less than 5%, or (0-5).

All of these values must total 100:

$$(75\text{-}85) - x + x + (35\text{-}40) - x + (0\text{-}5) = 100$$

Rearranging for 'x' gives:

$$x = (75\text{-}85) + (35\text{-}40) + (0\text{-}5) - 100$$

Considering the lowest and highest values x could take:

Lowest: $75 + 35 + 0 - 100 = 10$

Highest: $85 + 40 + 5 - 100 = 30$

This makes the correct answer A, between 10% and 30%.

19)   The correct answer is B (0.56 million)
There is a lot of irrelevant data to sift through in this question. The third bullet point is relevant here, regarding 2.23 million category A calls. The fourth bullet point is also relevant as it says that 74.9% of these were answered on time, meaning that around 25% were not. 25% of 2.23 million is just over 0.5 million, hence 'B' is the most appropriate answer.

20)   The correct answer is D
The third bullet point about the 2.23 million category A calls also states that around 33% of them were category A, 40% were B, and 27% were C. Therefore the correct pie chart shows A as being roughly 1/3 and C being just over ¼. Pie chart D fits both of these criteria.

21)   The correct answer is B (1.47 million calls did not result in an emergency response).
In option A, the given time limit for responding to calls should not affect the number that were transported or treated at the scene. Therefore this is not the correct answer.
Option B sounds the most reasonable out of all the options and follows the statement in the passage well.

Option C is a definitive statement that cannot completely be proven using the information provided. In any case, if something is a 'genuine emergency', it does not necessarily follow that there was a response to it.

Option D can be excluded on the basis that 27% of 8 million calls were category C, which is higher than 1.47 million calls.

22)   The correct answer is A (0.12 million)

Information from question 19 states that in 2011, 74.9% of the 2.23 million category A calls had a timely response. In 2010, there were 2.08 million category A calls, of which 74.3% were answered in timely fashion. These percentages are very similar, so the difference between the two total numbers can be compared: 2.23 – 2.08 = 0.15 million. If around 75% of them were answered in time, that is 75% of 0.15 million = 0.12 million.

23)   The correct answer is B (5)

The first step is to count how many grids have the same pattern; this is relatively simple when since many of the boxes are just rotated/inverted versions of each other.

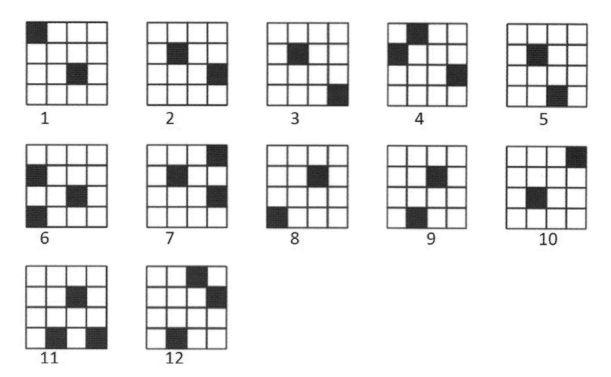

Looking at the options, grids 1, 3, 8 and 10 have the same pattern; 2, 5 and 9 have the same pattern; 6, 7 and 11 have the same pattern, while 4 and 12 have unique patterns. Thus five patterns are created, making the answer B.

24)   The correct answer is E (A survey of 2000 people carried out recently indicated strong public support for water cannons).

The best place to start when considering statements which would either weaken or in this case strengthen an argument is to identify the conclusion. From here, a reason can be identified which will increase the strength of the argument.

If water cannons were indiscriminate, statement A would then weaken the argument. Hence it can be excluded.

The expertise required to fire a water cannon does not really support whether they should be used or not. Therefore statement B can be excluded as it neither strengthens nor weakens the argument.

Statement C weakens the argument since it states that other methods are as effective as water cannons, meaning that there is no justification for their use.

The cost of each pair of water cannons weakens the argument. Thus statement D can also be discarded.

Statement E weakly supports the argument, and in comparison to the other options, is the best answer.

25)   The correct answer is C (13)

The easy way of doing this is to realise that the highest possible score is 18 and the lowest possible score is 2 (excluding zero). Therefore, there are potentially 17 plausible scores, all of which need to be assessed if they can be scored within the game:

2: 2 + 2 = 4, then miss = 2

3: 2, then miss = 3

4: 6 +2 =8, then miss = 4

5: 6 + 4 = 10, then miss = 5

6: 2 + 2 + 2 = 6

7: 6, then miss = 3. + 4 = 7

8, 10, 12, 14 and 16 can be made with combinations of 2, 4 and 6.

9: 6, then miss = 3. + 6 = 9

11, 13, 15 and 17 are impossible, therefore there are 13 possibilities.

26)   The correct answer is D (The French are European, and Spaniards are European, so the French is Spaniards).

This question needs to be considered in relation to which of the statements fit the logic of the argument, which is: 'art is copying; forgery is copying, so forgery is art'.

In statement A, the water analogy is very reasonable and makes sense.

The petrol analogy in statement B is not true (which is what is needed), but not really what the passage is trying to convey.

The weight analogy in statement C is quite reasonable. If 'A implies B', it be can reasonably concluded that 'not-A implies not-B'; so if being overweight is unhealthy, being 'not-overweight' (or having a normal weight) is 'not-unhealthy' (or healthy), which is what the passage is saying.

Statement D follows the line of logic that the passage is saying most accurately, as it assumes the fact two things may fit one category means that they are the same as each other. Obviously it is untrue and shows how flawed the art argument is.

27)   The correct answer is C ($20,000)

Two things are known in this question: that no sales were made in May and June, and that ½ of the amount for a piece of furniture is paid immediately, and a quarter each in the subsequent months. Let's draw a table and work backwards:

January	February	March	April	May	June
$4,000	$2,000	$2,000	$4,000	$2,000	$2,000
		$2,000	$1,000	$1,000	

$2,000 was made in June, which must have been a quarter of the amount of money paid in April (as the store was closed in May too). Therefore, $2,000 was received in May as well, and $4,000 was made in April *(italics)*. As there are $3,000 in total sales in May, he must have received $1,000 as a final ¼ payment from a purchase made in March; there must have been $1,000 in April and $2,000 in March for that purchase. April has now reached the $5,000 total given in the question.

March adds up to $4,000 in total, so another $2,000 needs to be added to this month, as well as another $2,000 in February and $4,000 in January (underlined). Combining all the money on the table, the total comes to $20,000.

28)   The correct answer is G (1, 2 and 3)

The conclusion for this passage is 'the ski holiday industry does not damage the environment', but the reasons given need to be used from the three statements to find a weakness.

Statement one shows a prominent weakness in the argument. The author says that saying that the ski holiday industry damages the environment is 'nonsense', but there is not a reasonable link to their belief that all travel damages the environment, hence it is weak.

Statement two is a reasonable comment to make as there is no positive comparison on the proportion of their energy consumption compared to other resorts, so it is unknown if 26% is a good or bad thing.

Statement three is a weakness as well, since the passage argues in favour of ski resorts with regards to energy consumption, but does not consider environmental damage that can be caused by ways unrelated to energy consumption.

As all of the options are weaknesses, the answer is G.

29)   The correct answer is C (£1360)

The total amount from sales is £12,240. The total number of sales can be termed, x. As 60% of the tickets were at £20 and 40% were at £15, the average price would be £18 (the difference between 20 and 15 is 5, and 60% of this is 3; which is added to 15). 12,240/18, with some long division, means that there were 680 tickets sold. So 40% of 680 is 272, and if all of these people received a £5 discount, there was 272 x 5 = £1360 was refunded.

30)   The correct answer is C (3 only)

Assumptions are simply unstated reasons, so first identify the conclusion (that the reasons support) of the passage and then see if the statements given are indeed reasons and if they have been stated already. The argument talks about how authors on health and treatments may be sponsored by pharmaceutical companies. The conclusion is along the lines of 'the public needs to know what weight they should put on these articles when they assess information from various sources'.

The passage says nothing about one-sided views, effectiveness or safety. Therefore statement one is not an assumption (unstated reason) that follows from the line of the argument to the conclusion. Also, 'authors give a one-sided view' is sweeping and quite an inflexible statement, hence it is incorrect.

When considering statement two, it can be seen that the passage does not say anything of the sort, and does not really assume this. It says that we should declare conflicts of interest so that informed decisions can be made. However, this is again quite a narrow statement and a little too cynical to be the right answer.

Statement three is a reasonable statement, and is not as narrow and sweeping as the other two statements, as it says that reliability 'cannot be fairly judged without information'. It links the argument and the conclusion well and is a reasonable statement to make. Thus, only this statement is correct as an assumption.

31)   The correct answer is C (19)

The information says that Jill is guaranteed to finish at least third, so the last placed player must be at least 7 points behind Jill at the end of the ninth round (as if this player won, and gained 6 points, they still would not overtake Jill; there are also no ties). For the same reason, Jill must be 7 points behind Karen and Gemma. Karen and Gemma must be on equal points at the end of the ninth round, as at the very least, either of them could get 1 point (by coming third) in the final round and the other could get no points (finishing last). This means that the person who 'finished ahead' would be the overall winner.

The total number of points awarded to all players must be (6 + 2 + 1 = 9) x 10 rounds = 90, and so all options need to be analysed to see which one fits this criteria.

If fourth place has 13 at the end of the tenth round, they must have at least 7 in the 9th round. Jill will, therefore, have 8 points, and the other two 15 each. The total here is 45, which means that this total is too small. Hence A can be excluded

If fourth place has 9 points in the ninth round; Jill will have 16 points, and the other two will have 23 each. This is a total of 71, which again is too small. Therefore option B can also be excluded.

If fourth place has 13 points in the ninth round; Jill will have 20 points, and the other two will have 27 each. This is a total of 87. This is close to 90 so is a viable option, if D and E are not going to work.

Options D and E will give totals of more than 90. Thus these answers are not correct.

32)   The correct answer is A (0.04)

By scouring the data, it can be found that in 1930, 7,000 people were killed out of 2.3 million vehicles (7/2,300). Today, 3,180 people were killed out of 27 million vehicles, so roughly half as many deaths with more than 10 times as many vehicles. Let's take the 1930 figure as a fraction (e.g. 10/10 to keep it simple). The numerator (number of deaths) for today will be half the amount in 1930, so it is 5. The denominator (number of vehicles) will be 10x more, so 100. So the fraction for today is 5/100, or 1/20. $1/20^{th}$ of the 1930 figure gives the answer.

33)   The correct answer is D (Hospital reporting of road accidents has become more accurate).

At first, all options seem pretty reasonable. By combing through the text and looking at the options in a little more detail, the best answer can be identified:

A lack of police recording for incidents where no incidents were sustained does not mean roads are getting safer but suggests the issue is being under-reported. Therefore statement A can be excluded.

Statement B is true, but words to that effect have already been mentioned in the text by Paul Smith from Safe Speed, who says: 'Cars are safer...' Therefore this statement does not strengthen the argument.

Statement C again, suggests the issue is under-reported and can be excluded.

The article mentions that the number killed or seriously injured fell from 1996 to 2004, but hospital admissions remained unchanged. If hospital reporting of accidents has become more accurate, this gives us more reason to trust the figures. Therefore statement D adds strength to the argument.

Statement E is true, but it has also been mentioned in the passage: 'paramedics [have become] better trained'. Therefore it too can be discarded.

34)   The correct answer is C (128,000)

We need to find 40% of 319,928. As the answer options are quite spaced out, one can afford to round up to 320,000 and find 40%, which will give the correct answer.

35)   The correct answer is A (The DfT collection method must underestimate the number of deaths and serious injuries).

Statement A is a possibility as underestimation that would explain the discrepancy between the hospital and DfT data.

Statement B is not an appropriate option as 'safer' is quite a vague term in this context. Even if the roads are getting safer, it does not account for the discrepancy between DfT and hospital figures. Thus this statement can be excluded

If statement C was true, it should really mean that the hospital figure decreases, but it stays constant here. Therefore it is incorrect.

If statement D was true and the hospital admission figures stayed stable, the DfT figures would have increased. As this has not happened, it is incorrect.

If statement E were true, it would again make the DfT figures higher than the hospital figures. Therefore this option can also be excluded.

BMAT Section 1 - 2013

1) **The correct answer is A (Tuesday, Thursday, Friday)**

As precisely two people have to be on duty on any day, and Carla is not working on Monday; Amy and Bob must work on Monday. As Bob only works a maximum of 3 days; the three days he works on are Monday, Tuesday and Friday. Thus, Amy and Carla both have to work on Wednesday and Thursday. Also, as none of the operators work for four consecutive days, Amy cannot work on Tuesday, so Carla musk work on Tuesday and Amy must work on Friday.

	Monday	Tuesday	Wednesday	Thursday	Friday
Amy	Y	N	Y	Y	Y
Bob	Y	Y	N	N	Y
Carla	N	Y	Y	Y	N

2) **The correct answer is C (The criteria cannot give an accurate judgement as to whether a planet is habitable).**

Option A cannot be concluded as the text only states that the new criteria makes Kepler-22b appear too hot for liquid water. Therefore, it cannot be implied that this means no life exists here as this was once deemed the second most habitable planet.

The phrase in option B 'The new criteria make many planets look too hot for liquid water' enables it to be ruled out, as fewer planets appear to be habitable than previously thought

The new criteria that makes Earth seem too hot for liquid water and consequently inhabitable are clearly untrue as there is currently life on Earth, and as a result, implies that this new criteria is not accurate. Thus option C is the correct answer.

The reference to clouds is used to explain why the criteria do not work with regards to Earth, so cannot be extended to Kepler-22b. Also, it cannot be assumed that life does not already exist on Kepler-22b. Thus option D can also be ruled out.

3) **The correct answer is C (Adam and Tara)**

If any two individuals are to have their birthdays on the same day of the week, the difference between their dates of birth must be a multiple of seven. For example if 281-218=63 (9 x 7), gives a multiple of 7, but all other differences do not give a multiple of 7. Adam's birthday is on the 218th day and Tara's birthday is on the 281st day, meaning their birthdays always fall on the same day of the week.

4) **The correct answer is C (Greater levels of activity and lower calorie consumption are the keys to weight loss).**

Statement A is stated in the text but is used as a comparison or explanation; it does not conclude the theme of the text in relation to weight loss and one's diet. Thus, it can be discarded as the main conclusion.

Although statement B can be drawn from the text, it is not the main conclusion as it only addresses one aspect of the text. When looking for a main conclusion, it should summarise the whole passage. Therefore it can also be excluded.

The conclusion is indicated by the precursor of 'therefore', and so the argument concludes one should lose weight by doing more and eating less. Only option C expresses this.

In option D, physical activity only partially summarises the text; the conclusion needs to refer to both physical activity and calorie consumption. Therefore this statement can also be discarded.

5)   The correct answer is D (171 Spruggles)

The number of items he sold on day 1 can be denoted as x. So, as he sold x number of items at £12 each, he made £12x. On the second day, he sold 2x number of items at £9 (25% reduction in price so 12-3= 9), and so he made £18x. The information states that 18x is 342 greater than 12x. Hence, 12x+342=18x and therefore, 6x=342 (take x values to one side). So, x=57 (divide both sides by 6). So, as he sold 3x goods over the 2 days, he sold 171 Spruggles (3 X 57). So, answer is D

6)   The correct answer is C (The discovery of a human settlement in America dating to around 12,000 BC/BCE).

At the time of this paper, it is 2013, so 13,500 years ago would mean the first settlements should be around 11,500 BC if the Clovis–First theory is true. Thus, the discovery of a settlement 500 years earlier in 12,000 BC would most seriously challenge this theory. Therefore, the answer is C.

7)   The correct answer is A (Doyle)

As no letter of the alphabet appears twice in any of the boys' full names, Eric's surname must be Floyd, as all other surnames have either an e or an r (or both). Dylan cannot have the surnames Doyle, Floyd or Hyde (all contain the letters d and y). Liam cannot have the surnames Doyle (repeated D), or Floyd (Eric's surname). Simon cannot have the surname Doyle, Floyd or Shore (all contain o). So, Ian must have the surname Doyle (as shown below)

	Doyle	Floyd	Hyde	Rush	Shore
Simon	X	X			X
Liam	X	X			
Ian	Y	X			
Dylan	X	X	X		
Eric	X	Y	X	X	X

8)   The correct answer is D (It is no surprise to hear that childhood is now less carefree than it was).

The question gives away the answer. By saying that it is a sarcastic comment, this means that the author is not surprised by this newest research because it is not a surprise to hear that childhood is now less carefree than it was. So, the answer is D.

9)   **The correct answer is A (We're not necessarily happier as we get richer).**
As the phrase says we've got unhappier by a greater amount than the money we've acquired, money isn't necessarily making anyone happy. Thus options C and D can be ruled out. However, it does not mean that less wealth would make anyone happier, ruling out D. Thus, the answer is A.

10)   **The correct answer is D (Neither 1 or 2)**
The psychologist is merely saying to get good at your job; you need to spend time and energy on it. So, neither assumption is needed for this argument to hold. Also, people who have more time may not necessarily give more time to their children, and they may be more stressed if they fail. So, the answer is D.

11)   **The correct answer is B (Anecdotal)**
The evidence used is an anecdote (a real story about a real person and event). Conclusive evidence is an irrefutable fact. Statistical uses figures as evidence. Irrelevant means the evidence is not related to the argument. In contrast, hearsay is not necessarily a true story. So, the answer is B.

12)   **The correct answer is B (1 pair)**
The cards show that there is only one pair: Tin-Jupiter; Saturn – symbol; symbol – gold.

13)   **The correct answer is D (Doctors should offer treatments on the basis of the outcome for the patient).**
Option A will not provide support, as the placebo might not work.
Option B is irrelevant, as the placebo has few or no side effects, and this statement is also adding no support to the argument.
Statement C provides an argument against the passage, so it is incorrect.
By ruling out all other option D, is the correct answer
Option E is irrelevant, as research has shown placebos can have a powerful therapeutic effect.

14)   **The correct answer is B (7)**
The alphabetical order of numbers is 8, 5, 4, 9, 1, 7, 6, 3, 2, and 0. Therefore, the other two numbers are 9, 1, 7, 6, 3 or 2. By presuming that the second number is 9, the sum of letters so far will be 12, and numerical sum of digits is 13. Thus, two can then be used as the third number: the pin is 4 9 2 0 and the total number of the letter than make up 9 and 2 are 7. So, the answer is B.

15)   **The correct answer is B (Most people want to escape from the modern obsession with safety at work).**
The argument has assumed that people do sports to counter stress at work. However, this argument is significantly weakened when reversed, and so most people want to escape the modern obsession by using the safety of work. Thus, the answer is B.

16) The correct answer is C (3 months)

Jenny was born in January, June or July. Alice was born in either April or August. Michael was born in either March or May. January and July are not two months away from either April or August. So, Jenny must have been born in June (which is 2 months apart from August and April). April is less than five months apart from March or May. So, Alice's birthday is in August and Michael's birthday must be in March for their birthdays to be five months apart. There are three months between March and June. So, the answer is C.

17) The correct answer is D (1 and 3)

The argument says lack of sleep causes impairment in memory. Statement one reverses this argument, so it has identified a weakness. Statement two is irrelevant to the argument. Statement three says there is a third factor (changes in the brain) which cause both sleep loss and memory impairment, so it has identified a weakness. Thus, both one and three identify a weakness.

18) The correct answer is B (36)

September is the ninth month, so the possible days it could happen are the 1st, 4th, 16th and 25th. On the 1st, the hours that can be taken are 4 and 16. For each hour, there are four possible times (with eight possibilities overall). The same reasoning applies for the 4th and 16th. So, there are 24 times so far. On the 25th, three possible hours can be taken (1, 4 and 16), so there are 12 possibilities on that day. Thus, there are 36 possibilities.

19) The correct answer is B (It could only be yellow, blue or red).

The large region next to X is touching blue, red and yellow. So, the large region must be green, and hence X cannot be green. The other region touching X can be either yellow or red. So, X could be yellow, blue or red. So, the answer is B.

20) The correct answer is C (Either none or one extra colour might be needed).

If the circle is placed inside a square, it can be the opposite colour to the square (so a white circle can be placed on a black square). However, if the circle is placed so it is crossing the boundary between a white square and a black square, the circle needs to be a different colour. So, either none or one extra colour might be needed depending on the circle's size and position. Thus, the answer is C.

21) The correct answer is A (Two colours will always be sufficient).

As only straight lines are used, and no curved lines are making up the boundaries between regions, only two colours are needed (much the same pattern as a chess board).

22) The correct answer is B (3)

By using the top half of the pentagonal dipyramid for the moment, it can be seen that three colours for the five sides will be needed, as only using two colours will always cause two adjacent sides to have the same colour. So, the same rule applies for the bottom half, and the same three colours could be used by simply changing the pattern (i.e. blue, red, green, blue, red on the top becomes red, green, blue, red, blue on the bottom). So, the answer is B.

23)   The correct answer is D (8)
There are 8 different tiles: all black, three-quarters black, half black, one-quarter black, half lined and quarter black, half lined, a quarter lined one way, and a quarter line going the other way. So, the answer is D.

24)   The correct answer is B (In Scotland consumption of alcohol has doubled over the past five decades as prices have fallen).
The first step is to identify the conclusion in the passage, which is that to reduce the harm caused by alcohol, the consumption must be reduced. The argument states that if the price of alcohol was increased, there will be less consumption. So, evidence that a decrease in price is correlated with an increase in consumption would strengthen the argument the most. Therefore, the answer is B.

25)   The correct answer is B (4)
The difference between the two clocks is 41 minutes. So, the times when eight different digits are displayed are: 19:56 and 20:37; and 19:57 and 20:38 - it must be these times, as it had to be a moment when it was close to going to 20:00 on the clock that was behind, for the hours and minutes to be different digits on both clocks. Thus, the number 4 does not appear which makes option B correct.

26)   The correct answer is A (1)
The number 5 is currently on the bottom face in the original diagram. It will roll onto 6 on when the octahedral lands on P, onto 7 on Q, 4 on R and finally onto 1 on S. So, the answer is A.

27)   The correct answer is C (Yes, because Beth was either unmarried and being looked at by Al or she was married and being looking at Charles).
If Beth is married, she is looking at Charles who is unmarried. If Beth is unmarried, Al (who is married) is looking at Beth. So, the answer is C.

28)   The correct answer is D (Children should be protected from harm).
The argument states that children should not be placed in situations where there can be damaging consequences, which agrees with the principle that children should be protected from harm.

29)   The correct answer is E (2, 4, 5, 6)
Use a rubber with 6 faces to draw on the patterns makes it clear that only cubes 2, 4, 5 and 6 can be made from the net above. So, the answer is E.

30)   The correct answer is D (1 and 3)

An assumption is an unstated fact in the argument.

The argument implies something evolves if it is an advantage, so point one can be assumed, as if that had not been assumed, then wrinkles would not have evolved according to the argument's theory. Also, another assumption here is that characteristics only evolve if they are advantageous (thus point three has been assumed). So, the answer is D.

31)   The correct answer is A (3)

The bottom row currently adds up to 22, so 7 more are needed. There is no number 0, and 6 and 5 have been allocated, so the remaining two seats go to numbers 3 and 4. If 3 was sitting adjacent to 6, that row would currently add up to 20, which cannot be achieved, as 12 is sitting elsewhere (a combination of 12 and 8 is not possible) and so is 9 (since a combination of 9 and 11 is not possible either). So, 3 must sit opposite 9. This means that the answer is A. (The rest of the seating arrangements are filled in to show that it works)

5	9	7	8
			11
			6
10	3	12	4

32)   The correct answer is B (28)

20% of young people use cannabis, so 2000 young people per 10000 take cannabis. Cannabis users are 41% more likely, so

$$1.41 \times 1 = 1.41\%$$

$$0.0141 \times 2000 = 28$$

So, the answer is B.

33)   The correct answer is A (8%)

20% of 41% is the same as 0.2 x 41 which equals 8. So, the answer is A.

34)   The correct answer is B (Those people who have a tendency to develop a psychotic illness often turn to drugs to ease their mental problems).

Statement A does not provide an alternative reason, as coincidence is not valid when there is such strong correlation between the two factors. Statement C is irrelevant, as the argument is about cannabis increasing the risk of suffering from psychosis not whether only cannabis causes psychosis. Statement D is an irrelevant fact that does not provide any alternative reason. Statement B offers a third reason, which causes both cannabis use and psychotic illness. Thus, the answer is B.

35) **The correct answer is C (A recent increase in the use of stronger types of cannabis has coincided with an increase in psychosis among users).**

Statement A could be the answer; however, it could just be related to the age demographic. Statement B is irrelevant to the question and thus can be discarded. Statement C shows there is a direct correlation between cannabis use and psychotic illness. Thus it strengthens the conclusion. Statement D has too many assumptions to be a valid argument and can be discarded. Statement E is also irrelevant to the question. So, the answer is C.

BMAT Section 1 - 2014

1) The correct answer is D (5)

When looking at the table, it should be immediately apparent that the columns are not in chronological order, so one must work from right to left when reading the table rather than left to right as done in a standard table.

The image below shows the sites which demonstrate both an increase in 'audience numbers' and time per visit; these have been highlighted to make counting them easy. In this example, there are five which show an increase in the two attributes of interest, therefore the correct answer is D.

Read the table in this direction

Site	February 2008		February 2007	
	Audience (000's)	Time per visit (hr:min:sec)	Audience (000's)	Time per visit (hr:min:sec)
myspace.com	55 419	2:12:19	53 362	2:00:24
Facebook	20 043	1:06:43	9 923	1:04:54
LinkedIn	7 392	0:10:31	1 990	0:05:10
Flixster	2 619	0:07:38	1 591	0:12:28
Reunion.com	4 323	0:04:34	4 348	0:04:49
Meetup.com	1 940	0:12:16	1 215	0:07:07
Last.fm	1 938	0:06:43	1 508	0:02:24
myYearbook	1 738	0:07:02	2 368	0:09:04

2) The correct answer is C (Herbivores are more at risk of extinction than carnivores).

This question requires the main idea of the argument to be identified, supported by reason. The most efficient way to recognise this is to look for words such as 'however,' 'so,' therefore' and other synonyms of these words in the text as they indicate a final decision.

Option A provides a partial or intermediate conclusion but also serves as the explanation for C (the correct answer). Incomplete conclusions are often seen in these types of articles, so a decision must be made at this point if this is a standalone conclusion or, part of another stronger conclusion. In this case, choices C and A are part of the same conclusion and can be put together as a statement and its explanation: "Herbivores are more at risk of extinction *because* herbivores are more threatened by environmental changes than carnivores."

B is incorrect as it is an opinion/viewpoint and therefore not a conclusion.

D is incorrect as it is a statement of fact relating to the general features that carnivores show.

E is the explanation for D and is also incorrect.

3)   The correct answer is E (Oscar, Rick, Bertha, Gavin, Yasmin)
From the information provided, the second (Rick), fourth (Gavin) and fifth (Yasmin) are correct, and since a name cannot be used twice or a have the same initial as any which have been already used, this narrows the options down considerably. This, therefore rules out option B, C, and D as they use the same initial twice, leaving options A and E. Since option B has been discarded, which has Bertha in first position, option A can also be removed, since it is the same name in the same position, leaving option E as the correct answer.

4)   The correct answer is B (Any claim that a sheep has been attacked by a wolf should be treated with caution).
There are many fact-based claims in this passage but very little that can be identified as a conclusion. The facts from the passage are as follows:

(1) Wolves are making a return to the Haute-France region;
(2) Farmers are compensated for sheep attacked by wolves;
(3) The reward is considerably more than the sheep's value;
(4) It is very difficult to distinguish between wolf and dog attacks; and
(5) The wild dog population exceeds that of the wolf population.

When considering all five facts together, it suggests farmers have a clear motive for making false claims regarding wolves attacking their sheep. Making option B the correct choice as it encompasses all of these facts and paints a clear picture of the situation.

5)   The correct answer is G
The key to solving this question is that "no black squares can touch either corner to corner or edge to edge." By drawing the 16 small tiles and shading them in as seen in the diagram below, we can begin to eliminate some of the options:

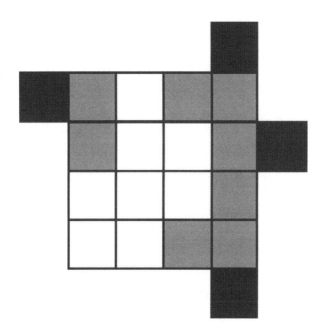

Using the rule that "one corner square and one edge square is to be black," it becomes apparent that the edge square on the left-hand side can be ruled out /shaded in. This action gives the location of two out of the three black squares seen shaded in the diagram below.

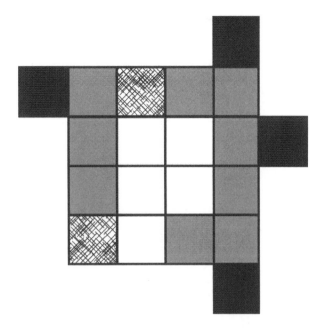

By doing this, all options are excluded except for G which, when rotated 90° to the left fits the requirements.

6)   The correct answer is B (It ignores the possibility that other factors may be necessary for acquiring perfect pitch).

To identify the flaws in the argument, one must first determine the conclusion. Therefore one must look for the keywords which indicate a conclusion as mentioned previously in question two, such as; 'because' 'therefore' or 'so.' The passage suggests that people who are taught music before age six will develop perfect pitch and it should, therefore, be made a priority in primary schools (this is the conclusion). Once this is identified, the argument can be taken apart to find the flaws.

Option A assumes that perfect pitch is important to acquire and worth primary school children spending time developing, is a viewpoint, not a fact. Therefore it can be excluded.

Option B is a clear flaw because even if music was taught to children under age of six, it would require them to continue learning music into adulthood, to maintain perfect pitch and ignores any other factors that relate to the development of perfect pitch. Therefore we can opt for choice B.

Answer C is incorrect as the article suggests no correlation between perfect pitch and success as a musician.

Answer D is incorrect as this is a specific factor which determines one's ability to develop perfect pitch.

7)   The correct answer is E (56 ¼ %)

To work out the options, first calculate the amount for each jar, with an added 25%

$$100g \times 1.25 = 125g$$

$$200 \times 1.25 = 250g$$

$$400 \times 1.25 = 500g + \text{an additional small jar containing } 125g$$

Therefore the customer purchasing a large jar of coffee gets 625g of coffee (or 225g more than usual, if the promotion was not on).

As a percentage:

$(225/400) \times 100 = 56.25\%$ more coffee than usual making the correct answer E

8)   The correct answer is B (9%)
The statistics for this question can be found in paragraph two of the article. A total of 632 patients from the original 7008 developed dementia in the eight years after anaesthesia, therefore $(632/7008) \times 100 = 9.02\%$ (Answer B)

9)   The correct answer is C (Other conditions or lifestyles which lead to the need for anaesthesia could also increase the risk of dementia).
Dr Karran reveals that there are many genetic and environmental factors which are known to lead to dementia. The passage does not say if these factors have been taken into consideration in this study; therefore there may be a link between one or more factors, anaesthesia and dementia, making answer C correct.

10)   The correct answer is D (The cohort studied was carefully selected to represent a typical demographic group with an average range of pre-existing medical conditions).
Answers A, B and C all suggest an alternative factor is responsible for the development of dementia. To rule out this effect, a sample which is representative of the general population of individuals, 65 and over, would remove the bias results.

11)   The correct answer is E (20%)
The article states that:
General anaesthesia increases the risk of developing dementia in later life by 35%, regardless of lifestyle. (Paragraph one).
A smoker undergoing general anaesthesia has a 27% likelihood of developing dementia in later life. (paragraph three).
Smokers have a 27% chance that they will develop dementia later in life if they have undergone general anaesthesia. On top of this, they have a 35% chance (or a probability of 1.35) of developing dementia in later life compared to a smoker who has not undergone general anaesthesia developing dementia

Therefore the answer is 27% / 1.35 = 20 %

12)   The correct answer is D (132)

Looking at the first and second place, it can be determined that the number of jellybeans is between 125 and 140. It can also be ascertained that it must be closer to 125, than 140 since Jessie is in first place and Saul is second. Making the range of answers:

$$140-125 = 15$$

The midpoint of the range is 7.5 (15/2 = 7.5), but since it is unlikely that there are half jellybeans we can assume that the answer must be either:

$$125 + 7 \text{ or } 125 + 8$$

Since Jessie (125) is closer than Saul (140), the 125+8 =133 (option E) can be ruled out as this would make Saul closer than Jessie. Therefore, the upper limit for the total number of jellybeans:

$$125 + 7 = 132$$

Options A and B can also be ruled out at this point as this would mean that Marie (currently in fourth position) would be closer than Saul, who is in second place. Option C can also be ruled out by following the same logic as it would mean that while Saul remained in second place, Imran would be displaced by Marie and placing him in equal position with Hank. Therefore option C is also incorrect.

13)   The correct answer is E (To find out whether crime levels are increasing we should survey people's experience of crime).

Assuming that the information provided is factual, one needs to ask what the most reasonable conclusion is, based on this evidence.

There are two critical points in this passage that can be used to identify the conclusion:

That recorded crime figures are not reliable when determining trends in crime

That the England and Wales crime survey is a more reliable source for determining crime rates than crime figures.

Based on these two ideas options A, B, and C attempt to provide a reason for the unreliability of the crime figures, but are not themselves conclusions. Therefore they can be ruled out.

Option D is an opinion/viewpoint and therefore not a conclusion as there is no evidence to support the idea that victims are fearful of reporting a crime, if this is fact, then this would also contribute to the inaccuracy of the crime figures held by police. This leaves option E, if more people are reporting that they have experienced crime, through the crime survey (assuming this is anonymous), it then stands to reason that crime rates are increasing.

14)   The correct answer is F (6 and 1)

The outline of diagram one matches the roofline of the back right-side of the house, showing the high point on the left and then a sloping roof to the right. Options one and five are mirror images of each other with diagram five

113

matching the view from the front left. However, the location of the windows and door are incorrect on diagram five when this view is examined from the back left. Therefore diagram one is correct.

For diagram three, the roof line matches what would be seen from the front right, but the door and window are incorrect. Diagram four is entirely incorrect with no matching roof line or window pattern. Therefore it can immediately rule out options C and D.

When looking at the diagrams in options two and six, they are fairly similar, but the lower roof profile on the right side of the diagram in option six fits better with the proportions of the house's back left wall. As there are no other options that are similar, option two can be ruled out and thus assume option six is the back left wall (which means that option F is the answer).

15)   The correct answer is A (Possible benefits that would come from improvements in medical science outweigh concerns about personal privacy).

This question requires an inference to be made on the missing step in the argument. To do this, first, identify the conclusion that the article is drawing; which is that 'the public should not be opposed to sharing their medical records'. Once the conclusion has been found, then identify the reason using the assumptions that are given. In this case, only one of these makes sense, which is the benefit of sharing their information – option A.

16)   The correct answer is D ($110)

There are two aspects to this problem:

To design the 8-page book in colour costs $60 more than in black and white (150-90 =60)

To print 500 booklets in colour costs $50 more than in black and white (30-20) x5 = 50

Therefore 60 + 50 = 110 making answer D correct

17)   The correct answer is D (It assumes that agile minds are equally effective with or without STEM training).

Four of the options can be ruled out by simply looking through the passage and finding the point of conflict for each:

Therefore, option A is incorrect since the article states that we should be "turning out agile minds." Option B is also incorrect due to the statement regarding the "world increasingly dominated by careers that involve these fields." Option C is incorrect as it does not use any data at all; apart from "anecdotal evidence". Statement E is also incorrect as it clearly states that "organisations and politicians repeatedly state that we must train more of these people." It can be inferred that the organisations they are referring to are STEM companies/organisations – which mean that this is their view.

Therefore option D is left; which is supported by the following:

"But STEM training is not the only answer: anecdotal evidence shows the STEM employees who do best are those most skilled in thinking and communicating. Instead of looking to produce scientists and engineers, we should focus on turning out agile minds."

It suggests an agile mind is more important than subject knowledge, and that mental agility can be taught. In many cases, this is incorrect as mental agility often has a lot to do with natural ability. In most situations, a scientist with or without an agile mind is still going to be more effective at solving a scientific problem than a person with an agile mind and no scientific background, simply due to the advantage of subject knowledge. Another point to consider here is that many STEM-based disciplines often allow the development of mental agility in a specific field.

18)   The correct answer is C (The Quavers will play the Flats, and the Minims will play the Crotchets).
There are several pieces of information that must be used to construct the order of players:
The quavers (6) were drawn out first, and the minims (5) were last
Therefore: 6 _ _ _ _ _ _ 5

The alternated between even and odd therefore it can be said that the quavers played an 'odd' team and the minims played an 'even' team. This limits the possible teams to 1, 3, 7 for the quavers and 2, 4, 8 for the minims

There is always at least a difference of three between each ball. Therefore it can be said with confidence that the quavers (6) played team (3) which is the flats. And the minims must have either played team (2) or team (8)
Therefore: 6 3 _ _ _ _ _ 5

To work out the rest of the sequence, the rules of the minimum difference of 3 between each ball and alternate odd and even numbers can be applied.

Therefore: 6 3 8 1 4 7 2 5

Which means that answer C is correct: the quavers will play the flats and the minims will play the crochets.

19)   The correct answer is F (2 and 3 only)
The question asks one to make an inference based on the information given. Therefore statement one cannot be assumed as it is referring to two different things; crime rate (in the statement) and sentencing (in the table). It is possible to commit a crime without being sentenced therefore the two are not a direct correlation. This means that options A, D, E, and G can be ruled out as correct answers.
When considering statement two, the figures for each area can be calculated:

Yorkshire: 5 million x 0.64% (or 0.0064) = 32000

Wales: 3 million x 0.5% (or 0.005) = 15000

Wales has roughly half the number of sentences as Yorkshire. Therefore, statement two can be inferred, ruling out options C and H and leaving option B and F as final possibilities.

For statement three, the sentencing rate of 0.62% is higher than 6 in every 1000 because (6/1000) x 100 = 0.6%. Therefore, statement three can also be inferred, making the correct answer F.

20)   The correct answer is C (1 for every 182 inhabitants)
The table tells shows that 0.55% of the 7.4 million in the population have been sentenced.

This means that for every 100 people 0.55 of them have been sentenced so it can be said that 100/0.55 = 181.8 which equals 1 in every 182 inhabitants making answer C correct.

21)   The correct answer is C (Both 1 and 2)
Arson 0.4%
South West 5 million x 0.5% = 25000
In order to get this number: 25000 x 0.4% = 100

The data for the offence type does not specify which region this information relates to. Therefore, it can be assumed that the information is the same nationwide. So, statement one can be assumed.
When considering the second statement, look again at the tables carefully as table one shows the percentage of sentences, whereas table two shows the offences. Therefore the information from both tables gives the outcome of 100, which means that statement two, must also be assumed, making the correct answer C.

22)   The correct answer is C (16:12)

$$1 \text{ day} = 24 \text{ hours} = 10 \text{ decidays}$$

Therefore 1 deciday in hours is:

$$24/10 = 2.4 \text{ hours old time}$$

75 millidays (from 1:75) is 75% of 1 deciday
Therefore:

$$2.4 \times 0.75 = 1.8 \text{ hours in old time}$$

Therefore:

$$2.4 + 1.8 = 4.2 \text{ hours past midday (since 0.00 is midday on the new clock)}$$

$$0.2 \times 60 \text{ minutes} = 12 \text{ minutes}$$

Therefore the time is 16.12 (option C)

23)   The correct answer is D (could be a contributory factor in the reduction of the incidence of new cases of dementia).
This question essentially asks its reader to link heart disease and dementia. When examining the last few sentences of the passage:
"Over the same period the rates of heart disease have fallen, and in general the health of the blood vessels in the elderly has improved. Given that brain function requires the supply of oxygen to the brain from blood vessels"

The article is hinting at a link between the health of the blood vessels and blood supply to the brain reducing dementia. Therefore, options A (as this is a highly generalised statement) and B can be safely ruled out as the passage focuses on heart disease and dementia, with no suggestion of any other factor. This leaves options C and D. Option C states that blood vessel health is the [only] cause of the reduction in dementia cases. This suggests that there is nothing else that is impacting on the falling numbers of dementia cases. This is unlikely since dementia is known to have many genetic and environmental factors.

Upon referring back to the articles last few sentences, it starts with the suggestive phrase "given that" which is used to infer a relationship. Therefore, choice D is the correct answer.

24)   The correct answer is B (Two double rooms)
Four single rooms will be:

$$£160 - 10\% \text{ discount} = £144$$

Two double rooms will be:

$$£130 - £10 = £120$$

Therefore option A can be ruled out.

1 double and two single rooms will be more expensive than both of these options as:

$$55 + 40 + 40 = £135 - 5\% \text{ discount} = £128$$

Thus, ruling out option C

One single and one family room:

$$= 90 + 40 = £130$$

Therefore the cheapest option is B.

25)   The correct answer is B (Taking painkillers increases the likelihood that flu sufferers will return to work while still infectious).
For this question, consider how each of the five statements supports the argument of reducing the number of painkillers used when one has the flu.

Option A does not support limiting the use of painkillers when one has the flu. Instead, it refers to reduced effectiveness on headaches, which can occur with or without the flu virus. Therefore statement A does nothing to support the case and be ruled out.

Option B references the return to work while still having the flu (in other words, prolonging the disease) and spreading it to co-workers (a reference to the amount of virus being passed onto others). Therefore, this statement strengthens the argument and is the correct answer.

Option C weakens the argument as it then becomes irrelevant to humans

Option D while itself being a true statement does nothing to support the argument for reducing painkillers and is an irrelevant statement, as the flu vaccine is taken before a person has the flu, rather than once the person has contracted it.

Option E, while it questions the use of painkillers when one is sick, does suggest this as a safety issue and does not support the ideas that they may prolong the disease or increase its transmission. Therefore this option can be ruled out as well.

26)   The correct answer is D (7)

To produce the 8 digits, each number from the 4 digit pin must be squared to give 2 numbers (therefore the squares of 1, 2 and 3 can be ruled out).

Leaving the options:

$$4^2 = 16$$
$$5^2 = 25$$
$$6^2 = 36$$
$$7^2 = 49$$
$$8^2 = 64$$
$$9^2 = 81$$

The information also reveals that there are 8 different numbers. Therefore, only one of 16, 36 or 64 can be used since they all contain 6.

This means that 25, 49 and 81 must be included. Since 81 is included, 16 can be excluded, as this would mean two 1's. 64 can also be ruled out since 49 is included, therefore the fourth number must be 36:

$$5^2 = 25$$
$$6^2 = 36$$
$$7^2 = 49$$
$$9^2 = 81$$

Therefore the missing digit in the account number apart from 0 will be 7 (option D)

27)   The correct answer is E (2 and 3 only)

This question requires careful analysis of each of the statements in line with the statistics. In terms of statistics, cyclists seriously injured 21 pedestrians compared to 24 pedestrians injured by motor vehicles every billion kilometres travelled, suggests that statement one could, in fact, be correct. However, in terms of frequency, there are likely to be many more cars on the road, compared to bikes leading to a higher chance that a pedestrian will be seriously injured by a car, rather than a bike. Therefore this statement is not correct.

For statement two, this is taken almost directly from the passage and therefore when comparing the two in the same distance, the risk is virtually the same. Thus this conclusion can be drawn.

Statement three again is a paraphrase of the statement "most collisions occur when pedestrians step into the road without seeing a cyclist," therefore it can be inferred that pedestrians are safer on the footpath making this statement also correct. Therefore option E is the right answer.

28)   The correct answer is A

Each of the images shows two faces which are next to each other on the outer surface. As the object is bent into its hexagonal shape, the two faces will be at an angle to each other, and parts of the shape adjacent can be seen. This is the shape that is two faces over from the surface in question.

Looking at each of the options:

A.   The shape two over from the square is the vertical rectangle.

The shape two over from the left pointing triangle is a diamond. Both of these shapes match what would be seen if they were laid on top of one another. Therefore, this is a potential answer.

B.   The upward pointing triangle would need to be adjacent to the vertical rectangle for the image to be seen. However, it is not – therefore B can be ruled out.

C.   The face has a hexagon inside this would mean that the shape two over would need to be the square which is not on this panel– therefore C can be ruled out

D.   Both inside shapes do not fit because the inside shapes are next to surface in question. Therefore, this option can also be ruled out.

E.   For this shape the horizontal rectangle and the vertical rectangle are adjacent to one another, so this fits, but the left pointing triangle and the diamond which are the adjacent shapes would not make this shape, therefore this option can be ruled out too.

Therefore A is the correct answer.

29)   The correct answer is E (1 and 3 only)

To answer this question, examine each statement and decide if it strengthens the theory in the passage, or weakens it. When looking at statement one, the article states that "in the past [morning sickness] would have helped to protect a foetus during the first three months of pregnancy when it is at its most vulnerable stage of development." Therefore the fact that statement one refers to morning sickness declining after the first three months (which is after the foetus has passed this stage of vulnerability) shows that it supports the argument.

When considering statement two, regarding strange food cravings, the theory does not suggest anything about 'strange food cravings.' Instead, it refers to 'harmful substances' which themselves may be part of the standard diet of a pregnant woman, for example, food poisoning from chicken or fruit that has insecticide spray on it. Therefore statement two can also be ruled out.

Statement three is taken almost directly from the passage; women with morning sickness tend to eat smaller amounts of food, which are simple and bland confirming the theory further. Therefore answer E is correct.

30)   The correct answer is D (12:45 pm)

For the express to get to Laydon, it takes 10/60 = 1/6 hr or 10 minutes since speed = distance /time. Therefore it will reach Laydon at 12.10

The post train takes 15/30 = 1/2 hr or 30 minutes to reach Laydon. Thus, it arrives at 12.30pm. Outside of Laydon, there is only a single rail line. Consequently the express train can only pass the post train at Laydon station as this is the only place where there are double tracks. Consequently, the express arrives at 12.10 but must wait 20 minutes for the post train to arrive before completing the second leg of its journey to Snelling.

The journey to Snelling takes 15/60 = ¼ hour, or 15 minutes, therefore, the entire trip takes:

10 minutes from Singlebourne to Laydon

20 minutes waiting at Laydon

15 minutes from Laydon to Snelling

Totalling 45 minutes (Answer D)

31)   The correct answer is C (9)

With some of the outer islands, there is the possibility of moving directly between them, however, where this is not the case one needs to backtrack to the main island Nolla. Therefore one possible route is as follows:

Nolla - Yksi - Kaksi - Yksi - Nolla - Kolme - Neija -Viisi - Neija -Nolla

OR

Nolla - Kolme - Neija -Viisi - Neija - Nolla - Yksi - Kaksi - Yksi - Nolla

Remember to count the trip between the island (the number of arrows) rather than the island itself as this will make the answer 10 rather than 9.

32)   The correct answer is D (1 hour)

Nolla - Neija - Viisi

The information states that the ferries between the outer islands leave on the hour; therefore if the person arrives in Neija on the hour, the maximum time they would need to wait to get onto the ferry to Viisi is 1 hour.

33)   The correct answer is C (2 hours and 45 minutes)

Kaksi - Yski - Nolla - Neija

Trips between the outer islands (Kaksi - Yski) take 45 minutes whereas trips between Nolla and the outer islands take 30 minutes in either direction.

Therefore:

45 +30+30 = 1 hour 45 travel time

However, in wait time between ferries also must be factored in.

The information states that the ferries from the outer islands leave on the hour. Therefore, if someone was leaving Kaksi on the 6 am ferry they would arrive at Yski at 6.45am, but would then need to wait until 7 am to catch the ferry to Nolla which arrives at Nolla at 7.30am. From here, they would then need to wait 45 minutes until 8.15 to catch the ferry to Neija, which takes another 30 minutes.

Therefore the total time taken is:

$$45 + 15 + 30 + 45 + 30 = 165 \text{ minutes (2 hours 45)}$$

34)   The correct answer is C (Both 1 and 2)
Kolme - Nolla - Yski

It takes 30 minutes on the ferry from Kolme to Nolla, and there is always at least 15 minutes waiting time at Nolla before the next leg of the journey, which also takes 30 minutes. Therefore, statement one is correct.
Knowing already that it takes at least 1 hour 15, the maximum wait time at Nolla must then be factored in. If a person was to miss the ferry but a few minutes and needed to wait for the next one, it would mean a maximum 45-minute wait, therefore making the entire journey take 1 hour 45 minutes. So, statement two is also correct. Thus option C is the best answer.

35)   The correct answer is B (1 hour)
Normal route: Yksi - Nolla - Neija
Alternate route: Yksi - Nolla - Kolme - Neija

The 7 am ferry docks in Nolla at 7.30, at this point, he would typically take the 8.15am ferry from Nolla which would dock in Neija at 8.45am.
Instead of taking the ferry to Neija he needs to take the alternate route to Kolme and then onto Neija. The ferry would still dock in Kolme at 8.45am, but he would have to catch the 9 am ferry to Neija after this, which takes another 45 minutes. Therefore he would arrive at 9.45am – one hour later than usual, making the correct choice C.

BMAT Section 1 - 2015

1)   The correct answer is D

For this question, it is easiest to draw everyone's names out in the order in which they appear. Straight away the order can be seen:

Stuart

Ruth

Margaret

Add in the following information about Tim being shorter than Ruth and taller than Adrian will give the following possibilities:

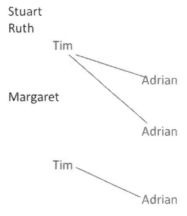

The lines denote the various possibilities of the heights of Tim and Adrian in relation to each other as well as the other children.

From this, it can be seen that Adrian must be shorter than Ruth and Stuart, but not necessarily Margaret which is option D.

2)   The correct answer is E (People born in the UK who are relatively affluent are unlikely to catch TB).

Option A states that TB is more common in endemic countries. It also says that the immune system may not be robust due to health problems and diet. It does not mention anything about a connection between the immune system and coming from a different country.

The passage states that people in deprived areas are more likely to have health problems or a poor diet. However, the opposite is not necessarily true. This is an example of needing to be careful about establishing a causal relationship unless it explicitly says. Thus statement B can be discarded.

Statement C only says that doctors do not think of it as a possibility, nothing about how seriously they take it.

The fact that it is not considered as a diagnosis means if anything it is underestimated which is the opposite of option D. Therefore this statement can also be discarded.

Statement E says that three-quarters of recorded cases were from deprived areas, clearly suggesting being affluent (not deprived) will mean you are less likely to get TB.

3)   The correct answer is A (Red Van)

September 1st to November 30th is the period of interest. Looking at the column for August shows all the mileage readings until September 1st. The November column shows all mileages up to and including November 30th. Therefore the difference between the August and November columns is the distance travelled in the period in question. The only two that are close to each other are the Red and Green vans. The Green van has a difference of 10319 miles whereas the Red one has 10,613 making A the answer.

4)   The correct answer is A (The study did not suggest attractiveness alone is sufficient to ensure success).

It helps to find the main conclusion and proceed from there; in this case, it is the last sentence.

Statement B can be discarded because the passage only talks about cycling experience, it does not extrapolate to all sports.

Statement C can also be discarded as once again; it does not talk about other sports at all. While this may be true, it does not mention other sports so this does not best express the flaw in the argument.

Statement D does not mention other sportsmen; it only suggests that those with cycling excellence are more attractive. Therefore this statement can also be excluded.

The passage says nothing about repeats; hence statement E is completely irrelevant.

The conclusion says that attractive people are likely to be successful cyclists as people with a higher placing are more attractive. However, this could be a coincidence. The passage does not say that attractiveness is the only prerequisite or even that it is required for cycling success, merely that this correlation has been found. The conclusion is clearly saying if you are attractive you will be a successful cyclist (so, not what the passage is saying and making incorrect assumptions). Therefore option A is the correct answer.

5)   The correct answer is D (8)

This question requires a keen eye and basic maths. It can be seen by scanning that the results are:

1st – 7.34m
2nd – 7.29
3rd – 7.17

Therefore anyone who gets above 7.17 – 0.5 = 6.67m will also be in.

Another look at the results can see five people meet this criterion, to add onto the 3 listed above giving 8 people, option D.

6)   The correct answer is C (Catalogued seed banks should be created and their contents trialled).

Statement A can be excluded as this is the opening statement, not the main conclusion.

While statement B is true, this is more of a statement and does not offer any action to be taken unlike the other options available.

Statement D is not true, it only says they will be worst affected. It does not specify which farmers should trial different crops. Also, this action can only be taken after the seed banks have catalogued plants.

Statement E is technically not true either, as it says the crops will be unable to grow. When in fact, the plants will grow; however, the yield will be lower. In any case, this is again just a statement and fails to incorporate the proposed solution of the seed bank.

Statements B or C, in reality, can be the answer as they are the only statements to mention seed banks. However, statement C is more advanced than B as it offers a solution and details the next steps that should be taken. Option C can be inferred from the last sentence.

7)   The correct answer is C (He made a loss of £300)

Using Helen's investment, the changes in share value can be mapped out for most of the days, as seen below:

M	£1000
T	£1200
W	£1080
T	£1350

This does require some mental maths. For example, calculating that Wednesday's price is 80% of Thursday's (0.8 x 1350) and that the increase of 20% from Monday gives £1200.

Using this method shows that there has been a drop of 10% from Tuesday to Wednesday. Therefore, Paul who bought his share on Tuesday and only had them for one day lost 10% of that which equals £300 making the answer C.

8)   The correct answer is B (It is a mistake to send offenders to prison when a non-custodial sentence is also appropriate for the crime).

Statement A says nothing about releasing prisoners early. Thus it can be discarded.

Statement B, although not successful, states that there are times when the crime is severe enough that prison is the only option.

Statement D is not necessarily true; the data suggests that 44% re-offend within one year which is less than half. It is impossible to determine the likelihood of each offender committing another crime.

Statement E is irrelevant to the passage. The passage only talks about alternatives to prison, nothing to do with recommending the prison length.

Statement B is the best answer, confirmed by the second paragraph. It states that prison is sometimes the only option when the crime is severe enough. However, the statistics used suggest the re-offending rate is less for the alternatives if the crime is appropriate. It is sending out a clear message about using non-custodial sentences, hence why there are three paragraphs on it.

9)   The correct answer is D (11,000)

Study one says 44% of former prisoners have reoffended within one year and 66% after five years. This shows that 66 – 44 = 22% re-offend after one year but before five years.

22% of 50,000 (population size) gives 11,000 which is option D

10) **The correct answer is A (Most offences which attract a prison sentence are not eligible for consideration of a non-custodial sentence as an alternative).**

While statement B may be true, the passage does not state this as fact. Instead, it says that non-custodial sentences are for crimes that are not that bad, nothing to do with the first time they commit a crime or not.

The passage implies the opposite to statement C; that most of the re-offenders have already served a custodial sentence and will then be given a non-custodial one.

Statement D may also be true, although it is not clear whether a suspended sentence counts as a custodial one or non-custodial. Also, it is unlikely to make up for such a large difference in figures.

Option A is the best answer. It says at the start of the second paragraph that some crimes can be given non-custodial sentences. It also says those given prison sentences are more likely to re-offend. These are also those individuals who commit worse crimes. Therefore it is reasonable to assume that a worse crime means more likely to re-offend. On the other hand, if the crime is not as bad, a non-custodial sentence is given, and the individual is less likely to re-offend.

11) **The correct answer is E (The study shows that subjecting an offender to restorative justice as well as issuing them with a community service order has the effect of reducing re-offending rates by 20%).**

Statement A can be excluded as it suggests prison in addition to restorative justice, which contradicts the text, which suggests restorative justice only.

Statement B can be excluded as natural justice would mean repeat offenders get worse sentences, for example, prison instead of offered other alternatives.

Statement C implies they should be imprisoned, thus weakening the argument.

Statement D could be a reason, but even if it is expensive, some crimes still require a prison sentence.

Statement E is the best answer as there is statistical proof that this reduces the re-offending rate and backs up the politician's statement.

12) **The correct answer is D (Solitaires)**

This requires some trial and error to find out which option cannot be made.

Option A: 9+3+5+5 = 22
Option B: 9+9+5-2 = 21
Option C: 9+5+5+5 = 24
Option D: It is not possible to make 23 (9+9+5 = 23), with one puzzle left and one cannot stay on 23.
Option E: 9+9+9-2 = 25

13) **The correct answer is D (The rights of the individual are less important than risks to society).**

While statement A may be true, the passage says it risks sending out the wrong message not that young people definitely cannot tell the difference.

Statement B contradicts the 'Unwritten Rule', and hence Option B cannot be regarded as an assumption since it is stated in the text. Football is just the example used here; it says high profile people towards the end. Thus statement C can be ruled out. Statement E would only be true if it were about high profile people, which is what the passage is specifically referring to.

Usually, the individual should be rehabilitated back into society unless they are high profile. This is because it says it may pose a risk to young children who may be influenced. This clearly shows that it is more important that the young children (society) do not get the wrong idea than if that one high profile individual is integrated back into society. Thus statement D is the best option.

14)   The correct answer is B (40 ml)

80ml of red paint has been used.

30% of the mural is brown but three colours are used, 10% of which is red.

Red % is therefore 10 + 20 (just red) + 5 + 5 (from orange & purple) = 40.

Therefore 40% equates to 80ml.

Blue % is 10 (from brown) + 10 (just blue) + 5 + 5 (from green & purple) = 30

Therefore using the red paint amount above, 30% is equal to 60ml.

Starting with a 100ml tube, therefore, means 40ml left over (Option B)

15)   The correct answer is A (Experimentation on primates should be considered as a means to develop treatments for brain disorders).

Statement B is true but not a conclusion, just a statement.

Statement C is also true but this is just restating the middle of the paragraph.

Statement D is not mentioned anywhere in the paragraph.

It is not certain that the conditions can be cured just that the potential treatments may help humans, thus ruling out statement E also.

The passage says that primates can be used to recreate lesions. It also says that using brain lesions may allow the development of treatments. Therefore statement A is indirectly saying that primates can be used to develop treatments.

16)   Correct Answer is D (12)

There are 16 girls and 10 boys in total = 26

Three girls have sisters so: G+ G +G +G+ G+G= 6

Two boys have brothers so: B+ B+ B+ B = 4

Two girls have brothers/Two brothers have sisters as stated:
B+B +G+G = 4

This gives 6 + 4 + 4 = 14. Therefore 26 – 14 = 12, (Option D)

17) **The correct answer is A (It assumes that the lower number of subsequent heart attacks will not be balanced by the higher recording of first heart attacks).**

Statement B is incorrect as the passage does not mention men at all. Thus it can be discarded.

Statement C is incorrect since the passage just says this method is an improved one.

Statement D is incorrect since the passage only says that it reduces the risk meaning that it could still happen even with treatment.

Statement E is incorrect as the passage makes no mention of men at all.

Statement A is the best answer since the conclusion is at the start saying the rate of heart attacks will fall in total. It also says more heart attacks are found, but the treatment will mean fewer future attacks. For the overall number to decline (the conclusion) then the number of future attacks prevented must be greater than those found (the assumption).

18) **The correct answer is E**

$$42 \times 8 = 336 \text{ points from spans.}$$

$$\text{This is } 336/720, \text{ which is just less than half.}$$

From here, a comparison of the pie charts will show that option E is the only option with the sector for spans being just less than half.

19) **The correct answer is C (54)**

$$330\text{ml} = 9 \text{ lumps.}$$

$$330 \times 6 = 1980 \approx 2000\text{ml}$$

$$9 \times 6 = 54 \text{ lumps}$$
$$\text{(Option C)}$$

20) **The correct answer is C (It would be 20% above the recommended level).**

Teenagers consume 150% of the RDA. Assume this is 150 units, and the RDA is 100 units for simplicity.

Therefore consuming 30% from sugary drinks would be 45 units.

Now, if they were to consume only one third as much sugar from soft drinks, then this would be 45/3 = 15 units, meaning that it has decreased by 45-15 = 30 units.

Subtract 30 units from 150 gives 120 units, which compared to original RDA of 100 is still 20 units or 20% over, therefore option C.

21) **The correct answer is C (£1031 million)**

10% of 5727 is 572.7

5727 − 572.7 = 5157

Multiply this by the £0.2, therefore:

0.2 x 5157 = 1031.4 (Option C)

22)   Correct Answer is A (When products are subject to a sales tax, retailers are known to reduce their purchase price in order to be competitive).

Option B can be ruled out as it cannot equate food to drink.

Option C can be ruled out as well as this has nothing to do with healthier options. Even if it increased by a minute amount, it would still represent an increase in tax money.

Option D is not related to the argument. Thus it can be excluded. The tax is there to provide health benefits. Even a volume tax would still not include those drinks, so there is still the same problem.

Option E actually strengthens the argument.

Option A is the best answer because the whole point is to direct the revenue towards the funding of health initiatives. The effect of A would mean less money on tax and therefore fewer benefits.

23)   The correct answer is E (Palace)

The palace and tower are furthest away from all other sites which can be deduced from scanning through the distances. From here it is trial and error of these two to find the right answer.

Hotel − Tower − Castle − Arch − Fountain − Courts − Hotel = 530m

Therefore not going to the palace (Option E)

24)   The correct answer is B (1 and 3)

Given that the passage says nothing about headaches affecting a student's performance, statement two can be discarded, thus eliminating options A and C.

Statement four actually supports the use of caffeine, and thus will not weaken the argument, thus confirming that C is not an appropriate option.

Statement five is a true statement and supports the use of caffeine given the claim in the passage regarding it boosting the effectiveness of short-term memory. Thus option D can also be discarded.

This leaves option B, which directly says that caffeine leads to reduced sleep and quality of sleep. This then follows onto statement three so that it can be read as if caffeine leads to a lack of focus and poor memory which directly opposes the paragraph (which is trying to outline the positives of caffeine).

25)   The correct answer is F (7)

Let start by drawing out what is known _ 8 _ _ _ _

The five blanks can be represented by a, c, d, e, and f. Therefore it would read a8cdef.

Therefore a8 + cd + ef = 80 (the letters are merely placeholders; this means that they cannot be multiplied like normal algebra). Also a8c + def = 800

Using the first equation (the one equalling 80), the information states that d + f must end in 2 to make 80 the product.

Also, the value of 8c has a range of 80-89.

It cannot be 80 (as f would have to be 0 and the numbers are all unique). For this reason, it cannot also be 81 (as it would require 19), 82 (would require 18), 85 (would require 15), 88 or 89 (would require 11). This only leaves four options of 83,84,86,87.   As a8c + def = 800 this means f has to end in 7, 6, 4 or 3.

Going back to d + f ending in 2, the combinations for the numbers d, f are thus (2,0)(0,2)(3,9)(9,3)(5,7)(7,5) again discounting other pairings as numbers can only be used once. Combining this with the above means the only possible combinations for d, f are (9, 3) or (5, 7). Therefore d cannot be 9 clearly as the 2 three digit numbers have to be less than 800 (otherwise 9ef > 800). Therefore d, f is (5, 7) making the last digit 7 (Option F)

26)   The correct answer is C (Other, more robust studies have not subsequently suggested a risk to health from saturated fat).

An assumption is an unwritten link between the reasoning and the conclusion. To identify an assumption in an argument the best place to start is work out the conclusion. In this passage, the conclusion is that 'butter and saturated fats do not damage our health as was previously thought.' From here, each statement can be considered:

Statement A is not an assumption as it is stated in the last line, where it suggests that enjoyment comes from having more saturated fat in the diet.

Statement B can be removed as the passage only talks about saturated fats nothing about other factors which are irrelevant here.

What the passage says is that saturated fat does not pose a threat to health; however, nothing suggests that people will actually take this advice. Thus statement D can also be discarded.

Given the contents of the passage, statement E is contradictory to this and therefore can also be discarded.

Option C is the best answer given that the passage says now the research has been discredited one can enjoy saturated fats. The studies are from the 1980s, yet it is concluding that in the present day saturated fats can be enjoyed. This suggests that in this time gap that either these are the only studies available or that the other studies have been completed but found nothing.

27)   The correct answer C (between 25 and 50%)
Easiest is to draw out the areas that may overlap. It says fewer than 5% have neither, so this could be as low as 0%.

Above shows the possibility if 0% of people have neither meaning that everyone has something. The 100 represents 100% of pupils. Using the smallest values for the % that own phones and tablets will give the smallest possible overlap and thus the lower boundary.

If 70% own a phone then there are 30% who do not. As the bar for those who own a laptop is 55% then this must mean the overlap is 55-30 = 25% which is the lower boundary.

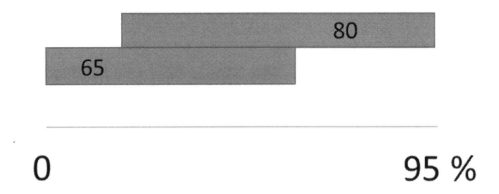

Above illustrates the possibility if 5% of people have neither (the maximum). This means 95% of the pupils have both a phone and laptop hence the bar going up to 95 instead of 100. For the greatest overlap, the highest value for those owning a phone or a laptop (80 and 65 respectively) must be used.

Simple maths shows that 95 − 80 = 15, therefore the overlap would be 65 − 15 = 50% which is the upper boundary. Therefore the % owning both is between 25 − 50% (Option C).

28)   Correct Answer is A (Melatonin levels rise and fall as a result of 'Owl' or 'Lark' behaviour).

The passage is saying that people get tired at different times. It is talking about regular sleep/wake cycles as opposed to those seen in jet-lagged passenger thus the information in the passage cannot be extrapolated to jet lag as this is different entirely to behaviour. This means that statement B is irrelevant.

Changing patterns of shift does not have anything to do with health, and if anything this statement supports the argument and agrees that there should be individual working hours. Thus, statement C can also be excluded. Statement D is entirely irrelevant to the discussion.

Given that shift working is not mentioned in the passage statement E can be excluded as well.

Therefore statement A is the best answer since the article suggests working when one is most awake so not working in shifts. It implies that the behaviour cannot be changed which is why employers need to be flexible, but if it turns out this is not true then this would weaken the argument.

29)   **Correct Answer is A (£85)**

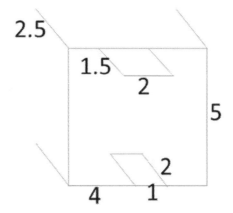

Make a rough drawing of the dimensions of the room (as seen above).

For the 5m long wall, it is 2.5m high and there are two of these so:

$$5 \times 2.5 \times 2 = 25m^2 \text{ to cover}$$

For the 4m wall it is slightly different:

$$4 \times 2.5 \times 2 = 20m$$

However there is a wall and a door which are:

$$1.5 \times 2 = 3 \text{ and } 2 \times 1 = 2$$
$$= 2 + 3 = 5m$$

Subtract the 4m wall from the wall with the door:

$$20-5 = 15m$$

Now it is known there cannot be an excess and that different numbers of layers can be used. Again a simple table will help. The table below shows multiples of 25 and 15 as they can either be painted over twice or thrice depending on the quality of paint to be used.

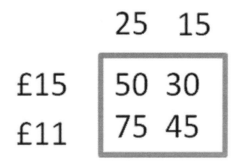

As paint cannot be left over, the values need to be divisible by 15. Therefore it can be seen that the more expensive paint needs to be used to cover the 15m walls and the cheaper one to do the 25m walls (as 50 is not divisible by 15). As the paint covers 15m and costs £11 for the cheaper tin and £15 for the more expensive one, this gives rise to....

75/15 = 5 tins needed at £11 each so £55

30/15 = 2 tins needed at £15 each so £ 30

£55 + £30 = £85, option A

30) **The correct answer is D (Some doctors choose to work for agencies in A&E to supplement their salaries).**
Statement A weakens the argument as financial incentives are explicitly mentioned in the passage and therefore can be excluded.
While statement B is true this does not address the central issue of pay. Thus it can also be excluded.
Statement C is irrelevant as it is not about the number of users of A&E services, but the number of doctors available.
While statement E may be true, the issue is not about the standard of care, it is about staffing issues. Therefore statement E can be excluded.
The best answer is option D as the article basically says that by paying better wages to A & E doctors will mean a reduction in the overall costs as well as fewer staff shortages. The passage is saying that paying more money would reduce shortages, therefore money is the main issue here. It is also saying that financial incentives are why people may work in A & E so it directly agrees with the passage by saying more money would solve the issue.

31) **The correct answer is B (2 is opposite 1; 4 is opposite 6)**
As there are two views of the dice both with a six, all sides of this one can be worked out. One and three are opposite each other, and so are four and two, since these have different totals. This leaves five and six as opposites of each other. These three combinations result in totals of four, six and eleven. It is easiest to make a table with all the possibilities and cross out the totals that cannot be obtained:

+	1	2	3	4	5	6
1	~~2~~	3	4	5	~~6~~	~~7~~
2	3	4	5	~~6~~	~~7~~	8
3	4	5	~~6~~	~~7~~	8	9
4	5	~~6~~	~~7~~	8	9	10
5	~~6~~	~~7~~	8	9	~~10~~	~~11~~
6	~~7~~	8	9	10	~~11~~	~~12~~

The information also states that none of the totals can add up to 7 so these have also been crossed out. It is also not possible to get the total of 2 or 12, so these are ruled out. This leaves 3,5,8,9 and 10 as possible totals. From here, it requires some trial and error to find the right combination.

Say for example one, and four were paired up giving a total of five. Then three would have to be paired up with either five or six. If the three was paired with five, this would provide a total of eight which is not possible as that would only leave six and two. If six was paired with three then giving a total of nine that would leave five and two giving a total of seven which is also not possible.

Therefore by eliminating all the other possibilities for three, it means three must be paired with two giving five. Therefore one must be paired with two giving three. Lastly, six must be paired with four giving ten. This gives option B.

32)   The correct answer is G (1,2 and 3)
Statement number one is true. The number of people convicted was:

$$1371 + 1552 + 1342 = 4265$$

Looking at the prosecution rates which are around 98% then it can be seen that 100% of people would be higher than 4300.
Statement two is also true. 1552 is 97.9% of people tried, therefore the total number is:

$$1552/0.979 = 1585. \ 1585 - 1552 = 33 > 30$$

Statement thee involves some addition to see it is true:

$$\frac{220+178+140}{88+86+74+220+178+140} = 538/786 = 0.68...$$

All 3 statements are true therefore G is correct.

33)   The correct answer is B (1274)

In the rest of England, the rate fell by 11.7%. By applying this to the 531 from the previous year in the north of England then this means the rate should have dropped by about 60 people (0.117 x 531). Thus, there should have been about 470 people convicted in the north of England.

The number was instead 566 which is 96 more, therefore subtract 96 from 1371 gives 1275 = 1274 which is B

34)   The correct answer is C (3 Only)

Statement one is false. The information says nothing about individual counties elsewhere. This means that one in the south could have had more total convictions but less as a percentage.

Statement two is also false. The increase could have been by 1; meaning the number could always have been high, but there is insufficient information to confirm this.

Statement three is true. 566/1371 = 0.412 which is roughly two fifths

Therefore only statement three is true (Option C).

35)   The correct answer is B (A higher proportion of complaints result in conviction in the north of England than in other regions of England and Wales).

Statement A can be excluded as it supports the argument.

Statement B can also be ruled out as one would expect more complaints with more animals.

Statement D can be ruled out as it could still mean they care more as a greater number of complaints can indicate a greater number of re-homed dogs. Also the argument is about animals in total and not just dog as the statement says.

Statement E does not specify which regions of the country and is it irrelevant whether the animals are categorised as working or not, as it is not mentioned in the paragraph.

Statement B can be inferred since if there is a conviction then cruelty has occurred. Therefore if a greater proportion of complaints lead to conviction then this means a greater proportion of cruelty, which weakens the argument.

BMAT Section 1 - 2016

1) The correct answer is D (3 in 8)

To answer this question, the table must first be completed. There are 72 boys in total; therefore there are six boys in year four, as the probability of picking a boy in year 4 is:

$$1/12 \times 72 = 6$$

From here other aspects of the table can be calculated using simple subtraction:

Year	Boys	Girls	Total
1	18	6	24
2	16	24	40
3	8	8	16
4	6	10	16
5	24	0	24
Total	72	48	120

The question is asking a 'given that' probability or in other words what fraction of year four pupils are boys. There are 6 year four boys and 10 year four girls, therefore, the chance of picking a year four that is a boy is 6/16 which can be simplified to 3 in 8

2) The correct answer is B (It is likely that some of the CO_2 from the fires in Indonesia will remain in the atmosphere).

Statement A cannot be confirmed as it is unknown if the contribution from other sources and the forest fires push the emissions over this 1000 gigatonne barrier.

The paragraph states that CO_2 is taken back up by plants as they grow and explains that this is not happening in Indonesia as the plants are burning. This and the increased addition of atmospheric CO_2 from peat suggest that not all of the released CO_2 is likely to be reabsorbed by plant growth. In confirming the conclusion, the 'therefore test' can be applied making statement B the correct answer.

The passage states that forest fires burn most fiercely when the region is drier, which has been the situation for this year, but it does not forecast how dry the region will be next year for a comparison. Thus statement C can be excluded.

Statement D is also incorrect as the passage does not mention prevention or the control of forest fires. It also does not claim that forest fires are the sole contributor to global warming, so it is unlikely that preventing them will prevent global warming altogether.

3) The correct answer is B ($105)

The first time John stayed the bill will be:

$$\text{Nights: } 50 + 50 + 40 + 40 + 40 = 220$$

135

Parking: 5 x 5 = 25

Total: 245

For the second stay, this will change to:

Nights: 40 x 8 = 320

Parking: 25 + 5

Total: 350

350 – 245 = a difference of $105

4)   The correct answer is B (Musical training may develop the tendency for the brain to synchronise to music).
Option B is the most appropriate flaw because their musical training may have developed the musicians' ability to synchronise with slow music, and therefore it is not an "innate tendency" and could be achieved by the non-musicians through training.

5)   The correct answer is A (Con)
From comparing the differences between points on the x-axis and the y-axis, it can be determined that the x-axis represents the practical test results and the y-axis represents the written results (the first five points on the x-axis match the difference between the five lowest points of the practical – 4,6,8,9,10). It shows that two people scored 10 in the practical with different results in the written; therefore there should be two vertical dots. However, there is only one. This dot, when compared with the left coordinate of (9,40) indicates that the student with a practical result of 10 plotted achieved a written result of less than 40 – indicating Fio is plotted. This would mean that Con has not been plotted.

6)   The correct answer is D (The government needs to reconsider, or justice will be inaccessible to most people).
The main conclusion of the argument is that "if justice is not to be out of reach for the majority of ordinary people, the government must think again". From here, each option can be examined to see if it is essentially giving the same message in a different way.
Option A is incorrect because the planned increase in fees is not an attack on the ability of the population to seek justice, and will only affect cases with claims of £200,000 or more, so this statement is too general. Option B is incorrect because this statement is not a conclusion and the argument also claims that the increase is equivalent to *treating* justice like a saleable object, rather than this being the actual or even desired outcome of the change, as the statement suggests. Again, C is too general as it suggests that the change will deter *all* individuals and businesses when in reality the richer ones will still be able to take their cases to court. While option E is not incorrect, the role of civil courts is not the main focus of this argument but is instead included to emphasise the main conclusion. The proposed changes are a threat to the accessibility of the legal system to many citizens and

businesses, which is the argument of option D. In confirming that D is the conclusion, the 'therefore rule' can be applied.

7) The correct answer is D ($38000)

To have paid less tax but earn more, Paul must have turned 50 – the tax brackets increase for this age group. Equations can be formed to work out how much he earned each year using the tax brackets.
When Paul was 49, he paid $5600 tax. This is equivalent to:

$$0.2 \times 25000 + 0.3 \times 'X' = 5600$$

$$0.3 \times 'X' = 600$$

$$'X' = 2,000 \text{ (his 'further income')}$$

Therefore Paul's total earnings were:

$$2,000 + 25,000 + 9,000 = 36,000$$

When he was 50, Paul paid 4800 tax. This is equivalent to:

$$0.2 \times 33,000 + 0.3 \times 'Y' = 4800$$

$$0.2 \times 33,000 = 6,600$$

Therefore Paul must have earned within this tax bracket between 14,000 and 47,000.

$$0.2 \times 'Y' = 4800$$
$$'Y' = 24,000 \text{ (his income within the 20\% tax bracket)}$$

Pauls total earnings when he was 50 in 2015:

$$14000 + 24000 = 38000$$

This is correct as it is 2000 more than he earned in 2014.

8) The correct answer is C (£40,000)

In the months from April to June, a total of 800 units of product one were sold, 800 of product two, and 800 of product three. The price for these products is 1500, 2000 and 1500 respectively per 100 units.

$$(8 \times 1500) + (8 \times 2000) + (8 \times 1500) = 40,000$$

9)   The correct answer is D (£7,000)
Product two started in March. 900 units were sold in the period from January to March therefore 900 were sold in March. This totalled 18000 of sales. As this is two-thirds of the number of sales for the first 3 months (March to May), then 9000 sales must have occurred in the months of April and May. In the period April to June, 800 units were sold totalling 16000. 9000 of these sales occurred in April and May, therefore, the remaining 7000 occurred in June.

10)   The correct answer is D (450)
Product six started selling at the beginning of November, therefore a total of 600 units sold in the months of November and December. To work out how many units were sold in December, look at the December income and unit six prices. Product six generated 6000 of income at a price of 4000 per 100 units. 6000/4000 = 1.5 meaning that 150 units were sold in December. This means that 450 units were sold in November.

11)   The correct answer is E (Product 5)

$$Product\ 1 = (1000 + 800 + 700 + 500)/12 = 250$$

$$Product\ 2 = (900 + 800 + 800 + 700)/10 = 320$$

$$Product\ 3 = (800 + 1100 + 700)/8 = 325$$

$$Product\ 4 = (700 + 500)/6 = 200$$

$$Product\ 5 = (700 + 700)/4 = 350$$

$$Product\ 6 = (600)/2 = 300$$

12)   The correct answer is D (4 hours 58 minutes)
The respective times are 10:39 pm and 3:37 am. Therefore she has slept for 4 hours and 58 minutes.

13)   The correct answer is A (A high level of intelligence is not required for a career in sport or entertainment).
The main conclusion of this passage is that "IQ is not largely due to genetics". Therefore the options must link to this idea in some way.
Option A is correct because it is argued that if the children of entertainers/athletes had low IQs, this could be taken as proof that IQ is hereditary, as they would have inherited this low IQ from their parents. Thus it is implied that those working in sports and entertainment have low IQs. Option B can be ruled out as the information suggests that those people are rich as a result of their intelligence, thus allowing them to enter highly selective careers such as medicine and law. This statement is fairly well documented in the passage. Option C can be ruled out as it contradicts what the passage is saying. Option D is very prescriptive, high levels of intelligence may increase the chance of entering these professions, but is not a guarantee. Therefore this statement can also be excluded.

14)   The correct answer is D (5)

This is cumulative, and so it would be useful to calculate and list how much she had at the end of each month:

Start – 1000
Jan – 1300
Feb – 1100
Mar – 1300
Apr – 1300
May – 1700
Jun – 1500
Jul – 1100
Aug – 1300
Sep – 1200
Oct – 1500
Nov – 1400
Dec – 1400

Therefore she had more than 1300 in the months May, Jun, Oct, Nov and Dec.

15)   The correct answer is B (On average, those elderly people who have lived a 'brain friendly' lifestyle would be expected to have a higher number of synapses in their brains).

Option A is incorrect, as the loss of synapses is presented as a natural process when ageing, rather than the product of a poor lifestyle. It is, however, argued that the right lifestyle can increase the number of synapses in the brain, which may be misleading. Option C is also incorrect, as the passage says that scientists have had opportunities to study the human brain, even if these were "rare", and have made important discoveries as a result – the paragraph suggests that deteriorating cognitive performance was reasonably well understood before the studies. Option D is incorrect as the passage does not link a higher number of synapses to a better quality of life. It is also not a guarantee of a higher quality of life. While many might agree with option E, the passage does not discuss the need for future donations, but simply praises past ones. Therefore this statement is irrelevant.

16)   The correct answer is A (Alun)

This is a question that will require visualisation as there is too much information to process. Draw the initials A, C, I, P and R in a circle. Process each outcome, so for Aluns' rolls, add two dots to Carmen and two to Ruthie as well as one to the centre. After processing each player's rolls, Alun will end up with 2 coins, Carmen with 4, Ian with 3, Prem with 3 and Ruthie with 4, with 9 in the centre.

17)   The correct answer is A (Governments will not allow routine sales of a new antibiotic, except in an emergency).

Statement B implies that the Government could not regulate the prescription of antibiotics efficiently; therefore it backs the argument that introducing penalties would not be enough. Statement C simply points out the inefficiency of antibiotics against viruses and their overuse in infections caused by mild bacteria. This suggests that their use could be decreased, but does not say by how much. Statement D is not directly related to the argument, as the problem of antibiotics in livestock production is not referenced. Statement A addresses an area the Government would be able to control – the sale of new antibiotics. By enforcing strict rules on sales, the Government would both be able to offer financial incentives and prevent the over-prescription of antibiotics.

18)   The correct answer is D (Mortgage 4)

The loan needed in each case will be 125,000. This is an 83.3% LTV (calculated using 125000/150000). Therefore mortgages 1 and 2 are not available.

Mortgage 3 = 500 + 0.05 x 125000 = 6750

Mortgage 4 = 2000 + .03 x 125000 = 5750

Mortgage 5 = 1000 + 0.04 x 125000 = 6000

19)   The correct answer is C (1,081)

In 2005 – 2011 (6 years), the number of wells drilled in Oklahoma rose by 2694.
In the same period, the number of wells in Texas grew by 33,753. In 2012, the number of wells in Texas grew by 13,540. This is a percentage increase of 40.11%
An increase of 40.11% on 2694 = 1080.6

20)   The correct answer is C (4,500,000 gallons per well)

The value for Louisiana was:

12,000 / (2327 + 139) = 4.87 million gallons per well

The value for Utah was:

590 / (1336 + 765) = 0.28 million gallons per well

Therefore the difference was 4.59 million gallons per well.

21)   The correct answer is E (1 and 3 only)

Statement one is correct because 110,000 million gallons of water were used in Texas during this period. If 0.8% is a mix of chemicals, this equates to:

0.008 x 110000 = 880 million gallons of chemicals

The global pollution is equal to the CO_2 emissions from 28 coal-fired power plants. Therefore: 100,551,000 / 28 should be equal to the average coal emission of a coal-fired power plant = 3,600,000 tonnes of CO_2, not 36,000,000 tonnes as statement two is stating.

In Colorado, the amount of water used for fracking was enough to meet the water needs of nearly 200,000 households. The amount of water used was 26,000 million gallons:

26000 / 200,000 = 0.13 million gallons = 130,000 gallons per household.

This makes statement three also correct, thus, the right answer is E.

22)   The correct answer is H (None of them)
Statement one is incorrect as states that with less access to water people are likely to import or store water. Also, the amount of water used for fracking is likely to be insignificant in comparison to the amount of water in each state.
Statement two is also incorrect as while the technology may have developed slowly; it would not show a difference between states – each state would have access to the same technology.
Statement three is also incorrect as the variation measured is water consumption per well – drilling more holes may lead to increased water consumption, but maybe not per well.

23)   The correct answer is D
Shape A cannot be made as the corners of the square are not showing.
Shape B cannot be made as the tip of the triangle is not showing.
Shape C cannot be made as again the tip of the triangle is not showing.
Shape E cannot be made as the corners of the square are not showing.

24)   The correct answer is C (People who play sport often drink beers together afterwards).
Although older people may prefer high impact walking, this does not mean that young people cannot participate in this form of exercise. Therefore statement A is incorrect. With regard to statement B, the paragraph also mentions that high impact walking is more efficient than running, which is not a stop-start activity – therefore this aspect of the activity is unlikely to be the reason, so statement B can be excluded as well. Statement C suggests the fattening effects of drinking beer would lessen the positive impact of the sport. If beer followed walking, then it is possible that it would not lead to a lower BMI than playing tennis. Thus statement C is the correct answer. Statement D does not address the argument, as the paragraph discusses the control of weight as an effect of, not a reason for, playing sport.

25)   The correct answer is D (12 minutes)
The total screening time of the six films was:

117 + 117 + 109 + 109 + 119 + 119 = 690 minutes = 11 and a half hours

The total time allocated for showing:

10:15 to 22:45 = 12 hours 30 minutes

This means there was one hour allocated to breaks, over a total of 5 breaks.

60 minutes / 5 = 12 minutes per break

26)   The correct answer is B (Being anxious and depressed may prompt people to read self-help books).
The paragraph does not align with statement A as it only explores one method people use in an attempt to become more contented with life. Statement B indicates that it is not the books that are making people depressed, but that readers were depressed and anxious before they read them (hence why they chose to read them). This explains why those who have read self-help books are more likely to have these problems. Again, statements C and D do not address the topic of the paragraph, which is the link between reading these books and depression (not ever reading the books and depression). The possibility that depressed people have not read or are unlikely to read these books is also almost certainly the case.

27)   The correct answer is F (86)
This simply involves going through each day and subtracting the diastolic value from the systolic value to calculate the difference. This difference is largest on Thursday pm (68), on which the pulse measures 86.

28)   The correct answer is D (People have some control over the influence of extrinsic factors such as stress or pollution).
The accuracy of this latest study is not mentioned in the paragraph. It also does not conclude that the risk of developing cancer is 100% down to extrinsic factors, but between 70 and 90%. It is mentioned that mistakes are inevitable, but it is not discussed whether these are preventable or not. However, because the passage claims that extrinsic factors cause cancer, then whether or not people develop it is partially within their control as they can control these extrinsic factors to a certain extent.

29)   The correct answer is B (7)
The green pen will mark the upper quarter and lower quarter of the string.
The blue pen will mark the (first, third, fifth and seventh) eights of the string.
The purple will mark the (1, 3, 5, 7, 9, 11, 13, 15) 16ths of the string.
In between the two green points will be the (third and fifth) eighths and the (5, 7, 11 and 13) 16ths, as well as the original half mark, totalling 7 marks.

30)   The correct answer is D (The argument depends on unwarranted claims about the mind and the brain).

Statement A is simply a contradiction and does not provide any evidence as to why the passage is wrong. Statement B also does not identify a flaw, as the paragraph states that the time frame is irrelevant. The paragraph also addresses technical progress directly 'every year machines get more and more complex' while it does not include science fiction. Thus statement C can be excluded. However, the argument makes unwarranted claims when it very boldly declares that "the brain is just a complicated machine" but does not go on to justify this assertion. This makes statement D the best option.

31)   The correct answer is D (10)

This information can be represented algebraically:

If the Sables scored the same number of fesses and pales, then their score is a multiple of 9 (7 + 2).

This also means that the Argents score is a multiple of 11 (2 pales for every fess = 2 + 2 + 7).

The information states that the Argents scored 1 less fess than the Sables. The information can be represented algebraically as:

$$9x = 11(x-1) -1$$

$$9x = 11x - 11 - 1$$

$$9x = 11x -12$$

$$2x = 12$$

$X = 6$ = the multiple of fess' that the Sables scored, therefore the Argents scored 5 fess'.

As they scored twice as many pales as fess' they must have scored 10 pales.

32)   The correct answer is A (37.9%)

The units given are the grams of fatty acids per 100 grams of oil.

100 grams of each oil equates to 10 + 65.7 = 75.7g of total polyunsaturated fat in a total of 200g of oil.

75.7/200 = 37.85%

33)   The correct answer is A (The balance of nutrients that humans had when they fed on hunter-gatherer diets was more appropriate than the balance they get from modern diets).

Statement A is correct as it implies that the 2:1 ratio of the diets of hunter-gatherers was more suitable.

Statement B can be excluded as global differences in diets is not discussed in the information.

Statement C can also be excluded since the information mentions that increasing the percentage of the typical fat consumption caused this decrease. Altering the ratio but not limiting the intake to this number is not mentioned and unlikely to have the same effect.

Statement D can be excluded as the information does not necessarily indicate this is due to the omega ratios – the increasing incidence of heart disease could be due to other properties of the vegetable oils.

Statement E is incorrect because the information does not suggest an optimum ratio of omega fats of 2:1, only that there is an optimum ratio.

34)   The correct answer is B (52%)

Canola oil contains 0.6% Erucic acid.

The tolerable amount is 500mg/day

The typical fat consumption was 143 grams per day, of which 30% is vegetable oils – if all the vegetable oil consumed was Canola oil, this would = 42.9 grams.

$$0.006 \times 42.9 = 257mg$$

$$257/500 = 51.5\%$$

35)   The correct answer is D (41%)

Again, this can be represented algebraically

$$(12.7x + 65.7y)/2 = 53.3x$$

$$12.7x + 65.7y = 106.6x$$

$$65.7y = 93.9x$$

Therefore $y/x = 1.429$. The amount of sunflower oil must be 1.429 times that of flaxseed oil.

If there is 1.49 of sunflower and 1 of flaxseed, then the flaxseed as a percentage is $100/2.49 = 41.16\%$

BMAT SECTION 1 - 2017

1)   The correct answer is C (450ml)

To answer this question, use the data given and work backwards to calculate the amount of red paint used for the room. Start by working out the amount of yellow paint used to paint the orange section (40%) of the room:

1500ml (yellow paint at the start) – 900ml (yellow paint at the end) = 600ml (yellow paint used)
Therefore: 600ml (yellow) + 600ml (red) = 1200ml (orange) (1:1 ratio)
40% = 1200ml (orange), so 60% = (1200 x 1.5) = 1800ml (pink)
Ratio red:white for pink = 1:3 which = 450:1350
Therefore: total red paint left = 1500 – (450 + 600)
=450ml

2)   The correct answer is D (Figures for drug prescriptions and disability claimants provide no evidence that antidepressant drugs are improving the long term mental health of people in the UK)

In the passage, we are only given figures for drug prescriptions between two years and the mental health disability claimants between two years. Correlation does not imply causation. Just because these two figures are presented next to each other, it does not necessarily mean that the figures are linked. Therefore, we can immediately eliminate A and C as viable options. The passage does not mention anything regarding doctors and increasing prescription numbers, therefore we can also rule out B as a viable option.

3)   The correct answer is D (Dayview)

To answer this question, start by using the table (simply add a column as shown below) to quickly work out which houses match at least 4 of the Joelson's wishes

House	No. of bedrooms	Garage	Garden	Distance to grocery store	Distance to sports facilities	Cost	Matches 4 wishes?
Acorns	5	Double	Large	2.0 km	8 km	$825,000	Yes
Bellavista	3	Single	Medium	2.5 km	4 km	$810, 000	No
Chestnuts	6	Double	Large	3.0 km	3 km	$930, 000	No (budget)
Dayview	4	Double	Medium	1.0 km	7 km	$640, 000	Yes
Everglade	4	None	Small	1.5 km	5 km	$860, 000	No

From the table, it is immediately evident that only Acorns and Dayview match at least 4 of the 5 wishes; now divide the cost of the house by the number of bedrooms:

Acorns: 825,000/5 = $165,000

Dayview: 640,000/4 = $160,000

Dayview has the lower price and is the house that the Joelson family should buy.

4)   **The correct answer is A (There are established procedures for managing and safely storing nuclear waste, funded by electricity users).**

The main argument in the text focuses upon the unacceptable risk that nuclear power poses to the environment and humanity, as stated in lines 5-6 of the passage: 'building enough nuclear power stations to make a meaningful reduction in greenhouse gas emissions would create tens of thousands of tons of lethal, high-level radioactive waste'. Hence, nuclear waste should not be used primarily because of this reason.

Option A, if true, most weakens the above argument because it states that there are already procedures in place to manage and safely store the 'lethal, nuclear waste' – therefore, the safety issues involved with using nuclear power have been taken care off.

Option B is somewhat irrelevant to the main argument, and simply supports the argument that nuclear power will deliver less energy globally.

Option C weakens the above argument, but not as much as Option A. The main concern with nuclear power is the production of nuclear waste, not the cost involved.

Option D supports the above argument which already draws attention to the fact that nuclear power is less air-polluting than fossil fuels.

5)   **The correct answer is D**

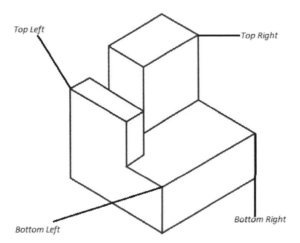

The puzzle piece shown has two notable features. The top right corner is taller than the top left corner and there is a gap between the blocks shown in the top left corner and the top right corner. Thus, the block of choice would add a small amount of height to the top left corner, additional height to the thin area between the top left and top right corner and a horizontal block between the bottom left and bottom right corner. This pattern is shown in example D, which when rotated 180 degrees completes the example block to form a complete cube.

146

6)   **The correct answer is C (It assumes that losing weight is sufficient to avoid developing prostate cancer).**

The passage states 'middle-aged men can prevent the development of prostate cancer by eating a healthy diet and taking regular exercise' – implying the following conclusion: prostate cancer can be prevented by eating a healthy diet and taking regular exercise. A flaw must therefore challenge this conclusion, such that even if all claims in the passage are true, the reasoning will still be flawed.

Option A may possibly be a flaw but does not impact the main conclusion which focuses upon prostate cancer, not other forms of cancer. Option B addresses some of the claims in the argument, but not the main reasoning of the argument. Option C is the best option and distinctly highlights the flaw in the reasoning of the argument. Option D lacks relevance to the argument and has no impact on its reasoning.

7)   **The correct answer is B (18)**

To complete this question, simply use the data given to determine the number of boys and girls who took part for each sport. Remember that there are equal numbers of boys and girls in the survey, and equal numbers of boys and girls who chose running.

Swimming: 28 boys, 0 girls
Rounders: 0 boys, 40 girls
Running: 14 boys, 14 girls

Therefore, football (48 people) must have 12 more boys than girls:
48-12 = 36

Number of boys = number of girls, so there are 18 girls who chose football

8)   **The correct answer is C (14.3)**

First, work out the number of re-offenders over the 9-year period:

74% of 42,721 = 0.74 x 42,721 = 31614 (approx. 75% of 42,000 = 31,500)

Then using the reconviction frequency rate: no. of offences per 100 offenders in the cohort, work out the number of reconvictions per re-offender:

(1,057 x 42,721) / 100 = 451,561 (approx. 10 x 43,000 = 430,000)

Reconvictions per re-offenders = 451,561/31,614 = 14.3 (approx. 430,000/30,430000 = 14.3)

9)   **The correct answer is E (1 and 3 only)**

To answer this question, evaluate each statement in turn.

Statement 1 requires simple maths:

1st year: 43% were reconvicted

2nd year 55% were reconvicted

43/55 = 78% (approx. 44/55 = 80%), which is greater than 77%, hence statement 1 is true.

Statement 2 requires the number of reconvicting offences between years 1 and 3:

Total offences during years 2 and 3: 61.9% - 43% = 18.9%

Total offences across the 9-year period: 74%

18.9% / 74% = 25.5% (approx. 20% / 80% = 25%) which is less than 1/3, hence statement 2 is false.

Statement 3 can be worked out by using the reconviction frequency rate for the first year:

Reconviction frequency rate is 1st year: 185.1

(185.1 x 42,721) / 100 = 79,034 which is greater than 77,000 (approx. 200 x 400 = 80,000)

Hence, statement 3 is true.

10) The correct answer is C (31,000)

The data states that 'offenders who received shorter sentences (less than 12 months) formed 24.2% of the cohort but committed 39% of all offences that led to a conviction in the 1st year of the follow-up. The answer can be worked out by finding the number of offences leading to a reconviction in the first year, and then calculating 39% of this value:

Reconviction frequency rate is 1st year: 185.1

(185.1 x 42,721) / 100 = 79,034 which is greater than 77,000 (approx. 200 x 400 = 80,000)

39% of 79,034 = 30,823 (approx. 40% of 80,000 = 32,000)

11) The correct answer is G (1, 2 and 3)

To answer this question, take each statement in turn and determine whether the factors, if true, will cause a decline in the year-on-year rate of reconvictions.

Statement 1: High numbers re-offenders being sent to prison mean that there can only be less reconvictions in the following years so statement 1 is true.

Statement 2: Natural mortality rate over a decade means that many of the re-offenders will pass away, and therefore resulting in a lower reconviction rate. Statement 2 is also true.

Statement 3: A harsher sentencing can cause a deterrent effect that results in less reconvictions as people become more wary of committing crimes. Statement 3 is true.

12) The correct answer is D (Graham and Carl)

Since the performer who plays Gracie cannot play any other roles, we can immediately eliminate option A.

We can thereafter eliminate options based on whether the two characters appear in the same scene.

B – Teddy and Guard 1 both appear in scene 1

C - The performer who plays Rose also plays Guard 1. As Sarah and Rose appear together in scene 10, option C is not viable.

F – Guard 1 and Guard 2 again also appear together in scene 1.

We can eliminate E as Sarah needs to be played by a female performer and Graham needs to be played by a male performer.

This leaves us with option D of Graham and Carl being the only viable option.

13)   The correct answer is B (...could be a contributory factor in the three incidences of extinction of marine animals)

Option A: The keyword in the statement is 'must'. Whilst the high levels of selenium overlapped with when marine animals first appeared, it does not define a causative event. Therefore A is not a valid conclusion.

Option B: A drop in selenium levels was found to correlate with the extinction events. However, we do not know for certain based on the information within the passage whether it caused the extinction events. The keyword 'could' makes this the most viable answer option.

Option C: The passage only says that the drop in selenium levels correlate with extinction events. It does not say whether it is more important than other tracer elements.

Option D: Correlation is not equal to causation. The keyword in this statement is again 'must'. Whilst drops in selenium levels may have contributed to the extinction events, we do not know this for certain just from the passage.

14)   The correct answer is B

There are three political parties in Xanthia: the Citron Party, the Jonquil Party and the

Saffron Party. Before last month's General Election the Jonquils held 126 of the 240 seats in the Xanthian Parliament, the Citrons held 80 and the Saffrons held 34.

In last month's General Election:

> Citrons gained 47 seats from the Jonquils and 10 seats from the Saffrons;
> Jonquils gained 11 seats from the Citrons and 15 seats from the Saffrons;
> Saffrons gained 18 seats from the Citrons and 33 seats from the Jonquils.

Before Election - Jonquils 126; Citrons 80; Saffrons 34; Total: 240

After Election:

> Jonquils: 126 + 11 (from Citrons) + 15 (from Saffrons) = 152
> 152 - 47 (to Citrons) - 33 (to Saffrons) = 72
> Citrons: 80 + 47 (from Jonquils) + 10 (from Saffrons) = 137
> 137 - 11 (to Jonquils) - 18 (to Saffrons) = 108
> Saffrons: 34 + 18 (from Citrons) + 33 (from Jonquils) = 85
> 85 - 10 (to Citrons) - 15 (to Jonquils) = 60

The entire circle represents 240. The Saffrons represents 60 of 240, which is the same of 1/4 of circle. The only pie chart showing 1/4 of circle is letter B.

15)   The correct answer is A (Soil is either acidic or alkaline, but there are camellias growing here, which cannot tolerate alkalinity, so this soil must be acidic)

This questions asks us to select from A-D which argument structure most resembles the argument in the above passage.

Let's assign meteorites the letter A, dust the letter B, and deuterium the letter C. From this, we can break down the argument into:

Either A or B could have occurred. However, as C is present, A cannot have occurred. Therefore B must have occurred.

The only argument that resembles this structure is option A:

We can assign acidic as A, alkaline as B, and camellias as C.

Soil is either A or B. However C is present, so B cannot be true. Therefore A must be true.

16)   The correct answer is D (7)

With the four digits in each combination adding up to 19, the total of both pins (or all 8 numbers) is 38. If we add all of the possible numbers (1 + 2 + 3 + 4 + 5 + 6 + 7 + 8 + 9) the total is 45. In order to make the required total of 45 from eight numbers, we omit or subtract the number 7.

17)   The correct answer is D (neither 1 nor 2)

Option 1: the statement doesn't relate to the subject matter of the argument. The main argument is that due to the damage done to the childhood stars, placing children in the industry should count as child abuse. The statement of mental breakdowns happening to anyone does not reflect the body of the argument.

Option 2: again, the statement doesn't address the main body of the argument. Whilst it may be true that being adored as a child does not offer an explanation for addictions, the main argument is about whether placing your child in the industry should count as child abuse.

18)   The correct answer is B (8)

We need to calculate how much of each ingredient we have left over:

Flour: 1000-225-400=375g
Sugar: 600-330-200=70g
Cocoa powder: 500-85-100=315g
Eggs: 12-2=10 eggs
Milk: 2500-250=2250ml
Butter: 600-150-400=50g

As we only have 50g of butter left over, we can only make one batch of 8 of pancakes.

19)   The correct answer is B (The study counted empty cells (which indicate that the data is unavailable and are perfectly normal) as spreadsheet errors)

A: Statement A actually strengthens the claim as it shows the field of genomics is most prone to spreadsheet errors

B: Significantly weakens the claim as empty cells are not counted as errors and the inclusion would vastly inflate the claim.

C: Just because findings have been significantly replicated, it does not mean that the spreadsheet errors would not cause a major issue in the future. The claim also described a 20% annual increase in error-ridden spreadsheets. Therefore even if the findings have not been an issue thus far, it does not mean they won't cause difficulties later on.

D: The 'SEPT2' issue was only one example of a spreadsheet error. Fixing this one issue will not solve the overall increase in error-ridden genomics spreadsheets.

20)   The correct answer is B (2 only)

Statement 1: The supplementary files graph only tells us the number of files per year. It does not tell us which or how many journals these supplementary files belonged to. Therefore this is not a statement that can be backed up.

Statement 2: In 2009, the number of files published with gene name errors was approximately 48. In 2011, the number has risen to approximately 104. 104 is more than double, 48 so this statement is supported.

Statement 3: In the observed period, Nature published 23 affected papers and BMC Bioinformatics published 21. Therefore this statement is not supported.

21)   The correct answer is D (63%)

The journals in which the proportion of papers affected was higher than average include; Nature, Genes Dev, Genome Res, Genome Biol, Nature Genet, Nucleic Acids Res and BMC Genomics.

Work out the number of papers affected in these journals:
23 + 55 + 68 + 63 + 9 + 67 + 158 = 443

Divide 443 by the total number of papers affected:
443/704 = 63% (approx. 450/700 = 64%)

22)   The correct answer is C (2018)

The data states that number of genomics papers packaged with error-ridden spreadsheets increased by 20% a year over the period, while there was a 10% annual growth rate in the number of genomics papers published. For 2015, 80% of all genomics papers published were affected.

Take 100 as the number of papers published in 2015, 80 of which would be affected. Using the growth rates, the number of papers affected in the following years can be calculated by multiplying the affected papers by 1.2 (20%) and the number of papers published by 1.1 (10%).

2015: 100 published, 80 affected
2016: 110 published (100 x 1.1), 96 affected (80 x 1.2)
2017: 121 published (110 x 1.1), 115.2 affected (96 x 1.2)
2018: 133.1 published (121 x 1.1), 138.24 affected (115.2 x 1.2)
As can be seen, in 2018, every genomics paper would be affected.

23)   The correct answer is E

The shaded region in the question indicates that two pieces are missing, and one piece must have 2 inward gaps, the other piece must have 1 inward gap. Options A-D all display jigsaw pieces with less than, or more than a total of 3 inward gaps, which will result in a crossover of the jigsaw edges. Hence the only possible option for the pieces are shown in Option E, whereby the first piece has 2 gaps, and the second has 1 inward gap.

24)   The correct answer is E (It fails to consider other factors that might have improved women's life expectancy)

The passage concludes that the more times women give birth, the more likely they are to die early. A flaw in the argument must challenge the reasoning of the conclusion.

Statement A challenges a claim in the passage but does not impact on the reasoning of the conclusion.

Statement B weakens the conclusion by challenging its basis, however it does not address the main flaw of the argument.

Statement C is irrelevant to the argument – infant mortality rates are not mentioned in the passage.

Statement D presents an implication of the argument, not a flaw.

Statement E directly challenges the reasoning of the conclusion – the reasoning of the argument is flawed as it suggests that women's life expectancy is solely dependant on the number of times they have given birth. By considering other factors that may have improved life expectancy over time, option E is the best expression of the flaw in the argument.

25)   The correct answer is E (36 kilometres)

This question involves setting up two simultaneous equations, then using algebra and fractions to work out the initial distance.

Using the formula speed = distance/time, we can setup a pair of simultaneous equations:

$$1: 30 = d \,/\, t$$
$$2: 27 = [d + 4] \,/\, 1.25t$$

Rearrange these equations to make 't' the subject, and then using substitution, work out the value of 'd':

$$1: t = d \,/\, 30$$
$$2: 1.25t = [d + 4] \,/\, 27$$
$$2: 5t \,/\, 4 = [d + 4] \,/\, 27$$
$$(\text{After simplifying}),\ 2: 5t = [4d + 16] \,/\, 27$$

Using substitution, make the two equations equal to each other, and then simplify:

$$1: t = d \,/\, 30,\ \text{so } 5t = d \,/\, 6$$
$$2: 5t = [4d + 16] \,/\, 27$$

Therefore:

$$[4d + 16] \,/\, 27 = d \,/\, 6$$
$$24d + 96 = 27d$$

$$3d = 96$$
$$d = 32 \text{ (original distance was 32km)}$$
New route distance $= d + 4$
$$= 32 + 4$$
$$= 36 \text{km}$$

26)   The correct answer is C (The cited study does not prove conclusively that the 'health checks' have prevented over 2,000 heart attacks and strokes)

Statement A cannot be concluded from the passage as it is mentioned that 'this level of detection of such risk factors *could* equate to the prevention of the over 2,000 heart attacks and strokes' – the key word in the passage is 'could'. There is no data regarding the impact of the 'health checks', hence the resources spent on them cannot be justified and statement A cannot be concluded.

Statement B also cannot be concluded for the same reason as statement A – there is no data regarding the impact of the 'health checks', therefore we cannot conclude whether the screening programmers can or cannot influence people's health related behaviours.

Statement C is correct and can be reliably concluded from the passage. It is inferred from the passage that 'health checks' can prevent over 2,000 heart attacks and strokes, however, this relationship has not been proven, as researchers did not monitor individuals who had been screened. Therefore, the cited study does not prove conclusively that the 'health checks' have prevented over 2,000 heart attacks and strokes – so statement C can be reliably drawn as a conclusion.

Statement D cannot be concluded, as there is no evidence of the impact of NHS resources on monitoring the long-term health outcomes of individuals. The main argument of the passage focuses upon the prevention of diseases, rather than the monitoring of long-term health outcomes of individuals, therefore statement D is somewhat irrelevant and cannot be concluded.

Statement E is irrelevant to the argument and cannot be supported by information in the passage, hence the statement cannot be drawn as a conclusion.

27)   The correct answer is B (€2.89)

First calculate the number of whole plates that can be prepared using the smallest number of packs without wasting food. This will be equal to the lowest common multiple (LCM) of 200, 300, 400.

LCM of 200, 300, 400 = 1,200
1 plate of seafood = 50g of each item
1,200 grams = 24 plates of seafood

Now the cost of the ingredients can be calculated (including the wholesaler's offer) - offer states 'buy any two packs of one item and get another pack of the same item free':

Prawns: $1,200 = 400 \times 3$
$= 2 \times €4.08$ (one pack is free)
$= €8.16$

Squid: $1,200 = 300 \times 4$
$= 3 \times €4.08$

= €12.24

Cockles, Whelks, Salmon: 3,600 = 200 x 18
12 packs = 12 x €4.08
= €48.96

Total cost = €48.96 + €12.24 + €8.16
= €69.36

Cost per plate = €69.36/24
= €2.89

28)   The correct answer is E (1 and 3 only)

An assumption is an **unstated** fact that must be true for the conclusion to be justified:

Statement 1 is an underlying assumption of the above argument. In the initial two sentences, it is stated that police officers should use body-worn cameras, primarily to lower levels of violence within police-public interactions. It can therefore be assumed that the need for body-worn cameras has arisen due to pre-existing excessive levels of force during police-public interactions.

Statement 2 is not an underlying assumption as it is not necessary for this statement to be true for the conclusion to be justified. Whether it is possible or not for police departments in different countries to agree on appropriate levels of force has no impact on whether the implementation of body-worn video cameras are preferable.

Statement 3 is an underlying assumption of the above argument. In the final two sentences, it is stated that a reason for implementation of body-worn cameras require that an officer issue a clear warning from the start that everyone in an interaction is being filmed. It can therefore be assumed that individuals being filmed by bystanders may have been unaware of the filming in previous cases. Thus this statement is an underlying assumption as it must be true for the implementation of body-worn cameras to be justified.

29)   The correct answer is E

A: If you observe side 4, the missing spot has side 1 on its left (opposite to side 6) and side 2 on the top (opposite to side 5). The only option that follows this pattern are options E and A.

But, when you observe the way the dice was turned, you can see that the missing spot on side 4 is near the lower spot on side 2 (view B)

So, the only option which shows the missing spot on side 4 near the lower spot on side 2 and with side 1 on the left is option E.

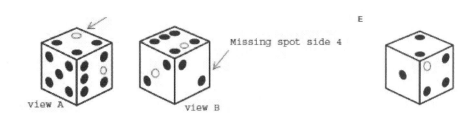

30)   The correct answer is C (It assumes that just because 'positive' traits are associated with strong brain connectivity these traits are caused by the strong connectivity)

The passage concludes that improving brain connectivity will result in more 'positive' lifestyle attributes. A flaw in the argument must challenge the reasoning of the conclusion.

Statement A challenges a claim in the passage but has no direct impact on the reasoning of the conclusion which centres upon the relationship between improving brain activity resulting in more 'positive' lifestyle attributes. However this statement addresses what factors constitute to a 'positive' lifestyle trait.

Statement B is irrelevant to the argument and does not address either improving brain activity or 'positive' lifestyle attributes.

Statement C is correct and best addresses the flaw in the above argument. The statement directly challenges the reasoning of the conclusion, which assumes that strong brain connectivity will cause 'positive' traits. Firstly, the passage only suggests a correlation between strong brain connectivity and 'positive' trains, not a cause. Secondly, there may be other factors involved which impact 'positive' traits – hence statement C is the best statement of the flaw in the above argument.

Statement D does not directly address the reasoning of the conclusion.

31)   The correct answer is D (George)

Let's make each friend's choice on table as a letter:

Cricket and Hokey = A
Golf and Rugby = B
Hockey and Snooker = C
Football and snooker = D
Cricket and Rugby = E
Football and Golf = F

And organise them:

```
          A --> Amir --> B        D --> David --> E
               |                       |
               C                       F
          F --> Eli --> D         C --> George --> A
               |                       |
               E                       B
          E --> Jess --> F        B --> Peter --> C
               |                       |
               D                       A
```

It was said that Jess shares one common interest with each friends on her side, it means she shares interest with "Cricket and Rugby" and "Football and Golf". The only option for this is "Golf and Rugby", making Jess the friend letter B.

George is the friend who has "B" as opposite side, which makes George as letter D.

The table is organized:

Amir -- Jess -- Peter -- Eli -- George – David

32)   The correct answer is C (both 1 and 2)

The reasons for previous increase in congestion are outlined in paragraph 4 of the passage.

Statement 1 is true as interventions to prioritise public transport could account for the increase in the problem of London's road congestion. This is proven in the passage, whereby the implementation of bus lanes and the resulting long-term loss of road space have contributed to recent increases in congestion.

Statement 2 is also true as an increase in road works by utility companies would increase in road congestion. This is highlighted in the text, whereby construction works have increased levels of congestion.

33)   The correct answer is E (92)

To answer this question, simply divide the cost of congestion to London's GVA in 2015 (£5.5bn) by the conservative estimate of the total cost of the tube strikes (£60m):

$$5.5bn/60m = 555/6$$
$$550/6 = 92 \text{ (approx. } 600/6 = 100)$$

34)   The correct answer is C (3 only)

Statement 1 cannot be inferred from the information given. Although car ownership has been falling in London, and the road congestion problem has not decreased, it cannot be inferred that the road congestion problem is solely dependant upon car ownership. The decline of car ownership in London may have reduced the capital's road problem, however other factors such as public transport implementations may have caused road congestion to increase.

Statement 2 cannot be inferred from the information given as there is no evidence to support the statement. Bicycle journeys only account for 2% of all travel, therefore converting traffic lanes into cycle tracks would most likely make London's congestion problem even worse.

Statement 3 can be inferred from the passage. In the third paragraph, it can be inferred that the road congestion problem has caused demands for the bus service, a method of public transport, to decline due to slower speeds and worse reliability.

35)   The correct answer is B (The original wider congestion charge zone encompassed some of London's profitable retail areas)

A: In 2014, 45% of journeys were taken by public transport. 300 extra buses running would reduce congestion and improve London's GVA.

B: Imposing a congestion charge in the profitable retail areas would reduce the amount of traffic going to those areas, and thus would decrease sales. This would lead to the loss of London's GVA. B is the correct answer because it is the only one out of the four that would explain an increase in the loss of profits.

C: Whilst this would lead to the loss of congestion charge, the practice would occur regardless of whether the wider congestion charge was put in place.

D: We cannot simply extrapolate the data from one year to discount any potential in the reduction of loss of profit

BMAT SECTION 2 WORKED SOLUTIONS

BMAT Section 2 - 2003

1) The correct answer is B

Starch is partially broken down in the mouth into sugars by amylase. For that reason, nutrient one must be starch as it shows partial digestion in the mouth. Protein and fats are not broken down in the mouth by amylase. Protein is digested primarily in the stomach into amino acids by protease enzymes such as pepsin making nutrient two, protein. Fat is digested in the small intestine into fatty acids and glycerol by lipase, therefore making nutrient three fat and option B the correct answer.

Reference: *BMAT Assumed Subject Knowledge Guide:* Organs and Systems: Digestive System Enzymes

2) The correct answer is E (3.2×10^{-12})

There are 1000 milligrams in one gram and 1000 grams in one kilogram therefore one milligram = 0.000001 kg (or 1×10^{-6}).

One atom of uranium = 4×10^{-25} kg x 1×10^{-6} = 4×10^{-19} mg

For 8 million atoms 4×10^{-19} x 8×10^6 = 3.2×10^{-12}

3) The correct answer is $a= 2$, $b =9$, $c= 6$

The first step is to count the number of atoms on each side of the equation:

$$a C_3H_6 + b O_2 \rightarrow 6CO_2 + cH_2O$$

	Left	Right
C	3	6
H	6	2
O	2	13

Given that none of the atoms in this equation are balanced, numbers need to be assigned to $a, b,$ and c to make both sides of the equation balanced.

Carbon:

There are three carbon atoms on the left-hand side and six carbon atoms on the right-hand side of the equation. $6/3 = 2$ making $a = 2$

This will have flow-on effects for other areas of the equation:

$$2C_3H_6 + b O_2 \rightarrow 6CO_2 + cH_2O$$

Placing a 2 in front of $2C_3H_6$ also affects H_6, now making it 12

Left	Right
6	6

159

12	2
2	13

Hydrogen:

There are now 12 Hydrogen atoms on the left-hand side of the equation and two on the right so:

$c = 12/2$

$c = 6$

$2C_3H_6 + bO_2 \rightarrow 6CO_2 + 6H_2O$

The six will have an impact on oxygen in $6H_2O$ (the 6 means six of everything in that compound)

Left	Right
6	6
12	12
2	18

Oxygen:

Having $6H_2O$ means that the left-hand side of the equation needs to be reviewed as the numbers of oxygen atoms on the right-hand side is greater than the left:

$b = 18/2 = 9$ making $b = 9$

The balanced equation is:

$2C_3H_6 + 9O_2 \rightarrow 6CO_2 + 6H_2O$

Reference: *BMAT Assumed Subject Knowledge Guide:* Chemical Concepts: Balancing Equations

4)   The correct answer is B (10cm)

The beam is balanced when the work done by one side of the beam is equal to the other (meaning that they cancel out or equal zero). The first step is to calculate the work (E) on the left-hand side (LHS) using the equation:

$$E = Fd$$

F = force in Newtons and d = distance in metres. For this question, the distances are in centimetres; hence they must be converted into metres first. Calculating work on the left-hand side of the fulcrum:

$$E_{LHS} = 500 \times 0.20$$

$$E_{LHS} = 100J$$

The unit is Joules as "work done is transferred to energy."

Next, calculate the work for the outermost weight on the right-hand side of the fulcrum (RHS2)

$$E_{RHS2} = 200 \times 0.4$$

$$E_{RHS2} = 80 \text{ J}$$

Since both sides of the fulcrum need to be equal, the above answer provides the work done and the distance for the inside weight on the right-hand side.

$$E_{RHS1} = 100-80 = 20J$$

$$d = E/F = 20/200 =$$

$$0.1m \text{ (10cm)}$$
$$\text{(Option B)}$$

Reference: *BMAT Assumed Subject Knowledge Guide:* Forces and Energy: Work Done

5)   The correct answer is D (yellow)

In pH 5.0, methyl orange would turn yellow since it changes from red to yellow at pH 4.0. Bromothymol blue would also turn yellow as a pH of 6.5 or higher is needed turn to it blue.

Phenolphthalein would remain colourless as it changes to pink at pH 9.0.

This means that the solution would appear yellow (answer D).

6)   The correct answer is 76.8kJ

The weight must be first be converted to mass by rearranging, and then using the equation W = mg (where g is the gravitational constant ($10Nkg^{-1}$).

$$W = mg$$
$$6000 = m \times 10$$

$$6000/10 = 600kg$$

To calculate kinetic energy:

$$E_k = {}^1\!/_2 mv^2$$

$$E_k = \tfrac{1}{2} (600 \times 16^2)$$

$$E_k = 76800 \text{ J}$$

The answer must be in kilojoules, 1000J equals 1kJ. Thus, the solution must be divided by 1000:

$$76800/1000$$

$$= 76.8 \text{kJ}$$

Reference: *BMAT Assumed Subject Knowledge Guide:* Forces and Energy: Mass, Weight, and Gravity; Kinetic Energy

7)   The correct answer is B

The female reproductive cycle is divided into 3 phases. The first phase is the follicular phase which begins on the first day of menstruation. During this phase, follicles (eggs) develop in the ovaries, stimulated by follicle stimulating hormone (FSH). The lining of the uterus is thick containing fluids and nutrients ready to nourish an embryo should the fertilisation of an egg occur.

If fertilisation does not occur and no embryo is present, the oestrogen and progesterone levels remain low (section A on the diagram), which triggers the lining of the uterus to be shed and bleeding to commence. In section B on the chart, the dominant follicle begins to secrete oestrogen which decreases the levels of FSH and increases the levels of oestrogen in the body, this occurs over 13-14 days. The follicular phase ends when the level of luteinizing hormone (LH) dramatically increases, stimulating the release of a follicle for fertilisation in the process called ovulation.

The ovulatory phase usually lasts 16 to 32 hours concluding when the egg is released. After ovulation, the luteal phase begins (sections C and D on the diagram), continuing for approximately 14 days and ends just before the menstrual period. During this phase, the egg travels along the fallopian tube to the uterus.

The remainder of the ruptured follicle forms a structure called the corpus luteum, which secretes progesterone and oestrogen and prepares the uterus for fertilisation. The levels of oestrogen secreted by the corpus luteum, however, are not as high as that seen in the follicular phase.

If the egg is not fertilised within the 12 -24-hour window after ovulation, the corpus luteum shrinks and begins to degenerate after 14 days. The unfertilised egg also dies and passes out of the uterus during menstruation. Oestrogen and progesterone levels fall, bleeding recommences to shed the uterine lining and the cycle starts over again.

8)   The correct answer is A, C, B, D

In a series circuit, the "resistance adds up" which means that the battery has to push charge through all three resistors. The total resistance can be calculated using the equation:

$$R_T = R_1 + R_2 + R_3$$

Therefore circuit D will have the largest resistance. In a parallel circuit, the charge has alternative routes through which it can move. Therefore, the total resistance is always less than that of the branch with the smallest resistance. In a parallel circuit with all resistors in parallel resistance can, therefore, be calculated using the equation:

$$R_T = 1/R_1 + 1/R_2 + 1/R_3$$

Therefore circuit A will have the smallest resistance. For circuits with resistors in both series and parallel conformations, the two above rules need to be combined. Circuit C has two resistors in series, so these will add together ($R1 + R2 = R_A$) to become one larger resistor (R_A). However, R_A is still in parallel with another resistor, so the parallel rule also applies:

$$R_{total} = 1/R_3 + 1/R_A.$$

This makes C the circuit with the next smallest resistance, as the current will have an alternate route. Circuit B is similar to circuit C except it is the opposite way around:

$$R_{total} = (1/R_1 + 1/R_2) + R_3$$

This makes B the second largest as the current still has to travel through two resistors. Therefore the order from smallest to largest resistance is: A, C, B, D

Reference: *BMAT Assumed Subject Knowledge Guide:* Electricity: Series Circuits; Parallel Circuits

9)   The correct answer is B (51g)
Calculate the number of moles hydrogen using the formula:

$$Number\ of\ moles = \frac{mass\ (g)}{relative\ formula\ mass}$$

Moles of hydrogen (H_2) = 9g/2 = 4.5

From the equation, the mole ratio is $3H_2$: 2N (or 3:2):

$$4.5 \times 2/3 = 3 \text{ moles of } N_2,$$

Therefore there must also be 3 moles of NH_3. This information can then be used to calculate the molar mass of NH_3:

$$14+3 =17$$

Place this value into the same equation as before rearranged to find mass rather than the number of moles:

$$3 \times 17 = 51g$$

Reference: *BMAT Assumed Subject Knowledge Guide:* Equations and Calculations: Formula Mass Calculations

10)   The correct answer is B
The function $y=2^x$ is an exponential graph, starting above the x-axis, thus immediately ruling out option C. These graphs "always go through the point (0, 1)" therefore option A can also be excluded. Because 2^x is positive, the graph will travel from left to right which rules out option D and leaves option B as the correct answer.

Reference: *BMAT Assumed Subject Knowledge Guide:* Graphs: Harder Graphs

11)   The correct answer is A (0)

"The frequency of a wave is set at its source" therefore none of the three phenomena mentioned can change it.

Reference: *BMAT Assumed Subject Knowledge Guide:* Waves and their Effects: Wave properties -Reflection; Wave properties – Refraction

12)   The correct answer is A (oxidation)

The citric acid cycle takes the acetyl group from acetyl CoA and joins it to oxaloacetate (4 carbon molecule) to form citrate (6 carbon molecule). Through eight different steps citrate is oxidised, releasing two carbon dioxide molecules for each acetyl CoA which is fed into the cycle. Succinic acid's (succinate) conversion to fumaric acid (or fumarate) is the sixth step in the citric acid cycle and removes two hydrogen atoms from succinate. The removal of the hydrogen atoms from a compound oxidises it. Therefore the formation of fumarate is considered to be an oxidation reaction.

13)   The correct answer is D (x>2 or x < -4)

$$x^2 > 8-2x$$

Make the inequality equal zero

$$x^2 + 2x- 8 = 0$$

As this is a quadratic inequality, it needs to be factorised:

$$(x+ 4) (x-2) = 0$$

Make each set of brackets = 0 and solve

$$X + 4 = 0 \text{ therefore } X = -4$$

$$X -2 = 0 \text{ therefore } X = 2$$
(Option D)

Reference: *BMAT Assumed Subject Knowledge Guide:* Algebra: Inequalities; Factorising

14) The correct answer is:

(i) Individuals 3,4 and 5

The condition shown in the diagram is recessive as it does not appear in every generation. For this couple (individuals three and four) to have an affected child, both individuals need to carry a copy of the recessive allele which then provides the zygote with two copies of the recessive allele (homozygous recessive). Individual five must also be heterozygous as they have one parent (individual two) who is affected (homozygous recessive) and would only have recessive alleles to contribute their offspring, and one unaffected parent.

(ii) The correct answer is E (1 in 8, 12.5%)

The previous question (14i) has already established that individual five is heterozygous. Assuming their partner is also heterozygous, the chance of producing offspring with two recessive alleles is 25% or ¼. The chance of having female offspring is 50% or 1/2.

To calculate the likelihood of the individual being female and affected, the two probabilities must be multiplied: 0.25 x 0.50 (x100) = 1/8 or 12.5%

Reference: *BMAT Assumed Subject Knowledge Guide:* Genes, Reproduction, and Evolution: More on Genetic Disorders; X and Y chromosomes

15) The correct answer is 4 minutes

The first step is to subtract the background radiation from the initial and final counts:

$$140 \text{ cpm} - 20 = 120 \text{ cpm}$$

$$35 - 20 = 15 \text{ cpm}$$

From here work out the cpm after each half-life:

$$120 / 2 \rightarrow 60/2 \rightarrow 30/2 \rightarrow 15$$

The arrows represent the number of half-lives (in this case there are three)

If it takes 12 minutes for the count rate to decrease from 120 to 15 counts per minute, this is three half-lives 12/3 = 4 minutes per half-life.

Reference: *BMAT Assumed Subject Knowledge Guide:* The Atom and Radioactivity: Half-Life

16) The correct answer is C (26g)

This problem requires the extrapolation of the data from the graph.

Draw a line with a ruler directly upwards to hit the graph at 20°C and then across to hit the y-axis at 26 g.

17)   The correct answer is E

Option A refers to the equation: voltage (volts) = work (Joules) / charge (coulombs) thus ruling this option out.

Option B refers to the equation: voltage = current (Amperes) x resistance (Ohms) therefore ruling option B out

Option C refers to the equation voltage = power (Watts)/current

Option D refers to the square root of power x resistance which also equals voltage

Option E refers to the square root of Power/ charge not a recognised equation in physics

Reference: *BMAT Assumed Subject Knowledge Guide:* Electricity: Current and Electricity; Potential Difference

18)   The correct answer is: E, B, C, A, D

The jugular vein collects blood from the brain and joins onto the vena cava (E) which then travels to the right side of the heart. Here, the blood enters the pulmonary circuit to become oxygenated, first moving through the pulmonary artery (B), through the capillaries in the lungs and then into the pulmonary vein (C). The blood then returns to the left side of the heart where it is pumped via the aorta (A) to the body, finally reaching the renal artery (D) leading to the kidney.

19)   The correct answer is C (3.32 x 10^{-20} J)

There are five waves of this radiation produced in 1×10^{-13} sec

Therefore $5 / 1 \times 10^{-13}$ = frequency for 1 wave = 5×10^{13}

$$E = f \, x \, h$$

$$5 \times 10^{13} \text{ x } 6.63 \times 10^{-34}$$

Therefore the answer is 3.32×10^{-20}J

20)   The correct answer is C (group 4, period 2)

The electron configuration for this atom is 2, 4

The group that an atom falls into is denoted by how many electrons it has in its valence shell. This atom has four and, as a result, it is located in group four on the periodic table.

The period tells us how many orbitals the atom has, in this case, it has two. Therefore, this atom belongs to period two.

Reference: *BMAT Assumed Subject Knowledge Guide:* Chemical Concepts: The Periodic Table

21)   The correct answer is E

The joint in the arm is a third class lever, where the bones in the forearm are the lever, the elbow joint is the pivot (or fulcrum), and the resistance (weight) is the load of the wrist and hand. Third class levers position the effort between the load and the fulcrum (thus ruling out option one). Force is exerted when the biceps and triceps muscles relax and contract to provide the effort (input) and move the load (output). The biceps muscle relaxes when the triceps muscle contracts and vice versa.

To move the lever upwards, the biceps muscle contracts (the effort is in an upward direction) and the weight of the load acts in a downward direction (ruling out option two). This leaves option three as the third class lever. The triceps is a first class lever system, where the load and the effort work in the same direction. The triceps muscle contracts as the arm straightens (ruling out option four) and leaving option five as the correct answer.

22)   The correct answer is E (1,2 and 3)

Coil rotation increases the frequency because there is a decrease in the revolution time. A higher frequency will also "increase the EMF as the field is reversing (changing direction) more frequently" – Faraday's law. Amplitude increases as the waves move further up and down away from the zero line. This also increases the voltage due to the coil moving through the field from the magnet at a faster speed.

Reference: *BMAT Assumed Subject Knowledge Guide:* Electricity: Generators

23)   The correct answer is E (The outer orbit/energy level is further from the nucleus)

All alkali metals have one valence electron in their outer orbital. With each additional orbital added to the alkali metal, the valence electron becomes a greater distance from the nucleus, thus the attraction between the positive nucleus and the negative valence electron decreases. This reduction in attraction means that the valence electron is easier to remove from the atom, and therefore will more readily participate in reactions, compared to those alkali metals higher on the periodic table.

Reference: *BMAT Assumed Subject Knowledge Guide:* Classifying materials: Group 1 – The Alkali Metals

24)   The correct answer is C

During exhalation (breathing out) air vacates the lungs. To do this, the volume of the chest (thorax) must decrease (ruling out options B, D and F). As the thoracic volume decreases, the pressure inside the thoracic cavity increases causing the air to move down its pressure gradient (from high pressure in the lungs to low pressure in the environment).

Breathing out also causes the diaphragm to relax and move upwards. As it moves upwards, it becomes more convex (ruling out option E). The ribcage and sternum drop down and inwards due to the decreased volume of the thorax (ruling out option A).

Reference: *BMAT Assumed Subject Knowledge Guide:* Organs and Systems: The Breathing System

25)   The correct answer is B

$$\frac{(2x^{3/2}y^3)^2}{\sqrt{z}}$$

Remove the brackets by squaring everything inside:

$$\frac{4x^3y^6}{z}$$

Reference: *BMAT Assumed Subject Knowledge Guide:* Algebra: Rearranging Formulas; Powers and Roots; Algebraic Fractions

26) The correct answer is C (kidney, lung)

The three chemicals that need to be considered for graph one are carbon dioxide, oxygen, and urea. The carbon dioxide concentration in the blood increases after moving through this organ indicating that it is a waste product that requires removal from the body. The oxygen concentration in the blood decreases after passing through this organ, meaning that the organ is using (not providing) oxygen. Urea is a waste product that is removed from the body as urine. The kidney is the organ which manufactures urine as a waste product; therefore Organ X is the kidney, which rules out all options except B and C. Organ Y then either becomes the liver (B) or the lungs (C). According to the second graph, the concentration of carbon dioxide and oxygen are dramatically changing, and the other three substances remain stable (unchanged) before and after the blood passes through the organ, indicating that this process is gas exchange. Since the lungs are the site of gas exchange, this means that option B is excluded, leaving option C as the correct answer.

Reference: *BMAT Assumed Subject Knowledge Guide:* Nerves, Hormones, and Homeostasis: The Kidney; Organs and Systems: The Lungs

27) The correct answer is A

When the skydiver first jumps out of the plane, the force accelerating them is greater than resistance slowing them down. As their speed increases, resistance also increases which gradually reduces acceleration until drag and acceleration are balanced. In other words, the skydiver has reached terminal velocity.
When the skydiver's parachute is closed, there is a small area (and therefore less drag) and the weight force/acceleration is pulling them downwards. Once the parachute opens, the area (and thus drag) increases (ruling out options B and D). The weight force however, remains the same, resulting in speed decreasing.

Reference: *BMAT Assumed Subject Knowledge Guide:* Forces and Energy: Resistive forces; Terminal Velocity

28) The correct answer is C ($Ca_5(PO_4)_3F$)

Ionic formulae must have an overall charge of zero (neutral). To achieve this, the positively charged ions must completely cancel out the negatively charged ions.
Option A has an overall charge of -2 since +2 + -3 + - 1 = -2 making this formula is incorrect.
Option B has an overall charge of -1 since (+2 x 3) + (-3 x 2) + - 1 = -1 and as a result, this formula is also incorrect.

Option C is correct as (+2 x 5) + (-3 x 3) + - 1 = 0 making this a neutral compound, where the number of positive and negative charges equal zero.

Option D is also incorrect as (+2 x 7) + (-3 x 5) + - 1 = -2

Reference: *BMAT Assumed Subject Knowledge Guide:* Classifying Materials: Ions: Formulas of Ions

29)   The correct answer is A (2)

To find the side of the triangle, the law of sines can be used where:

$$a/\sin A = b/\sin B = c/\sin C$$

The law of sines provides a formula that relates the sides with the angles of a triangle. This formula allows the side length or the angle of any triangle to be found. The side of the triangle is the angle it sits opposite.

Letters a,b,c represent the sides of a triangle and A, B, C are its angles.

Identify what is known in this equation:

$$\sqrt{6}/\sin (60) = PR/\sin (45) = c/\sin (75)$$

c / sin (75) can be ignored since it is not useful in solving PR

$$\sqrt{6}/\sin (60) = PR/\sin (45)$$

Flip the equation, so PR is on the left:

$$PR/\sin (45) = \sqrt{6}/\sin (60)$$

Solve for PR by multiplying both sides by sin (45):

$$PR = \left(\frac{\sqrt{6}}{\sin (60)}\right)x\sin (45)$$

$$PR = 2 \text{ (answer A)}$$

BMAT Section 2 - 2004

1)   The correct answer is B (2→ 3→ 4→ 1→7→ 6→ 5→ 8)

In a typical cardiac cycle, the blood returns from the lungs via the pulmonary vein (2) to the left atrium (3) and into the right ventricle (4). From here, it is pumped through the aorta (1) to the body at high pressure. Once the blood has delivered its oxygen and nutrients to the body, it returns to the heart via the vena cava (7) flowing into the right atrium (6). The right atrium releases blood into the right ventricle (5), from which it returns to the lungs to collect more oxygen via the pulmonary artery (8). Then the whole cycle repeats.

Reference: *BMAT Assumed Subject Knowledge Guide:* The Circulatory System – Heart

2)   The correct answer is B

The area of a triangle:

$$\frac{1}{2}base \; x \; height$$

Or:

$$\frac{base \; x \; height}{2}$$

Therefore to find the answer

$$A = \frac{(4 + \sqrt{2}) \; x \; (2 - \sqrt{2})}{2}$$

$$A = (2 + \sqrt{1}) \; x \; (1 - \sqrt{1})$$

$$\sqrt{1} + \; -\sqrt{1} = -\sqrt{2}$$

Therefore the area is:

$$(3 - \sqrt{2})cm^2$$

Reference: *BMAT Assumed Subject Knowledge Guide:* Areas

3)   The correct answers are q=3, r=12, s = 3, t = 6

qCu + rHNO$_3$ → sCu (NO$_3$)$_2$ + 6H$_2$O + tNO$_2$

First count up the number of each type of atom on both sides of the equation to identify which atoms need balancing:

	Left	Right
Cu	1	1
H	1	12
N	1	3
O	3	14

Next, add 12 to the left-hand side of the equation to balance hydrogen.

$r = 12$

$q\text{Cu} + 12\text{HNO}_3 \rightarrow s\text{Cu}(\text{NO}_3)_2 + 6\text{H}_2\text{O} + t\text{NO}_2$

Recount the atoms on each side:

	Left	Right
Cu	1	1
H	12	12
N	12	3
O	36	14

The next step is to balance the nitrogen by tentatively placing a 10 in front of NO_2

$q\text{Cu} + 12\text{HNO}_3 \rightarrow s\text{Cu}(\text{NO}_3)_2 + 6\text{H}_2\text{O} + 10\text{NO}_2$

Recount the atoms on each side:

	Left	Right
Cu	1	1
H	12	12
N	12	12
O	36	32

Next, consider oxygen; it requires another four atoms on the right to become balanced. Having $s = 2$ will give 38 oxygen atoms on the right side of the equation and will require nitrogen to be altered as a result, as this will become 14 (four from $\text{Cu}(\text{NO}_3)_2$ and ten from NO_2 – making it no longer balanced). Reducing t to 8 however, to rebalance it would only provide a total of 34 oxygen atoms where 36 are needed. Therefore the correct number for s is 3, which makes $t = 6$. t must be reduced for the number of nitrogen atoms to balance out.

	Left	Right
Cu	1	3
H	12	12
N	12	12
O	36	36

The final step is to make $q = 3$ to balance copper making the final equation:

$3\text{Cu} + 12\text{HNO}_3 \rightarrow 3\text{Cu}(\text{NO}_3)_2 + 6\text{H}_2\text{O} + 6\text{NO}_2$

Reference: *BMAT Assumed Subject Knowledge Guide:* Chemical Concepts: Balancing Equations

4)   The correct answer is E (300N)

Force applied is another way of asking for work done. In this case, the force is perpendicular to the distance, so the two distances can be added together:

$$16cm + 4cm = 20 \text{ cm or } 0.2m$$

$$w = F/d$$

$$w = 60 / 0.2$$

$$w = 300N$$

Reference: *BMAT Assumed Subject Knowledge Guide:* Forces and Energy: Work Done

5)   The correct answer is 0.32 A

Current can be calculated using the equation:

$$I = Q/t$$

The charge of one ion is 1.6×10^{-19}, and there are 10^{18} ions moving towards the cathode (or anode) each second:

$$1.6 \times 10^{-19} \times 10^{18} = 0.16 \text{ for one ion}$$

The rate for both the hydrogen and the chloride ions are needed therefore the charge for one ion must be multiplied by 2:

$$0.16 \times 2$$

$$= 0.32 \text{ or } 3.2 \times 10^{-1}A$$

Reference: *BMAT Assumed Subject Knowledge Guide:* Electricity: Current and Electricity

6)   The correct answer is E

To exhale, the air must be squeezed out of the lungs. Therefore, the thoracic cavity (Z) must reduce its volume, or increase the pressure on the lungs, thus ruling out options C and D. The ribs and intercostal muscles (X) and the diaphragm (Y) move inwards towards the spine and upwards in order to assist the thoracic cavity in reducing its volume. Therefore both of these muscles need to relax, making E the correct choice.

Reference: *BMAT Assumed Subject Knowledge Guide:* Organs and Systems: The Breathing System.

7)   **The correct answers are:**
i)   **E**
ii)   **B**
iii)   **A**
iv)   **C**

Ionic compounds have both high melting and boiling points and can conduct electricity when they are molten therefore A is an ionic compound (iii)

Metals are good conductors regardless of whether they are in a solid or liquid state. They also have low melting points, therefore B is a metal (ii).

'Liquid at room temperature' (around 20ᵒC) infers that the substance must melt at a temperature lower than this. Consequently, C is a liquid at room temperature (iii)

Option D does not match any of the properties of the listed substances and is therefore the odd one out.

Giant molecular structures have very high melting and boiling points, which makes E an inorganic substance (iv)

Reference: *BMAT Assumed Subject Knowledge Guide:* Classifying materials: Ionic Bonding; The Alkali Metals; Covalent Substances

8)   **The correct answer is E (WO_3)**
Work out the percentage of oxygen for this compound:

$$100 - 79.31 = 20.69\%$$

Divide the percentage for each element by its Ar

Tungsten (W)	Oxygen (O)
79.31/184 = 0.43	20.69/16 = 1.29

Multiply this value by 10 and then divide by 4

| 0.43 x 10 = 4.3 | 1.29 x 10 = 12.9 |
| 4.3/4 = 1.075 | 12.9/4 = 3.225 |

Round to the nearest whole number to get the ratio:

| 1 | 3 |

Therefore the empirical formula is WO_3

Reference: *BMAT Assumed Subject Knowledge Guide:* Equations and Calculations: Empirical Formulas and Molar Volume

9)   The correct answer is 7.2m

A change in speed is also known as acceleration. Therefore the first step is to use the equation:

$$a = (v - u)/t$$

v-u is sometimes represented as delta v. g= 10 N/kg is another way of referring to acceleration downwards. Therefore this value can be used as a substitute for a:

$$10 = (0-12) /t$$

Rearranged to find t this is:

$$t= (0-12)/10$$

$$t = 1.2 \text{ s}$$

This value can now be used to calculate the balls highest point (or displacement) using the equation:

$$d = \frac{\Delta v \; x \; t}{2}$$

$$d = 1.2 \text{x} 12/2$$

$$d = 7.2 \text{m}$$

Reference: *BMAT Assumed Subject Knowledge Guide:* Forces and Energy: Speed and velocity; Acceleration

10)   The correct answer is A and B

Begin by examining each of the angles and identifying which are alternate, allied or corresponding: alpha + gamma are allied angles so they will add up to 180°. This means that alpha + theta are also allied angles (u or c shape) and = 180°. Therefore Cos alpha and – Cos theta are equal making A correct. Sketching the graph to check, will verify the answer:

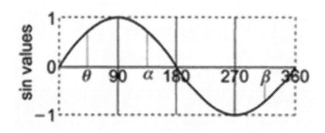

Theta and gamma are alternate angles (they form a Z shape), and as a result, they are equal. Consequently, theta and beta must also be equal, making B correct and C false. Since:

$$a + \theta = 180 \ and \sin 180 = 0$$

(from the graph below) then it can also be determined that D is false.

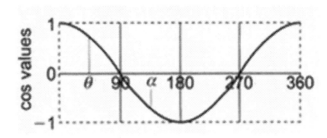

Reference: *BMAT Assumed Subject Knowledge Guide:* Geometry and Measures: Parallel Lines; Geometry Problems

11)   The correct answer is B (Reduction)

Converting pyruvic acid (CH_3COCO_2H) to lactic acid ($CH_3CH (OH) CO2H$) requires the addition of hydrogen from NADH when it becomes NAD^+ (meaning that it loses the hydrogen which pyruvic acid then gains). This conversion is an example of a reduction reaction.

12)   The correct answer is D (4,5,8,9)

The recessive condition is located on the X chromosome of the grandfather. Consequently, he can only pass the condition on to his female offspring since this is the only time he contributes his X chromosome to his offspring. In light of this, individuals four and five will have the defective allele as they are female. The male offspring, however, inherit their X chromosome from their mother, which means none of them will inherit the recessive X linked condition from their father.

Females have two different X chromosomes that they can contribute to their offspring (one maternal and one paternal). Therefore each time they have a child irrespective of gender, there is a chance that the affected X chromosome will be passed on. As a result, there is a chance that individuals eight and nine could also be affected.

Reference: *BMAT Assumed Subject Knowledge Guide:* Genes, Reproduction and Evolution: X and Y chromosomes; More on Genetic Disorders.

13)   The correct answer is D (x > 2 or x < -4)

$$x^2 > 8-2x$$

Make the inequality = to zero

$$x^2 + 2x - 8 = 0$$

As is a quadratic inequality, it needs to be factorised:

$$(x+4)(x-2) = 0$$

Make each set of brackets = 0 and solve:

$$X + 4 = 0 \text{ therefore } X = -4$$

$$X - 2 = 0 \text{ therefore } X = 2$$
(Option D)

Reference: *BMAT Assumed Subject Knowledge Guide:* Algebra: Inequalities; Factorising

14) **The correct answer is D (The mass of an ammonia molecule is less than that of a hydrogen chloride molecule.)**

This experiment is an example of the diffusion rates of two gases. The point at which the white ring appears shows where the gases have met. Hence, the ammonia has travelled a greater distance than the hydrogen chloride (hydrochloric acid). This is because molecules which are denser (heavier) will move a lot slower than molecules which are less dense. Denser molecules have a greater mass than those which are less dense; therefore their movement is much more gradual.

15) **The correct answers are:**
i)   **False**
ii)   **False**
iii)   **True**
iv)   **False**
v)   **False**

In circuit one, the voltmeter and the bulb are in parallel, meaning the voltage stays the same regardless of whether S1 is open or closed. Therefore statement i) is false.

In circuit two, closing S3 will create a short circuit as it is a path with no resistance. In this case, all of the current will flow through the top part of the circuit, meaning that the readings on the ammeters will decrease, making statement ii) also false.

Circuit three creates a parallel circuit which means that the current has two paths through which it can travel. Assuming that the light-bulbs are the same, the current will split, some moving through the lower circuit, and some through the upper circuit. The current will then converge (add) together before entering A_2, making statement iii) true.

In circuit four, closing the switch S_2 means that the A_3 is still in series with A_2. Therefore, the current will not decrease, making statement iv) false.

In circuit five, the reading on A_2 will decrease as closing S_3 creates a short circuit. Therefore, the current will take the path of least resistance through this loop instead of the other two paths containing the light-bulbs, making statement v) false.

Reference: *BMAT Assumed Subject Knowledge Guide*: Electricity: Series Circuits; Parallel Circuits

16)   The correct answer is B (27/64)
There is ¼ probability that someone will have a disability/long-term illness overall. Therefore the probabilities should be multiplied for each person in the group of three.
If there is ¼ probability that a person is affected, then there will be ¾ chance that they will be unaffected. Therefore for the three people:

$$¼ \times ¾ \times ¾ = 9/64$$

Each person has the same chance so the number is multiplied by three which gives the answer 27/64.

17)   The correct answer is D (900N)
Resistance is equal to the weight force and can, therefore, be calculated using the equation:

$$W = mg$$

$$w = 90 \times 10$$

$$w = 900 \text{ N}$$

Reference: *BMAT Assumed Subject Knowledge Guide:* Forces and Energy: Terminal Velocity

18)   The correct answer is D ($C_nH_{2n+3}N$)
Amines are classified according to the number of carbon atoms bonded directly to the nitrogen atom. A primary (1°) amine has one alkyl (aryl) group on the nitrogen atom.

19)   The correct answers are A, D & E
Ova and sperm (also known as gametes) have half the number of chromosomes as somatic (body) cells due to meiosis. Therefore they will have 23 chromosomes, with one of those being either X or Y.
The female (XX) parent produces the ova and can only contribute one or other of her X chromosomes; therefore A is the only normal ovum in the diagram. The female does not have a Y chromosome to contribute. Hence B and C are abnormal. The male (XY) parent can provide either an X OR Y chromosome to the offspring. Therefore sperm D and E are normal and option F is abnormal.

Reference: *BMAT Assumed Subject Knowledge Guide:* Genes, Reproduction and Evolution: Cell Division - Meiosis

20)   The correct answer is C (Q^2R/t)
The main equation used to calculate electrical power is: $P = VI$ making option D incorrect.

Options B and E can also be excluded as voltage is equal $I \times R$ and therefore can be substituted into the $P = VI$ equation to get $P = V^2/R$ or I^2R. Furthermore, $P = E/t$ which is the same as $P = Q V/t$, therefore, option A can also be used to calculate power. Thus the correct answer is C.

Reference: *BMAT Assumed Subject Knowledge Guide:* Electricity: Current and Electricity; Potential Difference

21)   The correct answer is D (Hepatic Portal Vein)
To identify the right answer, the structure of the circulatory system and to what each vessel is attached needs to be considered. Both the anterior (superior) vena cava and the aorta connect directly to the heart at one end. Therefore options A and B can be ruled out. The hepatic artery joins the aorta to the liver also excluding option C. The renal vein connects the kidney to the inferior vena cava to return blood to the heart, making option E is also incorrect. Option D is correct as the hepatic portal vein carries blood from the gastrointestinal tract, gallbladder, pancreas and spleen to the liver which all contain capillary beds.

22)   The correct answer is F
In alpha decay, two protons and two neutrons are lost making the atomic number decrease by two and the mass number decrease by four.
In beta decay, a neutron splits into a proton and an electron causing the atomic number to increase by one and the atomic mass to remain unchanged.
In the first decay, the atomic number has increased by one, and the mass number is still the same. Therefore this is a beta decay which rules out options A, B, and C.
In the second decay, the atomic number has decreased by two. To move from +1 to -1 on a number line, two must be subtracted, ruling out option D. In an alpha decay the atomic mass decreases by four (ruling out option E) therefore the value of x must be A – 4, making option F correct.

Reference: *BMAT Assumed Subject Knowledge Guide:* The Atom and Radioactivity: Ionising Radiation

23)   The correct answer is E (water, oxygen, carbon monoxide)
Oxygen can displace the water; thus water is weaker than oxygen, ruling out options B and C. Oxygen can be displaced by carbon monoxide, so it must be weaker than carbon monoxide but stronger than water ruling out options A and F.

24)   The correct answer is C
Muscles operate in pairs; when one contracts the other must relax. In the diagram, the quadriceps (R) must contract to straighten the leg, while its partner, the hamstring (P) must relax, which rules out options A, and B. The

calf or gastrocnemius (T) muscle must also contract while its partner the foot flexors (S) relax so that the foot can straighten out to push off the block thus ruling out D and E.

25)   **The correct answer is D**

$$T = 2\pi \frac{\sqrt{(k^2 + h^2)}}{gh}$$

Square both sides to remove the square root, the 2π becomes $4\pi^2$ since it is separate from the square root.

$$T^2 = 4\pi^2 \frac{(k^2 + h^2)}{gh}$$

Remove the fraction by multiplying both sides by gh

$$T^2 gh = 4\pi^2 (k^2 + h^2$$

Divide both sides by $4\pi^2$

$$\frac{T^2 gh}{4\pi^2} = k^2 + h^2$$

Subtract h² from both sides

$$\frac{T^2 gh}{4\pi^2} - h^2 = k^2$$

Remove the square by square rooting both sides:

$$k = \frac{\sqrt{T^2 gh - h^2}}{4\pi^2}$$

Therefore the correct answer is D.

Reference: *BMAT Assumed Subject Knowledge Guide*: Algebra: Rearranging formula

26)   **The correct answers are:**
i.   **Mitosis**
ii.   **Mitosis and meiosis**
iii.   **Meiosis**
iv.   **Meiosis**
v.   **Mitosis and meiosis**

In mitosis, the DNA coils up and become visible as chromosomes (v) before being replicated or copied (ii) the cell then divides into two identical daughter cells (i).

In meiosis, the DNA coils up and becomes visible as chromosomes (v) before being replicated (ii). They then line up along the equator and split into two daughter cells; this process then repeats, this time with no replication so that the resulting cells (called gametes iii) are haploid (iv).

Reference: *BMAT Assumed Subject Knowledge Guide:* Cell division – Mitosis; Cell division – Meiosis.

27) **The correct answer is C ($x^2 - 7x + 9 = 0$)**

A quadratic equation suggests x^2

The sum of the roots is 7 means: $7x$

The product of the roots is 9, meaning that this is the number on the end of the equation. Roots are the opposite signs of the numbers which means that it cannot be option A or D since these have the same sign for both. A positive root needs to either have two negative numbers for the product (since two negatives give a positive value) or two positive values for the product (this option has already been ruled out). Therefore the best answer is C.

Reference: *BMAT Assumed Subject Knowledge Guide:* Factorising quadratic equations

BMAT Section 2 - 2005

1) **The correct answer is A**

A.   Represents the tidal volume which is the movement of the air into and out of the lungs in one normal breath. Breathing in (inspiration) is shown as an upward trend on the graph while breathing out (expiration) appears as a downward trend.

B.   Represents the vital capacity of the individual, where the individual has exhaled the greatest volume of air by inhaling deeply.

C.   Represents the inspiration reserve volume – this is the average amount of air that can be inhaled (drawn into the lungs) after a typical inspiration in a healthy individual.

D.   Represents the expiratory reserve volume, the maximum volume of air exhaled from the lungs after one breath

E.   Represents the inspiration capacity, the total amount of air which can be inhaled (taken into the lungs) after a normal expiration.

2) **The correct answer is B (burning splint)**

A burning splint will be extinguished in carbon dioxide as it suffocates the flame. In the presence of hydrogen, a squeaky pop noise will be heard. The splint will need to be glowing (not alight) to test for oxygen. In the presence of oxygen, the flame will relight.

Reference: *BMAT Assumed Subject Knowledge Guide:* Chemical Analysis and Electrolysis: Flame Tests and Gas Tests

3) **The correct answer is D (four protons)**

Calculate the difference between the atomic (top) numbers

$$^{238}U - (^{95}Sr + ^{139}Xe) = 4 \text{ neutrons}$$

Therefore there are four neutrons emitted in this decay.

Reference: *BMAT Assumed Subject Knowledge Guide:* The Atom and Radioactivity: Ionising Radiation

4) **The correct answer is C (r and q)**

When resistors are connected in parallel, the current in the branches of a parallel circuit adds up to the supply current. Any components in parallel have the same potential difference across them:

$$R_{total} = 1/R_p + 1/R_r$$

Resistors in series are added together

$$R_{total} = R_p + R_q$$

To make current flow through the ammeter, the least possible resistance is needed which means that r would be 1/900 and q would also be 1/900

Reference *BMAT Assumed Subject Knowledge Guide:* Electricity: Series Circuits and Parallel Circuits

5)   The correct answer is D (Smoke particles cause coughing that can rupture alveoli)
Smoke is a known lung irritant; this irritation causes inflammation and damages the walls of the alveoli over time. As the alveoli are progressively damaged, they become weak and eventually rupture.

6)   The correct answer is C (2×10^9)
Substitute the numbers into the equation:

$$z = xy^2$$

$$1.2 \times 10^{13} = 3.0 \times 10^{-6} \, y^2$$

Rearrange the equation to find y^2:

$$y^2 = 1.2 \times 10^{13} / 3 \times 10^{-6}$$

$$y^2 = 4 \times 10^{18}$$

7)   The correct answer is A (oxidation and decomposition)
      The pyruvic acid (3C) enters the mitochondrial matrix where it is oxidised (2H are removed), and one molecule of carbon dioxide is lost. Glucose breaking into two molecules of pyruvic acid is considered decomposition as the molecule is breaking into two smaller molecules.

8)   The correct answer is A
A heterozygous individual can contribute both dominant and recessive alleles (long and short eyelashes) to their offspring while expressing the dominant trait of long eyelashes. This immediately rules out individuals B and D as they both have short eyelashes. Individual A has offspring with both short (individuals B and D) and long eyelashes (individual C) on the pedigree chart and therefore can be considered heterozygous. Individual E could also be heterozygous. However, the chance of this occurring is much less, as they only have one offspring, with long eyelashes.

Reference: *BMAT Assumed Subject Knowledge Guide:* Genes, Reproduction and Evolution: Genetic Diagrams; More on Genetic Disorders

9) **The correct answer is C (49% decrease)**

If B increases by 40%, that is the same as multiplying B by 1.4, the new equation then becomes:

$$A \propto 1/(B^2)(1.4^2) - \text{since B is increasing by 40\%}$$

$$= A \propto 1/(B^2 \times 1.96)$$

Therefore A has been multiplied by 1/1.96 when B is increased by 40%

$$1/(B^2) - 1/(B^2)(1.96) = 1/(B^2)(1-1/1.96)$$

The [1-1/1.96] = 0.49 which is the value that A has decreased, so this number must be multiplied by 100 to get 49% giving answer C

Reference: *BMAT Assumed Subject Knowledge Guide:* Numbers: Compound Growth and Decay

10) **The correct answer is 40cm**

In order for the 2 loads to be balanced (anticlockwise and clockwise movements must be equal)

$$800N \times 0.1 \text{ m} = 80Nm$$

$$80Nm = 200N \times d$$

$$80/200 = 0.4m \text{ (or 40cm)}$$

11) **The correct answer is D**

The molecular formula for Sodium Carbonate Decahydrate is $Na_2CO_3.10H_2O$
The Mr for the whole compound:

$$(23\times2) +12+ (13\times16) + (1 \times 20) = 286$$

The Mr for water $10H_2O$:

$$((10\times1) \times2) + (10 \times 160) = 180$$

To obtain a percentage x 100, so the final equation is:

$$\frac{180 \times 100}{(46+12+48+180)}$$

Reference: *BMAT Assumed Subject Knowledge Guide:* Equations and Calculations: Formula Mass Calculations

12)   The correct answer is B
The ciliary muscles relax which expands the space around the lens. The lens then thins, and the curvature decreases (less convex) and the suspensory ligaments tighten or stretch.

13)   The correct answer is A ($(by^2 + a^2)^{1/2} - a = x$)
Square both sides to remove brackets:

$$(Y^2)^{1/2} = (x + 2ax)/b$$

Remove fractions by multiplying both sides by b:

$$(by^2)^{1/2} = x + 2ax$$

Subtract 2ax from both sides

$$(by^2)^{1/2} - 2ax = x$$

Divide by 2x on both sides

$$(by^2)^{1/2} - a /2x = x /2x$$

$$(by^2)^{1/2} - a = x /2x$$

$$(by^2 + a^2)^{1/2} - a = x$$

Reference: *BMAT Assumed Subject Knowledge Guide:* Algebra: Algebra basics; Manipulating Surds; Solving Equations

14)   The correct answer is B (0.4ms)
Rearrange s= v x t to find t

$$t = s/v$$

$$t = 0.1/500$$

$$t = 0.0002$$

Multiply t by 2 (since the sound travels there and back):

$$t = 0.0002 \times 2 = 0.0004 \text{ (or } 0.4\text{ms)}$$

Reference: *BMAT Assumed Subject Knowledge Guide:* Other Applications of Physics: Ultrasound

15) **The correct answer is D (6z > x +3y)**

There is 1 N-N bond = x

There are 3 x H-H bonds = 3y

There are 2 x 3N-H bonds which = 6z

Therefore the answer is:
$$6z > x + 3y$$

Reference: *BMAT Assumed Subject Knowledge Guide:* Reaction Rates and Energy Changes: Bond Energies

16) **The correct answers are**
i.   **D**
ii.   **C**
iii.   **G**

D= tendons attach muscles to bones.
C = Ligaments connect two bones together.
G =Antagonistic muscles work in the opposite direction, so when one contracts the other relaxes.

17) **The correct answer is A (9)**
Evaluate means solve:

$$(\sqrt{5} - \sqrt{2})^2 \, (\sqrt{5} + \sqrt{2})^2$$

$$(2.24 - 1.41)^2 \, (2.24 + 1.41)^2$$

$$0.83^2 \, x \, 3.65^2$$

$$= 9.1 \text{ (9 rounded, therefore answer A is correct)}$$

18) **The correct answer is B (2.13x10⁹ years)**

The ratio of U: Pb is 1:7 which means that it has had three half-lives and would contain 87.5% Pb, therefore:

$$7.1 \times 10^8 \times 3 = 2.13 \times 10^9$$

Reference: *BMAT Assumed Subject Knowledge Guide:* The atom and radioactivity: Half-Life

19)   The correct answer is B (90)

$$50 cm^3/1000 = 0.05 dm^3$$

To find the mol of NaOH used:

$$2 \ mol/dm^3 \times 0.05 dm = 0.1 \ mol \ of \ NaOH$$

The mole ratio of H_2X to 2NaOH = 1:2. Therefore:

$$0.1/2 = 0.05 \ mol \ H_2X$$

Rearrange the equation:

$$Number \ of \ moles = \frac{mass \ (g)}{relative \ formula \ mass}$$

$$4.5/0.05 = 90 \ moles$$

Reference: *BMAT Assumed Subject Knowledge Guide:* Equations and Calculations: Relative Formula Mass

20)   The correct answer is C (magnesium ions from cell L to cell K)
Oxygen, as well as glucose, is required for cellular respiration inside a cell. Therefore both are necessary.

Reference: *BMAT Assumed Subject Knowledge Guide:* Cells and Cell Processes: Movement across Cells

21)   The correct answer is A

$$Area \ of \ semi-circle = \frac{\pi r^2}{2}$$

$$Area \ of \ equilateral \ triangle = \frac{\sqrt{3}}{4 \ x^2}$$

Add the two areas together

$$\frac{\sqrt{3}}{4x^2} + \left(\frac{\pi r^2}{2}\right)$$

$$R = 1/2x$$

Therefore:

$$\frac{\sqrt{3}}{4x^2} + \left(\frac{\frac{\pi 1}{2x^2}}{2}\right)$$

Multiply by 2 to remove /2:

$$\sqrt{3}x^2 + \left(\frac{\pi 1}{2x^2}\right)/8$$

Extract common x^2 value:

$$x^2\sqrt{3} + \left(\frac{\pi 1}{2}\right)/8$$

Simplify:

$$\frac{x^2(2\sqrt{3} + \pi)}{\cdot\ 8}$$

Reference: *BMAT Assumed Subject Knowledge Guide:* Pythagoras and Trigonometry: Pythagoras Theorem; Trigonometry Sin, Cos, Tan

22)   The correct answer is D (10.0 m/s)
Use the equations:

$$E_p = mgh$$

$$E_k = 1/2mv^2$$

Using g =10 for earth and 2.5 for other planet:

$$Ep = 1x\ 10\ x20 = 50$$

Ep is completely converted to Ek therefore Ek also = 50
Rearrange and solve Ek=1/2mv² to find v:

$$50 = \frac{1}{2} \times 1 \times v^2$$

$$50 \times 2 = v^2$$

$$100 = v^2$$

$$\sqrt{100} = v$$

$$V = 10 m/s$$

Reference: *BMAT Assumed Subject Knowledge Guide:* Forces and Energy: Kinetic Energy; Gravitational Potential Energy

23)   The correct answer is A (C_4H_9D)
Mr for C_4 =48
For C_4 to be 80% of the sample the Mr = 60 (48/0.8)
Remaining amount leftover for H: D ratio = 12 which therefore answer B is correct

24)   The correct answer is A (Blood in the aorta would not be fully oxygenated)
In the foetal heart, the foramen ovale allows the blood to travel from the right to left atrium without entering the pulmonary circuit. By remaining open, a small amount of blood is still able to move between the two atria, without being oxygenated. This results in blood in the aorta not being entirely oxygenated.

25)   The correct answer is B (4N)

$$P = F/A$$

Calculate P first if 760 mm Hg to be 1.0 atmosphere which is 100 kPa.
Substitute in the numbers.

$$P = 152/760 \times 100 = 20 \text{ kPa, } P = 20,000 \text{ Pa}$$

$$\text{Area} = 2.0 cm^2 / 1000 = 0.0002 \ m^2.$$

Substitute into equation

$$F = PA$$

$$F = 20,000 \times 0.0002,$$

$$F = 4N$$

26)   **The correct answer is D ($Na_2O \rightarrow 2Na + \frac{1}{2} O_2$)**

PbO_2 requires temperatures above 600°C to decompose thermally. The further down the reactivity series, the higher the temperature needed to decompose a metal thermally. Lead is also a transition metal, so it holds onto its electrons tightly and requires more energy to break the bonds in PbO_2.

27)   **The correct answer is 0.8**

$$a^2 + b^2 = c^2$$

$$12^2 + B^2 = 20^2$$

$$x = \sqrt{20^2 - 12^2}$$

$$= 16cm$$

$$A/H = 16/20$$

$$= 0.8$$

Reference: *BMAT Assumed Subject Knowledge Guide:* Pythagoras and Trigonometry: Pythagoras Theorem; Trigonometry Sin, Cos, Tan

BMAT Section 2- 2006

1)   The correct answer is E (3 and 5)
Insulin causes glucose to be taken up by the cells and stored as glycogen. Therefore, when there are higher insulin levels, the mass of glycogen will increase, and when there are low levels, the mass of glycogen will decrease. As a result, periods three and five of the graph correlate with low concentrations of insulin in the blood.

2)   The correct answer is C (the solubility in water)
The presence of a covalent bond and lack of electrical conductivity indicates this is not an ionic compound. Solubility is not usually a property associated with covalently bonded compounds but may occur if the products are soluble. This type of molecule normally contains a highly electronegative atom to interact with water molecules via H-bonds.

Reference: *BMAT Assumed Subject Knowledge Guide:* Classifying Materials: Covalent Substances

3)   The correct answer is F (28×10^{20})
After one half-life, half of the atoms of the radioisotope will remain.
In this case, the half-life is four years, therefore after eight years, only 25% of the original sample will remain. Assuming that the decay produces a 1:1 ratio of atoms X to atoms Y, then the number of atoms of Y produced by the decay of X can be calculated.
If 25% of X remains after eight years, there will be 8×10^{20} atoms of X remaining.
To work out the difference in X over the eight-year period:

$$32 \times 10^{20} - 8 \times 10^{20} = 24 \times 10^{20}$$

This means that 24×10^{20} of isotope X has been converted to Y.

To find the amount of Y present after eight years the starting amount of Y + increase in Y = current amount of Y.

$$4 \times 10^{20} + 24 \times 10^{20} = 28 \times 10^{20}$$

Reference: *BMAT Assumed Subject Knowledge Guide:* The Atom and Radioactivity: Half-Life

4)   The correct answer is B (see sequence)
The body retains water when it is dehydrated. This means that the blood contains a lower ratio of water than usual. Consequently, the levels of ADH will increase to stimulate the nephron to reabsorb more water, resulting in less water being excreted in the urine. As a result, the urine will become more concentrated.

Reference: *BMAT Assumed Subject Knowledge Guide:* Nerves, Hormones and Homeostasis: Controlling Water Content

5)   The correct answer is C (2, 7)

The most reactive non-metal is the element fluorine (this is the highest and furthest right of the non-metals, excluding the inert 'noble gases'). Fluorine's atomic number, atomic radius and electron shielding make it the most reactive and electronegative non-metal on the periodic table. It has an electronic configuration of 2, 7 since it is located in period two, group seven.

Reference: *BMAT Assumed Subject Knowledge Guide:* Classifying Materials: Group 17 – The Halogens

6)   The correct answer is A (-1/4)

It may help to draw out the triangle for this question.

First, rearrange the equation to get cos(A) on its own.

This becomes:

$$a^2 - b^2 - c^2 = -2bc \cos(A)$$

This can be rearranged to:

$$\cos(A) = (a^2 - b^2 - c^2)/-2bc$$

Inputting the given values gives:

$$\cos(A) = (16-9-4)/-12$$

$$\cos(A) = 3/-12$$

$$\cos(A) = -1/4$$

7)   The correct answer is A (2 only)

Microwaves are an electromagnetic wave, meaning that their oscillations are transverse, not longitudinal (such as sound waves) and as a result, statement one does not apply to microwaves.

However, all electromagnetic waves travel at the speed of light through air and can move through a vacuum (sound waves travel at ~300m/s and cannot travel in a vacuum where there are no particles). Therefore statement two is applicable and statement five is not applicable. Sound waves, not electromagnetic waves (which are ionising, to varying degrees) are used in pre-natal scanning, therefore statement three does not apply. Infra-red waves, not microwaves, are used in thermal imaging; making statement four is not applicable.

Reference: *BMAT Assumed Subject Knowledge Guide:* Waves and their Effects: Microwaves

8)   The correct answer is C (13/256)

165 is the upper quartile, meaning that a person has 25% or ¼ chance of having a heart rate above that and 75% or ¾ chance of not having a heart rate above 165.

Out of four people, if three people will have their heart rate above 165, and the first person is one with the chance of not having a heart rate above 165:

$$= 3/4 \times 1/4 \times 1/4 \times 1/4 = 3/256$$

Out of four people, if three people will have their heart rate above 165, and the second person is one with the chance of not having a heart rate above 165:

$$= 1/4 \times 3/4 \times 1/4 \times 1/4 = 3/256$$

Out of four people, if three people will have their heart rate above 165, and the third person is one with the chance of not having a heart rate above 165

$$= 1/4 \times 1/4 \times 3/4 \times 1/4 = 3/256$$

Out of four people, if three people will have their heart rate above 165, and the last person is one with the chance of not having a heart rate above 165:

$$= 1/4 \times 1/4 \times 1/4 \times 3/4 = 3/256$$

The question asks about at least three people, so the chance that all four people have a heart rate above 165 needs also to be considered:

$$(1/4) = 1/4 \times 1/4 \times 1/4 \times 1/4 = 1/256$$

Therefore the total probability:

$$= (3/4 \times 1/4 \times 1/4 \times 1/4) + (1/4 \times 3/4 \times 1/4 \times 1/4) + (1/4 \times 1/4 \times 3/4 \times 1/4) + (1/4 \times 1/4 \times 1/4 \times 3/4) + (1/4 \times 1/4 \times 1/4 \times 1/4)$$

$$= 3/256 + 3/256 + 3/256 + 3/256 + 1/256$$

$$= 13/256$$

9)   The correct answer is B (2 and 3 only)

Adding more ammonia will push the equilibrium in favour of the forward reaction, increase the amount of NH_4Cl produced and consequently the yield. Therefore statement two is correct. A catalyst does not change the equilibrium; instead, it speeds up the reaction process and thus reduces the time taken to reach equilibrium. Therefore statement one is incorrect. As the right-hand side is a solid and the left-hand side are gases, increasing the pressure will drive the reaction forward increasing the yield (based on the molar ratio of reactants and products), so statement three is correct. This is an exothermic reaction and so increasing the temperature would drive the equilibrium in favour of the formation of reactants, therefore reducing the yield and making statement four incorrect.

Reference: *BMAT Assumed Subject Knowledge Guide:* Reaction Rates and Energy Changes: Changing Equilibrium

10)   The correct answer is D (67%)
Drawing a Punnett square for this equation will assist with finding the answer. The result would be 25% CC, 25% Cc, 25% cC and 25% cc.
The provided numbers exhibit the expected ratio of 3:1.
The Punnett square reveals that 2/3 of the plants will be heterozygous Cc or cC, while 1/3 will be homozygous CC. Therefore the percentage of heterozygous is 66.6% (rounded to 67%).

Reference: *BMAT Assumed Subject Knowledge Guide:* Genes, Reproduction and Evolution: More on Genetic Disorders

11)   The correct answer is C ($3N/cm^2$)

$$P = F/A$$

The pressure applied by each piston will be the same, while the area the force is being exerted on will change. This means the force applied must also change proportionately.
As the pressure will remain the same, the pressure transmitted to Y will be $3N/cm^2$.

12)   The correct answer is E ($\sum d^2 = (1-r) \times (n^3 - n)/6$)
First, add and subtract to get 1 on the same side as r:

$$(6\sum d^2)/n \times (n^2-1) = 1-r$$

Then multiply both sides by $n (n^2 - 1)$:

$$6\sum d^2 = (1 - r) \times n \times (n^2 - 1)$$

Then divide both sides by 6:

$$\sum d^2 = (1-r) \times n \times (n^2 - 1)/6$$

Then n outside the bracket can then be brought into the bracket to give E.

$$\sum d^2 = (1-r) \times (n^3 - n)/6$$

13)   The correct answer is B (15.5g)

The Mr of potassium hydrogen carbonate is:

$$39 + 1 + 12 + (16 \times 3) = 100$$

To obtain the number of moles of potassium hydrogen carbonate, use the equation:

$$Number\ of\ moles = \frac{mass\ (g)}{relative\ formula\ mass}$$

$$50g/100 = 0.5\ moles\ of\ 2KHCO_3$$

The equation shows 2:1 molar ratio; therefore the decomposition will produce 0.25 moles of K_2CO_3, The Mr of K_2CO_3:

$$(39 \times 2) + 12 + (16 \times 3) = 138$$

Once again using the same equation number of moles = mass (g) / Mr rearranged to find mass (g):

$$0.25 \times 138 = 34.5g$$

This give the mass of solid product produced (the CO_2 and water would not be factored in as they are gases). Finally, the loss in mass can be calculated:

$$50 - 34.5 = 15.5$$

Reference: *BMAT Assumed Subject Knowledge Guide:* Equations and Calculations: Relative Formula Mass

14)   The correct answer is x = 3 and y = 1
Rearrange the bottom equation for 'y' and then input it into the above equation to work out 'x', then solve for 'y' and check both values work for both equations.

$$Y = 2x - 5$$

$$Y^2 = 4x^2 - 20x + 25$$

Input into the above equation:

$$4x^2 + 4x^2 - 20x + 25 + 20x - 50 = 47$$

$$8x^2 - 25 = 47$$

$$8x^2 = 72$$

$$X^2 = 9$$

$$X = -3 \text{ or } 3.$$

X must be positive therefore x = 3.

$$2x - 5 = y$$

$$6 - 5 = y$$

$$Y = 1$$

Reference: *BMAT Assumed Subject Knowledge Guide:* Algebra: Simultaneous Equations

15)   The correct answer is E (see table)

Arrow two will contain the highest concentration of glucose as a significant amount of glucose will have been absorbed in the stomach and intestines and will travel to the liver for storage as glycogen.

The highest concentration of urea will occur in arrow three, as the liver will have converted excess amino acids from the meal (which, unlike glucose, cannot be stored) to ammonium ions and urea for excretion.

The lowest concentration of oxygen will also occur in vessel three as oxygen will have been used by the liver to oxidise excess amino acids.

16)   The correct answer is 2ms^{-2}

The formula required for this question is:

$$F = m\,a$$

First, the net force must be calculated. The total upwards force on the mass =

$$120 \times 2 = 240 \text{ N}$$

The total downwards force on the mass =

$$20 \times 10 = 200$$

Therefore net force = 240-200 = 40 N upwards

As the mass is 20kg and the force applied is 40, the acceleration will be:

$$40 = 20 \times a$$

$$40/20 = a$$

$$a = 2\text{ms}^{-2}$$

Reference: *BMAT Assumed Subject Knowledge Guide:* Forces and Energy: Forces and Acceleration

17)   The correct answer is E (4 only)

The element with an atomic number of 20 and mass number of 40 is calcium. Mass number is another term used for relative mass (the number of protons and neutrons) since this is 40 for calcium, statement one is incorrect. Calcium is a group two earth metal, not a noble gas which are found in group 18 of the periodic table. Therefore statement two is incorrect. As a metal, with two electrons in its valence shell, calcium will lose these electrons to form a 2^+ ion, making statement three also incorrect. Calcium is located on the left-hand side of the table, making it a metal and hence making statement five false.

Reference: *BMAT Assumed Subject Knowledge Guide:* Classifying Materials: The Periodic Table

18)   The correct answer is C (1.4dm³)

$500cm^3$ of air 14 times a minute means the student is breathing $7000cm^3$ of air per minute = $7dm^3$.
Over four minutes this will be $28dm^3$ every four minutes.
The amount of oxygen absorbed is the percentage of inhaled air – the percentage of exhaled air = 21% - 16% = 5%

$$5\% \text{ of the } 28dm^3 = 0.05 \times 28 = 1.4dm^3$$

19)   The correct answer is C (see table)

When light levels are lowering, the pupils expand or dilate to allow more light to enter the eye. The circular muscles of the iris also relax while the radial muscles contract.

20)   The correct answer is E (V_3, V_1, V_2)

The voltage across two components in a parallel circuit is identical (voltage is the energy per charge carrier). Therefore:

$$R_1 \times 2 = R_2 + 1/(1/(2 \times R_3))$$

$$R_1 \times 2 = R_2 + 2R_3$$

Therefore R_3 must have the smallest resistance, R_1 must have the next largest, and R_2 must have the largest resistance.
Therefore the potential difference across each resistor must go in increasing order:

$$V_3, V_1, V_2$$

Reference: *BMAT Assumed Subject Knowledge Guide:* Electricity: Parallel Circuits

21) **The correct answer is 9**

Evaluate is another way of saying "solve." To solve this, BIDMAS needs to be used

To the power of 1/5 means the '5th root':

$$32^{1/5} = 2$$

Anything to the power of 0 = 1 - $81^{3/4}$ means the '4th root' of $81^3 = 3^3 = 27$

$$2 + 1/27 = 1/9$$

1/9 to the power of -1 = is the reciprocal of 1/9 = 9.

22) **The correct answer is D (X shows the route taken without a catalyst, V + W is the activation energy and V (the heat of reaction) has a positive sign)**

The reaction is endothermic. As the energy profile of the reaction increases; the heat is taken in from its surroundings. Hence the products have more energy than the reactants.

A catalyst reduces the activation energy required. Therefore Y demonstrates the energetic route taken in the presence of a catalyst.

The activation energy is the energy required to 'kick-start' the reaction. In this situation, it is W + V. Negative reaction energy (endothermic) has a positive sign while an exothermic reaction has a negative sign (loss of energy to the surroundings). This is an endothermic reaction and so would have a positive sign.

Reference: *BMAT Assumed Subject Knowledge Guide:* Reaction Rates and Energy Changes: Energy Transfer in Reactions; Energy

23) **The correct answer is C**

As the wavelength has stayed the same, the frequency of the light must also remain the same otherwise the colour of the light would change. The equation for the frequency of light is

$$f = c/\lambda$$

Blue light refracts more than red light, so the parallel component of its direction will be less than that of red light and therefore so will its speed: <2/3c.

Reference: *BMAT Assumed Subject Knowledge Guide:* Waves and their Effects: Wave Properties in Action

24) **The correct answer is E (1, 4 and 6 only)**

Aerobic respiration results in the complete oxidation of glucose, while anaerobic does not – aerobic always produces more energy per mole of glucose. Therefore statement one is correct.

Anaerobic respiration causes an oxygen debt to occur as there is an absence of oxygen, thus making statement two incorrect. The waste products of aerobic respiration are CO_2 and water, thereby making statement three also incorrect.

Statement four is correct because reabsorption requires active transport of molecules across barriers. Active transport also requires energy and so reduced aerobic respiration will limit the active uptake of mineral ions. When there is little oxygen, low rates of aerobic respiration occur as well as anaerobic respiration as it is more energy efficient. Therefore, statement five is incorrect. Statement six is correct because lactic acid is the only waste product formed during anaerobic respiration.

Reference: *BMAT Assumed Subject Knowledge Guide:* Cells and Cell Processes: Aerobic Respiration: Anaerobic Respiration in Animals

25) **The correct answer is B ($2p \rightarrow 2n + 2e^+$)**

In the last stage, when two 3He atoms are combined, the resulting atom is 4He. There are six protons in the reactants, but only four protons in the products and two neutrons. Therefore two protons have been converted to two neutrons and two positively charged electrons have been produced to account for the loss in positive charge.

26) **The correct answer is A (6)**

First turn the statement into proportionality:

$$a \propto 1\sqrt{b}$$

Substitute $a = 9$ and $b = 4$ into the above proportionality

$$9 \propto 1\sqrt{4}$$

If the increase is inversely proportional then

$$9/4 = x/16$$

Solve for x

$$144/4 = x$$

$$x = 36$$

Since a is inversely proportional to the square of b:

$$\sqrt{36}$$

$$b = 6.$$

Reference: *BMAT Assumed Subject Knowledge Guide:* Algebra: Direct and Inverse Proportion

27)   The correct answer is 5 seconds

If the surface area is $0.04m^2$, the charge needed for discharge would be:

$$0.04 \times 0.25 = 0.01$$

The rate of charge is 2mA = 0.002 C/s. Therefore:

$$0.01/0.002 = 5s.$$

Reference: *BMAT Assumed Subject Knowledge Guide:* Electricity: Current and Electricity

BMAT Section 2 - 2007

1)   The correct answer is B

Structure A is the afferent arteriole, B is the proximal convoluted tubule, C is the loop of Henle, D is the efferent arteriole and E is the collecting tubule. The nephron removes water, glucose, amino acids and other materials at the Bowman's capsule (proteins are too large to pass through the capillary walls), and reabsorbs water and many of these solutes later along the loop of Henle. This means that the concentration of substances is very low just after the Bowman's capsule, with high amounts of water.

Reference: *BMAT Assumed Subject Knowledge Guide:* Nerves, Hormones and Homeostasis: Kidney Function

2)   The correct answer is B (Elements X and Y have the same number of electrons in the first shell)

Element X is in the second row of the periodic table, which has eight elements. The question has not revealed in which group element X is located. Therefore it cannot be determined if element Y is in the same row. For example: if element X is in the 6th column (group) of the period, element Y would be in the following period, and thus have another orbital. As a result of this, statement A may or may not be correct, so it can be ruled out.

The groups (columns) along these rows represent the number of electrons in the atoms outer shell. Group two elements have two electrons, while group 8 have eight in their outer shell. Therefore elements X and Y would have a different number of electrons in their outer shell. However, shells fill from the inside first, and so the inner shell would be full. The innermost shell can house two electrons maximum and so elements X and Y would have the same number of electrons. Therefore statement B is correct.

As is the case for statement A, it is uncertain whether if Y is in the same period as element X (in which case it would have six more electrons in its outer shell) or not (in which case it would not). In light of this, statement C can be considered incorrect.

The nucleon number is the total number of protons and neutrons. The question reveals that element Y has six more protons that element X, but it would also have more neutrons, meaning the total number of protons and neutrons would be more than 6 of that of element X. Therefore statement D can be considered incorrect as well.

Reference: *BMAT Assumed Subject Knowledge Guide:* Chemical Concepts: The Periodic Table

3)   The answer is a= 220 and b =40

Alpha particles are much more ionising than beta particles and travel a much shorter distance in air because they are large and slow moving. They can be blocked by a thin sheet of paper while beta particles pass straight through. Therefore to find out the counts per minute caused by alpha and beta radiation, the background radiation must be subtracted first.

20 counts per minute (cpm) were caused by background radiation

40 (60-20) were caused by beta radiation (beta radiation can pass through paper)

220 (280 – 60) were created by alpha radiation.

Reference: *BMAT Assumed Subject Knowledge Guide:* The Atom and Radioactivity: Ionising Radiation

4)   The correct answer is A (10% decrease)
Increasing x and y by 50% is another way of saying that both have been multiplied by 1.5.
This means that $1.5^2 = 2.25x$ that of the original.

A decrease of 20% of this value means 80% remains

$$2.25 \times 0.8 = 1.8x \text{ the original value}$$

If P is doubled, then the original value is divided by twice as much, meaning the new value is now half of what it was

$$1.8/2 = 0.9x \text{ the original value.}$$

Q does not change, and so this is the final percentage of the original value.

$$\text{Therefore } 1 - 0.9 = 0.1 \text{ (or 10% decrease)}$$

5)   The correct answer is E (1 and 3 only)
As the volume of air in the chest cavity decreases, the ribs move down and inwards to replace this space, making statement one correct. Statement two is incorrect as exhaling causes the diaphragm muscles to relax.
The pressure in the lungs increases during exhalation – this is due to the difference in air pressure causing the air to be 'pushed' out the lungs. During inhalation, pressure decreases to produce an inflow of air due to the difference between internal and external air pressure. Therefore statement three is also correct.

Reference: *BMAT Assumed Subject Knowledge Guide:* Organs and Systems: The Breathing System

6)   The correct answer is A (W= nr⁴gt²/ 8πlR² –w/3)
Start by dividing both sides of the equation by 2π giving:

$$t/2\pi = \sqrt{(2lR^2(W+w/3)/n\pi r^4 g)}$$

Then square both sides to get rid of the right hand square root.

$$t^2/4\pi^2 = 2lR^2(W+w/3)/n\pi r^4 g$$

Multiply both sides by $n\pi r^4 g$

$$n\pi r^4 g\, t^2 /4\pi^2 = 2lR^2(W+w/3)$$

$$= nr^4 g\, t^2 /4\pi = 2lR^2(W+w/3)$$

201

Divide by $2lR^2$

$$= nr^4gt^2/8\pi lR^2 = W+w/3$$

Subtract $w/3$

$$= nr^4gt^2/8\pi lR^2 - w/3 = W$$

Reference: *BMAT Assumed Subject Knowledge Guide:* Rearranging Formulas: Powers and Roots; Algebraic Fractions

7) **The correct answer is 300 Turns**

$$\text{Power} = \text{voltage} \times \text{current}$$

Where current = 10A and Power = 0.5kW

The kilowatts need to first be converted into Watts before being used in the above equation:

$$0.5 \times 1000 = 500W$$

Rearrange the equation P = VI to find V:

$$V = P/I$$

Substitute the numbers into the above equation:

$$500/10 = 50V$$

The number of turns can be found using the equation:

$$\frac{coils\ on\ primary}{coils\ on\ secondary} = \frac{voltage\ on\ primary}{voltage\ on\ secondary}$$

$$1500/x = 250/50$$

$$1500/x = 5$$

$$x = 300$$

Reference: *BMAT Assumed Subject Knowledge Guide:* Electricity: Transformers

8) **The correct answer is B (1/3)**

The total negative charge from the oxide ion is (-2 x 4) = -8.

The compound has three Fe ions adding a positive charge of +8. These must be made up of both +3 and +2. Hence there is only one combination of Fe^{+3} and Fe^{+2} that combine to give a total charge of +8. This combination is two Fe^{+3} and one Fe^{+2}.

Therefore 1 / 3 of the Fe ions are in the 2+ state.

Reference: *BMAT Assumed Subject Knowledge Guide:* Classifying Compounds: Ions; Formulas of Ionic Compounds

9) **The correct answer is B**

Blood enters the right side of the heart in a deoxygenated state. From here, it is pumped to the lungs, before returning to the left side of the heart to be pumped around the body.

The semilunar valves allow blood to leave the respective sides of the heart and the atrioventricular valves allow blood to enter the left and right chambers of the heart. This stage is known as systole.

When the heart is pumping blood to the lungs, the right atrioventricular valve must be closed to avoid backflow of blood while the semilunar valve must be open to allow blood flow to the lungs. This eliminates options A, C, E, and F immediately. The situation is the same in the left side of the heart - the atrioventricular valve must be closed while the semilunar valve must be open to pump blood around the body. This eliminates option D and leaves option B as the correct answer.

Reference: *BMAT Assumed Subject Knowledge Guide:* Organs and Systems: The Circulatory System - Heart

10) **The correct answer is D**

The concentrations and volumes that contain the largest number of moles of reactants need to be calculated using the equation:

$$number\ of\ moles\ =\ concentration\ x\ volume.$$

Therefore for option:

A: 0.005 x 2 = 0.01

B: 0.0025 x 5 = 0.0125

C: 0.0075 x 3 = 0.0225

D: 0.005 x 4 = 0.02

This will produce the most substantial number of moles of products and the highest precipitate.

As the reactants are in a 1:2 molar ratio, the number of moles needs to be multiplied by 2 giving the following molar ratios:

A: 0.01:0.02

B: 0.0125:0.0125

C: 0.0225:0.025

D: 0.02: 0.0375

As a result, the largest number of moles can be created from solution combination D

Reference: *BMAT Assumed Subject Knowledge Guide:* Chemical Analysis and Electrolysis: Titration Calculations

11) The correct answer is E (all of the statements)

Temperature is a measure of the average kinetic energy of a substance. As heat energy is a form of energy and temperature is a measure of this energy, it is possible for a substance to lose heat energy without its temperature falling. Therefore statement one is correct.

Heat energy is transferred by radiation which can occur in a vacuum, making statement two also correct.

Steam has more energy than water at 100°C because of the energy required to overcome the hydrogen bonds holding the water molecules together. This is called the latent heat of vaporisation and makes statement three also correct.

Convection currents form as a result of water cooling, becoming more dense and falling to the bottom of the container. Warm water at the bottom of the container rises as it becomes less dense and takes the place of the cool water creating a current. Therefore statement four is also correct.

Reference: *BMAT Assumed Subject Knowledge Guide:* Heat and Energy: Heat and Temperature

12) The correct answer is E (1/64)

850 is the median value – 50% of the group will have walked more steps than this.
1000 is the upper quartile value. 75% of the data will be lower than this.
Therefore 25% of the members walked between 850 and 1000 steps. This means that each of the three members will have a 25% chance of having taken between 850 and 1000 steps:
0.25^3 is 1/64.

Reference: *BMAT Assumed Subject Knowledge Guide:* Statistics and Probability: Averages and Spread; Box Plots

13) The correct answer is C (The load is between the fulcrum and the effort)

The fulcrum, in this case, is the toes against the ground. The calf is exerting the effort, and so, the load (on the ankle) is between the fulcrum and the effort.

14) The correct answer is A (caesium and fluorine)

Elements in the lower periods of group one are more reactive due to the distance of the outer (valence) electron and the ease of losing this electron during a reaction. In contrast, elements in the higher periods of group seven are the most reactive due to the proximity of the outer electron shell and the stronger electron attraction experienced. Therefore the most reactive reaction would be between caesium and fluorine.

Reference: *BMAT Assumed Subject Knowledge Guide:* Classifying Materials: Group 1 – The Alkali Metals; Group 17 – The Halogens

15) The correct answer is B

Violet light has a higher level of energy, which refracts more than red light. The transition from water to an air medium causes the light to bend away from the normal, making B is the correct answer.

Reference: *BMAT Assumed Subject Knowledge Guide:* Waves and their Effects: Wave Properties in Action

16) The correct answer is C (1, 6)

Option A (-1, -6) does not satisfy the first equation as y is smaller than $x^2 + 3$
Option B (2, -1) also does not satisfy this equation for the same reason (-1 is not bigger than $2^2 + 3$)
Option C (1, 6) does satisfy the first equation, and 1 is greater than 1/6. Therefore, it also satisfies the second equation.
Option D (2, 2) again does not satisfy the first equation.

Reference: *BMAT Assumed Subject Knowledge Guide:* Algebra: Graphical Inequalities

17) The correct answer is D (4 and 8)

NPS must be a recessive gene in order for the third generation male to have NPS.
Individuals three and four must be heterozygous, as they would both need to contribute a recessive allele to produce a child with NPS. This same argument can be applied to individuals one and two, since they also have a child with NPS, but are themselves are unaffected by the condition. Individuals eight and nine must also be heterozygous as they have a parent who is affected, meaning that he could only contribute recessive alleles to his offspring. A dominant allele from the other parent would imply that individuals eight and nine are carriers of NPS and not affected.

Reference: *BMAT Assumed Subject Knowledge Guide:* Genes, Reproduction and Evolution: More on Genetic Disorders

18) The correct answer is D (8000 cm³)

The Ar of H_2O:

$$1 + 1 + 16 = 18$$

Mass = 6g so:

$$umber\ of\ moles = \frac{mass\ (g)}{relative\ formula\ mass}$$

$6/18 = 1/3$ moles of water

As 1 mole of gas takes up 24 dm cubed, the steam will take up:

$24dm^3 \times 1000 = 24000$

$24000/3\ cm^3 = 8000\ cm^3$

Reference: *BMAT Assumed Subject Knowledge Guide:* Equations and Calculations: Relative Formula Mass; Empirical Formula and Molar Volume

19)   The correct answer is 700N

Total moments about the pivot must be equal in equilibrium. 'w' = the weight of the bar

$1.5 \times 1000 = 4.5 \times 100 + 1.5 \times \text{'w'}$

$1500 = 450 + 1.5w$

$1.5w = 1050$

$w = 700N$

20)   The correct answer is A (2√3)

$$a^2 = c^2 - b^2$$

$$a = \sqrt{(36 + 5 - 9 - 20)}$$

$$= \sqrt{(12)}$$

$$= 2\sqrt{3}$$

Reference: *BMAT Assumed Subject Knowledge Guide:* Pythagoras and Trigonometry: Pythagoras Theorem

21)   The correct answer is E

Platelets are responsible for clotting blood. If the platelet level is low, the body will find it challenging to form blood clots and hence be unable to control bleeding. This eliminates options C, D and F as possible correct answers. White blood cells are integral to a person's immunity to disease. A high percentage of abnormal white blood cells will compromise the body's immune system, and they will, therefore, have a lower disease resistance. Thus, option B can also be ruled out. Red blood cells are responsible for the transport of oxygen. Since the question does not explicitly mention oxygen transport, it can be assumed that these are at a normal level, making E the correct answer.

Reference: *BMAT Assumed Subject Knowledge Guide:* Organs and Systems: The Circulatory System - Blood

22)   The correct answer is D (1, 3 and 6)

Statement one gives the right formula for ammonia. Statement two is incorrect as ammonia is slightly basic therefore the pH will be more than 7. Ammonia is a molecule and will, thus, have a molecular structure, making statement three correct. As it is slightly basic, it will turn damp red litmus paper blue (not the other way around), making statement four false. At room temperature ammonia is a gas; therefore statement five is also false. Nitrogen forms three covalent bonds, one with each of its hydrogen atoms, making statement six correct.

Reference: *BMAT Assumed Subject Knowledge Guide:* Classifying Materials: More Covalent Bonding

23)   The correct answer is E ($VT/x \times 10^3$)

An artery is cylindrical in shape. Therefore volume of a cylinder = cross-sectional area x length can be used. Multiplying the volume per second of blood flow V by the time taken for the blood to flow T would provide the volume of the length of the artery.

The volume must be multiplied by 1000 as 1 ml is equal to 1000 mm^3.

Dividing this volume by the length of the cylinder would give the cross-sectional area of the cylinder in mm squared.

Reference: *BMAT Assumed Subject Knowledge Guide:* Geometry and Measures: Volume

24)   The correct answer is A

The cylinder's volume is calculated by multiplying the cross-sectional area by the length, l.

$$= l\pi r^2$$

The hemisphere's volume is calculated by:

$$(4\pi \times r^2/3)/2$$

Therefore collating these two equations together produces:

$$l\pi \times r^2 + 2\pi\ r^3/3$$

The bracket (2r + 3l) can be taken out of this equation to produce:

$$\pi \times r^2/3 \times (2r + 3l)$$

Reference: *BMAT Assumed Subject Knowledge Guide:* Geometry and Measures: Volume

25)   The correct answer is A (83°C and 68°C)

The temperature of the liquid must be sufficient to cause hexane to boil (higher than 68°C) but less than the boiling point of heptane (98 °C) to provide successful distillation.

The temperature at the top of the flask must be equal to that of the boiling point of hexane (68°C) for hexane to condense.

26)   The correct answer is C

Increased levels of oestrogen are involved in the release of the egg from the ovary (ovulation). This coincides with the initiation of the thickening of the lining of the uterus, to receive the fertilised egg. Therefore option A can be ruled out. Oestrogen levels decline, once ovulation has occurred, thus ruling out option D. Progesterone levels remain high to maintain the uterine lining and nourish the fertilised egg. Hence options B, E and F can also be excluded. If the egg is not fertilised, the progesterone concentrations fall, causing the lining to break down and bleeding to commence, making option C the correct answer.

27)   The correct answer is D (1 and 2)

A beta particle consists of the emission of a high-speed electron following the decay of a neutron to a proton and an electron. In contrast, gamma radiation is the emission of a high energy wave (alpha is the emission of a helium nucleus). As beta decay would increase the atomic number of the atom statement one is correct.

Gamma radiation is highly penetrating and so would be able to pass through the patient's tissue to an internal tumour. However, it would not only attack the tumour but all the healthy cells in its flight path as well, making statement two correct and statement three incorrect.

Reference: *BMAT Assumed Subject Knowledge Guide:* The Atom and Radioactivity: Ionising Radiation

BMAT Section 2 - 2008

1)   The correct answer is D (reabsorption of glucose in the kidney tubules)
All options apart from D involve a positive concentration gradient and therefore indicate a passive form of transport. The reabsorption of glucose from the kidney occurs against the concentration gradient (active transport) and is thus the correct answer.

Reference: *BMAT Assumed Subject Knowledge Guide:* Nerves, Hormones and Homeostasis: Kidney Function

2)   The correct answer is C
Y^{3-} has gained three electrons and the configuration = 2, 8, 8. Under normal circumstances, it has a configuration of 2, 8, 5 meaning it is located in group five and period three.

Reference: *BMAT Assumed Subject Knowledge Guide:* Classifying Materials: The Periodic Table

3)   The correct answer is B
Isotope X decays into Y. This means that every 20 seconds the mass of Y will increase. However, as X decays, every 20 seconds, and the amount that Y increases by halves. This means that while the amount of Y continues to increase, the mass accumulated will slow down and level off over time. Therefore, the answer is graph B.

4)   The correct answer is D (4.5×10^{-1})

$$r^2 = 9 \times 10^{-6}$$

$$2r^2 = 1.8 \times 10^{-5}$$

$$2r^2t = 1.8 \times 10^{-5} \times 2.5 \times 10^4$$

$$P = 4.5 \times 10^{-1}$$

5)   The correct answer is C (33%)
Mice which are heterozygous will have the genotype Mm:

	M	m
M	MM	Mm
m	mM	mm

Mm crossed with Mm gives ¼ with MM; 2/4 with Mm; and ¼ with mm. Mice with homozygous recessive combination die, leaving three mice in the ratio = 1:2. Consequently, 33% are homozygous dominant

Reference: *BMAT Assumed Subject Knowledge Guide:* Genes, Reproduction and Evolution: More on Genetic Disorders

6)   The correct answer is E ($a = 2$, $b = 16$, $x = 8$, $y = 5$)

aKMnO$_4$ + bHCl → aKCl + aMnCl$_2$ + xH$_2$O + yCl$_2$

Count up the numbers of each atom on the right and left sides of the equation to identify which elements require balancing:

	Left	Right
K	1	1
Mn	1	1
O	4	1
H	1	2
Cl	1	5

The first atom to consider is chlorine, which has an uneven number of atoms on the left and right-hand side of the equation. This means a does not equal 1, as it must be an even number to make the number of chlorine atoms on the right side an even number. This immediately rules out options A, B and C. Upon ruling this out, $b = 16$ is also revealed, making the equation:

2KMnO$_4$ + 16HCl → 2KCl + 2MnCl$_2$ + xH$_2$O + yCl$_2$

	Left	Right
K	2	2
Mn	2	2
O	8	1
H	16	2
Cl	16	8

The next atom which requires balancing is oxygen, with eight atoms on the left and one atom on the ride side of the equation. It can be assumed that $x = 8$, making the oxygen atoms on both sides of the equation balanced. As a result, the number of hydrogen atoms changes to 16 (8 x 2 = 8), which is also balanced:

2KMnO$_4$ + 16HCl → 2KCl + 2MnCl$_2$ + 8H$_2$O + yCl$_2$

	Left	Right
K	2	2
Mn	2	2
O	8	8

H	16	16
Cl	16	8

The final step is to return to the chlorine atoms on the right-hand side of the equation, which can be balanced by when y = 5. Therefore the correct answer is E

Reference: *BMAT Assumed Subject Knowledge Guide:* Chemical Concepts: Balancing Equations

7)   The correct answer is B (1/(n+2)(n+1))

$$(n+1)/(n+2) - n/(n+1)$$

$$= 1/(n+2)(n+1)$$

Reference: *BMAT Assumed Subject Knowledge Guide:* Algebra: Sequences

8)   The correct answer is A (1 only)
The height lifted:
$$= 0.4 \times 5 = 2m.$$

Gravitational Potential Energy can be calculated using the equation = mass x gravity x height:

$$=100 \times 10 \times 2 = 2000J$$

This makes statement one correct.
Statement two is incorrect as the tension is equal to the weight:

$$100 \times 10 = 1000N$$

Statement three is also incorrect as there is no acceleration since the object is moving at a constant speed, which means acceleration = 0 ms^{-2}

Reference: *BMAT Assumed Subject Knowledge Guide:* Forces and Energy: Gravitational Potential Energy

9)   The correct answer is D (Both anaerobic and aerobic respiration are taking place)
Between 0 and 11 seconds, the oxygen demand exceeds the oxygen supply. When this occurs, the muscle cells use the oxygen that is available for aerobic respiration but must gain the extra energy required from anaerobic respiration, so both forms of respiration occur.

Reference: *BMAT Assumed Subject Knowledge Guide:* Cells and Cell Processes: Aerobic Respiration; Anaerobic Respiration in Animals

10)   The correct answer is C (C_6H_{16})

C_6H_{16} is not a reasonable product – even if a carbon atom molecule were fully saturated, it would only have 14 hydrogen atoms attached

11)   The correct answer is D (4 only)

Beta decay involves the changing of a neutron into a proton and a high-energy electron. It is this electron that leaves the atom, rather than the valence electron. Therefore statements one, two and three are incorrect. Statement four is correct because mass number = protons + neutrons. If a neutron is converted into a proton, the mass number is unchanged.

Reference: *BMAT Assumed Subject Knowledge Guide:* The Atom and Radioactivity: Ionising Radiation

12)   The correct answer is E

The breakdown of lipids into fatty acids would lower the pH. Likewise, protein breakdown gives amino acids also lowering pH. Carbohydrates molecules are broken down into sugars such as glucose, which does not affect pH. Therefore E is the correct answer.

Reference: *BMAT Assumed Subject Knowledge Guide:* Organs and Systems: The Digestive Systems - Enzymes

13)   The correct answer is D (2 followed by 5)

This is a transformation and can be achieved in the following ways: 270 degrees anticlockwise; 90 degrees clockwise. The answer must be D as although a direction has not been provided (clockwise or anticlockwise), the total of angles in D = 270 and so D is the most appropriate answer

Reference: *BMAT Assumed Subject Knowledge Guide:* Geometry and Measures: The Four Transformations

14)   The correct answer is D (Decreasing temperature)

Adding a catalyst does not change the equilibrium. Therefore option A is incorrect.
Decreasing pressure will cause the equilibrium to increase it, producing more carbon monoxide making option B also incorrect.
Decreasing temperature favours exothermic reactions, as the equilibrium will move to produce more heat, which will remove more carbon monoxide, which makes option D correct.
Adding nitrogen will cause the equilibrium to shift in the opposite position. Hence option E is also incorrect.

Reference: *BMAT Assumed Subject Knowledge Guide:* Reaction Rates and Energy Changes: Changing Equilibrium

15)   The correct answer is F

Graph Z reflects *weight* as it remains constant and is indicated by the horizontal line. Y is velocity or drag force, which increases as the car increases in speed. X can be acceleration or resultant force. Thus, the only possible combination is F

Reference: *BMAT Assumed Subject Knowledge Guide:* Forces and Energy: Forces and Acceleration

16) **The correct answer is A (9 − √6)**

$$Area\ of\ a\ triangle\ =\ ½\ base\ x\ height$$

$$= ½\ (4\text{-}√6)\ x\ (6\text{+}√6)$$

$$= 9\ \text{-}√6$$

Reference: *BMAT Assumed Subject Knowledge Guide:* Geometry and Measures: Area

17) **The correct answer is B**
The correct pathway is stimulus-receptor-CNS-muscles-response, which is B.

Reference: *BMAT Assumed Subject Knowledge Guide:* Nerves, Hormones and Homeostasis: Neurons

18) **The correct answer is F ($C_{n+1}H_{2n+3}ON$)**
The general formula for an alkane is C_nH_{2n+2}. To find the general formula for the amide hydrogen must be removed and replaced with $CONH_2$. Therefore the formula must reflect the net addition of 1 C, 1O, 1N, and 1H.

This makes the total formula $C_{n+1}H_{2n+3}ON$ - answer F.

19) **The correct answer is C (10 cos θ)**
A bearing is a clockwise angle from North. Draw a diagram which has the angle θ from the original position, go 5km north, and the new bearing is 2θ. This will create an isosceles triangle where with two angles in the triangle as angle θ, one side as 5 and one side as x. By drawing a line from the side x to make 2 right-angled triangles, then

$$x/2 = 5\cos\theta$$

therefore x = 10 cos θ

Reference: *BMAT Assumed Subject Knowledge Guide:* Geometry and Measures: Bearings

20) **The correct answer is F**

Closing the switch forces all current via the path of least resistance and the 12V will be divided between X and Z resistors. Making the resistance in Z:

$$12 / 2 = 6V$$

As a result, the current in X increases by a factor of 1.5, as the current is travelling through two resistors as opposed to three. This makes the current at resistor X:

$$20 \times 1.5 = 30mA.$$

Therefore the correct answer is F.

Reference: *BMAT Assumed Subject Knowledge Guide:* Electricity: Series Circuits

21) **The correct answer is B (1 and 3 only)**
In double circulation, one complete circuit means that blood goes through the heart twice making statement one right.
Lungs receive 100% of the CO (cardiac output) whereas the kidney receives less making statement two incorrect. Statement three is correct as the blood must first go through the lungs to be oxygenated. Statement four is incorrect as blood is received from the hepatic artery which branches off from the abdominal aorta.

Reference: *BMAT Assumed Subject Knowledge Guide:* Organs and Systems: The Circulatory System – Heart

22) **The correct answer is D (They all react with O_2 to give the same products)**
A is incorrect as there are strong covalent bonds between the atoms in all three allotropes.
In graphite, carbon is only bonded to three other carbon atoms making statement B incorrect.
Graphite conducts electricity, which is a physical property. This is in contrast to diamond and buckminster fullerene which are electrical insulators. This fact rules out statement C and E, leaving statement D as the correct answer.

Reference: *BMAT Assumed Subject Knowledge Guide:* Classifying Materials: Covalent Structures

23) **Correct answer is C ($mv^2/2f$)**

$$E_k = 1/2mv^2$$

And

$$Work\ Done = Fd$$

Therefore Work done = KE

$$d = 1/2mv^2$$

$$d = mv^2/2F$$

Reference: *BMAT Assumed Subject Knowledge Guide:* Forces and Energy: Kinetic Energy

24) The correct answer is A ($x^2 + 5x + 3 = 0$)

Quadratic equations follow the format: $ax^2 + bx + c = 0$

The products must add to make: -5. This is represented by the term -b therefore making b = 5

The products multiply to make 3, so c = 3

Reference: *BMAT Assumed Subject Knowledge Guide:* Algebra: Factorising Quadratics

25) The correct answer is D (Mother and daughter)

The man received the Y allele from his father and got the colour blindness X allele from his mother, which means she must at least carry the recessive allele. Males only have one X chromosome which is contributed to all their female offspring. As a result, the affected X chromosome passed onto all of this man's female offspring, making D the correct answer.

Reference: *BMAT Assumed Subject Knowledge Guide:* Genes, Reproduction and Evolution: Genetic Disorders; More on Genetic Disorders

26) The correct answer is C (39)

First, the volume of sulfuric acid must be converted to dm^3:

$$12.5/1000 = 0.0125 \ dm^3$$

$$Number\ of\ moles\ =\ volume\ used \times concentration$$

$$0.0125 \times 2 = 0.025 \text{ moles of sulfuric acid}$$

The ratio of XOH: H_2SO_4 = 2:1 so:

$$0.025 \times 2 = 0.05 \text{ moles of XOH}$$

$$Number\ of\ moles = \frac{mass\ (g)}{relative\ formula\ mass}$$

$$2.8/0.05 = 56 \text{ (Mr of XOH)}$$

Known Ar values are H = 1 O = 16

$$56 - 16 - 1 = Mr\ of\ X$$

$$Therefore,\ X = 39$$

Reference: *BMAT Assumed Subject Knowledge Guide:* Chemical Analysis and Electrolysis; Equations and Calculations: Relative Formula Mass

27) **The correct answer is C (480m)**

Sound through steel distance s and time t.

Sound through air - distance s and time t + 1.5.

The distances are constant so:

$$t\ (1.5) \times 300 = t \times 4800$$

$$300t + 450 = 4800t$$

$$4500t = 450$$

$$t = 0.1$$

$$Distance = 4800m/s \times 0.1 = 480m.$$

Reference: *BMAT Assumed Subject Knowledge Guide:* Waves and Their Effects: Wave Basics

BMAT Section 2 - 2009

1) The correct answer is C

A is homozygous dominant so can be denoted by AA and as B is recessive can be represented by aa. The progeny will be as follows:

	A	A
A	Aa	Aa
A	Aa	Aa

Therefore all the progeny are Aa

If E is homozygous recessive, then the progeny (F) can be as follows:

	A	a
A	Aa	aa
A	Aa	aa

Therefore it can be seen the probability of F being recessive is 2/4 or 50%.

If E is heterozygous, then the table is shown below

	A	a
A	AA	Aa
A	Aa	aa

Therefore the probability of being homozygous recessive is ¼ or 25%.

This makes the answer C.

Reference: *BMAT Assumed Subject Knowledge Guide:* Genes, Reproduction and Evolution: Genetic Diagrams

2) The correct answer is E (2,4 and 5)

Molecules lacking double bonds cannot take part in an addition reaction. In light of this, C_nH_{2n+2} can be eliminated. The hydrogen atom can be replaced by other elements, but the general formula still applies. If there are 2n+2 other atoms not including carbon, then these are excluded.

If the compound can be represented by C_nH_{2n} using the same principles as above, then it is eligible. This shows that compounds 2,4 and 5 can take part. Therefore E is the correct answer.

Reference: *BMAT Assumed Subject Knowledge Guide:* Carbon Chemistry: Alkenes

3) The correct answer is C (5.0 upwards)

The equation required is:

Force = mass x acceleration

$$900 - 600 = 300N$$

As there is a net force upwards, it means the acceleration is upwards. Rearranging the force equation, acceleration is force/mass:

$$300/60 = 5ms^{-2}$$
(Option C)

Reference: *BMAT Assumed Subject Knowledge Guide:* Forces and Energy: Forces and Acceleration

4)   The correct answer is C (xy/(x+y+z)2)

The balls are being replaced, so the denominator (x+y+z) when finding out the probability will remain the same. To find out the probability of two independent events, each is multiplied:

Therefore the probability is:

$$\frac{xx}{x+y+z}\frac{y}{x+y+z} = \frac{xy}{(x+y+z)^2}$$

(Option C)

Reference: *BMAT Assumed Subject Knowledge Guide:* Statistics and Probability: The AND/OR Rules

5)   The correct answer is E

Statement A is false because, after birth, the environment affects the phenotype of an individual, changing their features by the time of maturation.

Multiple births can involve multiple eggs in the womb which are fertilised, not necessarily the traditional idea of a twin which is a natural clone. If there were to be separate eggs in the same womb this would mean a multiple birth but the children would have different genetics meaning statement B is also incorrect.

Certain species of plants reproduce naturally by cloning; hence statement C is also false.

Statement D is false because clones do not contain mutations, their DNA is identical.

In a clone the DNA gets replicated which is what makes them identical. Therefore statement E is correct.

Reference: *BMAT Assumed Subject Knowledge Guide:* Genes, Reproduction and Evolution: Cell Division - Mitosis

6)   The correct answer is B

All the other structures except option B have simple covalent structures which can be drawn out. Silicon dioxide, graphite and diamond are all examples of giant covalent structures.

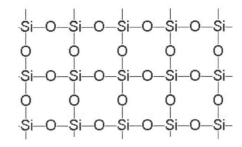

The structure above shows silicon dioxide. It is hard at room temperature with very high melting and boiling points.

Reference: *BMAT Assumed Subject Knowledge Guide:* Classifying Materials: Covalent Substances

7) **The correct answer is E**

$$Power = current \; x \; voltage$$

Therefore voltage is equal to power/current. As power is measured in watts and current is measured in Amperes, then this means the units would be watt per amp or E.

Reference: *BMAT Assumed Subject Knowledge Guide:* Electricity: Power Ratings

8) **The correct answer is B**
The distance between the midpoint and the vertex must be found to complete the triangle. Both the sides will be ½, so the hypotenuse can be found using Pythagoras' theorem which is $a^2 + b^2 = c^2$.

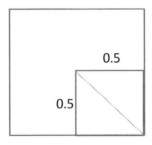

$$0.5^2 + 0.5^2 = 0.25 + 0.25 = 0.5$$

$$0.5 = c^2 \text{ so c (hypotenuse) is equal to the square root of } 0.5.$$

Now another triangle must be used to find the dotted line. One side is known as the square root of 0.5, and the other is 1 (the vertical line). Therefore c^2 here is:

$$(\sqrt{0.5})^2 + 1^2 = 3/2 \text{ so } c = \sqrt{3}/2 =$$
$$\text{(Option B)}$$

Reference: *BMAT Assumed Subject Knowledge Guide:* Pythagoras and Trigonometry: Pythagoras' Theorem

9)   The correct answer is D

Statement A is correct as the table shows that for both light and heavy drinkers, the presence of mutations causes the risk to increase. A positive correlation can also be seen between risk and alcohol intake, therefore statement B is also correct.

For a light drinker, the risk increases by 0.5 when going from having 0 to 1 mutant allele. From 1 to 2 mutant alleles the risk increases by 0.3, giving a total of 1.8. However, when considering a heavy drinker, the risk at 0 mutations is already four times higher than that of a light drinker (4.0) and more than double the risk of a light drinker with two mutant alleles.

This shows clearly that drinking causes more risk than having more mutations (At least until 2) and thus makes statement C correct.

A light drinker with 2 mutations has a risk value of 1.8 compared to 6 for a heavy drinker with 2 mutations. 6 is greater than 1.8, therefore, statement E is correct.

Statement D is incorrect because the table shows an increase in risk value by 0.5 (for 1 mutation) for both heavy and light drinkers. However, having 0 mutations but being a heavy drinker increases the risk by 3 compared to having no mutations and being a light drinker. In view of this, a risk value of 3 is greater than 0.5, showing drinking would be the primary factor and not the number of mutations.

10)   The correct answer is E (65%)

$$Mass = Moles \, x \, Relative \, formula \, mass$$

Therefore the number of moles of carbon dioxide is:

$$4.77/44 = 0.1089$$

With combustion of carbon compounds, there is the same number of moles of the compound and carbon dioxide.

$$CH_{4(g)} + 2O_{2(g)} \rightarrow 2H_2O_{(l)} + CO_{2(g)}$$

Above is an example, to show the molar ratios.
The mass of carbon can be calculated:

$$0.1089... \, x \, 12 = 1.3g$$

As a percentage this is:

$$(1.3/2) \, x100 \approx 65\%$$
$$(Option \, E)$$

Reference: *BMAT Assumed Subject Knowledge Guide*: Equations and Calculations: Relative Formula Mass

11)   The correct answer is C

To identify the type of radiation, the properties of each type must be considered. Alpha particles are the least penetrative and can be stopped by a few centimetres of air. They would not reach the 30cm distance to detector one and give no reading thus options A and B can be excluded. Conversely, gamma rays can only be stopped by concrete/metal, with air having no effect. It would, therefore, be expected that the radiation would reach detector two, and decrease as appropriate with time. However, detector two shows a straight line so options E and F can also be excluded. This leaves options C and D, both of which are beta radiation.

The beta particles are not reaching detector two, if they were, the graph would show a curve, and instead, the graph shows the background radiation (with a value of 20). Therefore this needs to be subtracted from the count:

$$220 - 20 = 200$$

$$200 / 2 = 100$$

From here the background radiation needs to be added in again:

$$100 + 20 = 120 \text{ counts}$$

Therefore the value on the graph corresponding to 120 counts per minute is 2.4 hours - option C.

Reference: *BMAT Assumed Subject Knowledge Guide:* The Atom and Radioactivity: Ionising Radiation; Half-Life

12)   The correct answer is C (32/9)

$$y \lozenge x = y^x / X$$

This shows that the symbol will involve division as well as the first number to the power of the second number.

$$y^x / x = \lozenge$$

This means that:

$$2 \lozenge 3 = 2^3 / 3 = 8/3$$

$$8/3 \lozenge 2$$

$$(8/3)^2 / 2$$

$$64/9 / 2$$

$$= 39/2$$
(Option C)

13)   The correct answer is B

When the oxygen concentration in the blood becomes low, the body tries to compensate by diverting blood away from non-essential organs. Both statements A and C involve the lungs so these will be compensated and the hypoxia will not affect them immediately, ruling out both of these options. Statements D and F involve the kidneys. These processes do not involve oxygen; instead, they involve the osmotic and oncotic pressures across the nephron. This means that they are independent of a drop in oxygen, making these options incorrect. Statement E requires osmosis which again does not involve oxygen or blood; therefore it can also be excluded. Statement B is correct as the blood is diverted away from the intestine. This will mean less oxygen is available and hence less energy to transport glucose across the intestinal wall.

Reference: *BMAT Assumed Subject Knowledge Guide:* Cells and Cell Processes: Osmosis

14)   The correct answer is B

The reaction will only take place if the element on its own is more reactive than the element already in the compound, essentially making this a displacement reaction. From here it can easily be seen that only options two, three and four fulfil this requirement making the correct answer B.

15)   The correct answer is D

To find the distance, the area under the graph must be calculated. The middle section of the graph has a constant velocity. It lasts for 3 minutes (or 180 seconds). There is a constant velocity of 20 m/s, so the distance for this period would be:

$$180 \times 20 = 3600 \text{ metres}$$

For the first part of the graph, the area of the rectangle can be worked out, and the area of the triangle overhang subtracted. This gives:

$$(60 \times 20) - (0.5 \times 60 \times (20\text{-}15)) = 1200 - 150 = 1050 \text{ metres.}$$

Finally, the triangle for deceleration needs to be calculated. Although it is curved, it will give a close estimate. This occurs for 3 minutes again so the area of this triangle will be:

$$0.5 \times 180 \times (20\text{-}0) = 1800 \text{ metres.}$$

From here the areas from each step can be added to give a total distance:

$$3600+1050+1800=6450 \text{ metres}$$

However, looking at the graph, it is evident that the result is slightly overestimated, due to the final triangle being curved. Therefore the answer is not 6450m but would be a few metres below this value, the nearest of which is 6.00 km which is D.

Reference: *BMAT Assumed Subject Knowledge Guide:* Forces and Energy: Velocity-Time Graphs

16) **The correct answer is F**

Evaluate is another way of saying "solve". The most straightforward way to do this is by expanding each of the aspects of the equation:

Expand the standard form:

$$2x10^3 = 2000$$

$$8x10^2 = 800$$

Add the top line of the equation:

$$2000 + 800 = 2800$$

Expand the standard form in the denominator:

$$3x10^{-4} = 3/10000$$

Simplify:

$$\frac{2800}{1/2500 + 3/10000}$$

Or

$$\frac{2800}{7/10000}$$

Multiply each side by 10000:

$$28000000/7 \text{ or } 4000000 = 4x10^6$$

Finally, take the square root:

$$\sqrt{4x10^6}$$

$$2x10^3 = 2000 \text{ (Option F)}$$

17) **The correct answer is F (All of the above)**

Statements one and two relate to both intra-specific and inter-specific competition respectively. Animals compete with animals of the same and different species to survive. Statement three is Darwin's theory of evolution. Diversity in the gene pool can mean some animals are better suited to survive and some are less so. Natural selection means those with traits that enable them to survive will do so and pass these favourable characteristics on to their offspring. However, the opposite is also true; those without desirable characteristics will not survive causing them to become extinct. As all statements are true, the correct option is F.

Reference: *BMAT Assumed Subject Knowledge Guide:* Genes, Reproduction and Evolution: Evolution

18)   The correct answer is D (8)

a Cu + b HNO$_3$ → a Cu(NO$_3$)$_2$ + c H$_2$O + 2NO

To work out the value of b, the different atoms on each side of the equation need to be counted:

	Left	Right
Cu	1	1
H	1	2
N	1	4
O	3	9

Option d (b = 8) is the only option which allows the equation to be completely balanced. This is due to HNO$_3$ being the single source of hydrogen, nitrogen and oxygen atoms on the left side of the equation.

a Cu + 8 HNO$_3$ → a Cu(NO$_3$)$_2$ + c H$_2$O + 2NO

	Left	Right
Cu	1	1
H	8	2
N	8	4
O	24	9

If b is less than eight then the number of these atoms cannot be cancelled out on the right-hand side of the equation. From here a = 3 and c = 4.

Reference: *BMAT Assumed Subject Knowledge Guide:* Chemical Concepts: Balancing Equations

19)   The correct answer is B (20m)
The initial velocity will be 0 m/s, and the end velocity will be 20m/s. The acceleration will be 10m/s^2 (since gravity is acceleration in a downward direction).
In order to find out displacement (distance) use the equation:

$$v^2 = u^2 + 2as.$$

Substituting the values in:

$$20^2 = 0 + 2 \times 10s$$

Simplified:

$$400 = 20s, \text{ so } s = 20 \text{ metres (B)}$$

Reference: *BMAT Assumed Subject Knowledge Guide:* Forces and Energy: Speed and Velocity; Acceleration

20)   The correct answer is D (2/3)

The volume of a sphere is:

$$4/3\pi r^3$$

The volume of the cylinder is:

$$\pi r^2 h$$

As the sphere fits inside the cylinder, this means the height of the cylinder will be the diameter of the sphere which will be 2r. This means the volume of the cylinder will be:

$$\pi r^2 \times 2r = 2\pi r^3$$

Calculate the volume of the sphere as a fraction of the cylinder's volume:

$$\frac{4\,\pi r^3}{3} / 2\pi r^3$$

$$= (4/3) \div 2$$

$$= 2/3$$
(Option D)

Reference: *BMAT Assumed Subject Knowledge Guide:* Geometry and Measures: Volume

21)   The correct answer is D

The purpose of gas exchange in the alveoli is primarily to get oxygen into the blood. Immediately after inhalation, the concentration of oxygen will be high. This will diffuse through the capillary into the blood which has just come from the rest of the body via the pulmonary artery and right side of the heart. As the blood has come from the rest of the body, all the oxygen will have been delivered to the tissues so its concentration will be low. However, the blood will now be full of carbon dioxide, ready to diffuse back into the lungs to be exhaled. This makes the correct answer option D in the table.

Reference: *BMAT Assumed Subject Knowledge Guide:* Organs and Systems: The Lungs

22) The correct answer is D (2 and 3)

In equation one, the hydrogen and iodine bonds have to be broken before being reformed into 2HI. Therefore this reaction will be slow and can be excluded. In reaction four, the Br in the CH_3Br is broken as it exists in its ionic form Br^- after the reaction has taken place, therefore it can also be excluded. Reactions two and three are addition reactions with bonds being formed and none being broken. These two reactions will occur quickly, making the correct answer D.

23) Correct answer is A (2500N)

The forces acting between the engine and carriage one is called 'x'. The question states that the engine is providing 15000N of force but force x is opposing it. This is slowing the powered engine down but at the same time is the driving force for carriage one. This phenomenon is known as tension. Therefore the value of the tension in the coupling x needs to be calculated followed by T.

F = ma can be used to work out for the acceleration for powered engine:

$$F = 15000N, \quad m = 20000 \text{ kg}$$

$$15000 - x = 20000a.$$

For carriage one it will be:

$$x - T = 5000a.$$

For carriage T there is no opposing force behind the carriage so:

$$T = 5000a.$$

Therefore:

$$x - T = T \text{ so } x = 2T$$

This gives:

$$x = 10000a$$

Substituting this into the equation for the powered engine:

$$15000-10000a = 20000a$$

Cancelled out this gives:

$$15-10a = 20a, \text{ so } 15 = 30a \text{ so } a = 0.5/ms^2.$$

$$\text{This means } T = 5000 \times 0.5 = 2500N = A.$$

Reference: *BMAT Assumed Subject Knowledge Guide:* Forces and Energy: Forces and Acceleration

24)   The correct answer is A ($\pm 2\sqrt{(y+10)}/5 + 6$)

Rearrange this equation step by step.

$$y = 5 (x/2 - 3)^2 - 10$$

First add 10 to both sides:

$$y + 10 = 5 (x/2 - 3)^2$$

Next, divide both sides by 5:

$$(y + 10)/5 = (x/2 - 3)^2$$

From here, take the square root of both sides:

$$\pm\sqrt{(y+10)}/5 = (x/2) - 3$$

Add three from both sides

$$\pm\sqrt{(y+10)}/5 = (x/2) - 3$$

Multiply both sides by two:

$$\pm\sqrt{(y+10)}/5 + 3 = x/2.$$
$$\text{(Option A)}$$

Reference: *BMAT Assumed Subject Knowledge Guide:* Algebra: Rearranging Equations

25)   The correct answer is F (3, 4 and 5 only)
Statement one is incorrect because insulin regulates blood glucose levels.

Homeostasis relies on input from the nervous system as well as from hormones; hence statement two is also incorrect. The role of the pancreas is to make and release insulin. Since insulin is the hormone responsible for controlling blood glucose, statement three is correct.

The hormonal system releases chemicals such as insulin to control glucose, while the nervous system receives signals relating to the regulation of body processes via the hypothalamus. For example, in the control of body temperature, impulses are sent which cause surface blood vessels to constrict/dilate. In light of this, statement four is correct.

Statement five is also true since the skin hairs can be made to either lie flat when the body is warm or stand on end (piloerection) when it is cold to trap air for insulation.

Reference: *BMAT Assumed Subject Knowledge Guide:* Nerves, Hormones and Homeostasis: Hormones

26) The correct answer is C (3/8)

First, subtract the relative formula mass of the CH_2 to leave the elements that have different isotopes:

$$12 + 1 + 1 = 14$$

Thus the relative formula mass of the compound left is:

$$128 - 14 = 114$$

From here, work out how the numbers 35&37 and 79&81 add to give a total of 114. The only way this occurs is by using 35 and 79.

The isotope with mass number 35 is three times as common this means that ¾ of the naturally occurring chlorine will have a relative formula mass of 35. For bromine ½ of the naturally occurring form will have the relative formula mass 79. By multiplying these numbers together to work out what fraction of the compound will have the relative formula mass of 114.

$$¾ \times ½ = 3/8 = C$$

Reference: *BMAT Assumed Subject Knowledge Guide:* Classifying Materials: Isotopes and Relative Atomic Mass

27) Correct answer is E (150m/s)

Use the formula $v = f\lambda$ where lambda is the wavelength to calculate the wavelength using the first graph. The wavelength is the distance for the whole wave to be completed; it can be calculated using any two points (from peak to peak, or trough to trough). It can be seen there are two complete waves in 60 metres, so the wavelength is, therefore, half of this (30 metres).

The frequency is how many waves there are in one second. The second graph shows that there are three complete waves in 0.6 seconds. Therefore in one second, there will be five waves, giving a frequency of 5Hz. This means the velocity of the wave will be:

5 x 30 = 150m/s = E

Reference: *BMAT Assumed Subject Knowledge Guide:* Waves and Their Effects: Wave Basics

BMAT Section 2 - 2010

1)   The correct answer is E

The thermoregulatory centre of the brain is located in the hypothalamus which is where internal temperature changes are detected. The result is a homeostatic response to maintain the constancy of the internal environment via the process of vasodilation. This means that the small arterioles close to the surface of the body (skin) dilate to help dissipate heat from the surface of the skin by increasing blood flow. This does not affect the position of the capillaries in the skin, which remains in position. The hair erector muscles relax, causing the hair to stay flat against the skin.

Reference: *BMAT Assumed Subject Knowledge Guide:* Nerves, Hormones and Homeostasis: Controlling Body Temperature

2)   The correct answer is E (I_2O_5)

The relative atomic masses provided can be used to determine that a compound with 63.5g of iodine contains 0.5 moles of iodine using the equation:

$$Number\ of\ moles = \frac{mass\ (g)}{relative\ formula\ mass}$$

$$63.5/127 = 0.5\ moles$$

20g of oxygen translates to 1.25 moles of oxygen atoms:

$$(20/16) = 1.25\ moles$$

Therefore the molar ratio of iodine to oxygen is

$$0.5\ to\ 1.25,\ alternatively,\ 2\ to\ 5$$

$$\Rightarrow I_2O_5$$

Reference: *BMAT Assumed Subject Knowledge Guide:* Equations and Calculations: Relative Formula Mass

3)   The correct answer is A (1.2 minutes)

Protactinium 234 and uranium 234 have the same relative atomic mass so for every gram of protactinium 234 that undergoes decay; exactly one gram of uranium 234 will be formed. As the experiment proceeds, the mass of uranium 234 approaches 16 grams exponentially, suggesting that this is the maximum weight possible. Thus the experiment must have begun with 16g of protactinium 234. The half-life is the time taken for half of this amount to decay, so in this instance, for 8g of protactinium to decay and form a corresponding 8g of uranium. This is given in the table as 1.2 minutes.

Reference: *BMAT Assumed Subject Knowledge Guide:* The Atom and Radioactivity: Half-Life

4)   The correct answer is C (p = 0.5 and q > 0.5)

This question can be illustrated using an artificial example. Assume that the larger container had a capacity of 100ml and so contained 100ml of liquid. The smaller one can be assumed to have a capacity of 50ml. 50ml must now be poured from the larger container to the small one. In this instance, p=0.5 as the larger container now contains 50 out of its original 100ml. q=1 as the smaller container contains 50ml out of its 50ml capacity. In this example, p + q=1.5 so A cannot be true. q=1 so B is also incorrect. P necessarily equals 0.5 as it has lost half its fluid, and q is greater than 0.5 as it represents the smaller container; both of these conditions will be true for any given example, and so the correct answer is C. D and E are incorrect as illustrated by the example.

5)   The correct answer is C (2 and 3)

Insulin acts to decrease blood glucose levels by increasing glucose uptake in the muscles and the liver and reducing glucose production, so statement one is incorrect. Oestrogen levels rise prior to ovulation in response to rising Follicle stimulating hormone (FSH) levels to increase the thickness of the uterine lining. This is to prepare the uterus for implantation by a fertilised ovum following ovulation. Therefore statement two is correct. Adrenaline is released as part of the 'fight or flight' response to perceived danger. This acts directly on heart muscle to increase heart rate and strength of contraction of the heart tissue to enhance the delivery of oxygen to the muscles. Therefore statement three is also correct.

Reference: *BMAT Assumed Subject Knowledge Guide:* Nerves, Hormones and Homeostasis: Hormones

6)   The correct answer is D (88g)

The 12g of carbon used in stage two represents 1 mole of carbon as calculated using the equation:

$$Number\ of\ moles = \frac{mass\ (g)}{relative\ formula\ mass}$$

12/12 =1 mole carbon

This will react completely with 1 mole of carbon dioxide:

$$Mr = 12+16+16 = 44$$

CO_2 weighs 46g and forms two moles of carbon monoxide weighing 56g in total (44+12). If two moles of carbon monoxide are used in stage three, then two moles of carbon dioxide will also be produced as the ratio of CO to CO_2 is 3:3 in the stage three equation. Thus, two moles of CO_2 weighing 88g:

$$[16+16+12]x2 = 88g$$
(Option D)

Reference: *BMAT Assumed Subject Knowledge Guide:* Equations and Calculations: Relative Formula Mass

7) The correct answer is A (Amplitude = 3m; Frequency = 1/(12 x 3600))

The amplitude of a wave is the distance from the rest position to the peak (or trough) of the wave, which is equivalent to half the height between the peak and the trough in this case:

$$6/2 = 3m$$

The frequency is given in Hertz which is the number of waves per second. Since there is one wave in 12 hours (measured horizontally between peaks) there are 1/12 waves in one hour:

$$1/(12 \times 60) \text{ waves in a minute}$$

$$\text{or } 1/(12 \times 60 \times 60) \text{ waves in a second,}$$

$$\text{This is equivalent to } 1/(12 \times 3600)$$

Reference: *BMAT Assumed Subject Knowledge Guide:* Waves and Their Effects: Wave Basics

8) The correct answer is C (1/16)

To get back to where they started in this game, a player must roll a left followed by a right (or vice versa) or an up followed by a down (or vice versa). This can occur in four possible ways as LR, RL, UD or DU out of a total of 16 possible combinations of L, R, D and U. Thus, the probability of achieving this combination is ¼. Additionally, the number rolled on both occasions must be the same. For whichever number is rolled on the first occasion, there is a ¼ probability of rolling that same number again. Thus, the probability of ending up at the start position is ¼ x ¼ = 1/16 (option C).

Reference: *BMAT Assumed Subject Knowledge Guide:* Statistics and Probability: The AND/OR Rules

9) The correct answer is B (an advantageous allele)

The gene pool is a term that applies exclusively to a population or species, and not to an individual. Therefore A cannot be used to complete the statement. B is the correct answer as individuals with an advantageous allele (a version of a gene) will have a reproductive/survival advantage and be more likely to pass this allele on to their offspring thus affecting evolution by the mechanism of natural selection. C is incorrect as a high reproductive capacity is not sufficient for evolutionary advantage as these offspring may be weak and unable to survive. D and E have little relevance to the issue of global natural selection.

Reference: *BMAT Assumed Subject Knowledge Guide:* Genes, Reproduction and Evolution: Evolution

10) The correct answer is D (3 and 4)

The complete combustion of a fuel is when the carbon-containing compound burns completely in oxygen to form carbon dioxide and water, so the answer is D. An example would be the combustion of methane: $CH_4 + 2O_2 \rightarrow CO_2 + 2H_2O$.

Reference: *BMAT Assumed Subject Knowledge Guide:* Carbon Chemistry: Burning Fuels

11)   The correct answer is C (Atomic number 82; Mass number 207)

Two protons and two neutrons are lost from a nucleus when it emits an alpha particle which means the mass number (the number of neutrons + protons) decreases by four, and the atomic number (the number of protons) decreases by 2. In beta decay, a neutron changes into a proton and an electron, so the mass number stays the same but the atomic number increases by 1 (a proton has been gained). For radon 219, decay results in the emission of three alpha and two beta particles, resulting in a decrease in the mass number by 12 (3 x -4) to 219 and the atomic number by 4 ([3 x -2]+[2x1]) to 82, making the answer C.

Reference: *BMAT Assumed Subject Knowledge Guide:* The Atom and Radioactivity: Ionising Radiation

12)   The correct answer is C

The sum of the times of the 20 people in the first group is 1080 seconds (20 x 54) and the sum of the times of the people in the second group is T x P. The mean of the combined group of first and second groups is calculated by dividing the total sum of times by the total number of people in both groups, or 1080+TP/20+P = 56. This can be arranged to solve for P as below:

$$\frac{1080 + TP}{20 + P} = 56$$

$$1080 + TP = 56(20 + P) = 1120 + 56P$$

$$TP - 56P = 40$$

$$P(T - 56) = 40$$

$$P = \frac{40}{T - 56}$$

13)   The correct answer is F (4 and 5)

Neurotransmitter molecules are formed in the 'presynaptic knob' in the axon terminal before a synapse and not in a receptor, so statement one is false. The signal is then transmitted by diffusion of these molecules, not osmosis, so statement two is also false whereas statement five is true. These transmitter molecules are not released 'once the signal has been transmitted across the synapse' making statement three false as well. These transmitters are released before any signal has been transmitted, they are the signal themselves. Finally, statement four is correct – an action potential (impulse) causes the release of neurotransmitters from the 'presynaptic knob' into the synapse.

Reference: *BMAT Assumed Subject Knowledge Guide:* Nerves, Hormones and Homeostasis: Synapses and Reflexes

14) The correct answer is A (1,2 and 6)

All ionic equations must balance for charge as well as mass, meaning the sum of the positive and negative charges must be equal on both sides of the equation. This is not true of equation three, which has a total charge of -4 on the left and 0 on the right. The same goes for equation four, which has a total charge of -1 (-2- -1=-2+1) on the left and 0 on the right. Equation five is balanced for charge, however, there are two iodine species on the left and only one on the right, so the equation is not balanced for mass and is incorrect. The remaining equations are correctly balanced for mass and charge, so the answer is A.

Reference: *BMAT Assumed Subject Knowledge Guide:* Classifying Materials: Formulas of Ionic Compounds

15) The correct answer is B (Bulb X: brighter; Bulb Y: dimmer)

Electric current will always take the path of least resistance in any given circuit and since the light bulbs represent resistance the current will always bypass any bulbs if possible, thus reducing their brightness. Initially, while switch P is open and Q is closed, the current will flow around the circuit, through switch Q, bypassing bulb X and all other bulbs except Y, since this is in the main branch of the circuit. Once switch Q opens, this path is no longer available. Instead the current will flow through X and the now closed switch P and then through bulb Y, still bypassing all the remaining bulbs. As a result, X will shine brighter as the current flowing through it has increased and Y will be dimmer as it was previously the only bulb in the circuit but now must share current with X. Therefore the answer is B.

Reference: *BMAT Assumed Subject Knowledge Guide:* Electricity: Current and Electricity

16) The correct answer is C (9cm)

Triangles ABC and ADE share angle BAC (=angle DAE) and angle ABC=angle ADE because line BC is parallel to line DE. Angle ACB=angle AED for the same reason. Since both triangles have three equivalent angles, they are similar triangles, and their side lengths are related to each other by a single ratio. Side AB of triangle ABC corresponds to side AD of triangle ADE, and the ratio between them is 4/x (because AD = x-4+4). Side BC of triangle ABC corresponds to side DE of triangle ADE and the ratio between them is x/(x+3). These two ratios are necessarily equivalent because they represent a pair of similar triangles. The following equation can be constructed and solved as below.

$$\frac{4}{x} = \frac{x}{x+3}$$

$$4 = \frac{x^2}{x+3}$$

$$4x + 12 = x^2$$

$$x^2 - 4x - 12 = 0$$

$$(x - 6)(x + 2) = 0$$

$$x = 6 \ or - 2$$

x cannot be equal to -2 as then side DB would have length -6cm, therefore x= 6 and DE has a length of 9cm (6+3) so the answer is C.

Reference: *BMAT Assumed Subject Knowledge Guide:* Geometry and Measures: Similar Shapes

17)   The correct answer is E (S = 50; T = 50; U = 100)

An individual with two heterozygous parents has a 50% chance of being a carrier, 25% chance of being affected by the condition and, 25% chance of being homozygous dominant. Thus the probability of individual S or T being a carrier is 50%. Individual X is homozygous recessive and consequently, has the condition. This means that both her parents (individuals U and V) have a 100% chance of being carriers of the condition as this is the only way for her to inherit two recessive alleles since neither parent is affected, hence the answer is E.

Reference: *BMAT Assumed Subject Knowledge Guide:* Genes, Reproduction and Evolution: More on Genetic Disorders

18)   The correct answer is B $Mg(H_2PO_4)_2$

To identify the possible formula, the net charges for each option must be calculated. In an ionic compound, the number of positive charges and negative charges must cancel each other out, to give an overall (net) charge of zero. Option A has a net charge of -2 (2-2 x 2) when the respective charges of all the species in the molecule are added together, so is not correct. Option B has a net charge of 0 (2-1 x 2) and is the correct answer. Option C has a net charge of 2 (2+1x3-3) so is also incorrect. Option D has a net charge of 2 (2+ [1x3-3] x2) making it also incorrect. Option E has a net charge of 2 (2x2+1-3) making it incorrect. Finally, option F has a net charge of 3 (2x2+1x2-3) so is incorrect. Therefore the correct answer is B.

Reference: *BMAT Assumed Subject Knowledge Guide:* Classifying Materials: Formulas of Ionic Compounds

19)   The correct answer is B (Q only)

Velocity is the change in the directional distance within a specific period of time, whereas acceleration is a measure of how quickly the velocity is changing with time. These 'rates of change' can be derived by calculating the gradient of a graph which shows the above parameters plotted against each other, so acceleration is equivalent to the gradient of a velocity versus time graph. This can be seen for graphs P and Q: P has a gradient of 10/24 m/s/s, or, $0.42 m/s^2$ whereas Q has a gradient of (58-10)/20 m/s/s or 2.4 m/s^2. Graphs R and S are straight line graphs and their gradient signifies velocity as they are distance versus time graphs. Since their gradients are constant throughout the graph, their velocity is constant, which signifies an acceleration of 0 m/s^2. If a distance versus time graphs shows a non-zero acceleration, it would be curved not straight. Therefore only Q shows the correct acceleration.

Reference: *BMAT Assumed Subject Knowledge Guide:* Forces and Energy: Speed and Velocity; Distance-Time Graphs; Acceleration; Velocity-Time Graphs

20) The correct answer is A

The surface area of a cylinder is given as the sum of the areas of both of its faces added to the remaining area:

$$(\pi r^2 + \pi r^2)$$

This can be expressed as the circumference of the face of the cylinder multiplied by the height (*h*) of the cylinder by thinking of the remaining area as a curled up rectangle. Thus the surface area of a cylinder is:

$$2\pi r^2 + 2\pi rh$$

The volume of a cylinder is the area of its face multiplied by its height. If the volume and surface area of this cylinder are equivalent the following equation can be constructed and solved to illustrate that the answer is A.

$$2\pi r^2 + 2\pi rh = \pi r^2 h$$

$$2\pi r + 2\pi h = \pi rh$$

$$2r + 2h = rh$$

$$rh - 2h = 2r$$

$$h(r - 2) = 2r$$

$$h = \frac{2r}{r - 2}$$

Reference: *BMAT Assumed Subject Knowledge Guide:* Geometry and Measures: Surface Area; Volume

21) The correct answer is B (1,2 and 5)

Meiosis is the form of cell division which creates haploid gametes for the process of sexual reproduction. It occurs in the reproductive organs (testes or ovaries) therefore statement one is correct. Mitosis is the form of cell division which creates diploid daughter cells which are identical to the cells they originated from and has a variety of uses including cell replacement, growth and cloning making statement two is also correct. During meiosis, each cell undergoes two stages of division; the first stage is similar to mitosis and splits the cell into two diploid counterparts. The second stage splits each of these diploid cells into two haploid cells, resulting in four haploid cells with half the genetic material of a normal cell. As with all cells (except those just about to undergo cytokinesis - or cell splitting), each new cell has one nucleus. Therefore statement three is incorrect because there are four nuclei are formed in total. Statement four is also incorrect, as each cell undergoing mitosis splits into two diploid daughter cells, each with one nucleus. Statement five is correct as asexual reproduction involves diploid cells and is comparable to 'cloning' using the process of mitosis. Asexual reproduction results in identical offspring and does not use meiosis as this would lead to offspring which are unique. Therefore the answer is B.

Reference: *BMAT Assumed Subject Knowledge Guide:* Genes, Reproduction and Evolution: Cell Division – Mitosis; Cell Division - Meiosis

22)   The correct answer is C (60%)

To answer this question the first step is to calculate the relative formula mass of benzene:

$$(12 \times 6) + 6 = 78$$

Then the following equation must be used to work out the number of moles of benzene:

$$Number\ of\ moles = \frac{mass\ (g)}{relative\ formula\ mass}$$

$$number\ of\ moles = \frac{3.9}{78}$$

$$= 0.05 \text{ moles of benzene}$$

Nitrobenzene has a relative formula mass of:

$$(12 \times 6) + (5 \times 1) + 14 + (16 \times 2) = 123$$

Therefore the expected yield of nitrobenzene will be:

$$0.05 \times 123 = 6.15g$$

Using the following equation to calculate yield:

$$percentage\ yield = \frac{actual\ yield\ (g)}{predicted\ yield\ (g)} \times 100$$

$$\frac{3.69}{6.15} \times 100 = 60\%$$

Making the answer C

23)   The correct answer is G (Power of pump = 250; speed of water = 10)

Power in Watts can be defined as

$$Power = \frac{work\ done\ (Nm)}{time(s)}$$

Work done is equivalent to the force applied (N) multiplied by the distance through which this force is applied (m).

These two equations can be combined to derive a third equation:

$$Power = force\ applied \times velocity$$

The force in this example is 25N (5kg x 10N/kg), so the power of the pump is 25x where x is the speed of the water. Therefore the correct option will have a number in the power column which is 25 times greater than the number in the speed column and option G is the only response which satisfies this criterion.

Reference: *BMAT Assumed Subject Knowledge Guide:* Forces and Energy: Power

24)   The correct answer is C (125/729)

Let the side length of the original (first) square be x so that this square has area x^2. The second square can be cut out of the first square leaving four right angled triangles adjacent to each edge of equal area. These triangles each have an area of:

$$(\tfrac{1}{3}x \times \tfrac{2}{3}x) \div 2 = \tfrac{1}{9}x^2$$

The total area of the second square is equal to the area of the first square minus the area of four of these triangles:

$$x^2 - \frac{4}{9}x^2 = \frac{5}{9}x^2$$

Thus the second square has an area which is 5/9 of the first square. If this process was repeated, the third square would have an area which is also 5/9 of the second square, or

$$\frac{5}{9} \times \frac{5}{9}$$ of the first square

Consequently, the fourth square will have an area which is:

$$\frac{5}{9} \times \frac{5}{9} \times \frac{5}{9}$$ of the first square

$$= \frac{125}{729}$$ of the first square

238

Therefore the answer is C.

25)   The correct answer is E (2,3 and 5)

Statements one and four are incorrect as the nervous system uses electrical impulses to trigger neurotransmitter release across synapses. These are chemical impulses and can be similar to hormones meaning electrical impulses alone are not used. Statement two is correct as the nervous system activates target structures (for example muscle fibres for movement) as does the hormonal system (for example heart muscle is 'activated' by adrenaline). Statement three is correct as the nervous system can convey messages along neurones in milliseconds, whereas the hormonal system can take days or even weeks to cause a response. Statement five is correct – for example, the sympathetic nervous system (a branch of the central nervous system) can act on the adrenal glands to cause the release of the hormone adrenaline during times of stress.

Reference: *BMAT Assumed Subject Knowledge Guide:* Nerves, Hormones and Homeostasis: Hormones

26)   The correct answer is B (20)

Each vertex (corner) in a drawn organic structure represents a carbon atom, as do the letters C when they appear attached to a vertex. The molecule in question consists of three hexagons and one pentagon, with three additional carbon atoms (in 2 x CH_3 and 1 CO_2H). Since some of the corners of these shapes overlap, there are only 17 independent vertices and three additional carbon atoms, so a total of 20 carbon atoms in the molecule. Therefore the answer is B.

27)   The correct answer is D (45kJ)

A car of mass 800kg will have a weight of 8000N. The car is moving at a constant speed and is therefore not accelerating. Since the car is moving up an incline, work is being done to increase the car's gravitational potential energy (GPE). In 50m, the car will gain 2.5m of height (50/20), and since:

$$GPE = weight \; x \; height$$

This corresponds to 20000 Nm. The car must also oppose a frictional force of 500N across the 50m distance, which corresponds to a further 25000 Nm of work (500 x50). Adding up these figures = 45000 Nm (20000+25000), and since 1 Nm is equivalent to 1 joule, 45000 Nm is equal to 45 kJ.

Reference: *BMAT Assumed Subject Knowledge Guide:* Forces and Energy: Gravitational Potential Energy

BMAT Section 2 - 2011

1) **The correct answer is F (Carbohydrase)**

Gland	Hormone	One function
Adrenal	Adrenaline	B
E	Oestrogen	Female secondary sexual characteristics
C	ADH	G
Testes	D	Male secondary sexual characteristics
Pancreas	A	Regulates blood glucose level

2) **The correct answer is B (X_2Y_3)**

Since metal X is in group three of the periodic table, it will have an ionic charge of +3 as it loses three electrons. Element Y will have a charge of -2 as elements in group six need to gain two electrons to fill their valence shell. The charges on any ionic compound must cancel out, giving a net charge of zero. To achieve this for this compound, two Xs and three Ys are required. Hence, the answer is B.

Reference: *BMAT Assumed Subject Knowledge Guide:* Classifying Materials: Formulas of Ionic Compounds

3) **The correct answer is C**

$$E_k = \tfrac{1}{2}\, mv^2$$

Thus, car Q has four times as much KE as car P, since 'v' is twice as big.
Gravitational potential energy (GPE) is directly proportional to height; so car Q has twice as much GPE as car P. Therefore, the answer is C.

Reference: *BMAT Assumed Subject Knowledge Guide:* Forces and Energy: Kinetic Energy

4) **The correct answer is C (81)**

$$3x\, (3x^{-1/3})^3$$

$$= 3x\, (27x^{-1})$$

$$= 3 \times 27$$

$$= 81$$
(Option C)

5)   The correct answer is F (3,4 and 5 only)

Meiosis results in variation within the species thus making statement one false. Mitosis, on the other hand, results in the production of genetically identical daughter cells making statement two false. When mitotic cell division occurs, the outcome is two diploid cells, whereas meiosis results in four haploid cells, making statements three, four and five correct (option F).

Reference: *BMAT Assumed Subject Knowledge Guide:* Genes, Reproduction and Evolution: Cell Division – Mitosis; Cell Division - Meiosis

6)   The correct answer is D (1 and 2 only)

Increasing the temperature increases the kinetic energy of molecules. Hence, they move faster, and more collisions take place with more energy on average. Temperature, however, has no impact on the orientation in which the molecules collide. Thus, the answer is D.

Reference: *BMAT Assumed Subject Knowledge Guide:* Reaction Rates and Energy Changes: Collision Theory

7)   The correct answer is E (When a nucleus emits a beta particle, there is no change in the number of particles it contains)

Nuclear fission is the decaying of a nucleus. Therefore, statement A is false. Half-life is defined as the time taken for half the nuclei of a substance to decay; making statement B also false. The number of protons is known as the atomic number. The mass number, by contrast, is the number of protons and neutrons in the nucleus, making statement C false. Nuclear fission is used in nuclear power stations, not nuclear fusion. Therefore, statement D is also false. The emission of a beta particle results in a neutron turning into a proton. As this particle remains in the nucleus, there is no change to the number of particles present. Thus statement E is correct. An alpha particle consists of two neutrons and two protons. Therefore statement F is incorrect.

Reference: *BMAT Assumed Subject Knowledge Guide:* The Atom and Radiation: Ionising Radiation

8)   The correct answer is D (22.5°)

There are twelve hours and 360^0 in a circle. Hence, the angle between any two adjacent hours is 30^0. This means that 45/60 of 30^0 is 22.5^0. Thus, the answer is D.

9)   The correct answer is C (1,2,3 and 5 only)

Individuals within a sexually reproducing species are unique due to meiosis, making statement one correct. Intra-specific competition occurs between members of the same species; therefore statement two is also correct. Statement three is correct because individuals with advantageous adaptations are better suited to the prevailing environment as they can exploit resources more efficiently; therefore they will have a higher chance of survival. Breeding within a population is not restricted to individuals with advantageous adaptations. Individuals without beneficial adaptations can still reproduce, however, their survival and that of their offspring may be limited, due to them lacking these adaptations. Therefore this statement (four) is false. Statement five is also true, because individuals with advantageous adaptations are more likely to survive, and are often more successful at attracting mates, thus passing on these favourable alleles.

Reference: *BMAT Assumed Subject Knowledge Guide:* Genes, Reproduction and Evolution: Evolution

10)   The correct answer is D (138)
Each corner of the structure in the question represents a carbon atom. Carbon can bond to four atoms; therefore each of the carbon atoms on the outside of the ring will also have two hydrogen atoms attached to it as well. The two carbons in the middle of the hydrocarbon will have three carbons joined to it and only one hydrogen atom. Consequently, the carbon skeleton has ten carbon atoms and 18 hydrogen atoms. Therefore the relative molecular mass will be: $(10 \times 12) + 18 = 138$

11)   The correct answer is B
When the switch is open, no current flows through the ammeter, as the diode is the wrong way round. When the switch is closed, and since $I = V/R$ ($V = 6V$ and $R = 3$), the current is 2A. Hence, the answer is B.

12)   The correct answer is D (x>y)
The easiest way to identify which statement is correct is to assign numbers to w, x, y and z.
Statement A does not need to be true, for example, 'w' could be 4, and 'x' could be -3, and this would still satisfy the inequalities given. Similarly, using substitution one can see that B, C, and E do not need to be true. However, $x > y$ must be true, as $y^2 > y$, and $x > y^2$.

13)   The correct answer is E
Blood which enters the muscle will be high in oxygen (to allow maximum aerobic respiration) and low carbon dioxide, as this a waste-product of respiration. This immediately rules out options A, B and C. Gas exchange is made possible by diffusion of gases, which thus eliminates option F. For the muscle cells to absorb maximum oxygen from the blood, a steep concentration gradient must be present. Therefore, oxygen levels will be low in the muscle cells to facilitate this. Likewise, for carbon dioxide, the concentration will be high in the muscle cell and low in the plasma, making option E correct.

Reference: *BMAT Assumed Subject Knowledge Guide:* Organs and Systems: The Lungs

14) **The correct answer is C**

Compounds in which the species share a pair of valence electrons form covalent bonds.

The structures that contain covalent bonds are: CO_2, $Ca(OH)_2$, H_2SO_4, $MgCO_3$, Na_3PO_4, SO_2, and SiO_2.

15) **The correct answer is B (3.75×10^3N)**

$$Force \ x \ distance \ = \frac{1}{2}mv^2$$

$$Force \ x \ 0.6 \ = \ \frac{1}{2} \ x \ 0.05 \ x \ 300^2$$

$$Force = 3750 \ N$$

Reference: *BMAT Assumed Subject Knowledge Guide:* Forces and Energy: Kinetic Energy

16) **The correct answer is E (3 and 4)**

Option A: Make equations 1 and 2 equal

$$x^2 = 3x - 2$$

$$x^2 - 3x + 2 = 0$$

$$(x - 2)(x - 1) = 0 \text{ (graphs intersect)}$$

Option B: Make equations 1 and 3 equal

$$1 - x^2 = 3x - 2$$

$$x^2 + 3x - 3 = 0$$

Using $b^2 - 4ac$:

$$3^2 - (4 \ x \ 1 \ x \ -3) = 21 > 0 \text{ (graphs intersect)}$$

Option C: Make equations 2 and 3 equal

$$x^2 = 1 - x^2$$

$$2x^2 - 1 = 0$$

Using $b^2 - 4ac$:

$$0 - (4 \ x \ 2 \ x \ -1) = 8 > 0 \text{ (graphs intersect)}$$

243

Option D:

$$x^2 = x + 6$$

$$x^2 - x - 6 = 0$$

$$(x - 3)(x + 2) = 0 \text{ (graphs intersect)}$$

Option E:

$$1 - x^2 = x + 6$$

$$x^2 + x + 5 = 0$$

Using $b^2 - 4ac$:

$$1^2 - (4 \times 1 \times 5) = -19 < 0 \text{ (graphs do not intersect)}$$

Reference: *BMAT Assumed Subject Knowledge Guide:* Graphs: "y=mx + c"

17)   The correct answer is D (1,2 and 3)

If the condition were dominant, U would only need to inherit the dominant allele from her father (T) via his sperm. Thus, statements one and two are correct. Alternatively, individual U could have inherited the condition through a spontaneous mutation in the mother's egg, or if the condition was recessive and the individual's mother was a carrier (the recessive alleles would be passed to U via a sperm from T and an egg from S that both had the recessive allele). Hence, the answer is D as all the three statements are possible reasons.

Reference: *BMAT Assumed Subject Knowledge Guide:* Genes, Reproduction and Evolution: More on Genetic Disorders

18)   The correct answer is E (a = 3, b = 8, x = 3, y = 4)

The first step is to total each of the species on each side of the equation.

	Left	Right
Cu	1	1
H	1	2
N	1	4
O	3	9

$a=x$ as only these two substances have Cu. Since b controls the number of hydrogen, nitrogen and oxygen atoms on the left-hand side of the equation, this number will limit the combinations possible. b cannot = 4 as this would mean that $y = 2$ to balance out the hydrogen atoms on the right-hand side. This would then require x = 2 as well, which makes the number of nitrogen atoms on the right-hand side unbalanced, therefore options A and C can be excluded.

b cannot = 16 as this would mean that $y = 8$ and $x = 6$ to balance out the hydrogen and nitrogen atoms respectively. This would leave the oxygen atoms on the right-hand side unbalanced by 2. Therefore option B can also be excluded.

Option D can also be ruled out as it fails to allow the oxygen atoms on the right side to be balance out.

Option E where b = 8 means that, $y = 4$. This allows the hydrogen atoms on the right side of the equation to balance, having a total of 8 (4x2) and both a and $x = 3$. Therefore the correct answer is E.

Reference: *BMAT Assumed Subject Knowledge Guide:* Chemical Concepts: Balancing Equations

19)   The correct answer is A

In a circuit, the resistance increases with temperature because the flow of current is restricted in high temperatures. When the temperature is constant, the resistance in the circuit will remain constant also, making graph A the correct option.

Reference: *BMAT Assumed Subject Knowledge Guide:* Electricity: Resistance and V = I x R

20)   The correct answer is B

$$a^2 + b^2 = c^2$$

The base of the middle triangle =

$$(1^2 + 3^2)^{\frac{1}{2}} = 10^{\frac{1}{2}}$$

The base of the largest triangle =

$$(10 + 10/9)^{\frac{1}{2}} = 10/3$$

Area of the largest triangle =

$$(10/3 \times 10/9) \times \frac{1}{2} = 50/27 \text{ cm}^2$$

The answer is B

21)   The correct answer is D

The quantity of nuclear DNA depends on whether the cell in question is haploid (one quantity) or diploid (two quantities). Both the sperm and egg cells (known as gametes) will only have one quantity of nuclear DNA since both the zygote and red blood cell are diploid; thus excluding options B and E. Cell R contains no nuclear DNA, which rules out options A, C and E as these cells are diploid. Hence the answer will be D.

Reference: *BMAT Assumed Subject Knowledge Guide:* Genes, Reproduction and Evolution: Cell Division – Mitosis; Cell Division - Meiosis

22)   The correct answer is D (289.80kg)
First find 70% of PbS:

$$0.7 \times 478 = 334.6 \text{ kg}$$

Calculate the relative molar mass for PbS:

$$207 + 32 = 239$$

Find the proportion of Pb in PbS

$$207/239 = 0.866$$

Calculate the mass that can be extracted:

$$0.866 \times 334.6 = 289.8$$

23)   The correct answer is C
The frequency of orange light remains constant. However, the wavelength and speed will decrease as the glass is denser than air.

$$Wave\ speed = Frequency \ x \ Wavelength$$

$$Frequency = \frac{3.0 \times^{8}}{600 \times 10^{-9}}$$

$$Frequency = 5.0 \times 10^{14} \text{ Hz}$$

The frequency and the reduced wave speed can now be used to determine the new wavelength

$$Wavelength = \frac{2.0 \times^{8}}{5.0 \times 10^{14}}$$

$$Wavelength = 400 \text{ nm}$$

Hence, the answer is C.

Reference: *BMAT Assumed Subject Knowledge Guide:* Waves and their effects: Wave Properties - Refraction

24)   The correct answer is B (1/45)

The possibility of getting two 6's is 1/18 (probability A and B)

The chance of rolling a six on the fair dice is 1/6 (probability A)

Therefore to work out the probability for the unfair dice (probability B), the following equation can be used:

$$P (A \text{ and } B) = P (A) \times P (B)$$

$$1/18 = 1/6 \times 1/3$$

The probability of getting 1 -5 on the unfair dice is:

$$(2/3)/5 = 2/15$$

To find the probability of getting a total of 2 requires the same equation, used previously:

$$1/6 \times 2/15 = 1/45 \text{ (answer B)}$$

Reference: *BMAT Assumed Subject Knowledge Guide:* Statistics and Probability: The AND/OR Rules

25)   The correct answer is D (2 would be higher)

Part one of the graph would be steeper as the body would need to respond more aggressively to compensate for the lack of response to the stimulus. Part two on the graph would be higher as the level of this factor would continue to rise for an extended period (for example: blood glucose levels, continuing to rise until insulin is released). Part three would be less steep as it would take the body longer to return to its normal state. Hence, the answer is D.

Reference: *BMAT Assumed Subject Knowledge Guide:* Nerves, Hormones and Homeostasis: Homeostasis and Negative Feedback

26)   The correct answer is E ($2CH_3SCH_3 + 9O_2 \rightarrow 4CO_2 + 6H_2O + 2SO_2$)

$aCH_3SCH_3 + bO_2 \rightarrow cCO_2 + dH_2O + eSO_2$ is the unbalanced equation that will result when dimethylsulphide is burnt in an excess of air. This means that there is sufficient O_2 to produce the products of a complete combustion reaction, allowing, H_2O, CO_2 and SO_2 to form. Only E has the correct equation, which includes all three products. Hence, the answer is E.

Reference: *BMAT Assumed Subject Knowledge Guide:* Carbon Chemistry: Burning Fuels

27)   The correct answer is B (198m)

$$60 \text{ seconds}/50 \text{ beats} = 1.2$$

247

Since there is a beat every 1.2 seconds; the soldiers at the front must put down their right foot in half this time (0.6 seconds). Hence, it takes 0.6 seconds for sound to reach the soldiers at the back.

$$Speed = distance/time$$

Distance = 0.6 seconds x 330 m/s = 198m

Reference: *BMAT Assumed Subject Knowledge Guide:* Waves and their Effects: Wave Basics

BMAT Section 2 - 2012

1) **The correct answer is F (1, 2, 3 and 4)**

All of these options are correct and have physiological examples that support each effect. For instance, a rise or fall in blood pressure initiates homeostatic responses, and a rise or fall in outside temperature also initiates homeostatic responses. Therefore the correct answer is F.

Reference: *BMAT Assumed Subject Knowledge Guide:* Nerves, Hormones and Homeostasis: Homeostasis and Negative Feedback

2) **The correct answer is D (75%)**

The molar amounts of 1-bromobutane and butan-1-ol are equal (1:1 ratio). The equation to calculate the number of moles (n) =

$$Number\ of\ moles = \frac{mass\ (g)}{relative\ formula\ mass}$$

For 1-bromobutane, the M_r is

$$(12 \times 4) + 9 + 80 = 137$$

So the number of moles (n =

$$2.74/137 = 0.02\ moles$$

For butan-1-ol:

$$1.11/74 = 0.015$$

$$0.015/0.02 \times 100 = 75\%\ yield,\ which\ is\ option\ 'D'$$

Reference: *BMAT Assumed Subject Knowledge Guide:* Equations and Calculations: Relative Formula Mass

3) **The correct answer is B.**

N is the mass number (the number of protons and neutrons in the nucleus), and R is the atomic number (the number of protons only). The number of protons defines what the element is, while isotopes are versions of that element which all have the same atomic number but different mass numbers.

In the first stage, X has two more protons than Y, which is commonly associated with alpha decay (where two protons and two neutrons are lost – so P, the mass number, is N-4). Between Y and Z, there is no change in mass number (which stays at P, or N-4) which suggests beta radiation, where a neutron changes into a proton, and so one proton is gained from Y to Z. This changes the atomic number from R-2 to R-1, making the correct answer B.

Reference: *BMAT Assumed Subject Knowledge Guide:* The Atom and Radioactivity: Ionising Radiation

4)   The correct answer is A

For the smallest circle, the area is:

$$\pi \; x \; (1/2d)^2$$

Therefore the radius, which is half the diameter =

$$1/4\pi d^2$$

The second circle is:

$$\pi \; x \; d2 \; = \; \pi d^2$$

Subtracting the smallest circle from the second circle =

$$3/4\pi d^2$$

This is the smaller shaded area. For the third circle the area =

$$\pi \; x$$

$$= \frac{9}{4}\pi d^2$$

$$= 2.25\pi d^2$$

For the largest circle, the area =

$$\pi \; x \; (2d)^2 = \; 4d^2$$

The difference between these is 1.75πd^2 which gives the larger shaded area.
Adding these two =

$$2.5\pi d^2$$

$$\text{or} \; \frac{5}{2}\pi \; d^2$$

(Option A)

Reference: *BMAT Assumed Subject Knowledge Guide:* Geometry and Measures: Area

5)   The correct answer is B.

A general knowledge of the dangers of smoking and the chemicals it contains is required. It is well known that nicotine is the addictive substance in cigarettes, which must mean that it affects the brain, so 'Area 1'. 'Area 2' points to the bronchi, thus suggesting bronchitis, which is the irritation and inflammation of the bronchi. 'Area 3' refers to the alveoli, which break down, leading to a reduced surface area for gas exchange resulting in emphysema. 'Area 4' points to the blood vessels required for gas exchange, which carbon monoxide disrupts by binding to red blood cells.

6)   The correct answer is C.

The 'head' of the lecithin is meant to represent the charged part of the molecule that will dissolve in water, termed hydrophilic, and the tail is meant to represent the uncharged part of the molecule that will not dissolve, termed hydrophobic.

7)   The correct answer is F (β and γ).

A piece of paper can stop alpha particles; beta particles are stopped by a sheet of aluminium, while some gamma can be absorbed by a thick slab of lead. Looking at the data, there is hardly any difference between the readings for 'nothing' and 'paper', suggesting that no alpha radiation is present. The fact that the numbers decrease significantly after going through an aluminium sheet, but do not fall close to zero, suggests that both beta radiation and gamma radiation is present here.

Reference: *BMAT Assumed Subject Knowledge Guide:* The Atom and Radiation: Ionising Radiation

8)   The correct answer is E

$$G = 5 + \sqrt{7(9-R)^2 + 9}$$

The first steps are to move the 5 and the square root to the other side of the equation.

$$(G-5)^2 = 7(9-R)^2 + 9$$

Move the 9 that is being added to the bracket and the 7 that is being multiplied by the bracket:

$$\frac{(G-5)^2 - 9}{7} = (9-R)^2$$

Square root the left-hand side

$$\sqrt{\frac{(G-5)^2 - 9}{7}} = (9-R)^2$$

Finally, swap the '-R' for everything on the left-hand side, making 'R' the subject:

$$R = 9 - \sqrt{\frac{(G-5)^2 - 9}{7}}$$

Reference: *BMAT Assumed Subject Knowledge Guide:* Algebra: Rearranging Formulas

9)   The correct answer is A (1 and 2).

Statement one is true. Since the stimulus cannot be detected, a reflex arc cannot follow as a result and a reflex action or output cannot occur.

Statement two is also true because the visual cues can also cause actions/outputs. For instance, if someone could not sense a hot frying pan but saw it (especially with flames underneath), it would act as a visual stimulus to move their hand away from the frying pan, as they can see that it is hot, even if they cannot feel it.

Statement three is incorrect because the problem is with the detection (sensing) of pain rather than being able to 'act' or respond to it.

Statement four is also false because the problem is not with the communication to the brain, but the 'sensing' of pain in the first place.

Therefore the best answer is A (1 and 2 only)

Reference: *BMAT Assumed Subject Knowledge Guide:* Nerves, Hormones and Homeostasis: Synapses and Reflexes

10)   The correct answer is D (1, 2, 1, 2).

The first step to balancing any equation is to count up the species on each side of the equation. Therefore:

	Left	Right
Na	3	5
H	3	2
P	2	3
O	8	11

The best place to start is with hydrogen as only water contains it on the right-hand side compared to both reactants on the left-hand side. Many of the options for hydrogen can be eliminated quickly (especially the ones where the first is equal to or more than the last number because this cannot possibly balance) because the hydrogen atoms do not balance, apart from 'D'.

Reference: *BMAT Assumed Subject Knowledge Guide:* Chemical Concepts: Balancing Equations

11) **The correct answer is D.**

Work done (wd) is more than just wd = f xd. Distance (d) is the distance moved and wd provides the energy transfer. Thus in diagram one, when the person is sitting down, there is no energy transfer, and so no work being done.

In diagram two, the distance is incorrect – technically, he is doing no work. There is no energy transfer for spinning around a point, so the distance should be the height he moves the handle, not the distance from the pivot. This is the turning moment that needs to be calculated. There is work done by the force required to swivel the wheelbarrow as shown in the diagram, but as explained, no distance is being moved.

Diagram three, as seen in diagram two, the motor is doing work by using force to pull the object. Unlike all the others, however, an actual distance is being moved (vertically upwards), so this is the only case of wd = f xd. Therefore, 'D' is correct.

Reference: *BMAT Assumed Subject Knowledge Guide:* Forces and Energy: Work Done

12) **The correct answer is E (1940)**

$$\sqrt[3]{\frac{2 \times 10^5}{(5 \times 10^{-3})^2}} - \sqrt{(4 \times 10^3) - (4 \times 10^2)}$$

The first step is to tidy up the numbers inside the square root on the left by removing the brackets and multiplying the power -3 (on the 10) by the 2 outside the bracket and squaring the 5; giving 25 x 10^{-6} as the denominator.

$$\sqrt[3]{\frac{2 \times 10^5}{25 \times 10^{-6}}} - \sqrt{(4 \times 10^3) - (4 \times 10^2)}$$

The next step is to remove the powers, by using the rule of indices. Since this is division, the powers must be subtracted so 5 - - 6 = 11 (10^{11}). Giving:

$$\sqrt[3]{\frac{2 \times 10^{11}}{25}} - \sqrt{(4 \times 10^3) - (4 \times 10^2)}$$

2 divided by 25 is 0.08; 0.08 x 10^{11} is the same as 8 x 10^9

$$\sqrt[3]{8 \times 10^9} - \sqrt{(4 \times 10^3) - (4 \times 10^2)}$$

Cube root this to give:

$$2 \times 10^3 - \sqrt{(4 \times 10^3) - (4 \times 10^2)}$$

Looking at the second square root, it is simpler to work out. 4×10^3 is 4,000, while 4×10^2 is 400, so the difference between them is 3,600. The square root is 60.

$$2 \times 10^3 - 60 =$$

$$2 \times 10^3 (2,000) - 60$$

$$= 1940$$

Reference: *BMAT Assumed Subject Knowledge Guide:* Algebra: Solving Equations

13) The correct answer is E (1 and 3 only).
There is an equal distance around the outside of disc Q and R, suggesting that antibiotics at X and ½ X strengths appear to be equal, so as a result, statement one can be considered correct.
There is no indication that antibiotic resistance occurs at all three strengths, given that two of the three discs show a clear space around their circumference, indicating no bacterial growth in this area. In light of this evidence, statement two is incorrect.
This option is a possibility as had the antibiotic diffused further out of the disc; there may be a larger 'halo circumference' around disc R. Hence statement three is correct.

14) The correct answer is F ($Cu_3C_2H_2O_8$).
Since there are three coppers in all options, there must be three moles altogether of $CuCO_3$ and $Cu(OH)_2$. This may be as two moles of the former and one of the latter, or vice versa, as it is a mixture.
Two moles of $CuCO_3$ and one mole of $Cu(OH)_2$, will give three moles of copper, two moles of carbon, eight moles of oxygen and two moles of hydrogen; this is option F.
For the alternative option, there is one mole of $CuCO_3$ and two moles of $Cu(OH)_2$. This results in three moles of copper, one mole of carbon, seven moles of oxygen and four hydrogen. This is option not available, thus, option F is the correct answer.

15) The correct answer is B.
When a wave travels through an object, its frequency is unaltered but its wavelength changes. In light of this, the following formula can be used to find out the wavelength of the wave when it passes through the food containers.

$$wave\ speed\ =\ frequency\ x\ wavelength$$

The initial frequency of the wave:

$$3.0 \times 10^8 = 12 \times \lambda.$$

$$\frac{3.0 \times 10^8}{12} = 12 \times \lambda.$$

$$\lambda = 0.25 \, x \, 10^8 \rightarrow 2.5 \, x \, 10^7$$

This frequency value can now be used with the decreased speed when the wave passes through the plastic container, thus providing the new wavelength value:

$$2.0 \, x \, 10^8 = f \, x \, 2.5 \, x \, 10^7$$

$$f = 2.0 \, x \, 10^8 / 2.5 \, x \, 10^7$$

$$= 0.8 \times 10 = 8 \text{ cm.}$$
(Option B)

Reference: *BMAT Assumed Subject Knowledge Guide:* Waves and their Effects: Wave Basics

16)   The correct answer is C (4/9)

The key to this problem is to realise that each tan ratio is referring to a different triangle. Tan A refers to the triangle ACM; then CM can be labelled as 1 and AC as 6 (tan = opposite/adjacent). Tan B refers to triangle ABC, and can hence be labelled AC as 2 and BC as 3. Because each of these numbers are nominal ratios, tan A can be changed to 4/24 and tan B to 6/9. Tan θ is CB/CM, or 4/9.

Reference: *BMAT Assumed Subject Knowledge Guide:* Pythagoras and Trigonometry: Trigonometry – Sin, Cos, Tan

17)   The correct answer is C (1 and 4 only).

ADH is a hormone that is produced by the pituitary gland and regulates urination. Statement one is correct as alcohol travels in the bloodstream, causing a reduction in ADH hormone. Therefore, for this communication to occur, ADH must also move through the bloodstream.

Statement two is false as the preamble to the statement reveals that an increase in alcohol consumption reduces ADH levels.

Statement three also contradicts the information stated in the preamble; increased alcohol (and therefore, decreased ADH) causes more dilute urine production. Hence this statement is also false.

Statement four is correct because ADH reduces urine output. When there is less ADH, there will be more urination/water loss, and therefore more dehydration.
Therefore, only one and four are correct.

Reference: *BMAT Assumed Subject Knowledge Guide:* Nerves, Hormones and Homeostasis: Controlling Water Content

18) **The correct answer is D (treating a solution of vanadium sulfate with metallic iron).**

Zinc is above iron in the reactivity series, and therefore iron cannot displace the vanadium from vanadium sulfate, consequently no reaction will occur. All of the other options are possible because the elements and the methods used (such as electrolysis) facilitate displacement of vanadium.

Reference: *BMAT Assumed Subject Knowledge Guide:* Products from Rocks: The Reactivity Series; Classifying Materials: The Periodic Table

19) **The correct option is D.**

There are many things to consider in this question, which makes it difficult. In a parallel circuit, voltage is the same across each of the branches and current is variable. Furthermore, the total resistance of a parallel circuit is calculated by adding the reciprocals of the individual resistances together:

$$1/total\ resistance\ =\ 1/resistance\ `a'\ +\ 1/resistance\ `b'\ ...$$

Firstly, if Lamp X blows, the resistance for the branch for X increases. In this situation:
1/total resistance = 1/big number (for the resistance for the circuit in X) + 1/normal number (for the other parallel circuit). This is in comparison to total resistance = 1/normal number + 1/normal number, so relatively, the overall resistance would increase (because the formula is 1/total resistance, so the reciprocal would be a bigger number). Given that the total resistance increases, this will affect both Ammeter 1 and 2. Ammeter 1 measures the total current, and because of the increased total resistance, it will give a lower reading. This is because V = IR where voltage throughout the circuit stays the same, the total resistance increases, thus the total current must decrease. Equally, however, all current now flows through the bottom branch of the circuit as well, where Ammeter 2 is concerned. Voltage is constant along branches, and because the individual resistance of this branch does not increase like the one in X, current must increase. Therefore the answer is 'D'.

Reference: *BMAT Assumed Subject Knowledge Guide:* Electricity: Parallel Circuits; Resistance and V = I x R

20) **The correct option is B (1/4).**

The key information required here is that the player is equally likely to choose each bag, and the game is set up, so the player has the smallest possible chance of winning. A win is defined as either two red balls or two yellow balls. The way to set up the reds, so the player has the least chance of winning is to put two reds in each bag. If there were three in one, and one in the other, there is a ½ chance the player will get the bag with 3 red balls (out of 4 balls in total) – the same if all four was in one bag. Therefore, the probability is:
½ (probability of picking either bag) x ½ (2 out of 4 red balls) x 1/3 (1 out of 3 red balls) = 1/12
For yellow balls, the feasible option is to put two balls in one bag and one in the other. So if the player was to win:
½ x 2/3 (two out of three yellow balls) x ½ (one out of two yellow balls) = 1/6
Adding 1/12 and 1/6 give a probability of ¼.

Reference: *BMAT Assumed Subject Knowledge Guide:* Statistics and Probability: The AND/OR Rules

21)   The correct answer is D (2 and 3 only).

The ratio refers to dominant: recessive phenotypes. The situation given has 3:0 ratio – so no recessive phenotypes have appeared, thus reason one is incorrect. Reason two is correct, a smaller sample size of offspring may not reflect the monohybrid ratio of 3:1. The chance of producing a recessive phenotype offspring is ¼, compared to ¾ for the dominant phenotype, if more offspring are produced; it is still possible, due to chance, that no recessive phenotypes will be produced. This also verifies reason three. Therefore the correct option is D.

Reference: *BMAT Assumed Subject Knowledge Guide:* Genes, Reproduction and Evolution: More on Genetic Disorders

22)   The correct answer is B (2 only).

In beta decay, the number of protons increases by one and the number of neutrons decreases by one. So for tritium, its mass number will stay the same, but its atomic number will increase by one (as the number of protons has increased). Therefore it turns into helium-3, and gives off an electron (see below):

$$_1^3H \rightarrow \, _2^3He + \, _{-1}^{0}e$$

Oxygen in the HTO is in the -2 state and is a strong electron acceptor. If it accepts the electron from the decay, it becomes unstable and splits into molecular oxygen (O_2) and an oxide ion (O^{2-}) – obviously more than one mole of tritium has to decay. It then makes sense that the O^{2-} ion is accepted with the H^{2+} ions to make water, and molecular oxygen also forms, as said above.

Reference: *BMAT Assumed Subject Knowledge Guide:* The Atom and Radioactivity: Ionising Radiation

23)   The correct answer is D.

The question states that the cyclist freewheels down the slope at a constant speed. The cyclist gets all his energy from gravitational potential energy, which is either converted into kinetic energy (which can be calculated by ½ mv^2) or work done against friction (which is $wd = f \times d$, where d is the distance travelled, and so is parallel to the slope). Therefore:

Gravitational Potential Energy = weight × height

GPE = 100kg x 10 x 100 m = 100,000 J

100,000 J is also Work done, which is Work done = force x distance.
The force can be calculated from the information given in the question: for every one metre covered vertically, 10 metres are covered on the road. So if 100 metres are covered vertically, 1000 metres are covered along the road. Therefore:

wd = f xd = 100,000

$$d = 1000m$$

$$f = wd/d$$

$$= 100,000/1,000$$

$$= 100 \text{ N}$$

Reference: *BMAT Assumed Subject Knowledge Guide:* Forces and Energy: Work Done; Kinetic Energy; Gravitational Potential Energy

24)   The correct answer is A (25%).

The cost of metal (M) + the cost of wood (W) = the total cost (C):

$$M_{COST} + W_{COST} + C$$

The cost of M is proportional to the diameter: $M_{COST} = kD$ and the cost of W is proportional to the square of the diameter: $W_{COST}= uD^2$.

When the diameter doubles, the cost triples, so the new cost of metal is 2kD, and for W:

$$4uD^2 \text{ x } 2kD + 4uD^2 = 3C$$

Since $kD + uD^2 = C$, simultaneous equations can be used to remove one of the variables and allow the other to be worked out:

$$2kD + 4uD^2 = 3C$$

$$kD + uD^2 = C \text{ (x2)} \rightarrow 2kD + 2uD^2 = 2C$$

Subtracting these

$$= 2uD^2 = C$$

The value of C can then be substituted again:

$$2uD^2 = kD + uD^2$$

$$uD^2 = kD$$

uD^2 represents the cost of wood and kD represents the cost of metal.

Therefore the cost per unit of metal is three times that of wood, the ratio of the cost must be 3:1 and so metal must make up 25% (of one out of four parts) of the cost of the sign.

Reference: *BMAT Assumed Subject Knowledge Guide:* Algebra: Simultaneous Equations

25)   The correct answer is E.

Recessive conditions only show their phenotype (physical effect) when the genotype is homozygous recessive; that is, the sufferer has inherited two recessive alleles, one from each parent. Therefore, both parents must carry at least one recessive allele and one dominant allele (hence being heterozygous). The heterozygous parents must gain their recessive allele from their parents (the 'grandparents'), and in this generation, at least one of the grandparents must be heterozygous to produce a heterozygous offspring (the 'parent') if they do not suffer from the disease. Other family members (such as the other grandparent, uncles, or the like) can be homozygous dominant or heterozygous if they do not also suffer from the condition.

Thus if 'U' has the condition, 'S' and 'T' must both be heterozygous. 'S' must have gained her recessive allele from one of 'P' or 'Q', but as there is no indication that either 'P' or 'Q' suffered from the disease, one of them must have been heterozygous. The other relatives do not have to be heterozygous, so overall three of the people in the pedigree must be heterozygous.

If both 'R' and 'U' have the condition, 'S' and 'T' must again be heterozygous (for 'U') and 'P' and 'Q' must be heterozygous (for 'R'); this gives us four individuals who must be heterozygous.

Reference: *BMAT Assumed Subject Knowledge Guide:* Genes, Reproduction and Evolution: More on Genetic Disorders

26)   The correct answer is E.

This question relates to understanding how pressure affects equilibrium. In general, the reaction is favoured towards the direction that produces less pressure (in other words, the direction producing fewer moles of gas). At the start of the reaction, the forward reaction is favoured because two gaseous moles of reactants are converted to one gaseous mole of product. There is a high amount of pressure initially because there is little product compared to two moles of reactants. As the reaction progresses (and is catalysed by the nickel), more of the one mole of ethane is produced, giving less pressure. Thus E is the correct option.

Reference: *BMAT Assumed Subject Knowledge Guide:* Reaction Rates and Energy Changes: Changing Equilibrium

27)   The correct answer is G (S only).

Frequency can be calculated by:

$$Frequency = 1/time\ period$$

The time period is 0.2 ms, so the frequency is 5 kHz, making statement 'S' is true. Statement 'P' is incorrect because the speed of sound is constant in air – this is 340m/s. X and Y are two extreme points, so the amplitude would be half the distance between X and Y – 2.5mm, thus making statement 'Q' incorrect as well. Wavelength is calculated by:

$$velocity\ of\ wave/frequency = \lambda$$

$$= 340m/s \; /5kHz$$

$$= 68mm$$

This means that statement 'R' is incorrect.

Reference: *BMAT Assumed Subject Knowledge Guide:* Waves and their Effects: Wave Basics

BMAT Section 2 - 2013

1) **The correct answer is H (1, 2 and 3)**

All three statements apply to both the nervous and endocrine system. These systems work together to maintain homeostasis in the body. Both systems involve chemicals; for the nervous system, this could be neurotransmitters such as dopamine, whereas it could be hormones such as insulin or ADH for the endocrine system. The brain coordinates the functioning of the nervous system. Hormones such as ADH are produced in the pituitary gland of the brain.

Reference: *BMAT Assumed Subject Knowledge Guide:* Nerves, Hormones and Homeostasis: Hormones

2) **The correct answer is D (1 and 4 only)**

Displacement reactions are determined by a chemical's relative reactivity. Aluminium is more reactive than lead and zinc is more reactive than copper, so the first and fourth equations are displacement reactions. However, iron is less reactive than aluminium, and fluorine cannot bind to chlorine. Hence, the answer is D.

Reference: *BMAT Assumed Subject Knowledge Guide:* Products from Rocks: The Reactivity Series

3) **The correct answer is D (1 and 2 only)**

Statements one and two are correct because living tissues contain water molecules and ionising radiation can damage the DNA in the nucleus. Statement three, however, is incorrect because infra-red damages living tissue through heat. So, the answer is D.

Reference: *BMAT Assumed Subject Knowledge Guide:* Waves and their Effects: Microwaves; Infrared

4) **The correct answer is A (10/7)**

$$X + 7y = 6 \times 10^7 \text{ and } x - 2y = 4.2 \times 10^7$$

$$(6 \times 10^7)/(4.2 \times 10^7) =$$

$$6/4.2 = 10/7.$$

Making the answer A

5) **The correct answer is F (2 or 3 only)**

Carbohydrase breaks down carbohydrates into monosaccharides, this does not affect pH. Protease breaks down proteins to amino acids, decreasing the pH.
Lipase breaks down lipids to glycerol and fatty acids, also decreasing the pH. Therefore, the answer is F

Reference: *BMAT Assumed Subject Knowledge Guide:* Organs and Systems: The Digestive System - Enzymes

6)   The correct answer is B
Delta H is negative, so the forward reaction is exothermic. Therefore, decreasing the temperature shifts the position of the equilibrium to the right. Also, there are fewer moles of gas on the right, so increasing the pressure or increasing the concentration of R and S will also encourage the equilibrium to shift to the right. Hence, the correct answer is B.

Reference: *BMAT Assumed Subject Knowledge Guide:* Reaction Rates and Energy Changes: Energy Transfer in Reactions; Bond Energies

7)   The correct answer is H (P increases, Q increases, R decreases)
Closing the switch provides a new path of least resistance that allows the current to bypass the first resistor (R). Therefore, when resistance decreases, and current increases, the total voltage will stay the same (Current=voltage/resistance). The reading on the ammeter (P) will consequently increase. There is no voltage across the first resistor, and all the voltage is connected across the second resistor, so as Q and R are voltmeters (connected in parallel), the readings increase and decrease respectively. Thus, the answer is H.

Reference: *BMAT Assumed Subject Knowledge Guide:* Electricity: Resistance and V = I x R

8)   The correct answer is F (6 + 1/2x)

$$\frac{4 - (X^2(1 - 16x^2)}{(4x - 1)2x^3}$$

Open the brackets:

$$\frac{(1 - 4x)(1 + 4x)}{2x(4x - 1)}$$

Simplify:

$$\frac{4 + (1 + 4x)}{2x}$$

Form a top heavy fraction:

$$\frac{(12x + 1)}{2x}$$

Split the numerator

$$6 - \frac{1}{2x}$$
(Answer F)

9)   The correct answer is F

The longest neuron is the sensory neuron as its runs from the hand to the spinal cord. The shortest neuron is the relay neuron which connects the sensory neuron to the motor neuron, running to the biceps muscle, making the answer F.

Reference: *BMAT Assumed Subject Knowledge Guide:* Nerves, Hormones and Homeostasis: Neurons

10)   The correct answer is B (560 cm³)

The equation for this problem is

$$Number\ of\ moles = \frac{mass\ (g)}{relative\ formula\ mass}$$

$$1.15\ /23$$

$$= 0.05\ moles$$

$2Na + 2H_2O \rightarrow 2NaOH + H_2$ so, 0.05/2= 0.025 moles of hydrogen gas are produced.

$$Moles\ x\ STP\ =\ volume$$

$$0.025\ x\ 22400 = 560cm^3$$
(Answer B)

Reference: *BMAT Assumed Subject Knowledge Guide:* Equations and Calculations: Relative Formula Mass;

11)   The correct answer is C

The critical angle for the glass/air boundary is 42° when the ray of light is travelling from a medium of high density (glass) to a medium of low density (air). However, there is no critical angle when the ray of light travels from air to glass. In diagram one, 40° is less than the critical angle of 42°, so total internal reflection will not take place, and most of the light will be refracted (P). In diagram two, total internal reflection also cannot take place, so most of the light will be refracted (S), thus making the answer C.

Reference: *BMAT Assumed Subject Knowledge Guide:* Waves and their Effects: Wave Properties - Refraction

12)   The correct answer is B (A reflection in the y-axis)

Rotating clockwise through 90° about the origin results in points A, B, C, D having coordinates: (1, -1), (1, 1), (-1, 1), and (-1, -1) respectively. A reflection in line y=x will result in points A, B, C, D having coordinates: (-1, 1), (1, 1), (1, -1), and (-1, -1) respectively. Therefore, to transform the square back to its original orientation, a reflection in the y-axis is needed. So, the answer is B.

Reference: *BMAT Assumed Subject Knowledge Guide:* Geometry and Measures: The Four Transformations

13)   The correct answer is C (Fluorescent protein from a jellyfish)

Enzymes (also known as restriction enzymes) are used to cut the DNA molecule at a specific locus to get the desired gene, and the ligase enzyme is needed to insert the gene into a plasmid or viral genome. To produce a fluorescent protein, the gene for the protein is required, rather than the protein itself. So, the answer is C.

Reference: *BMAT Assumed Subject Knowledge Guide:* Genes, Reproduction and Evolution: Genetic Engineering

14)   The correct answer is A ($MgCl_2$ and three atoms of argon)

$MgCl_2$ is an ionic compound consisting of Mg^{2+} and $2Cl^-$, which is equivalent to two atoms of argon and one atom of neon. So, the answer is A.

Reference: *BMAT Assumed Subject Knowledge Guide:* Classifying Materials: The Periodic Table

15)   The correct answer is D (70 counts per minute)

After 24 hours, isotope X has undergone:

$$24/4.8 = 5 \text{ half-lives}$$

Isotope Y has undergone:

$$24/8 = 3 \text{ half-lives}$$

Therefore the amount remaining:

$$320/2^5 = 10 \text{ and } 480/2^3 = 60$$

The combined amount remaining after 24 hours =

$$60 + 10 = 70$$
(Option D)

Reference: *BMAT Assumed Subject Knowledge Guide:* The Atom and Radioactivity: Half-Life

16)   The correct answer is D (The cube of x is inversely proportional to the square of y)

The statements can be summarised by the formulae:

$$X = kz^2 \text{ (where k is a constant)}$$
$$\text{and}$$
$$y = c/z^3 \text{ (where c is a constant)}$$

This means that:

$$z = (c/y)^{1/3} \text{ and } x = k(c/y)^{2/3}$$

Resulting in:

$$x^3 = (k^3 c^2)/y^2$$
$$\text{(Answer D)}$$

Reference: *BMAT Assumed Subject Knowledge Guide:* Algebra: Variables; Direct and Inverse Proportion

17)   The correct answer is A (1, 3 and 5 only)

Statement one is true, as the quality of the oocyte and the newly transferred material can vary significantly from case to case. Somatic cell nuclear transfer does not involve fertilisation, making statement two irrelevant. Implantation is also an important aspect which determines the success the embryo, as this provides it with vital nutrients to develop correctly. Hence statement three is correct

Statement four is also irrelevant, as somatic cell nuclear transfer does not involve the use of stem cells. Statement five is also true since there are many processes involved to ensure that the nucleus is accepted into the enucleated egg. So, the answer is A.

18)   The correct answer is E (83.3%)

The balanced equation for this reaction is: $NaOH + HCl \rightarrow NaCl + H_2O$.

To calculate the number of moles of hydrochloric acid:

$$Number\ of\ moles = concentration\ \times volume$$

$$= 0.05 \times 0.5 = 0.025 \text{ moles}$$

To find the mass of pure sodium hydroxide:

$$mass = Number\ of\ moles\ \times relative\ formula\ mass$$

The Mr of sodium hydroxide =

$$23 + 16 + 1 = 40$$

Therefore the pure mass =

$$0.025 \times 40 = 1 \text{ g}$$

$$Percentage\ purity = \frac{pure\ mass}{impure\ mass} \times 100\%$$

$$= 1/1.2 = 83.3\%$$

(Option E)

Reference: *BMAT Assumed Subject Knowledge Guide:* Equations and Calculation: Relative Formula Mass

19) **The correct answer is D**

$$P = VI, and\ I = V/(R_1 + R_2)$$

Combining these equations gives:

$$P = V^2/(R_1 + R_2)$$

The voltage across the resistor R_1 is IR_1, so the power dissipated by R_1 is I^2R_1 (as P = VI and $V = IR_1$).

$$I = \frac{V}{R_1 + R_2}$$

Giving the end result of:

$$P = \frac{V^2 R_1}{(R_2 + R2)^2}$$

(Option D)

Reference: *BMAT Assumed Subject Knowledge Guide:* Electricity: Resistance and V = I x R

20) **The correct answer is D (36cm²)**
The surface area of the smallest cube is 5cm² (1cm² x 5)

The side length of the medium sized cube is x

$$1^2 + 1^2 = x^2$$

$$x = 2^{1/2}$$

Therefore the surface area of the middle sized cube is:

$$(4 \times 2) + (2-1) = 9 \text{ cm}^2$$

The side length of the largest cube is y:

$$2 + 2 = y^2 \text{ So, } y = 2.$$

This means that the surface area of the largest cube is:

$$(5 \times 2^2) + (2^2 - 2) = 22 \text{cm}^2$$

Therefore the total surface area of the shape is:

$$5 + 9 + 22 = 36 \text{ cm}^2$$

(Option B)

21)   The correct answer is E (1 and 2 only)

Liver cells are somatic cells and therefore contain a diploid number of chromosomes (46 in humans). This means that the genes for all enzymes and proteins as well as the sex chromosomes (XX or XY) can be found in every somatic cell in the body, with the liver being no exception to this. However, the liver cells store glycogen and not starch. So, the answer is E.

22)   The correct answer is C (4)

The first step is to count up the number of atoms of each species, on each side of the table:

	Left	Right
C	2	2
H	5	6
Cr	2	1
O	8	3

There are two atoms of chromium on the left-hand side; so, there must be two on the right-hand side, d = 2. This makes the total charge on the right-hand side 6+. Since only $C_2H_4O_2$ and C_2H_4O are the only sources of carbon atoms a = c, therefore if b = 8 H^+ then e = 4 which means that the number of hydrogen atoms on the right-hand side is now balanced with the left-hand side. This action impacts the number of oxygen atoms on the right, bringing it to 6, still two atoms short of being balanced with the left-hand side. Because a = c, both of these will = 3 to balance the numbers of oxygen atoms on both sides. Therefore the answer is C (e = 4)

Reference: *BMAT Assumed Subject Knowledge Guide:* Chemical Concepts: Balancing Equations

23)   The correct answer is D (The variation of the wavelength (y-axis) of waves with a speed of 0.2m/s with their frequency (x-axis))

The graph can represent F=ma as mass is constant. Therefore option A can be considered correct. Option B can also be considered a correct option as I=V/R with resistance remaining constant. Kinetic energy = ½ mv^2 is also a correct option (C) as the mass in this equation remains constant. For the equation W=Fd, force remains constant, therefore option E is also valid.

In option D, wavelength = speed/frequency. This option is not valid as although speed is constant, the frequency is inversely proportional to the wavelength, therefore this option is incorrect.

24)   The correct answer is C (8/15)

There are a total of 10 balls from which to choose. To select two blue balls and a red ball in any order, the probability for each ball must be calculated and then multiplied by three (the number of balls being selected).

The chance of selecting a blue ball first is 8/10. Since all three balls are chosen at once, they are not replaced. Therefore the chance of getting a blue ball the second time is 7/9. The chance of getting a red ball as the third choice is 2/8.

The three balls above can be chosen in any order, therefore the total probability for this combination is:

$$(3 \times (8/10 \times 7/9 \times 2/8)) = 7/15$$

The chance of selecting two red balls and one blue ball is as follows:

$$(3 \times (2/10 \times 1/9 \times 1)) = 1/15$$

Therefore the total probability =

$$7/15 + 1/15 = 8/15$$
(Option C)

Reference: *BMAT Assumed Subject Knowledge Guide:* Statistics and Probability: The AND/OR Rules

25)   The correct answer is C

The dominant allele for this problem can be represented by T, and the recessive allele is t. Crossing genotype tt with Tt results in 50% Tt and 50% tt (resulting 50% without tails). Crossing Tt with Tt produces 25% TT (dead), 25% tt and 50% Tt (therefore 2/3 of living cats do not have tails). So, the answer is C.

Reference: *BMAT Assumed Subject Knowledge Guide:* Genes, Reproduction and Evolution: More on Genetic Disorders

26)   The correct answer is B (3,6)

NO is more likely to form the intermediate product NO_2 than N_2. So, equation three is the first step, and as NO is a catalyst, it needs to be regenerated, and NO_2 needs to react with SO_2. So, equation six is the next step. This gives the answer B.

27)   The correct answer is E (1400J)

$$F = ma$$

$$a = 20/4$$

$$a = 5ms^{-2}$$

$$E_k = 1/2mv^2$$

$$1800 = 0.5 \times 4v^2$$

$$v = 30$$

The body will gain another 10m/s in two seconds. So, the new kinetic energy:

$$= 2 \times 40^2 = 3200J$$

Therefore the difference =

$$3200 - 1800$$

$$= 1400 \text{ J}$$

Option E

Reference: *BMAT Assumed Subject Knowledge Guide:* Forces and Energy: Forces and Acceleration; Kinetic Energy

BMAT Section 2 - 2014

1)   The correct answer is C (4 only)

The deoxygenated blood travels from the body through the vena cava and enters the right atrium making statement two false (ruling out option B, F, and G). The deoxygenated blood enters the right side of the heart, before going to the lungs, making statement one incorrect (thereby ruling out A, D, and E). From the right ventricle, the blood then travels to the lungs via the pulmonary artery (making statement three false). Once the blood has been oxygenated, it returns to the left side of the heart when it moves through the left atrium and ventricle. The aorta is the major vessel in which oxygenated blood leaves the heart at high pressure. The aortic valve prevents the blood from flowing backwards into the left ventricle as it exits the heart by way of the aorta. Therefore statement four is correct.

Reference: *BMAT Assumed Subject Knowledge Guide:* Organs and Systems: The Circulatory System – Heart

2)   The correct answer is B (1 and 3 only)

For a redox reaction to occur, there must be electrons transferred.

In reaction one the copper changes from Cu^{2+} to Cu (meaning it is reduced) and the zinc changes from Zn to Zn^{+2} (oxidation), therefore this is a redox reaction, ruling out options D, E, and F

Reaction two has no electrons transferred, and the ionic charges remain the same. Therefore this is not a redox reaction and rules out option A.

Reaction three is similar to reaction one where the magnesium is oxidised since it changes from Mg to Mg^{2+} when it becomes $MgSO_4$. The H_2SO_4 is reduced because it changes from H_2SO_4 (this molecule contains 2 x H^+ ions) to H_2 gas. Reaction four is not a redox reaction because there is no transfer of electrons.

Reference: *BMAT Assumed Subject Knowledge Guide*: Chemical change: Redox Reactions

3)   The correct answer is D (4 only)

Statement one is incorrect because microwaves have one of the longest wavelengths (and therefore have one of the lowest energy levels) when compared to other waves in the electromagnetic spectrum. This excludes options A, E, and F.

The higher the frequency and the energy it can transfer, the shorter the wavelength, therefore statement two is also incorrect, ruling out options B, G, and H.

Statement three is false as the wavelength and frequency of a wave are inversely proportional to each other, but both are directly proportional to the velocity of the wave according to the equation velocity = frequency × wavelength, making option C incorrect.

Statement four is correct as ultraviolet waves have a higher frequency than visible light, so carry more energy and can, therefore, damage the cornea (transparent layer in the front of the eye) causing cataracts. Therefore option D is the correct answer.

Reference: *BMAT Assumed Subject Knowledge Guide*: Waves and their Effects: Wave Basics

4) **The correct answer is B (x/x+4)**

$$\frac{x^2 - 4x}{x^2 - 16}$$

Factorise both the top and the bottom:

$$\frac{x(x-4)}{(x+4)(x-4)}$$

Cancel out (x- 4) leaving:

$$\frac{x}{(x+4)}$$

Reference: *BMAT Assumed Subject Knowledge Guide:* Algebra: Algebraic Fractions

5) **The correct answer is D (K, M, N)**

During DNA synthesis the DNA doubles through the process of DNA replication. As a result, the number on the graph increases from 1 to 2 AU. The only place this occurs in the graph is at M, which immediately rules out options A, B, C, G and H. Once DNA replication occurs, the next stage is for it to separate to either pole of the cell. However, the amount of DNA is still going to be the same (so 2 AU), on the graph this appears as either J or N (as these lines are the only two at 2 AU which is horizontal). When the cell divides the DNA content will decrease, meaning that there must be a decline on the graph, which is K as the content decreases from 2 AU to 1 AU. Therefore the correct option is D.

Reference: *BMAT Assumed Subject Knowledge Guide:* Genes, Reproduction and Evolution: Cell Division - Mitosis

6) **The correct answer is H**

Temperature is a measure of the average kinetic energy of the particles. Therefore by increasing the temperature the kinetic energy, the particles possess also increases. When these particles have a higher level of kinetic energy, they move around at a much faster speed. This increases both the frequency of collisions and the force of these collisions, thereby excluding options A, B, E and F. With a greater number of collisions occurring, with greater force, the chance of the collisions being successful also increases (ruling out options C, and D). The activation energy is the amount of energy that is required to allow the reaction to occur; this is fixed and therefore does not change when the temperature is adjusted thus ruling out G and making H correct.

Reference: *BMAT Assumed Subject Knowledge Guide*: Reaction Rates and Energy Changes: Collision Theory

7) The correct answer is F (watt/volt)

A is incorrect as this infers the equation I = Q /t which is coulomb/second

B is incorrect as this infers the same equation: I = Q /t is coulomb per second, not coulomb x second as is written in B.

C is incorrect as this implies the equation: W/Q = V which calculates voltage not current.

D is incorrect as it uses the equation V=IR rearranged for I = V/R, this equation has been inverted and is therefore incorrect.

E is incorrect as it uses the equation V=IR rearranged for I = V/R but it is stated as VxR which is incorrect.

F is correct as this uses P = VI rearranged for I = P/V or power/voltage, so watts/volt is correct.

Reference: *BMAT Assumed Subject Knowledge Guide:* Electricity: Current and Electricity; Potential Difference; Resistance and V = I x R; Power Ratings;

8) The correct answer is B (n =2p + 3q)

$$4^p \times 8^q = 2^n$$

A number which is an exponent of an exponent is the same as multiplying the exponents:

$$\text{Since } 2^3 = 8 \text{ and } 2^2 = 4$$

$$8^q = (2^3)^q = 2^{3q}$$

$$4^p = (2^2)^p = 2^{2p}$$

$$= 2^{2p} \times 2^{3q}$$

Multiply the two numbers together that have the same base (also known as adding the exponents).

$$2^{p} + 3^{q} = 2^n$$

If the value of the bases is the same, the value of the exponents must also be the same.

$$2p + 3q = n$$
(Option B)

Reference: *BMAT Assumed Subject Knowledge Guide:* Algebra: Powers & Roots

9) The correct answer is D

To manufacture the protein insulin, the DNA (gene) for insulin is first acquired from a human chromosome, thus ruling out options A and B. Option A also refers insulin DNA as the end product which makes this statement further incorrect. The insulin gene must then be inserted into the circular DNA of a bacterium, which will express the gene

272

when it reproduces by binary fission. This fact makes statement E incorrect as it suggests that the insulin gene can be removed from one human and then placed directly into another human. The bacterial expression of the gene leads to the insulin protein being made as a result, not the insulin DNA as is suggested by option C, therefore making it incorrect and option D correct.

10) The correct answer is C (b=5)
The first step when balancing any equation is to count up the atoms on each side of the reaction (arrow).

$a\text{CH}_3\text{OH} + 3\text{H}_2\text{O}_2 \rightarrow \text{CO}_2 + b\text{H}_2\text{O}$

	Left	Right
C	1	1
H	10	2
O	7	1

When balancing a chemical equation, there must be the same number of carbon atoms, hydrogen atoms and oxygen atoms on both sides of the chemical reaction.

$a\text{CH}_3\text{OH} + 3\text{H}_2\text{O}_2 \rightarrow \text{CO}_2 + b\text{H}_2\text{O}$

Making $b = 5$ gives:

$a\text{CH}_3\text{OH} + 3\text{H}_2\text{O}_2 \rightarrow \text{CO}_2 + 5\text{H}_2\text{O}$

	Left	Right
C	1	1
H	10	10
O	7	7

Which makes C correct.

Reference: *BMAT Assumed Subject Knowledge Guide:* Chemical Concepts: Balancing equations

11) The correct answer is F (Rod X loses electrons to the cloth and rod Y is positively charged.)
When an object becomes charged, electrons are transferred to that object, therefore options C, D, G, and H are incorrect as they state that protons have been transferred. The gain of electrons means the object will have a negative charge (since the number of negative charges will outnumber the positive charges). The loss of electrons will confer a positive charge since the number of positive charges will now outweigh the negative charges. Therefore rod X will either gain electrons and become negatively charged or lose electrons and become positively charged. For the two rods X and Y to repel each other, they must have the same charge. Therefore A and E are incorrect as this would mean rod X and Y have the opposite charges and attract each other. Option B is also

incorrect as both must have a charge to repel. This leaves option F as the correct answer which makes rod X positive as it loses electrons and rod Y positive.

Reference: *BMAT Assumed Subject Knowledge Guide:* Electricity: Static Electricity

12)   The correct answer is F (225 + x/2)

On the diagram in the question, draw a vertical line downwards from point L (see red on diagram) to create another 90° angle. This shows that the angle of SLT is 90° + x since they are alternate angles.

Draw a straight line from point S to point T to create an isosceles triangle (black dotted line). The interior angles of a triangle add up to 180°, therefore:

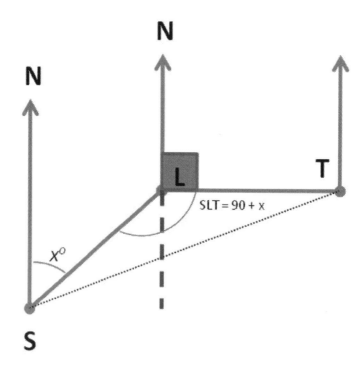

Angle LTS + Angle LST = 180 − SLT which is (90 + x)

Which means that angle LTS + LST = 90 + x or

$$\frac{90 + x}{2}$$

Since there are 2 'x' angles, to get from T to S:

$$\frac{270 - (90 + x)}{2}$$

$$270 - 45 + \frac{x}{2}$$

$$225 + \frac{x}{2}$$

Reference: *BMAT Assumed Subject Knowledge Guide:* Geometry and Measures: Bearings

13)   The correct answer is B (2 and 3 only)
ADH or antidiuretic hormone controls the amount of water in the blood and tells the kidneys how much water they should conserve. When the blood-water levels are too low the pituitary gland releases more ADH, ruling out statement one and making statement two correct. The ADH acts on the kidneys causing them to decrease the amount of water in urine, thus making it more concentrated. This increases the amount of water that is reabsorbed into the blood, making statement three also correct and statement four incorrect. The reabsorption of glucose is not related to the concentration of water in the blood, therefore statements five and six are also incorrect.

Reference: *BMAT Assumed Subject Knowledge Guide:* Nerves, Hormones and Homeostasis: The Kidneys and Homeostasis; Controlling Water Content

14)   The correct answer is C (1, 3 and 4 only)
But-1-ene is an alkene. Therefore, it will contain the C=C double bond, making statement two false. But-1-ene follows the general formula for alkenes of C_nH_{2n}, making statement three correct. The C=C bond decolourises bromine water (the test for alkenes) making statement five incorrect and statement four correct. But-1-ene undergoes polymerisation reactions to form the polymers polybutene or polyisobutylene, making statement one correct. Because statements 1, 3, and 4 are correct the answer is C

Reference: *BMAT Assumed Subject Knowledge Guide:* Carbon Chemistry: Alkenes; Using Alkenes to make Polymers

15)   The correct answer is B
Cold water is denser than hot water, therefore as the water cools it will sink to the bottom of the container, creating a convection current. For this reason, the best position for the cooling unit can be seen in position (p) as this will allow the hot water to be cooled and then sink. If the unit was placed in one of the other two positions (Q or R), the hot water at the top of the unit would remain hot. The outside of the container should be shiny as this would assist with keeping the water cooler. A dark surface would encourage the absorption of infra-red heat from the containers surroundings, causing the water to remain at room temperature (if not higher). Therefore the best answer is option B
Reference: *BMAT Assumed Subject Knowledge Guide:* Heat and Energy: Convection; Heat and Radiation

16)   The correct answer is D (Class 3 contains the same number of students as class 1.)
Since there are twice as many students in class 1 as class 2:

Class 1 = 2n

Class 2 = n

If the mean (or average) score for class 1 is 61, then:

$$61 \times 2n = 122n$$

To find the mean, add up all the scores and divide by the number of students, for class 2 this will be

$$63 \times n = 63n$$

Class 3 = m (the number of students in the class). So the total of all the scores in the class will be the mean multiplied by the number of students (m)

$$70 \times m = 70\ m$$

Place this into the same equation since the mean for the three classes is 65:

$$65m \times (2n + n + m)$$

From here, substitute the numbers in and rearrange:

$$65m \times (122n + 63\ n + 70m)$$

The total score for the three classes =

$$65 \times 3 = 195n$$

$$195n + 65m = 122n + 63n + 70m$$

Simplify the equation by collecting like terms:

$$195n - 122n - 63n = 10\ n$$

$$10n + 65\ m = 70\ m$$

$$70\ m - 65\ m = 5\ m$$

$$10n = 5m$$

$$10/5 = 2$$

$$2n = m$$

The number of students in Class 3 is 2n, which is the same as the number of students in Class 1.

Reference: *BMAT Assumed Subject Knowledge Guide:* Statistics and Probability: Averages and Spread

17) The correct answer is B (1 only)

Emulsification increases the overall surface area of the lipid by breaking a large droplet up into many smaller droplets. Each droplet has a lower surface area than the bigger droplet. Therefore statement one is correct. Bile is an alkaline substance and acts to neutralise the acidic contents of the stomach upon entry to the small intestine. Thus, the pH of the food will increase when it enters the small intestine, making statement two incorrect. Lipase is an enzyme which is not found in bile. Instead, it is found in pancreatic juice along with trypsin and intestinal amylase. Therefore, statement three is incorrect and option B the correct answer.

Reference: *BMAT Assumed Subject Knowledge Guide:* Organs and Systems: The Digestive System – Enzymes; The Digestive System - Structure

18) The correct answer is B ($C_2H_4O_2$)

One mole of the gas =$24dm^3$, and we have 2.4 dm^3 in a 6g sample, therefore:

$$24/2.4 = 0.1 \text{ mole of the gas weighs 6g}$$

This means that one mole of the compound = 60g and the relative molecular mass will be 60.
The C: H: O ratio of for this compound is 6:1:8

Therefore: 6+1+8 = 15

Therefore the mass of each element in the 60g sample is:

$$C= 60/15 \times 6 = 24$$

$$H = 60 / 15 \times 1 = 4$$

$$O = 60/ 15 \times 8 = 32$$

So the relative masses for each element are: C: 24 H: 4 O: 32

The Ar values of each element are:

C: 12
H = 1
O = 16

From here, divide each relative mass by the Ar value to find molecular formula of the compound:

$$\text{Carbon} = 24/ 12 = 2 \ (C_2)$$

Hydrogen = 4 / 1 = 4 (H_4)

Oxygen = 32 /16 = 2 (O_2)

Hence the molecular formula is $C_2H_4O_2$

Reference: *BMAT Assumed Subject Knowledge Guide*: Equations and Calculations: Empirical Formulas & Molar Volume

19)   The correct answer is C

The period = 2.0s (taken from the graph) therefore:

$$Frequency = (1 / 2.0) = 0.50Hz$$

$$v = f \times \lambda$$

$$= 0.50 \times 1.5 = 0.75cm/s$$

Reference: *BMAT Assumed Subject Knowledge Guide*: Waves and their Effects: Wave Basics

20)   The correct answer is A (1/3)

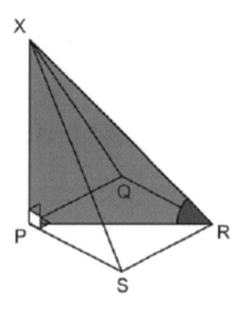 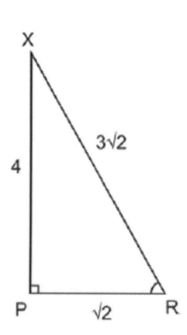

The first step is to draw a line joining P and R and make a right angle triangle. The angle in question is XRP. From here Pythagoras' theorem can be used since it is a right-angled triangle:
Length PR equals the square root of two since PR is the diagonal of the square PQRS.

$$R^2 = XP^2 + PR^2$$

$$XR = \sqrt{18} = 3\sqrt{2}$$

$$Cos\,(XRP) = \frac{PR}{XR}$$

$$Cos\,\frac{\sqrt{2}}{3\sqrt{2}}$$

$$= 1/3$$

Reference: *BMAT Assumed Subject Knowledge Guide*: Geometry and Measures: Pythagoras Theorem; Trigonometry

21)   The correct answer is G (2,3 and 4 only)
This question is largely based around cellular respiration and the reactants and products of this equation. Statement one can be ruled out immediately since anaerobic respiration occurs in low oxygen levels and the neurons require oxygen to function for longer than 5-10 seconds. When cells respire, they generate a significant amount of heat, which increases the temperature of the body. Thus, statement two is true. The brains primary food source is glucose; insulin works to lower the levels of glucose in the body. Low glucose levels due to too much insulin could prevent cellular respiration, thus making statement three also correct. One of the products of cellular respiration is CO_2, hence statement four is also correct.

Reference: *BMAT Assumed Subject Knowledge Guide*: Cells and Cell Processes: Aerobic Respiration; Anaerobic Respiration in Animals

22)   The correct answer is D (1 and 2 only)
The diagram of graphene and the properties listed suggest that it is a giant covalent structure. Graphene also looks similar in structure to graphite in that it has a hexagonal shape. Each carbon atom is covalently bonded to three other carbon atoms, leaving one free electron allowing it to be an electrical conductor; therefore property number two is correct. Giant covalent structures also have a high melting point and are insoluble in water; therefore property number one is correct and property number three is incorrect.

Reference: *BMAT Assumed Subject Knowledge Guide*: Classifying Materials: Covalent Substances; Identifying Structures

23)   The correct answer is E
The total mass of the particles before and after fission must be the same as mass is conserved.

$$U_{235} + 1_n \rightarrow 236$$

Therefore, the total mass after fission must also be 236

A = 2 + 141 + 92 = 235 - incorrect
B = 2 + 142 + 94 = 238 - incorrect
C = 3 + 140 + 92 = 235 - incorrect
D = 3 + 140 + 94 = 237 - incorrect
E = 3 + 141 + 92 = 236 - correct
F = 3 + 142 + 94 = 239 – incorrect

Reference: *BMAT Assumed Subject Knowledge Guide*: The Atom and Radioactivity: Nuclear Fission

24)   The correct answer is E

First, add the additional information provided in the question to the probability tree:

- 1/100 x 1000 = 10 people per 1000 have the condition
- 10 x 4/5 (or 80%) will test positive = 8 people will test positive (true positive)
- If 10 people per 1000 have the condition, this means that 1000-10 = 990 (99/100) do not have the condition
- Of the 990 who do not have the condition, 1/10 will test positive 990 x 1/10 = 99 people who will have a false positive.

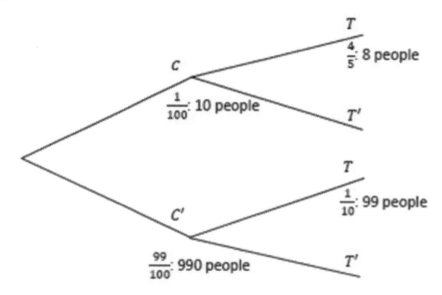

Therefore there will be 8 + 99 = 107 people who will test positive for the condition.
Only 8 of these people have the condition. Therefore the probability will be 8/107.

Reference: *BMAT Assumed Subject Knowledge Guide*: Statistics and Probability: Tree Diagrams

25)   The correct answer is E (Both parents are homozygous, and mutation occurred in the DNA of a gamete from one of her parents)

A recessive condition is only expressed if the individual has two copies of the recessive allele, one maternal (from the mother's side) and one paternal (from the father's side). Since neither of the woman's parents are affected by the condition, they must be carriers (heterozygous) for the condition. Hence statement A is correct. The woman's parents would have received the recessive allele from their parents (the woman's grandparents), meaning that they too could either be carriers (heterozygous) or be affected by the condition. In light of this, statements B, C, and D are also correct.

For a gametic mutation to be seen in the offspring, both parents would require the same mutation in their gametes, or the mutation would need to be dominant. Since it is suggested that only one of the parents has the mutation and the condition is recessive, statement E can be deemed false.

Reference: *BMAT Assumed Subject Knowledge Guide*: Genes, Reproduction and Evolution: Genetic Disorders

26)   The correct answer is E (4 and 5 only)

The atomic number reveals how many electrons the atom has, making options one, two and three incorrect. Negatively charged ions gain electrons to fill their valence shell and thus have a greater number of electrons than protons which gives them their negative charge. Cl^- has 17 electrons as a chlorine atom but when chlorine becomes an ion, it gains an additional electron to fill its valence shell, resulting in a total of 18 making option four correct. Positively charged ions do the opposite; losing electrons to fill their valence shell and so they have a higher number of protons compared to electrons. Calcium as an atom has 20 electrons, however, when it becomes an ion, it loses two electrons to become Ca^{2+}, thus giving it a total of 18 electrons making option five also correct.

Reference: *BMAT Assumed Subject Knowledge Guide*: Classifying Materials: Ions

27)   The correct answer is D

The first step to solving this problem is to calculate gravitational potential energy using the equation

$$E_p = mgh$$

$$E_P = 20 \times 10 \times 10$$

$$E_P = 2000 \text{ J}$$

From here, the equation p =W/t can be used to calculated power since work done (W) is the same as gravitational potential energy. The information on the graph to allows t to be found. Because the change in height is not constant from 0m to 50 m, consider a point around 10 m that is constant.

The graph shows the change in height over time between 15-35 s is constant; therefore this time interval can be used to calculate power.

The height changes 10 m (15 – 5 m) in 20 s, therefore t = 20 s

$$P = W/t$$

$$P = 2000 / 20$$

$$P = 100 \text{ W}$$

Reference: *BMAT Assumed Knowledge Guide:* Forces and Energy: Gravitational Potential Energy; Power

BMAT Section 2 - 2015

1)   **The correct answer is E (Brain transmits electrical impulse to relay neuron)**

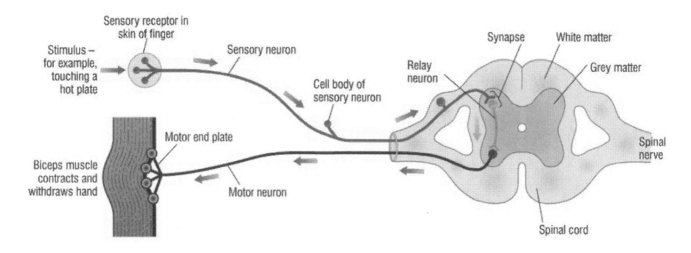

Option E is the only statement not included in the diagram above and hence is the correct answer.

2)   **The correct answer is C (1 and 3 only)**

Polypropene has the formula $(C_3H_6)_n$ and has no C=C double bonds, thus it cannot decolourise bromine water. Compound number four also lacks a C=C double bond, hence this will not discolour the bromine water either. However, compounds one and three (drawn below) do have C=C double bonds which will be able to decolourise bromine water, therefore option C is correct.

Reference: *BMAT Assumed Subject Knowledge Guide*: Carbon Chemistry: Alkenes

3)   **The correct answer is B**

Dark surfaces absorb and emit infrared wavelengths well (unlike light surfaces). Therefore the options can be narrowed down to either A or B.

Option A can then be excluded due to light surfaces being good reflectors of heat. With a white jacket, the heat will be reflected from the inside of the person off the jacket and back to the person keeping them warm. The light coloured jacket emits the heat energy poorly also so little of the person's heat energy is lost to the environment. Body temperature is warmer than the environmental temperature thus the heat needs to be retained rather than absorbed and emitted (which a dark surface would do), hence Option B is correct.

Reference: *BMAT Assumed Subject Knowledge Guide*: Heat and Energy: Heat Radiation

4)   The correct answer is B (3/28)

3 out of 8 of the beads in the bag are black, which means that the probability of selecting a black bead is 3/8. Once a black bead is removed, the chance of getting a second black bead then becomes 2/7 since the beads are not being replaced after each selection. The probability of both beads being black is found by multiplying the probability for each bead with the other:

$$3/8 \times 2/7$$

$$= 6/56$$

$$= 3/28$$

(Option B)

Reference: *BMAT Assumed Subject Knowledge Guide*: Statistics and Probability: The AND/OR Rules

5)   The correct answer is A

Anaerobic respiration is the incomplete breakdown of glucose due to the absence of oxygen; hence options C, D, G and H can be excluded. It can be summarised by the equation:

$$Glucose \rightarrow lactic\ acid\ (+\ energy\ released)$$

As seen in the above equation, anaerobic respiration only produces lactic acid as a product, unlike aerobic respiration which produces carbon dioxide and water. In light of this, options B, E and F can also be ruled out, leaving A as the correct option.

Reference: *BMAT Assumed Subject Knowledge Guide*: Cells and Cell Processes: Anaerobic Respiration in Animals

6)   The correct answer is A (-a)

The graph below shows that the energy change for the reaction (delta H) is positive. This indicates that the reaction is endothermic, meaning that heat energy has been absorbed. This is the difference between the energy of the products and the reactants. The energy change of the reverse reaction will be the opposite, written as −delta H since the energy change value is the same, just in the opposite direction. Therefore option A is correct.

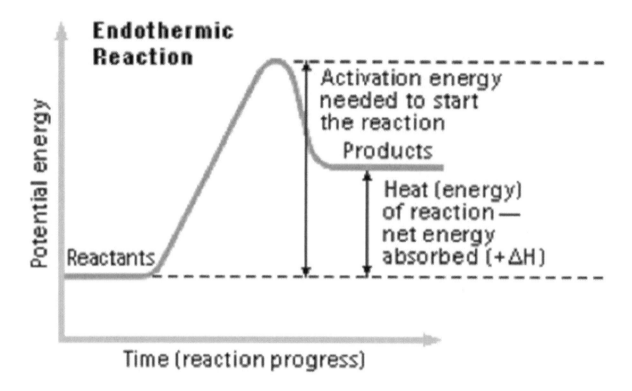

Reference: *BMAT Assumed Subject Knowledge Guide*: Reaction Rates and Energy Changes: Bond Energies

7) **The correct answer is D**

A step-down transformer decreases the voltage so the energy can be used in households. As it is 100% efficient, no energy is lost as heat, meaning that power in is equal to power out. Since power = voltage x current, the current must increase for the power to remain the same. Therefore option D is correct.

Reference: *BMAT Assumed Subject Knowledge Guide*: Electricity: Transformers

8) **The correct answer is E**

Use Pythagoras' theorem to find the length of the dotted line. Half the length of QR is 4.

$$a^2 + b^2 = c^2$$

$$6^2 = 4^2 + c^2$$

$$36 = 16 + c^2$$

$$c = \sqrt{20}$$

$$= 2\sqrt{5}$$

To find the tangent to the angle use the opposite and adjacent lengths (SOHCAHTOA)

$$tan\theta = 2\sqrt{5}/4$$

$$= \sqrt{5}/2 = E$$

Reference: *BMAT Assumed Subject Knowledge Guide*: Pythagoras and Trigonometry: Trigonometry – Sin, Cos, Tan

9)   The correct answer is D

Mouse one is homozygous; therefore it will be either CC or cc. As 100% of the offspring are also black, mouse one is CC, since at least one dominant allele needs to be present to deposit the black colouration into the fur. Therefore each of the offspring will receive a dominant allele (C) from mouse one, making them black and a recessive allele (white, c) from its other parent making the offspring 100% Cc.

When mouse one (CC) is crossed with mouse two (Cc), each of their offspring will receive at least one dominant allele, since this is the only allele that mouse one can contribute. Mouse two on the other hand, can contribute either C or c, but the recessive colour will be masked by the dominant black allele giving 100% black offspring. The Punnett square below shows the possible genotypes for the offspring of mouse one and two.

	C	c
C	CC	Cc
C	CC	Cc

The Punnett square shows that 50% of the offspring are heterozygous, with the black phenotype and 50% will be homozygous dominant, also with the black phenotype. Hence option D is the correct answer.

Reference: *BMAT Assumed Subject Knowledge Guide*: Genes, Reproduction and Evolution: More on Genetic Disorders

10)   The correct answer is D (rubidium is stored under oil)

Option A is incorrect because the electrolysis of aqueous RbCl shows that the rubidium ions would be formed and rather than rubidium metal.

$$RbCl_{(aq)} + H_2O_{(l)} \rightarrow Rb^+_{(aq)} + OH^-_{(aq)} + H_{2(g)} + \frac{1}{2}Cl_{2\,(g)}$$

For group one metals, both the boiling and melting points decrease with each subsequent period down the group, making statement B incorrect. The opposite is true for reactivity, the further down the group, the more reactive the metal becomes, and hence statement C is also incorrect. Group one metals are stored in oil as they react violently with both water and oxygen (air), therefore statement D is correct. Statement E is incorrect as rubidium forms a +1 ion; it takes two rubidium ions to bond with a sulfate ion to give the ionic compound an overall charge of zero.

Reference: *BMAT Assumed Subject Knowledge Guide*: Classifying Materials: Group 1 – The Alkali Metals

11) The correct answer is A (1 Only)
Statement one is correct, this is known as a nuclear chain reaction.

Statement two is incorrect. Half-life is defined as the time taken for the nuclei to decay by half. Statement three is also incorrect as the reactions in the sun involve nuclei joining together, known as nuclear fusion.

Reference: *BMAT Assumed Subject Knowledge Guide*: The Atom and Radioactivity: Nuclear Fission; Nuclear Fusion

12) The correct answer is B (a<c<b for all values of X)

$$c = (3+x)/(5+x)$$

Since b = (3+x)/5 it can be seen they have the same numerator but that for any number of x above 0 that c will have a larger denominator making c < b.

C can be split up.

$$C = (3+x)/(5+x)$$

$$= 3/(5+x) + x/(5+x)$$

$$= a + x/(5+x)$$

As x/(5+x) will be greater than 0 for all values of x above 0 this means that c>a giving rise to a<c<b

13) The correct answer is B
Given that the same amount of food and drink has been consumed, the total amount of urea produced will remain constant. However, on a hot day, more water will be lost through sweat. This means that the body will try to retain water by secreting ADH which will work to reabsorb water in the collecting ducts in the kidney, and back into the body. Therefore less water will be in the urine (the urine will be more concentrated) making option B correct.

Reference: *BMAT Assumed Subject Knowledge Guide*: Nerves, Hormones and Homeostasis; The Kidneys and Homeostasis;

14) The correct answer is C (They are saturated compounds).
Statement A is false, as the general formula for cycloalkanes is C_nH_{2n}.

Cycloalkanes are saturated compounds; therefore they do not react with bromine water, making statement B false and C true. Burning in excess oxygen is known as complete combustion, hence the products of this reaction will be CO_2 and H_2O, making statement D false.

Cyclohexane, cyclopentane and cyclobutane are members of the homologous series known as cycloalkanes, meaning that statement E is also false. The compounds in question are held together by simple covalent bonds, therefore statement F is incorrect.

Reference: *BMAT Assumed Subject Knowledge Guide*: Carbon Chemistry: Alkanes; Burning Fuels

15)   The correct answer is A

$$Force = mass \; x \; acceleration$$

Vertical force:

$$25-20= 5N.$$

Therefore acceleration:

$$= 5/2 = 2.5m/s^2$$

Horizontal force:

$$50-40= 10N$$

$$=10/2$$

$$= 5m/s^2$$
(Option A)

Reference: *BMAT Assumed Subject Knowledge Guide*: Forces and Energy: Resultant forces; Forces and Acceleration

16)   The correct answer is E (9250)
The ratio for charities A, B and C = 1: 2/3: 4/5. Charity C is received 4/5 of the money which is 3000 which means:
4/5 x 3000 = 3750

This means that 5/5 (or 1) = 3750, which is the amount received by charity A
It also means that 2/3 of 3750 = 2500, which is the amount that charity B received.
Therefore the total amount collected will be 3750+ 2500+3000= 9250 (option E)

17)   The correct answer is H
Process number one in the diagram is photosynthesis which can be summarised by the equation:

$$arbon\ Dioxide + Water \xrightarrow{Light} Glucose + Oxygen$$

$$6CO_2 + 6H_2O \xrightarrow{Chlorophyll} C_6H_{12}O_6 + 6O_2$$

This process does not involve either digestive or respiratory enzymes, therefore it can be excluded. Process number two is feeding, and thus requires digestive enzymes, so it must be included. Process three is decomposition, which involves digestion by decomposers such as bacteria and fungi. Therefore, process three must also be included. Process four involves respiration. This process releases carbon dioxide into the atmosphere; consequently it requires respiratory enzymes and must be included as well. Thus the correct answer is H.

Reference: *BMAT Assumed Subject Knowledge Guide*: Energy Flow: Carbon Cycle

18)   The correct answer is C (A high activation energy would give a slower rate than a lower activation energy)
Statement A is false because a catalyst would speed up the reaction. Statement B is also false as this only applies to solids. A lower energy requirement will result in a faster reaction rate. Therefore statement C is correct. Increasing the temperature increases the number of collisions per unit time, and as a result, the reaction will speed up, so statement D is incorrect.
The reaction rate can be measured by the amount of gas collected in a specific time frame, rather than in just collecting a volume of gas. Hence statement E is also false.

Reference: *BMAT Assumed Subject Knowledge Guide*: Reaction Rates and Energy Changes: Measuring Rates of Reaction; Collision Theory; Catalysts

19)   The correct answer is G

An alpha particle is made up of two protons and two neutrons and is represented by: $^{4}_{2}\alpha$.

A beta particle is an electron or e⁻ and is represented by $^{0}_{-1}\beta$.

In the first stage of decay, nucleus M emits a beta particle to become nucleus N, therefore X = W+1. In the second stage of decay, nucleus N emits an alpha particle to become nucleus Q. Since an alpha particle has been lost, the mass number decreases by four meaning Y = V-4 (as the electron has a mass of 0). Therefore the answer is G.

Reference: *BMAT Assumed Subject Knowledge Guide*: The Atom and Radioactivity: Ionising Radiation

20)   The correct answer is D
The code mn is the total score at present (number of pupils x mean score)
Adding in this new pupil and there score means the total score is now mn+n, and the total number of pupils is n+1. The mean is now m-2.

Put this into an equation:

$$\frac{mn + n = m - 2}{n + 1}$$

Rearrange this to get:

$$mn + n = (m-2)(n+1)$$

Expand the brackets to get:

$$mn + n = mn - 2n + m - 2$$

Simplify:

$$3n = m-2 \text{ or}$$
$$n = (m-2)/3$$
$$\text{(Option D)}$$

Reference: *BMAT Assumed Subject Knowledge Guide*: Algebra: Variables

21)   The correct answer is A (1 and 4 only)

Statement one is true because DNA has a double helix structure. This structure would need to be identical for it to be incorporated into the human cell.

Statement two is false since human cells lack a cell wall

Bacteria are prokaryotes with circular chromosomes and plasmids which contain their DNA, not a nucleus, making statement three false.

Since all cells have a cell membrane, statement four is true. Since statements one and four are both true, the correct option is A

Reference: *BMAT Assumed Subject Knowledge Guide*: Cells and Cell Processes: Cells

22)   The correct answer is C

With each subsequent group to the right in the periodic table, one electron is added to the outer ring. Therefore, Cl, which is usually in Group 17 now becomes Cl^- meaning that it has gained an electron so has the same configuration as the group 18 element Ar. Using this same principle Cl^+ moves left a group and becomes similar to group 16 elements. K^+ loses an electron so moves left one group from group one to group 18, making it similar to Ar and Cl^-. Ca^+ will become similar to Group 1 elements while K^- becomes like group 2 elements. Therefore this reveals that K^+, Ar and Cl^- have the same electron arrangement making option C the correct choice.

Reference: *BMAT Assumed Subject Knowledge Guide*: Chemical Concepts: The Periodic Table

23)   Correct Answer is D (61m)

Reaction time is now 0.7 x 2 = 1.4s. The car will initially travel 1.4 x 20 = 28m before the brakes are applied. The equation needed to calculate the distance required to stop is:

$$s = 0.5(u + v)t$$

Substituting in the values:

0.5 x (20+0) x 3.3 = 33.

Add this onto the 28m for the distance before the brakes are applied:

28 + 33 = 61m

(Option D)

Reference: *BMAT Assumed Subject Knowledge Guide*: Forces and Energy: Speed and Velocity

24) The correct answer is D

Start by finding a common denominator for all the terms to create one equation as the numerator. Since there is 2x-3 and 2x+3, the denominator becomes (2x-3)(2x+3) so multiply each term appropriately giving...

$$\frac{(2x + 3)(2x + 3)}{(2x + 3)(2x - 3)} + \frac{(2x - 3)(2x - 3)}{(2x + 3)(2x - 3)} - 2\frac{(2x + 3)(2x - 3)}{(2x + 3)(2x - 3)}$$

Expanding the numerator gives...

$$4x^2 + 12x + 9 + 4x^2 - 12x + 9 - 8x^2 + 18$$

$$= 36 / (2x-3)(2x+3)$$

(Option D)

Reference: *BMAT Assumed Subject Knowledge Guide*: Algebra: Multiplying Out Brackets

25) The correct answer is G

To be male, there must be an X chromosome for every two A chromosomes, so XAA and XYAA which only leaves options G or H.

The information also states that the X: A ratio is 1:1 for females, meaning that XXAA, XXYAA and XXYYAA are female fruit flies since they have an equal number of X and A chromosomes.

This means that option G is the correct answer.

26) The correct answer is B (1.60g)

Mass = number of moles x relative formula mass

Relative formula mass of CH_4:

$$(12 + (4 \times 1)) = 16$$

Therefore the number of moles of methane is

$$1.6/16 = 0.1 \text{ moles}$$

According to the chemical equation, for one mole of methane, there are two moles of oxygen so there must be 0.2 moles of oxygen. The molar mass of oxygen is:

$$16 \times 2 = 32.$$

Therefore the mass of oxygen used is:

$$0.2 \times 32 = 6.4g$$

To find the amount remaining, subtract the amount used from the original amount:

$$8-6.4 = 1.6g \text{ left}$$
$$(\text{Option B})$$

Reference: *BMAT Assumed Subject Knowledge Guide*: Equations and Calculations: Relative Formula Mass

27)   Correct Answer is D (1 and 2 only)
Statement one is correct since F = ma, $4 \times 1.25 = 5N$.
velocity = frequency multiplied by the wavelength, $5 = 4 \times 1.25$, making statement two also true.
Statement three is false since V=IR, voltage = current x resistance $4 \neq 1.25 \times 5$
As only statements one and two are true, D is correct.

Reference: *BMAT Assumed Subject Knowledge Guide*: Forces and Energy: Forces and Acceleration; Waves and their Effects: Wave Basics; Electricity: Resistance and $V = I \times R$

BMAT Section 2 - 2016

1) The correct answer is D

Urea is a natural waste product of protein metabolism. It is removed from the blood by the kidneys. The aorta and renal artery carry blood to the kidney to carry out this process, while the renal vein and vena cava transport the now deoxygenated blood back to the heart for oxygenation. Due to the higher blood pressure that the aorta and renal artery have to deal with from the heart, the muscular walls of the vessels are much thicker than that of the vena cava and renal veins. The renal arteries and veins transport blood from the aorta and vena cava to the kidneys and vice versa, therefore with this information it can be deduced that:

1 = the vena cava

2 = the aorta

3 = the renal vein

4 = the renal artery

Vessel five transports urine from the kidney to the bladder. This is the ureter, not to be confused with the urethra which transports urine from the bladder out of the body during excretion. This will have the highest concentration of urea following removal from the blood and concentration by the kidneys. The vena cava and renal vein will have the lowest concentrations of urea as they contain blood that has just been processed by the kidneys, while the aorta and renal artery contain intermediate levels as the blood is yet to be processed and the urea removed.

Reference: *BMAT Assumed Subject Knowledge Guide*: Nerves, Hormones and Homeostasis: The Kidneys and Homeostasis

2) The correct answer is F (2, 3 and 4 only)

This element has three shells, with the innermost containing two electrons, the middle holding eight electrons, and the outer containing three electrons (giving a total of 13). An element is uncharged, and so the number of electrons must equal the number of protons in the atom, meaning the atomic number (number of protons) is 13. Therefore statement number four is correct – the element is Aluminium.

There is no element present in Group (column) 12, period (row) three; Aluminium is grouped with the non-metals or poor metals, in group 13. Thus statement one is incorrect.

When elements react to form compounds, they do so in such a way that the individual atoms form 'complete' outer shells. This is guided by electronegativity and depends on the elements reacting. In the case of Aluminium and Oxygen, Aluminium is the less electronegative of the two (has a lower tendency to attract electrons), and will, therefore, 'donate' its outer three electrons to oxygen, providing it with a full outer ring of eight. To form this full outer ring, each oxygen atom must receive 2 electrons. Therefore the ratio of aluminium atoms to oxygen atoms in the compound must be 2:3 (2 x 3 electrons = six donated by aluminium, 3 x 2 electrons = 6 received by oxygen), making statement two correct.

The same is the case for the reaction of Aluminium with Bromine. In this case, Bromine is more electronegative than Aluminium and so will attract and receive electrons, while Aluminium will again donate. Bromine atoms need one electron to form a full outer shell, and hence the ratio will be 1:3 (1 x 3 electrons donated by aluminium, 3 x 1 electron received by Bromine), hence statement three is correct.

Reference: *BMAT Assumed Subject Knowledge Guide*: Chemical Concepts: The Periodic Table: Ionic Bonding

3)   The correct answer is D (300/50 g/cm³)

Density is defined as mass per unit volume. In this example, the mass of the system increases by 300g for each weight added and the volume of the weights and water increases by 50cm cubed for each weight added. This means that the mass of each weight is 300g while the volume is 50cm³. To work out density using these values, divide mass by volume: 300/50 g/cm³.

Reference: *BMAT Assumed Subject Knowledge Guide*: Geometry and Measures: Density and Speed

4)   The correct answer is A

If two lines are parallel on a graph, it means their gradients are the same. Alternatively, if the two lines are perpendicular, the two gradients are the negative reciprocal of one another. Gradient is defined as the change in Y divided by the change in X. In this case, the change in Y is (9 − 3 =6) while the change in X is (6 - -3 =) 9. 6/9 would give the line a gradient of 2/3 or two thirds. Straight lines are written in the form y = mx + c, where 'm' is the value of the gradient. In this case, A contains 'm' with a value of 2/3.

Reference: *BMAT Assumed Subject Knowledge Guide*: Graphs: Finding the Gradient; "y=mx + c"

5)   The correct answer is B

DNA is packaged into structures called chromosomes within the nucleus of a cell. Therefore W is a chromosome (genes are sections of a chromosome).

Restriction enzymes are used to cut DNA at specific points, depending on the restriction enzyme. Both the enzyme used to cut the DNA and the (in this case) plasmid must be the same to produce complementary 'sticky ends'. Therefore X and Y are restriction enzymes.

These complementary ends on the plasmid and the removed section of DNA are 'stuck' (ligated) together using an enzyme called DNA ligase, which is Z.

Reference: *BMAT Assumed Subject Knowledge Guide*: Genes, Reproduction and Evolution: Genetic Engineering

6)   The correct answer is E

Mixture A could be separated by evaporation as calcium carbonate is a rock (solid) and the water (liquid) can be boiled off, hence this option can be excluded.

Pentane and octane are both liquids at room temperature. This means that they can be distilled (evaporated and condensed). Fractional distillation works by using the different boiling points of two liquids to separate and then condense them. As pentane and octane have a different molecular formula, they will have different boiling points, and therefore fractional distillation will be a suitable separation technique. This means that mixture B can be ruled out.

Silicon dioxide and water contain a solid and a liquid. Filtration would allow the liquid to pass through a filtration material such as filter paper while trapping the solid silicon dioxide. Hence mixture C has a suitable form of separation.

Sodium chloride and water consists of a solvent (water) with a dissolved solute (sodium chloride) forming a solution. In a solution with a dissolved solid, boiling the solution will remove the solvent liquid and leave the solute behind. Distillation involves boiling the solution and so this would be a suitable separation technique, thereby excluding mixture D.

Ethanol and water are both liquids. Because they both contain OH groups, they can form hydrogen bonds with one another and form a miscible mixture. Separating funnels work on immiscible liquids by collecting the different layers formed one by one – this would not be possible with an ethanol/water mixture. Hence mixture E is the correct option

Reference: *BMAT Assumed Subject Knowledge Guide*: Chemical Analysis and Electrolysis: Separating Techniques

7) The correct answer is D (1 and 2 only)

An isotope is an atom of an element that contains a different number of neutrons than those most commonly found in nature. These contain the same number of protons and electrons as usual and thus have the same chemical properties – neutrons do not affect this, thus making statement one correct.

The atomic number of an element is the number of protons present. Since each isotope of an atom will have the same number of protons, statement two can be deemed correct. The mass number of an element is the number of protons and the number of neutrons together (the mass of an electron is insignificant in comparison). Therefore the mass number will be affected by a change in the number of neutrons while the atomic number will remain the same (28 in this case).

As there are 28 protons, and the largest mass number is 62, the isotope with the maximum number of neutrons the element can contain is 34. In light of this, statement three is incorrect.

Reference: *BMAT Assumed Subject Knowledge Guide*: Classifying Materials: Isotopes and Relative Atomic Mass

8) The correct answer is B (12)

The mean is the total of all the values divided by the number of values. The total mass of Jim, Karen and Leroy must be (90 x 3 =) 270kg. This can be placed into the equation:

$$(n + 3) \times 78 = 75n + 270$$

$$78n + 234 = 75n + 270$$

$$3n + 234 = 270$$

$$3n = 36.$$

$$n = 12$$

Reference: *BMAT Assumed Subject Knowledge Guide*: Algebra: Variables

9)   The correct answer is F (protease from the stomach)

A pH lower than seven means the environment must be acidic for the enzyme to work effectively. Therefore, options A and B can immediately be ruled out; as amylase works best to digest carbohydrates into simple sugars such as glucose both in the mouth and small intestine at a pH around 7-8.

Lipase is produced by the pancreas, but is found in the stomach as well as the mouth and breaks down fats into fatty acids and glycerol in the small intestine; hence options C and D can also be excluded.

The conditions in the stomach are acidic, so the addition of bile in the small intestine increases the pH back to approximately seven. Therefore, it can be deduced that the enzyme in question is a protease found in the stomach without even using the last piece of information, which is not helpful as the core body temperature of (and therefore the temperature of all these locations) the body is 37°C. Hence the correct answer is F.

Reference: *BMAT Assumed Subject Knowledge Guide*: Organs and Systems: The Digestive System -Enzymes

10)   The correct answer is F (392)

This question simply requires adding the mass numbers of all the individual atoms in the molecule together:

$$((14 \times 1) + (1 \times 4)) \times 2 + (56 \times 1) + ((32 \times 1) + (16 \times 4)) \times 2 + ((1 \times 2) + (16 \times 1)) \times 6$$
$$= 392$$

Reference: *BMAT Assumed Subject Knowledge Guide*: Equations and Calculations: Relative Formula Mass

11)   The correct answer is B

Increasing the speed of rotation of the coil will increase the size of the induced voltage as a higher rate of change in flux is created.

The 'wavelength' or oscillation of AC would increase as there would now be more turns per unit time.

Reference: *BMAT Assumed Subject Knowledge Guide*: Electricity: Generators

12)   The correct answer is D (49πmm²)

Subtracting the thickness of the artery wall from the total radius of (1.6 / 2 = 8mm) will give the radius of the internal cross-sectional area of the artery:

$$(8 - 1) = 7mm$$

Using area $- \pi \times r^2$ the internal area can be calculated as:

$$(\pi \times 7^2 =) 49\pi \ mm^2$$

(Option D)

Reference: *BMAT Assumed Subject Knowledge Guide*: Geometry and Measures: Area

13)   The correct answer is B (2 only)

The equation for aerobic respiration:

$$glucose \ + \ oxygen \ \rightarrow water \ + \ carbon\,dioxide\ (\ +\ energy)$$

In contrast, the equation for anaerobic respiration:

$$glucose\ \rightarrow lactic\,acid\ (\ +\ energy)$$

Only glucose is present in both equations, therefore the correct answer is B.

Reference: *BMAT Assumed Subject Knowledge Guide*: Cells and Cell Processes: Aerobic Respiration; Anaerobic Respiration in Animals

14)   The correct answer is C

The electrolysis of an electrolyte causes the negative ions migrate towards the positive electrode (anode) and become neutrally charged while the positive ions migrate towards the negative electrode (cathode) and also become positively charged – the ions are the charge carriers in this circuit.
With an aqueous solution, water is present, and as it can be oxidised and reduced, therefore, hydrogen is produced instead of copper at the cathode. Likewise, with calcium bromide, hydrogen would be produced at the cathode, not calcium, thus making options A and B incorrect.
Option C is an aqueous solution, thus the product will be hydrogen, making this option correct.
With molten ionic solids, only the ions present in the molten solid are found at the electrodes as there is no water to carry the charge. This means that sodium would be present instead of hydrogen at the cathode, thus ruling out option D.
In the hydrolysis of aluminium oxide, aluminium would be present on the cathode, since it is the positive ion, not the anode thus option E is also incorrect.

Reference: *BMAT Assumed Subject Knowledge Guide*: Products from Rocks: Extraction of Metals

15)   The correct answer is D

Only microwaves and radio waves are used for communication, as their wavelength is long enough and their frequency low enough. These waves are not ionising enough to lose their energy and dissipate before reaching their intended target (like gamma rays). This is shown by the frequency of 1.5×10^{10} Hz, which falls into the range of microwaves.

$$Speed \ = \ distance\ /\ time.$$

$$3.0 \times 10^8 = 45,000,000 \times 2 \text{ m / time}$$

$$= 90,000,000\ /\ 3.0 \times 10^8 = 0.30 \text{ seconds}$$

Reference: *BMAT Assumed Subject Knowledge Guide*: Waves and their Effects: Wave Basics; Microwaves

16)   The correct answer is C (64cm²)

First split the shape up into a triangle and a rectangle. Take P, Q and the midpoint of P → S as a right-angled triangle with base 6cm.

From tan (opposite over adjacent), the opposite side will be larger than the base by a ratio of 4:3. As the base is 6cm, the height of the right angle triangle can be calculated, and therefore the original shape will be 8cm.

Add the area of the triangle and the rectangle together.

$$The\ area\ of\ a\ triangle\ =\ half\ base\ x\ height$$

$$= 0.5 \times 6 \times 8 = 24cm^2$$

$$The\ area\ of\ the\ rectangle\ =\ base\ x\ height$$

$$8 \times 5 = 40cm^2$$

Therefore the total area of the shape

$$= 24 + 40 = 64cm^2$$

Reference: *BMAT Assumed Subject Knowledge Guide*: Geometry and Measures: Areas; Pythagoras and Trigonometry: Trigonometry – Sin, Cos, Tan

17)   The correct answer is G (1,2,3 and 4)

Mutations in DNA cause differences between the template strand and the copied strand and thus differences between the parent and daughter cells. Differences may be beneficial, for example increasing the efficiency or expression of the gene, but more likely than not they are detrimental resulting in a reduction in efficiency of a gene, sometimes to such an extent that the cell dies. Mutations can reduce the efficiency of the allele of the gene to such a level that it knocks out the function of the gene altogether. This could range from having no effect on the cell, to a positive effect on the cell, or an adverse effect, depending on the role of the protein. In light of these facts, all four statements can be considered correct.

Reference: *BMAT Assumed Subject Knowledge Guide*: Genes, Reproduction and Evolution: Genes, Chromosomes and DNA

18)   The correct answer is E (120cm³)

First, convert the volume from cm^3 to dm^3 by dividing by 1000:

$$30/1000 = 0.03dm^3$$

From here, calculate the number of moles of acid present using the equation:

$$Number\ of\ moles = concentration \times volume$$

Number of moles = 0.2 x 0.03

= 0.006 moles

Because this is a diprotic acid, meaning it contains two Hydrogen atoms, it doubles the number of moles of acid present as two atoms of hydrogen can dissociate per acid molecule. An example of a diprotic acid is H_2SO4. Therefore the total number of moles is:

0.006 x 2 = 0.012 moles of acid

This means that 0.012 moles of base is required to neutralise this acid.
This can be calculated by using the same equation as before rearranged for volume:

0.012 / 0.1 = 0.12 dm³

0.12 x 1000 = 120 cm³
(Option E)

Reference: *BMAT Assumed Subject Knowledge Guide*: Chemical Analysis and Electrolysis: Titration Calculations

19)   The correct answer is (25A)
The equations required for this problem are:

$$Energy = voltage \times charge$$

And

$$Charge = current \times time$$

The charge present is therefore

125 / 500 = 0.25

The current is therefore:

0.25 / 0.01 (converted to seconds)

= 25 Amps
(Option D)

Reference: *BMAT Assumed Subject Knowledge Guide*: Electricity: Current and Electricity; Energy Transfer in Circuits

20)   The correct answer is C

$$a/b = c/d + e/f$$

First, get e/f on one side by subtracting c/d:

$$a/b - c/d = e/f$$

Then multiply by f to get rid of the fraction:

$$Af/b - cf/d = e$$

Then multiply by both b and d to get rid of the left side denominators:

$$Afd - cfb = ebd$$

Factor out f:

$$F(ad - cb) = ebd$$

And then divide by the bracket:

$$F = ebd/(ad\text{-}cb)$$

Or
$$F = bcd/(ad\text{-}bc)$$
(Option C)

Reference: *BMAT Assumed Subject Knowledge Guide*: Algebra: Rearranging Formulas

21)   The correct answer is A (1 and 4 only)
There are two types of cell division – mitosis and meiosis. Meiosis is involved in the formation of four haploid gametes, while mitosis forms two diploid cells.
Mitosis is therefore involved in stem cell division (no gametes are formed) and asexual reproduction of single-celled organisms, making statements one and four correct. However, mitosis is not involved in the growth and repair of individual cells – this is down to the S and G phases of the interphase, which is a part of the mitotic cycle.

Reference: *BMAT Assumed Subject Knowledge Guide*: Genes, Reproduction and Evolution: Cell Division - Mitosis

22)   The correct answer is B (Line B)

As there is an excess of calcium carbonate chips, the reaction is limited by the HCl. In this case, there is the same number of moles of HCl in both samples – 2.0 x .05 = 1.0 x 0.1 (= 0.1 moles). Therefore there will be the same amount of carbon dioxide produced.

The higher concentration will drive the reaction forward faster because the equilibrium will shift to the right. A decrease in surface area contact due to the reduction in volume will slow down the reaction, and therefore the initial reaction rate will be faster.

Reference: *BMAT Assumed Subject Knowledge Guide*: Reaction Rates and Energy Changes: Changing Equilibrium

23)   The correct answer is E

The mass of an object is unchanged in different gravitational fields – it is an inherent property dependant on the amount of matter present. Only the weight is affected by the strength of the gravitational field.

The mass of the object can be calculated using the gravitational field strength and the weight of the object on earth:

$$Weight = mass \ x \ gravitational \ field \ strength.$$

$$15 = mass \ x \ 10$$

$$Mass = 0.15 \ Kg$$

As an object falls, its gravitational potential energy is converted to kinetic energy. The gravitational potential energy gained by raising 10m will, therefore, be equivalent to the KE gained by falling 10m. We can calculate this increase in GPE by the equation:

$E_p = mgh$

$$Or$$

$$weight \ x \ height$$

$$= 3 \ x \ 10 = 30 \ J$$

Reference: *BMAT Assumed Subject Knowledge Guide*: Forces and Energy: Weight, Mass and Gravity; Gravitational Potential Energy

24)   The correct answer is D (1/4)

This is the probability that A and B antigens are present given B antigens are present.

12% of people have B antigens present (9% have B but not A + 3% have both).

3% have both B and A.

This means that for every 12 people with B antigens, three will have A antigens as well

3/12 = ¼

25)   The correct answer is H (12)

The diagram suggests that the dark coloured allele is dominant and the white allele recessive.

Start by assigning genotypes to the mice (from left to right); parent one has to be homozygous recessive as the only way that it can be white is by having two recessive alleles. Parent two could either be homozygous dominant given that all of its offspring have dark coloured coats, or it could be heterozygous. Parent three must also be heterozygous given that it has a mix of dark and white offspring and must be able to contribute both the dark allele to produce dark coloured offspring and the recessive allele to produce white offspring. Parent four is homozygous recessive as it has a white coat.

Family P must be all heterozygous, since they have both a white and a dark parent and they will contribute an allele from each parent.

Family Q - although it is likely that at least one is homozygous (given natural probability), in theory, all four could be heterozygous, and this question asks for the maximum possible number of heterozygous mice.

Family R - the two dark-coloured mice have to be heterozygous, and the two white coats, homozygous.

Thus, the maximum possible number of heterozygous mice is 12.

Reference: *BMAT Assumed Subject Knowledge Guide*: Genes, Reproduction and Evolution: Genetic Diagrams

26)   The correct answer is D (100cm^3)

The limiting reagent in this reaction is the gas Y – only 10cm is present to react.

The reaction goes to completion, so all of Y reacts with 20cm of X to produce 20cm of Z.

$$Final\ volume\ of\ X = 100cm^3 - 20cm^3$$

$$= 80cm^3$$

$$Final\ volume\ of\ Y = 10cm^3 - 10cm^3$$

$$= 0\ cm^3$$

$$Final\ volume\ of\ Z = 0cm^3 + 20\ cm^3$$

$$= 20\ cm^3$$

Therefore the total final volume is 100cm^3

27)   The correct answer is C (320nm)

The wavelength of the ray of light through air will be 4/3 x that of the wavelength through water

$$= 4/3\ x\ 360nm = 480nm$$

The wavelength of the ray of light through glass will be 2/3 x that of the wavelength through air

= 2/3 x 480nm = 320nm

BMAT SECTION 2 - 2017

1) **The correct answer is A (P=bile, Q=protease, high hydrogen ion concentration, R=insulin, protease, lipase, amylase)**

P labels the gallbladder, which secretes bile.

Q labels the stomach. Gastric secretions include mucus, hydrochloric acid from parietal cells, proteases (pepsinogen), and gastrin (hormone that controls acid secretion and motility).

R labels the pancreas. The pancreas secretes pancreatic juice, which contains proteases, lipases, and amylases. Alpha cells in the pancreatic islets secrete glucagon and beta cells in the pancreatic islets secrete insulin.

2) **The correct answer is E (Cu → Cu2+ + 2e + Cu2+ + 2e– → Cu)**

This question requires an understanding of electrolysis. We know that both the anode and the cathode are made of copper and the solution is copper (II) sulfate, which makes this a copper purification electrolysis. The anode is the positively charged electrode where electrons will leave, which creates copper ions (Cu^{2+}) and 2 electrons. The cathode is the negatively charge electrode where electrons are gained. Copper ions (Cu^{2+}) at the cathode gain 2 electrons to form copper atoms (Cu).

3) **The correct answer is A (none of them)**

On the electromagnetic spectrum the wavelength from shortest to longest is:
Gamma→X-ray→UV→Visible light→Microwaves→Radio waves

Therefore we know that options 1 and 3 are incorrect.

X-rays are used in hospitals to examine broken bones so option 4 is incorrect.

All types of electromagnetic waves travel at the same speed in a vacuum (around 300,000,000 m/s) so option 2 is also incorrect.

4) **The correct answer is F ($9-4\sqrt{5}$)**

$(\sqrt{5} - 2)^2 = (\sqrt{5} - 2)(\sqrt{5} - 2) = 5 - 4\sqrt{5} + 4 = 9 - 4\sqrt{5}$

5) **The correct answer is G (1, 2, 3, and 4)**

Changes in any of these four options can potentially affect whether healthy white blood cells can be produced by the body

6) **The correct answer is D (2 and 4 only)**

The atomic number at the top left gives the number of protons as well as the number of electrons in an atom. Below the atomic number is the mass number, which gives the total number of protons and electrons. However, any electrons gained or lost must also be accounted for in ions.

Option 1: The sulfide has gained 2 electrons to equal 18 electrons, but it also only has 18 neutrons (mass number-atomic number).

Option 2: The chloride ion has gained an electron to make 18 as well as having 20 neutrons (37-17)

Option 3: The argon atom has 18 electrons but has 22 neutrons

Option 4: The potassium ion has lost an electron to make 18 and has 20 neutrons

Option 5: The calcium atom has 20 neutrons and 20 electrons

7)   The correct answer is F (1 and 3 only)

Rate of evaporation is higher when the temperature is higher as the particles have more kinetic energy to overcome the intermolecular forces, so option 1 is correct. Rate of evaporation is higher if there is a higher flow of air above the liquid as it decreases the concentration of other substances in the air, therefore option 2 is incorrect. Rate of evaporation is higher if there is a larger surface area as there is more space for molecules to potentially escape.

8)   The correct answer is A ($\frac{1}{19}$)

This is a question dealing with conditional probability. Probability that a patient at the centre has a migraine is $\frac{5}{20}$. After the first patient is picked, we need to adjust the new probability of another patient being picked who has a migraine. The new probability is $\frac{4}{19}$. The probability of picking two patients with migraines is equal to $\frac{5}{20}*\frac{4}{19}=\frac{1}{19}$.

9)   The correct answer is E (2, 3 and 4 only + 1, 2, 3, and 4)

This question requires an understanding of osmosis.

Experiment 1: There is no glucose, only water. Although there is distilled water in both the partially permeable membrane and in the dialysis tubing, there is still a movement of water. The rate of movement in will equal the rate of movement out.

Experiment 2: There is 10% glucose solution in both the dialysis tubing and in the partially permeable membrane. Same principle applies as in experiment 1. 10% glucose solution will be made up of 90% water, so there will still be movement of water in addition to the movement of glucose.

Experiment 3 & 4: There is only glucose solution in the partially permeable membrane. Therefore glucose will move out into the dialysis tubing. However, as there is a lower concentration of water in the partially permeable membrane, distilled water from the dialysis tubing will move into the membrane.

10) The correct answer is C (2 only)

The equation of the reaction is: $Mg(s) + 2 HCl(aq) \rightarrow MgCl_2(aq) + H_2(g)$.

Option 1: There is no change to the energy of the particles so this is incorrect.

Option 2: As the magnesium reacts with hydrochloric acid, magnesium chloride and hydrogen gas is formed. Therefore, there will be a reduction in the concentration of hydrochloric acid, which ultimately means less hydrogen gas will be given off. Option 2 is correct.

Option 3: Activation energy does not change through the reaction so this is incorrect.

11) The correct answer is C (2 and 4 only)

In a series circuit, there is only one path for the current to take which means the current will remain the same every part of the circuit (eliminating options 5 and 6).

The total resistance in a series circuit is simply $R = R_1+R_2+R_3...$

Using the equation of I (current) = V(voltage)/R(Resistance), we can rearrange to find the voltage. V=IR. Therefore as the resistance in R1 is double that of R2, we can see that voltage will also double (eliminating options 1 and 2).

The only two viable options are 2 and 4.

12) The correct answer is F (2.25cm)

We can see that triangles PQT and PRS are congruent. RS is 5x longer than QT. Therefore PS will be 5x longer than PT. TS is then $\frac{4}{5}$ of PS. 1.8cm divided by $\frac{4}{5}$ gives you 2.25cm, which is the overall length of PS.

13) The correct answer is E (1 and 2 only)

Option 1: We know that sheep have 54 chromosomes in their body cells. The gamete cell nucleus contains the haploid number of chromosomes, which is 27. Option 1 is correct.

Option 2: Stem cells are undifferentiated cells that are able to differentiate into other specialised cell types. The cell produced in step four grows into an embryo therefore option 2 is also correct.

Option 3: We know that meiosis creates daughter cells with half the number of chromosomes compared with the parent cell. From option one, we already know that the gamete cell only contains half the number of chromosomes. Therefore option 3 is incorrect.

14) The correct answer is E (2, 3 and 5 only)

A disproportionation reaction must feature an element being both oxidised (loss of electrons) and reduced (gain of electrons)

Option 1: None of the elements are both oxidised and reduced

Option 2: Copper has oxidation state of -1 in Cu_2O and goes to an oxidation state of 0 in Cu and an oxidation state of -2 in CuO

Option 3: Cl_2 goes from an oxidation state of 0 to an oxidation state of -1 in HCl and an oxidation state of +1 in HClO

Option 4: Same as option 1, none of the elements are both oxidised and reduced

Option 5: Hg goes from an oxidation state of -1 to an oxidation state of 0 in Hg and an oxidation state of -2 in HgCl.

15)   The correct answer is F (absorption of a neutron, emission of a beta particle, emission of a beta particle)
In beta decay, a neutron will change into a proton and an electron. Whilst the atomic mass number will stay the same, the atomic number will increase by one. We know from the atomic numbers given to us that we need to increase the atomic number of uranium by two to make it into plutonium. Therefore, two beta particle emissions are needed.

However, we also need to increase the atomic mass number by one from 238 to 239, so we also need to absorb a neutron.

F is the only option with one neutron absorption and two beta particle emissions.

16)   The correct answer is A ($5*10^{24}$ kg)

Rearranging the equation, we get $$\frac{gR^2}{G} = M$$

Therefore: $$M = \frac{10 * (6 * 10^6)^2}{7 * 10^{-11}} = 5.14286*10^{24}$$

Correct to 1 significant figure gives us $5*10^{24}$ kg.

17)   The correct answer is G (2 and 3 only)
Option 1: Whilst coronary arteries supply the heart muscles with oxygenated blood, glucose enters heart muscles through specialised glucose transporters (GLUT4) and not through passive diffusion.

Option 2: Coronary arteries do pump blood at high pressure so this is correct

Options 3: Coronary arteries contain many layers of smooth muscle cells in order to maintain the high pressure so option 3 is correct.

18)   The correct answer is C (2C3H6O2 + MgCO3 → Mg(C3H5O2)2 + CO2 + H2O)
We know that propanoic acid is a monoprotic acid, whereas magnesium belongs in Group 2. Therefore magnesium ions will have a charge of -2 and propanoate ions will have a charge of +1. The end product of B ($MgC_3H_5O_2$) does not balance out the charges so we can eliminate B as a viable answer option.

Reaction between propanoic acid and a carbonate will release CO2, so we can eliminate A. We can also eliminate D as 2CH3COOH does not give us the chemical formula for propanoic acid.

The end product of E ($Mg_3C_3O_2$) is not the chemical formula for magnesium propanoate as it lacks any hydrogens so we can eliminate this option.

The only option that remains is C, with all products present and balanced correctly.

19)   The correct answer is E (1200 m/2)

The equation of speed is S=D/T

As the microphone records the reflection, we need to double the distance travelled, giving us 12 metres.

S=12m/0.01secods=1200 m/s

20)   The correct answer is E ($\dfrac{x+1}{2x(x-1)}$)

We need to find the least common multiplier between the three fractions, which is 2x(x-1). We then multiply each fraction by 2x(x-1)

$$\frac{1}{2x}+\frac{1}{x-1}-\frac{1}{x}=\frac{x-1}{2x(x-1)}+\frac{2x}{2x(x-1)}-\frac{2(x-1)}{2x(x-1)}=\frac{x-1+2x-2(x-1)}{2x(x-1)}=\frac{x+1}{2x(x-1)}$$

21)   The correct answer is D (0.5 and 0.750)

As two of the children from 1 and 2 have freckles, we can conclude that the gene for having freckles is dominant. However, as 4 doesn't have freckles, we know that 1 is heterozygous dominant for freckles and 2 is homozygous not having freckles. Labelling F as the dominant allele for having freckles as f as the recessive allele for not having freckles:

	F	f
f	Ff	ff
f	Ff	ff

From the table we can deduce that the children of 1 and 2 will only have 0.5 chance of having freckles.

We know 5 must be heterozygous dominant from the table above. 6 must also be heterozygous dominant as 7 and 8 both do not have freckles.

From this table we can deduce that the children of 5 and 6 will have 0.75 chance of having freckles

22)   The correct answer is B (0.400 mol/dm³)

Molar mass of the copper (II) sulfate is: 64+32+(4*16)+(5*2)+(5*16) = 250

10/250 = 0.04 moles of copper (II) sulfate in 100cm³ solution.

The concentration required is in moles per cubic decimetre (litre), so we need to multiply the 0.04 moles by a factor of ten. This gives us 0.400 moles of copper (II) sulfate per dm³.

23)   The correct answer is F (the force that the table exerts on the floor)

Newton's Third Law: If an object (A) exerts a force on another object (B), then object (B) will exert an equal force in the opposite direction on to object (A).

The opposite force to P (the force that the floor exerts on the table) is the force that the table exerts on the floor.

24)   The correct answer is C ($9\pi+9\sqrt{5}$)

Area of triangle: rearranging Pythagoras theorem of $a^2 + b^2 = c^2$, we know that 9^2-6^2=b^2
$b=\sqrt{45}$

To calculate the area of the triangle, we need to do ½bh = 0.5* $\sqrt{45}$ *6=3$\sqrt{45}$ = 3$\sqrt{9}\sqrt{5}$=9$\sqrt{5}$

Area of sector: We know that the sector is ¼ of a circle due to the right angle. Area of the entire circle = 6^2 *π=36π. Therefore area of the sector is a quarter of the size, giving 9π.

Adding these two together we get 9π+9$\sqrt{5}$

25)   The correct answer is G (2 and 3 only)

Option 1: The cat is a warm blooded mammal, therefore the internal temperature will be regulated. Option 1 is therefore incorrect.

Option 2: We know from the information in the passage that the gene is sensitive to temperature, with warmer temperatures resulting in a paler colour. Therefore we can conclude that as the ears, front of face, paws, and tail are of cooler temperature, the colour in comparison to the rest of the body becomes darker.

Option 3: We know that the coat colour is sensitive to temperature, which is an environmental factor. Therefore option 3 is also correct.

26)   The correct answer is B (0.12dm³)

The balanced equation for the reaction is 2Na + 2H2O ---> H2 + 2NaOH

0.23g of sodium equals 0.01 moles of sodium. From the equation, we know that 0.005 moles of hydrogen was made. The questions tells us to assume that the molar volume of gas is 24dm³.

$$24*0.005=0.12dm^3$$

27) **The correct answer is C (1.25)**

Kinetic energy (KE) = 0.5 * mass (m) * velocity (v)^2.

The mass of the object here is 2.5kg therefore KE = 0.5 *2.5*v^2=1.25v^2

This gives us the gradient of 1.2.

BMAT SECTION 3 ESSAY PLANS

BMAT Section 3 – 2003

1) 'Is the sale of body parts wrong?'

Discussion of the sale of organs is overshadowed by cases of murder, and corruption. But there is also a serious ethical issue about whether people should be allowed to sell parts of the body. It applies not only to organs, such as the kidney or parts of the liver, but also to tissues, such as bone marrow, gametes (eggs and sperm) and even genetic material. The usual argument in favour of allowing the sale of organs is that we need to increase supply. In the US, as few as 15% of people who need kidney transplants ever get a kidney. Some have proposed an "ethical market" in organs. There would be only one purchaser, which would buy all organs and distribute according to some fair conception of medical priority. There would be no direct sales, no exploitation of low-income countries and their populations.

But there may be a stronger argument in favour of sale of body parts. People have a right to make a decision to sell a body part. If we should be allowed to sell our labour, why not sell the means to that labour? If we should be allowed to risk damaging our body for pleasure (by smoking or skiing), why not for money which we could use to realise other goods in life? If we allow people to die for their country, it seems we should allow them to risk death or injury for the chance to improve the quality of their lives or their children's lives or for anything else they value. Money for these people is just a means to realise what they value in life. Whether or not a private market in organs will increase supply or improve its quality, it seems that people have a right to sell them.

The above article was taken from: Savulescu J. Is the sale of body parts wrong? *J Med Ethics*, 2003; 29: 138-139.

Explain what you think the author means by the term 'ethical market'. Present an argument against the legalised sale of organs. What is your own view of the author's assertion that individuals have the right to sell their own body parts?

Explain what you think the author means by the term 'ethical market.'
An 'ethical market' may suggest a regulated service for the purchasing and selling of non-essential organs, where all involved parties provide informed consent.

Present an argument against the legalised sale of organs.
- Poverty Pressure – Legalising the sale of organs would likely increase pressure on those in poverty, who may feel obliged to sell their organs to feed their families. It may ultimately be regarded as an 'alternative' to social welfare.
- 'Non-essential' – It is almost impossible to determine what should be regarded as a non-essential organ, as this will largely vary from individual to individual. Furthermore, whilst one kidney may be regarded as non-essential today, following a severe kidney infection or metastatic cancer one year later, the original kidney may be much required.

What is your own view of the author's assertion that individuals have the right to sell their own body parts?
- Increased Supply – The creation of a legal market would increase the supply of organs, thus reducing the number of people dying on waiting lists.

- Increased organ transplants – With a greater supply, biological and mechanical organ matching would likely be more specific resulting in improved long-term outcomes and survival rates. There would also be greater economies of scale and the creation of more specialist transplant surgeons, rather than 'general transplant surgeons'.

- The benefits of such policies can be seen in countries like Iran which have a legal market for non-essential organs (for example, kidneys) and have much shorter waiting lists, with more than 1,400 kidneys bought and sold each year (Statnews, 2016)

- Reduced black market – With a legal, regulated market, this will reduce the scope for a black market where transplant success rates are much lower, expenses are higher ($3,000 up to $150,000 for a kidney), and exploitation is common.

Conclusion

Whilst there are pitfalls of an ethical, legal market for organs, undoubtedly without such a market, a black market will remain where only the rich will benefit. Legalising this market will allow it to be regulated, increasingly organ supply, success rates as well as allowing all members of the population to benefit.

2) *A little learning is a dangerous thing* (Alexander Pope)

Explain what you think the author means by this statement. Advance an argument against the statement above, i.e. in support of the proposition 'a little learning is *not* a dangerous thing'. What do you think determines whether or not learning can be a dangerous thing?

Explain what you think the author means by this statement.
- This statement suggests that limited knowledge can often result in more harm than good, and as such, it may be more beneficial to either know nothing or a substantial amount.

Advance an argument against the statement above, i.e. in support of the proposition 'a little learning is *not* a dangerous thing.'
- When someone knows 'a little' and appreciates that they only know a little, this can be beneficial.
  For example, knowing first aid skills in an appropriate situation or recognising that sharp left sided chest pain at rest could suggest a myocardial infarction. Therefore one should call an ambulance.
- Learning curve – to know a lot you must first know a little, no-one is born knowing everything.
- If everyone followed this concept, nobody would learn anything

Arguments in favour of the statement
- It is dangerous when people think that they know more than they do. For example, a medical student who tries to treat family members, or even a consultant neurosurgeon attempting cardiothoracic surgery.
- Knowing only half of the symptoms may lead to the wrong diagnosis:
  For example chest pain may suggest a myocardial infarction (MI). However chest pain following chest trauma may indicate an impact injury.

What do you think determines whether or not learning can be a dangerous thing?

- The focus of knowledge – learning about first aid and basic life support is likely to be useful and unlikely dangerous. On the other hand, learning about designing military weapons is more likely to be dangerous.
- Moral Compass – Irrespective of the knowledge topic, an ethical focus is essential in ensuring that knowledge is not abused. Whilst Dr Harold Shipman was very knowledgeable, he abused his knowledge and contributed to the deaths of approximately 200 trusting patients.
- Personal Insight – In addition to the content of knowledge, it is important to understand one's level of knowledge objectively. For example, a medical student who believes that he can perform cardiothoracic surgery after completing a first aid course is likely to represent a danger to others, whereas another student who recognises the limitation of his first aid qualification is likely to be a more useful contributor to society.

Conclusion

It is not a matter of 'a little' or 'a lot' of knowledge, but rather it is most important to recognise one's level of knowledge and their limitations.

3) *It is ridiculous to treat the living body as a mechanism.*

What does the above statement imply? Give examples that illustrate why it might sometimes be sensible to treat the body as a mechanism and others that illustrate the opposite. How might you resolve this apparent contradiction?

What does the above statement imply?

- This statement suggests that each body should be thought of as an individual unique being, rather than a technical entity, whereby any input will generate an identical output irrespective of the body involved.

Arguments against this statement

- Health guidelines such as those proposed by the National Institute for Health and Clinical Excellence (NICE) are reliant on the assumption that each body will respond in a similar way to a given treatment and hence can be regarded as a mechanism. For example, antibiotics are suggested for those who have a severe bacterial infection, and statins are suggested for those with elevated cholesterol with the hope of tackling the infection and reducing one's cholesterol respectively.
- Similarly, our understanding of the gastrointestinal (GI) tract is based on a general mechanism rather than investigation of each individual. For example, if a patient has a bowel resection, our general understanding of the GI tract would lead us to conclude that the patient may develop diarrhoea through an inability to reabsorb water.

Arguments in favour of the statement

- Whilst NICE guidelines do rely on the body having a mechanistic response; they further acknowledge that each person is unique and additional factors such as ethnicity, age and co-morbidities must be taken into account when advising on treatment. This is supported by NICE guidelines on high blood pressure which suggest different medication depending on the individual's age and ethnicity.
- Human understanding of the human body and the world is always changing. Regarding the body as a mechanism would suggest that we have a complete understanding; contrastingly, with many diseases such as Alzheimer's Dementia not having any cure, this would suggest otherwise.

313

- There is far more to treating a patient than providing medication. The biopsychosocial approach suggests that medical professionals need to manage the social and psychological impact of each condition, and that this impact will vary from individual to individual and as such cannot be addressed with identical mechanisms.

- Genetic and environmental factors often play a role in diseases. They cannot always be predicted and can influence whether patients will develop a disease, and how they respond to treatment.
  For example, two siblings growing up in a troubled family, one may develop depression and personality disorder – whilst the other could be completely normal. (Sullivan et al., 2000).
  - o The rationale as to why one sibling did, and the other did not develop the condition cannot be explained by any mechanism.

Conclusion

Whilst the body is not an exact mechanism, it is required to consider it as such to propose and implement appropriate medical guidelines and manage patients.

4) *Our belief in any particular natural law cannot have a safer basis than our unsuccessful critical attempts to refute it. (Karl Popper)*

What do you understand by the statement above? Can you suggest examples where a scientific experiment might not proceed by attempting to refute a hypothesis? To what extent do you think the statement accurately reflects the nature of scientific method?

What do you understand by the statement above?
- This statement suggests that no beliefs, laws or perceptions should be regarded as definite and all should be open to criticism as well as opposing research.

Can you suggest examples where scientific experiment might not proceed by attempting to refute a hypothesis?
- Scientific research is largely dependent on funding, and it is generally unlikely that one will obtain funding to explore further theories to the contrary of something as well founded as Newton's Laws, or other similarly held principles.
- In every failed attempt to negate/refute natural laws, we provide evidence to strengthen the basis of the natural law, and thus indirectly future efforts to refute it.

To what extent do you think the statement accurately reflects the nature of scientific method?
- On the other hand, almost all research is available to challenge including material published in highly regarded journals such as The Lancet, for example, Dr Andrew Wakefield's publication on the association between the MMR vaccine and Autism was later retracted following challenges (Wakefield et al., 1998).
- Away from Medicine, previously held beliefs about the world have also been challenged through investigative research, for example, Christopher Columbus established that there was far more on Earth than was previously accepted and believed.

- Much of science today is not about refuting existing laws, but about verifying new laws and hypotheses. For example, significant research has gone into the development of medications to slow the progression of Alzheimer's Dementia (for instance cholinesterase inhibitors). These medications do not challenge any existing natural law; they merely attempt to add to current practice and knowledge.

BMAT Section 3 – 2004

1) *Individual freedom and the rule of law are mutually incompatible.*

Write a unified essay in which you address the following:
What might be the grounds for making this assertion? Give a reasoned argument against the proposition. How can the concepts of freedom and law be reconciled in a real society?

What might be the grounds for making this assertion?

- The law may be regarded as a set of rules limiting what individuals in a society are allowed to do, which restricts their freedom because some people would inevitably wish to do things that are outside the law.

- This assertion is supported by the fact that many laws restrict individual freedoms. For example, there have been many cases of individuals seeking euthanasia who have been forced to travel to the Dignitas clinic in Switzerland as a result of laws preventing euthanasia in the United Kingdom.

Give a reasoned argument against the proposition.

- The law does not necessarily limit freedom, in fact, it often protects individual freedom because, in a lawless society, certain individuals may be given the means to control/enslave/dominate others, which would restrict individual freedom more than the law would:

   For example, laws protecting the press/journalists (in many democratic countries) exist to maintain individual freedom of speech, and freedom for the public to be informed about global events, without large corporations and politicians being able to silence them.

   o Laws about needing a trial before conviction also protect individual freedom from wrongful imprisonment.

   o Laws against slavery limit the ability of some to own cheap labour, but also protect the freedom of the would be slaves

- In many cases, it is not laws but other factors restricting freedom such as cultural beliefs and financial inequality. For example, a child born into one family may receive access to the very best healthcare and have the opportunity to pursue a career in any field of their preference. In contrast, another child born at the same time to another family in a nearby town may have almost no available health care or long-term prospects as a result of cultural and financial limitations rather than legal frameworks.

How can the concepts of freedom and law be reconciled in a real society?

- People should be free to do as they wish, but within reason, as long as this is not destructive/ harmful/ freedom limiting to others.

- The constitutions of many countries dictate some degree of protection of individual freedoms, but also for the 'common defence' (US constitution), and the law must balance these two needs.

- A duty-based framework can also be applied: lawmakers must fulfil their duties to all the people they represent to ensure the fairest and freest society possible. Therefore they may pass laws to allow this even if this restricts certain individual freedoms.

Conclusion

- Whilst some laws restrict freedom, others very much protect individual freedom, and as such, an all-encompassing blanket statement regarding laws and freedom cannot be reliably concluded.
- It is up to policymakers and high court judges to balance individual freedom and the maintenance of an orderly society when shaping legislation. They must consider a wide range of viewpoints and ethical frameworks to effectively do so.

2) *There is more to healing than the application of scientific knowledge.*

Write a unified essay in which you address the following:
Briefly define 'scientific knowledge'. Explain how it might be argued that medical treatment that is not wholly based on scientific knowledge is worthless. Discuss whether there can be approaches to healing that are valid but not amenable to scientific experiment.

Briefly define 'scientific knowledge.'
- Scientific knowledge involves dissecting the interactions that take place in the world through cause and effect and the empirical study of natural and man-made phenomena.

Explain how it might be argued that medical treatment that is not wholly based on scientific knowledge is worthless.
- Scientific knowledge is widely directly involved in medicine especially diagnostics, for example, blood tests and computerised imaging.
- One cannot heal with communication skills alone – there is a need for a scientific basis to support the action, such as the case in prescribing antibiotics.
- Without scientific knowledge at the forefront of medical treatment, medical capacity to intervene is very limited.

Discuss whether there can be approaches to healing that are valid but not amenable to scientific experiment.
- There are many 'non-scientific' approaches to healing such as homeopathy, which many patients find beneficial where conventional medicine has failed to offer benefit.
- Good communication is essential; having knowledge alone and being unable to convey it to patients is insufficient and often leads to medication errors and patient non-compliance
- Healing relies on patient compliance with treatment, (such as avoiding alcohol in the case of liver disease) – in this case, advice is arguably more important than scientific knowledge
- Another aspect of 'healing'/treating is palliative (end of life) care which requires more humanity and social assistance than the scientific input.

Conclusion
Communication, compliance and humanity are all important – but without the application of scientific knowledge, the aforementioned have limited benefit and thus are more important as auxiliary measures.

3) *Our genes evolved for a Stone Age lifestyle. Therefore, we must adopt Stone Age habits if we are to be healthy.*

Write a unified essay in which you address the following:

Explain the logical connection between the two sentences.
What might be the practical implications if we were to agree with the reasoning? Discuss the extent to which the argument is valid.

Explain the logical connection between the two sentences.

- These statements suggest that genetics contribute significantly to the outcome, and thus, to optimise this outcome, one should follow their genetic predisposition.
- The first statement controversially suggests that human genes are more suited to a more primitive lifestyle.

What might be the practical implications if we were to agree with the reasoning?

- In practical terms, following this rationale would involve adopting a more primitive life approach involving less technological involvement with everything from preparing food to travelling and our home habitat.
- As such, we would likely have more active lifestyles due to the requirements to source our own food, water and travel between locations.
- With regards to healthcare, we would revert to less scientific focused treatments, with a more significant role for alternative medicine.

Arguments in favour of the statement

- Our attempts to adopt more 'advanced' lifestyles have led to increased pollution, toxicity and water contamination, all of which has resulted in increased morbidity.
- People who currently employ 'Stone Age habits' such as healthier eating and more exercise generally live longer, and this is promoted by Public Health England (PHE)/doctors.
- Current skills that mankind have learnt are not 'primitive' ones that would aid in our survival. We are designed to be hunter-gatherers and to be able to find food/water, build shelter, and procreate. We have learnt to do other tasks, but they are not innate.

Arguments against this statement

- The increased life expectancy compared to during the Stone Age suggests that our present lifestyle approaches are more supportive of our environment. The average life expectancy in the UK is 81 presently and has increased significantly over the last 2,000 years (World Bank, 2016).
- Our current circumstances are very different to those faced in the Stone Age, and we are not under constant threat from our environment as in the Stone Age, in that we do not risk death on a daily basis.
  - In the same way, our ancestors adapted to their environment; we must do the same with ours which means forming our own habits
- Stone Age habits may mean leaving the weakest behind, which would probably result in a smaller, healthier population. Such an approach may be regarded as unethical and would also make the medical profession redundant.

Conclusion

- The statement is well-meaning but should not be taken literally.
- Instead, it should be interpreted as try and live life as healthily as possible.
- However, one can disagree that it is essential, as both genes and environment dictate how to survive. Genetics are no longer as important as they once were.
- Overall, one can disagree with the statement – for the benefit of human progress we must continue to develop our own habits appropriate for this era.

BMAT Section 3 – 2005

1) *Animals do not feel pain as we do.*

Write a unified essay in which you address the following:

In what way might 'feel' here have a different meaning from 'sense'?

What kinds of experiments or observations might support such a view?

Advance an argument against the statement above, i.e. that animals feel pain of the same kind and to the same extent as we do.

In what way might 'feel' here have a different meaning from 'sense'?

- Pain is a complex experience with both sensory and emotional components
- 'Sense' refers to detecting noxious stimuli as is seen in the physical damage to the body through sensory organs/nerve endings connecting to spinal reflex arcs and 'lower' brain areas, such as the brainstem
- 'Feel' refers to the secondary emotion/state of mind experienced as a result of detecting this noxious stimulus that is, being aware of the sensation of pain, and controlled by 'higher' brain areas, for example, the amygdala and cerebral cortex.
- Suffering is caused by the feeling of pain, not by merely sensing it- hence it is possible to feel pain/ suffering without physical harm (for example emotional pain; phantom limb syndrome), and not all physical harm results in suffering (for example some women in childbirth).

What kinds of experiments or observations might support such a view?

- Descartes, in the 17th century, infamously described animals as 'automata', incapable of feeling or suffering.
- The experience of pain is a subjective emotional experience. Therefore our understanding of it comes from individual patient reports.
- Animals are unable to communicate their experience of pain verbally, and even non-verbal manifestations can be subtle, different to those in humans, which can be misinterpreted as indifference/ lack of feeling of pain.

  For example, prey species may have evolved to show very little pain behaviour, such as inappetence and social withdrawal without obvious vocalisation, to not 'advertise' injury to predators.

  o Predator species, such as wolves, may also hide pain to avoid appearing weak to the rest of the pack.
- For a long time in the 20th century, cognitive ability was thought to be a prerequisite for sentience.
- Many 'lower' animals have a less developed/ no cerebral cortex (the main part of the brain attributed to higher cognition and sentience in humans), so were thought incapable of cognition and feeling pain (Proctor, 2012 in a review: Animal sentience: Where are we and where are we headed?)

Advance an argument against the statement above, i.e. that animals feel pain of the same kind and to the same extent as we do.

- Although animals are unable to communicate verbally, there is a whole field of study into measuring how they manifest pain. Such as the Glasgow Composite pain scale for dogs (2007), or the 'Grimace scale' for rabbit pain facial expressions- so we are now reasonably good at assessing pain in mammalian species.

- Studies on small animals after surgery show pain behaviours when not given sufficient pain relief, which is alleviated when given analgesics (Proctor, 2012)
- Studies in many non-mammalian species including birds and fish, where pain behaviour is alleviated by the administration of analgesics (painkillers)
  For example, lame chickens (foot pain) preferentially eat food mixed with analgesics rather than non-analgesic food and show reduced pain behaviour (Danbury et al., 2000).
- The 'feeling' of pain is even documented in fish, who have no cerebral cortex: trout have impaired attention to other threats when in pain showing they are aware of feeling pain – this shows other nervous system structures can evolve to perform the same role as the cerebral cortex (Sneddon, 2003).
- Animals may in fact experience more severe pain given that they are unable to communicate with the vet. For example: for a human patient, the experience of the pain of a fracture repair surgery may be mitigated by the knowledge that the procedure will ameliorate their pain.

Conclusion

- Despite differing views throughout the centuries, the current consensus is that for vertebrates, pain causes suffering, which underpins animal welfare legislation in most countries (Proctor, 2012)
- Because the feeling of pain is a personal experience, there is still have no way of knowing exactly how other animals experience pain, and whether this is the same as or different to humans, but this should not stop us from endeavouring to minimise pain and suffering of all animals that are part of society.

2) *Science should leave off making pronouncements: the river of knowledge has too often turned back on itself. (Sir James Jeans, 1877-1946)*

Write a unified essay in which you address the following:

What do you understand by the word 'pronouncement'?
Give an example of a biomedical pronouncement that has subsequently turned out to be false.
Advance an argument against the statement above, i.e. that scientists should nevertheless not feel inhibited in making pronouncements of what they believe to be the truth.

What do you understand by the word 'pronouncement'?

- A pronouncement is to make a statement of declaration. It is more firm than simply announcing.
- This statement suggests that science has been wrong in the past only to have to backtrack later when other evidence to the contrary has appeared.

Give an example of a biomedical pronouncement that has subsequently turned out to be false.

- Smoking was initially thought to be beneficial and could keep people slim. This turned out to be incorrect (British Doctors study conducted by Doll and Hill, 1951-2001) proved the link between smoking and lung cancer.
  - o This can mislead the public, especially if you always have to correct yourself later.
  - o The public may lose trust in the scientific community and not know what to believe.

- Pronouncing something too early can be harmful (going against the nonmaleficence principle) In the case of thalidomide initially being considered safe, and the erroneous autism-MMR (Measles, Mumps, Rubella) vaccine paper (Wakefield et al., 1998) which unfortunately some people still believe today.

Advance an argument against the statement above, that scientists should nevertheless not feel inhibited in making pronouncements of what they believe to be the truth.

- You need to make pronouncements so that others in the scientific community can verify/disprove it; this is all part of human advancement.
  - o Someone needs to make a statement first for others to be able to disseminate it
- If we had this fear of failure, individuals would be afraid to do research or to publish their findings.
- Many times, science has been right such as the Framingham heart study (1948-present) means that the effects of diet, exercise on atherosclerosis and coronary artery disease are now known.
- Most of the time scientific pronouncements are right, unfortunately, in many cases, they only achieve significant media attention when they are wrong, and thus people often remember these unfortunate incidents.

Conclusion
- Whilst science should still make pronouncements, they should be cautious in doing so.
- This way it gives an accurate representation, by saying they have shown x, but there is still further work that needs to be done to prove the hypothesis.
- This is the norm now when scientific work is published, with all findings being somewhat cautious. Only when multiple groups have reproduced the work, can it start to be considered factual and endorsed by regulatory bodies such as NICE.
- Even if the initial pronouncement is wrong, it still benefits humanity as other researchers including themselves will develop a greater understanding including with 'negative research papers' (papers which find no association between tested factors) which are findings in their own right.

3) *With limited resources and increasing demand, doctors will not in the future be concerned about how to cure, so much as whether to cure.*

Write a unified essay in which you address the following:
Explain what you think this statement means.
What factors might contribute to 'limited resources' and 'increasing demand'.
Advance an argument that governments should ensure that resources for medical care should always match demand.

Explain what you think this statement means.
- This statement suggests that resource restraints will largely dictate provision of medical care as opposed to knowledge and technological limitations.

What factors might contribute to 'limited resources' and 'increasing demand'.
- Limited resources
  - o Economic climate changes – global recession

- o Increasing the cost of many health supplies as technology advances (for example, before the widespread use of MRI scanners, other more simplistic imaging modalities were used which were significantly less costly).
- Increasing demand
  - o Aging Population – There has been a combination of living longer with the average life expectancy of 82 in the United Kingdom and 84 in Japan (WHO, 2016) as well as a shift in the population demographics with more of the population older than 50 than ever before. In comparison to younger demographics, health resource requirements are much more significant in those over 50 and are driving the increased demand for healthcare.
  - o Patient expectation – The global media has played a significant role in raising patient expectations with regular coverage of 'cancer-beating wonder-drugs'.
  - o Health promotion and preventative medicine– There are many more screening programmes as well as health promotion campaigns which not only result in the earlier diagnosis of many conditions but also detect many incidental findings which require resources and would possibly have minimal impact on a patient's quality of life.

Advance an argument that governments should ensure that resources for medical care should always match demand.

- The health of a population impacts productivity. Hence, whilst it may cost money to finance medical care, it will lead to higher productivity, GDP and thus tax returns.
- Failure to fund medical care sufficiently would be a regressive policy that would be to the detriment of the less affluent, whilst the wealthier members of society will be able to self-fund private healthcare. This may indirectly result in a perpetuating cycle where the poorer members of community are more likely to remain poor due to health challenges and as such, reduced progression opportunities.
- One of the core principles of medical ethics is beneficence; there are few things better for patients that providing the best available healthcare provisions.

On the other hand,

- Every expense has an opportunity cost, and significant healthcare investment may result in reduced investment into education or other vital areas.
- Providing the services that patients desire (for example elective non-emergency surgeries the very next day) would not only be very costly but also require a higher supply of medical professionals. Whilst it may be possible to recruit doctors and auxiliary professionals from abroad, this would likely result in shortages in other countries damaging their healthcare systems.

Conclusion

It is essential to invest adequately into healthcare to preserve and encourage a healthy, productive population with minimal inequality. However, it would be naïve to expect that health investment should match patient demands, especially given the ever-increasing patient expectations and significant expenses associated with medical equipment that would restrict budgets for other important areas.

BMAT Section 3 – 2006

1) ***Our zeal to make things work better will not be our anthem: it will be our epitaph.***
(Bryan Appleyard, Countdown to Catastrophe, Sunday Times, 15/12/02)

Write a unified essay in which you address the following:
The above statement was made in reference to modern technology; explain what you think it means. Advance an argument against the statement above, i.e. in support of the proposition 'our zeal to make things work better will be our anthem'.

The above statement was made in reference to modern technology; explain what you think it means.

- The statement implies that our eagerness to develop or improve things will take us to our destruction instead of victory.

Advance an argument against the statement above, i.e. in support of the proposition 'our zeal to make things work better will be our anthem'.

- With advancing modern technology, we have created a toxic atmosphere for nature and all living beings.
  - Daily increasing carbon dioxide emission.
  - Greenhouse gases.
  - Modern warfare.
  - Nuclear power plants.

- Technology has also greatly influenced man's natural lifestyle.
  - Social media, internet and television, have reduced human to human interactions and have increased overall inactivity.
  - 'Watching TV occupied an average of 2.8 hours per day' (Bureau of Labour Statistics, 2017)
  - Improved transportation and electronic housework aids (washing machines, robotic cleaners) have reduced daily exercise with sedentary lifestyles having a strong association with hospitalisations, all-cause mortality, cardiovascular disease, diabetes, and many cancers (Biswas et al., 2015)
  - Technological advancements have resulted in the widespread provision of 'fast food' which is often responsible for delivering unhealthy constituents to the human body.

- The deviation from the natural lifestyle along with increased environmental pollution has contributed to:
  - Chronic diseases like diabetes, hypertension.
  - High mental stress.

Arguments against the statement

- The rapid evolution of science and technology in recent years has made the majority of the world's life easier. For example advances in transportation, sanitation and medicine.
- Humanity's perseverance and dedication to improving things have led to improvements in healthcare and sanitation having a positive impact on life expectancy.

324

- The increased life expectancy compared to during the Stone Age suggests that our present lifestyle approaches are more supportive of our environment. The average life expectancy in the UK is 81 presently and has increased significantly over the last 2,000 years (World Bank, 2016).

Conclusion

It is crucial to encourage technological and medical advancements with the intention of 'making things better'. However, there is equally a requirement for regulation and moderation to avoid the development of potentially harmful technological advancements.

2) *Higher education and great numbers that is a contradiction in terms. (Friedrich Nietzsche)*

Write a unified essay in which you address the following:
Expand the argument underlying this assertion. What do you understand by 'higher Education'? Is it qualitatively different from other kinds of education? Present an argument that it is, in fact, possible to provide higher education for a large proportion of the population.

Expand the argument underlying this assertion. What do you understand by 'higher Education'? Is it qualitatively different from other kinds of education?

- This statement means you cannot have a large section of the population in higher education.
- Higher education (HE) – after secondary school is traditionally optional. Specialising in a particular field and delivered by a university or other learning institution.
- Although mainly content based, university is also for educating yourself about how to live independently, live and work with other people, and gain independence.
- Even if you are not didactically taught these skills, higher education is intended to broaden the person's mind not just academically advance one.

Present an argument that it is, in fact, possible to provide higher education for a large proportion of the population.

- There is a funnel-like plot from primary to secondary to tertiary education, with the numbers declining at each stage
- Like most disciplines, the more specialised the work, the fewer numbers there will be doing it. Thus we cannot expect a large majority to undertake HE especially now fees are in excess of £9000 with many students being saddled with debt.
- If everyone completes HE, it loses its value and becomes the 'norm', and you no longer stand out from the crowd. It merely just becomes education as such. There are also disadvantages such as rising unemployment and grade inflation as a result.
- Nietzsche argued that pupils lose their individual personality and become a process if lots of people go through HE. Pupils are not being 'educated' but just doing it because it is the norm and will ensure financial security. We are guilty of this in the West where it is expected of most of us to pursue HE rather than making a conscientious choice to do so.

Argument against the statement

- The United Nations says everyone has the right to HE.
- In western developed countries, we currently can do this. In 2006, 25% of 18-year-olds went to university compared to 31% in 2015.
- Education is correlated with economic growth. Therefore, the more people in a population you educate, the more a country will prosper.
- Encouraging HE creates competition whereby the general standard of the candidate is raised. For skilled jobs, there will be many competent candidates, ensuring quality control. We see this today where many highly qualified graduates cannot get jobs. This point can go either way.
- HE means people make more informed decisions and are more actively involved in politics and society which may be reflected in elections, in the community. This means that everyone's baseline knowledge increases and people are more understanding, tolerant, educated about the world and others that live in it.

Conclusion

- It is possible to have a society where most people receive HE
- Whilst there may be pitfalls like we see today with regards to unemployment and student debt, overall greater levels of knowledge benefits everyone.

3) *The main benefit of patient consent is that it relieves doctors of blame for bad decisions.*

Write a unified essay in which you address the following:
Explain the argument underlying this statement. What is conventionally regarded as the benefits of 'patient consent'? Give an example of a situation in which a patient's consent would be meaningful, and another in which it would not. How should clinical decisions be made?

Explain the argument underlying this statement.

- This statement suggests that patient consent is a safeguard for medical negligence rather than a measure of the benefit of patients.

Arguments in favour of the statement:

- Following medical and surgical errors, the consequences (litigious and financial) are generally less in cases where consent has been sought and documented compared to cases in which appropriate consent has not been obtained.
- Patient consent enables shared responsibility and 'transfer of care'. With patients involved in the ultimate decision, they are partly responsible for the outcome even though they may not have the same level of understanding as the doctor who suggested/offered the therapy.

What is conventionally regarded as the benefits of 'patient consent'? Give an example of a situation in which a patient's consent would be meaningful, and another in which it would not.

- Without the requirement for consent, there is an unclear boundary between mutually agreeable procedures and assault.

- Consent means patients can make informed decisions about their care, moving from paternalistic medicine to one where the patient is as much a key part as the doctor (GMC guidelines on consent from 2008).
- Consent also allows life-saving treatment to occur such as many acute surgical procedures (For example; treating a ruptured abdominal aortic aneurysm). If there are risks of death involved, then it is not necessarily to absolve the doctor of blame, but an optimist can think of it as allowing the doctor to save the patient's life. Without consent and 'shared responsibility' it is likely that many doctors would not proceed with these procedures for fear of ultimate responsibility despite well understood prior risks.
- Consent also follows autonomy (the patient dictating what happens to themselves). Involving the patient in the decision-making process also increases trust in the doctor and therefore compliance with medications. (Etchells et al., 1996)

How should clinical decisions be made?
- Decisions should always be made with the patient (if they have capacity).
- Capacity and whether a patient can consent needs to be assessed thoroughly where it is not clear or if there are multiple treatments which could be life-changing.
- There are many benefits of obtaining patient consent, including preventing unnecessary litigation against doctors. However, there are undoubtedly a number of patient benefits

BMAT Section 3 – 2007

1) *The technology of medicine has outrun its sociology.* (Henry E. Sigerist, 1891-1957)

Write a unified essay in which you address the following:
What do you understand by this statement? Give an example of a technological advance to which it might apply. How might this problem be addressed?

What do you understand by this statement?

- This statement suggests that medical advancements have superseded the population and social structure that they were intended to serve.
- It may also suggest that parts of society may not be willing to accept specific medical technologies or treatments because of their cultural values or beliefs.

Give an example of a technological advance to which it might apply

- Advanced medical technologies are expensive and are limited only to those who can afford it. For example, the medication Provenge which can be used for metastatic prostate cancer costs between £250,000 and £500,000/QALY and as such is not funded by the NHS (NICE, 2015)
- Even basic medical technologies such as vaccinations and antibiotics which may be life-saving may not be available to specific poorer communities.
    - A study led by the University of Liverpool found out that the prices charged by drugs companies for some of the most crucial treatments have risen more than 1000% over the last five years (The Telegraph, 2017)

- Societies are comprised of a range of religious and cultural values, some of which oppose current medical practice and advances.
    - This includes contraception and abortion which current medical technology enables, however many religious and societal views oppose their use.
    - Jehovah's Witnesses are not allowed to accept blood transfusions including in emergency situations, despite current medical technology making this a very safe and often lifesaving measure.

How might this problem be addressed?

- Improved funding for the NHS can ensure that wider society has access to the very best medical advancements as opposed to only societies' elite who have private health insurance.
- In endeavouring to address religious views which oppose the current medical practice, it may be possible to use technology to develop religion compliant medical products for example substitute fluids which have the same physiological benefit as blood transfusions without being religiously unacceptable for Jehovah's Witnesses.
- On a separate point, public health education regarding medical advancements is important to portray realistic expectations of medical advances as well as to dispel any fears as a result of 'sensationalist media headlines'.

Conclusion

The value of medical advancements is proportionate to its societal benefit. As such, discovering cancer-curing medications which are to the benefit of a minority (as a result of expense) are of less value than 'simpler' medical advancements which benefit wider society.

---

2) *Our unprecedented survival has produced a revolution in longevity which is shaking the foundations of societies around the world and profoundly altering our attitudes to life and death. (Tom Kirkwood, BBC Reith Lectures, 2001)*

Write a unified essay in which you address the following:
This is a statement concerning ageing and longevity; explain what you think it means.
Advance an argument against this statement, i.e. in favour of the proposition that 'a revolution in longevity is *not* shaking the foundations of societies around the world'.

This is a statement concerning ageing and longevity; explain what you think it means.
- This statement suggests that with the increasing global life expectancy, personal, societal and political perspectives are being re-evaluated.

Advance an argument against this statement, i.e. in favour of the proposition that 'a revolution in longevity is *not* shaking the foundations of societies around the world'.
- Varying attitudes to life and death have been present for many years, long before life expectancy reached the current age of 82 in the UK (WHO, 2016). One of the most controversial topics pertaining to life and death is abortion with the abortion act legislated in 1967, with illegal abortions being prevalent far before then when life expectancy was much lower.
- Global longevity has resulted in a spiralling global population with resultant shortages and inflation for food, fuel and health provisions. Some countries have previously attempted to combat this population challenge through political measures, such as the 'One child policy' present in China until 2015.

Arguments in favour of the statement
- As a result of our increased life expectancy and ageing population, there is a political budget transition with more than ever before being spent on social care and pensions. For example, the Department of Health budget was £124.7 Billion in 2017/18, more than double the budget of £54.9 Billion in 1997/98 (The Kings Fund, 2017).
- Within the medical practice, there is greater emphasis on palliative care and end of life social and medical support to cater for the increasing number of people living longer (and often with significant morbidity).
- As a result of global longevity, retirement ages and support are continually being re-considered with the expectation that people should be working until later than ever before. The current retirement age for those born after 1978 is 68 in the United Kingdom, with the anticipation of further rises in the near future (The Telegraph, 2017).

Conclusion

Varying attitudes towards life and death have been present for hundreds of years. Nonetheless, global longevity has had a profound impact on health, social and economic policies worldwide.

3) Irrationally held truths may be more harmful than reasoned errors. *(Thomas Henry Huxley)*

Write a unified essay in which you address the following:
This is a statement concerning truth in science; explain what you think it means. From what Huxley says in this statement, what do you think he means by 'irrationally held truths'? Advance a contrary argument, that reasoned errors are more harmful than irrationally held truths.

From what Huxley says in this statement, what do you think he means by 'irrationally held truths'?

- Huxley's statement suggests that having a method of finding the answer is more important than the final answer itself.
- Huxley was a 19th-century biologist who was dubbed 'Darwin's Bulldog' for his strong advocacy of Darwin's theory of evolution, the scientific method and science education in schools (Encyclopaedia Britannica Online, 2006). He was also one of the founders of agnosticism, (Huxley, 1889), all of which caused some tension with the Church
- Therefore, by 'irrationally held truths', Huxley is probably primarily referring to blind belief in God, and religious views that have been instilled by a strict traditional Christian education
- However, Huxley's words should not necessarily be interpreted as anti-religion, but rather as pro-science. Therefore he could be referring to any belief that is not demonstrated by scientific evidence, including superstitions and pseudoscience.

Advance a contrary argument, that reasoned errors are more harmful than irrationally held truths.

- This argument will focus primarily on the scientific interpretation of the question rather than the religious one
- In the practical applications of science, the end result may be more important than the methodology. Hence a reasoned error may have more harmful consequences:
  - If a doctor miscalculates the drug dosage for a patient, the patient may still experience adverse effects, even if the correct equation was used, whereas the patient will be medically safe if they receive the proper dosage, even if the doctor performed the wrong calculation.
- Also, having reasoning behind an erroneous belief may give one the false belief that they must be correct, and less likely to consider the correct answer, whereas it may be easier to get an individual to understand the reasoning behind their beliefs if you are not telling them their ideas are wrong.

In favour of the statement

- Believing something is true 'irrationally', without question, and without asking why, is dangerous because one stops thinking logically or for themselves, and could thereafter be led to believe almost anything.
- It is better to be wrong, but have gone through a method of inquiry to find the answer for oneself, as this equips one with critical thinking which will allow the correct answer to be found in the future.
- For example, it is worse if a school student knows 8x7=56 because the teacher has made him repeat his time's tables, compared to a student who tries to work it out for himself and obtains an answer of 55. At

least the latter student knows *how* to solve the problem, and is equipped to find the correct answer in the future, whereas the former student only knows the answer because he blindly believes in what his teacher has told him, which will limit his ability to obtain further knowledge.

Conclusion

- Both reasoned errors and irrationally held truths can be extremely harmful in science, but in different ways, so clearly, the best option is to arrive at a reasoned truth.
- Arguably, 'truths' do not even exist in science, and all we believe to be true are reasoned errors, even in the form of imprecise measurements.

BMAT Section 3 – 2008

1) When you can measure what you are speaking about, and express it in numbers, you know something about it; but when you cannot ... your knowledge is of a meagre and unsatisfactory kind. *(Lord Kelvin, 1824-1907)*

Explain what you think Lord Kelvin means. In particular discuss the extent to which Lord Kelvin's remark applies to biology and medicine, with specific examples of topics that do or do not require to be treated quantitatively.

Explain what you think Lord Kelvin means.

This statement suggests that the value of all knowledge is underpinned by being quantifiable. For example, scoring this essay as '5' indicates that the information enclosed is of value, whereas providing comment-based feedback is of no value, according to Lord Kelvin who is accredited for determining a value for absolute zero temperature.

In particular discuss the extent to which Lord Kelvin's remark applies to biology and medicine, with specific examples of topics that do or do not require to be treated quantitatively.

- Biology and medicine are sciences based on evidence from research and long-term experience which are presented statistically.
  - In a patient with an incurable or significant illness, the prognosis is given as a percentage of survival after studying survival rates of patients with similar conditions.
    For example, the five-year survival rate for bowel cancer in England and Wales is shown to be 59% for patients diagnosed during 2010-2011 with the five-year survival rate for women slightly lower (Cancer Research UK).
  - Several scoring systems are used in talking about the prognosis of patients.
    For example, 2014 data for breast cancer survival in England show 100% of patients diagnosed at stage I survived for at least one year, versus 63% of patients diagnosed at stage IV (Cancer Research UK).
  - In the development of pharmaceuticals, the effects are given as quantifiable data as what percentage responded, what percentage showed major side effects and so on. This allows one treatment to be compared to another such as the current first-line treatment for any particular condition.
  - A patient's condition is discussed depending on a variety of quantifiable elements together which determines if the patient is stable or needs further treatments such as, blood pressure, heart rate, body temperature.
  - Many authors have offered similar views including Robert Heinlein who famously stated "If it can't be expressed in figures, it is not science; it is opinion" (Time Enough for Love (1973)).

- On the contrary, medicine deals with complex human emotions which cannot be given a quantifiable value.
  - In the management of a terminally ill patient, the emotional support needed for the patient and family cannot be quantified, but nonetheless plays a significant role in holistic patient management.
  - The response to stimuli such as pain (although often subjectively scored) tends to be subjective and emotion based. Thus, pain management based on strict quantified values prove to be less beneficial to patients.

For example, a study by Department of Emergency Medicine, Medical Center Boulevard concluded that "The visual analog scale cannot adequately discriminate between those patients who do and do not desire analgesia"and speculates it's best to "simply ask the patient about his or her need for pain medication" (Howard et al., 2003)

- When managing a person with suicidal thoughts, the extent to which the psychiatrist has to intervene, the sensitivity to be shown and the swiftness with which to make decisions are not measurable (to date) and are unlikely to be quantifiable in the future. Nonetheless, the effective acute management of such patients is vital.

2) Life has a natural end, and doctors and others caring for a patient need to recognise that the point may come in the progression of a patient's condition where death is drawing near. *(UK General Medical Council, Good Practice)*

Explain what you think this statement means and why it is of relevance to good medical practice.
What are the risks and consequences of doctors and others caring for patients not recognising the point where death is drawing near? Give a reasoned answer.

Explain what you think this statement means and why it is of relevance to good medical practice.

- Natural end implies that it is normal for life to end this way and that there is not always something a doctor can do.
- It essentially means that instead of trying to cure a patient, one should focus on palliative care to make their last few days/weeks comfortable.
- Good medical practice means respecting this even if it goes against the doctor's wishes or their natural instincts.

What are the risks and consequences of doctors and others caring for patients not recognising the point where death is drawing near? Give a reasoned answer.

- Arguments in favour of the statement
  - As people approach the end of their life, more often than not, they want comfort and dignity. More medications/procedures can cause more pain which may oppose the patient's wishes (autonomy) but also nonmaleficence (not doing harm).
  - In modern medicine, shared decision-making is employed whereby the patient, medical team and relevant family members agree on a management plan. Respecting this often means accepting that little further medical intervention should be taken.
  - Also, in applying the ethical principle of justice; the same time and resources could be better spent on other patients who have reversible illnesses and have a better chance of survival.
  - Prolonging life unnecessarily may result in unintentional and avoidable patient harm. This can be seen in the case of Charlie Gard where the paediatric team felt that keeping the child on a ventilator was prolonging the child's suffering and was not in his interests.
  - GMC guidelines also state if a patient has capacity then they have to be allowed to make their own decision even if the doctor does not understand the reasoning. Therefore it is the law that sometimes treatment must be stopped even if a medical professional does not agree.

- Arguments against the statement
  - Death is often seen as the ultimate harm, and thus allowing patients to die contradicts the ethical principle of nonmaleficence.
  - Some patients can recover extraordinarily well even on the 'brink of death'. This is particularly common in patients with infection-induced delirium as well as intracranial bleeds which after medical and surgical intervention respectively can demonstrate significant improvement.
  - Where do you draw the line? It is challenging to determine when patients are reaching the end of their life even for experienced consultants. 'Over-detection' will likely result in patients not receiving the best possible medical care available.
  - If a capacitous patient wishes to try every treatment option, including experimental treatments to prolong their life and wishes to self-fund, it would be an infringement on patient autonomy to prevent them from doing so.

Conclusion

Recognising when patients reach the end of their life is invaluable in allowing the patient and family preparation as well as ensuring the patient's comfort in their last days. Nonetheless, this recognition should not be at the expense of optimal medical care, whereby patients are not being offered potentially beneficial medical care for fear of causing harm in what may be their finals days.

3) *Science is the great antidote to the poison of enthusiasm and superstition.*
   (Adam Smith, The Wealth of Nations, 1776)

Explain what you think this statement means. What do you think Smith is referring to when he talks about enthusiasm and superstition, and to what extent is science an antidote to these?

Explain what you think this statement means.

- This statement suggests that non-scientific perspectives are of little value and provide society with counter-productive positivity without a factual basis. Furthermore, it is the requirement of science to neutralise this misinformation.

What do you think Smith is referring to when he talks about enthusiasm and superstition?

- In relation to enthusiasm, Smith may be referring to sensationalist media headlines which are regularly found in tabloid newspapers and often reference early-stage research and misinterpret them as being the 'cure for all cancers'.
- Enthusiasm may also relate to inherent hope. Many patients and families find it difficult to accept that they or a loved one will pass away as a result of a medical condition, despite being advised so by medical professionals. The consequence of this is the sub-optimal end of life planning.
  - Scientists who are over enthusiastic may resort to attempting dangerous acts of adverse outcomes or become unethical to provide the evidence needed.
    Tuskegee Syphilis study (1932 – 1972) was a study conducted by U.S. Public Health Service under the guise of offering free health care with the intention to observe the natural progression and long-term manifestations of untreated syphilis in rural African-American men in Alabama whilst denying them the appropriate treatment.

    ○   Historically, over-enthusiastic or superstitious individuals have been noted to carry out destructive acts without evidence and proper understanding.

          For example, witch hunts were a search for evidence of witchcraft, often involving moral panic or mass hysteria as it was believed certain people were given power by the devil to harm others. It is estimated more than 200,000 were tortured, burnt or hanged in the Western world from 1500 until around 1800.

To what extent is science an antidote to these?

- Science is primarily based on evidence, and as such many 'wonder drugs' referenced in sensationalist headlines are later disproved by science in larger-scale research.
- Science has also disproved many superstitions and unfounded historical beliefs. For example, hopping twice on the service line or bouncing the ball seven times has not been found to be correlated with being a better tennis player.
- On the other hand, some individuals have little faith in evidence-based medical practice, and as such, irrespective of scientific research, they remain enthused and undeterred regarding the benefits of homeopathic therapeutic approaches.
- It is often enthusiasm that fuels science. For example, many medications which are presently widely used (for example, antiretrovirals for HIV) were previously developed on the hope and enthusiasm that one day we would be able to manage this progressive and debilitating condition better.
- This statement may represent a false dichotomy. In many cases, superstitions are used alongside science, for example, some surgeons employ superstitious practices during lifesaving surgeries.

Conclusion

Science is a useful counterbalance to over-enthusiastic and superstitious beliefs. Nonetheless, it would be inaccurate to consider these three core pillars as mutually exclusive especially given the significant contribution of prior enthusiasm and optimism towards current scientific practice.

BMAT Section 3 – 2009

1) *You must be honest and open and act with integrity.*
(UK General Medical Council, Good Medical Practice 2006)

Explain what is meant by the above statement. Why might honesty, openness and integrity be important in a good doctor? Under what circumstances might a good doctor be justified in being less than perfectly honest or open in the course of their professional practice?

Explain what is meant by the above statement.
- This statement suggests that truthfulness and professionalism should be at the heart of all medical practice.

Why might honesty, openness and integrity be important in a good doctor?
- These characteristics are vital in maintaining patient confidence in the medical profession. Without social confidence that one's medical history is being managed confidentially, patients would be less forthcoming regarding their medical history, thus reducing the ability to diagnose and treat patients optimally.
- Within the medical profession, one relies on the honesty of colleagues in providing an accurate handover and documentation of patient information. Without this, good medical care will be compromised.
- In cases where errors have been made, it is essential to be open and forthcoming towards patients, correcting, acknowledging and apologising for the error made. This is supported by studies which have found that patients are far less likely to complain about an error if the medical team has been forthcoming and honest regarding the error (Witman et al., 1996).
- All three characteristics are essential in ensuring uniform patient care, where there is no discrimination between the manner in which patients are managed.

Under what circumstances might a good doctor be justified in being less than perfectly honest or open in the course of their professional practice?
- In cases of 'near misses' for example when an incorrect medication has been prescribed, however, detected before patient administration, it is widely believed that being honest with the patient and advising them regarding this potential error is not in their or the medical team's benefit, as it may undermine patient confidence in medical practice unnecessarily.
- Medical research often involves the use of placebo medication to ascertain therapeutic benefit. Whilst prior informed consent ensures that this is not dishonest, the use of placebos must be patient-blind and thus not open or known to the patient.
- In patients who have acquired hospital-acquired infections (For example, hospital-acquired pneumonia, norovirus or MRSA), full openness would likely involve advising the patient of the possible infectious source which would probably be another patient or health professional on the ward. In these cases, it would not alter patient management and would merely infringe on the other patients right to confidentiality, and as such, full openness is not of benefit.

Conclusion

Honesty, openness and integrity are absolute requirements for doctors and all medical professionals. Nonetheless, there are a range of scenarios where complete disclosure would not be of the patient or therapeutic benefit and as such these cases should be managed accordingly, without misinforming or denying patients of essential information.

2) *Science is a way of trying not to fool yourself. (Richard Feynman, 1964)*

Explain why not fooling oneself is necessary for a scientist. Why might it be easy for scientists to make the mistake of fooling themselves? How might scientists guard against this mistake?

Explain why not fooling oneself is necessary for a scientist.
- This statement suggests that science is the basis for factual accuracy, and thus non-scientific conclusions are unfounded.
- Scientists, such as medical practitioners are not only caring for themselves but also the welfare of others. Thus, they have a greater responsibility and requirement to provide accurate information and advice.
- Scientists who 'fool oneself' are at risk of fooling others. For example, Dr Andrew Wakefield published a study in the Lancet associating the MMR vaccine with autism. Despite being a previously well-regarded gastroenterologist, it is arguable that Dr Wakefield was fooled himself and thereafter millions of others, ignoring the small sample size and lack of reproducibility (The Lancet, 1998).

Why might it be easy for scientists to make the mistake of fooling themselves?
- There is strong positive publication bias. Studies with findings are far more likely to be published than studies which find no correlation between two factors. Thus, there is an incentive for researchers to find a correlation between two variables, even if no such correlation exists.
- Scientists may also be influenced by their personal social, religious and cultural perspectives allowing these to cloud their objective scientific perspective.
- Scientists may bias the results of their research to satisfy the research funding party. Sponsorship bias is a well-recognised contributor to the publication of misinformation. (Lexchin, 2012)

How might scientists guard against this mistake?
- Strict regulation and declaration of potential conflicts of interests and funding sources can help to reduce the publication of misinformation.
- Education initiatives at various stages including in medical school to make future doctors and scientists aware of the various biases and factors that may cloud their objective judgement.
- The involvement of regulatory bodies such as the GMC and GPhC and others ensure that medical professionals do not abuse their position for personal and monetary gains at the expense of the wider population.
- Use of appropriate methods to minimise bias (for example, double-blind clinical trials).
- Involving colleagues for a second opinion, especially in cases where a clinician may have a strong personal or religious pre-founded opinion.

3) *It is an obscenity that rich people can buy better medical treatment than poor people.*

Explain the argument behind the statement. What assumptions does it make? Argue to the contrary, that patients are entitled to spend money on better healthcare if they choose to.

Explain the argument behind this statement
- This statement is based on the argument that access to healthcare is a basic human right.
    - One of NHS core principles – " Good healthcare should be available for all regardless of wealth, and it should be based on clinical needs, not the ability to pay."
    - Both the rich and poor contribute to society.
    - All members of society pay taxes (whether through income tax or VAT) thus funding the public health sector.
    For example, research by the Equality Trust has found that poorer individuals pay proportionally more tax than wealthy individuals; 7% compared to 1.5% of total income respectively (The Guardian, 2017)

What assumptions does it make?
- The statement assumes that the private health sector provides better care in comparison to the public sector. Whilst in general, waiting lists are shorter in the private sector, recent investigations into private health care such as the case of Dr Ian Patterson who carried out unnecessary breast procedures has highlighted that private health provisions are not as well regulated as NHS services.
    - A study investigating the performance of private and public health sector delivery in low and middle-income countries found evidence against the claim that the private sector is usually more efficient, accountable, or medically efficient than the public sector. However, the public sector appeared frequently to lack timeliness and hospitality towards patients (Basu et al., 2012).
- It also assumes that rich people are more likely to prioritise spending on healthcare compared to less affluent individuals.

Argue to the contrary, that patients are entitled to spend money on better health care if they choose to.
- With the limited NHS resources and stretched DOH budget, the decision by individuals to purchase private healthcare is of benefit to society as it reduces the number of patients on NHS waiting lists as well as saving the NHS substantial money.
- Furthermore, with these patients being able to have their health procedures sooner, it enables them to continue working and thus contributing through additional tax revenues.
- One of the core medical ethics principles is autonomy; it would be an infringement on patient autonomy if one were to deny someone access to private healthcare.
- Where do you draw the line? Others may argue that it is unfair that some individuals can purchase better education than others as well; should this also be restricted?
- Private healthcare (especially in the UK) is an essential source of 'export' income, attracting many wealthy individuals from around the world and thus increasing total GDP, government tax revenue and capital for further health research.

BMAT Section 3 – 2010

1) *Anyone who has a serious ambition to be a president or prime minister is the wrong kind of person for the job.*

What is the reasoning behind this statement? Argue to the contrary that without serious ambition to be a leader a person would not be suited to the job. To what extent is ambition required to succeed as a political leader?

What is the reasoning behind this statement?

- This statement is based on the rationale that the characteristics required to become an admirable prime minister or president is in opposition to the necessary attributes to reach such a position. For example, a prime minister should be selfless and wholly committed to serving others, whereas, to become the leader of a political party, one (generally) must highlight their strengths as well as the weaknesses of their competitors.

Argue to the contrary that without serious ambition to be a leader, a person would not be suited to the job

- The job of president or prime minister is an undoubtedly challenging post which requires commitment and resilience. Without underlying ambition, it is unlikely that one would be able to withstand the inherent pressures of such a position.
- In parallel, similarly becoming a doctor requires significant commitment and determination. Without the initial challenges of securing a position in medical school and passing university medical exams, arguably one would not be prepared for the challenges to be faced as a medical practitioner.

To what extent is ambition required to succeed as a political leader?

- As discussed, ambition and resilience are essential to succeed in any position of power, scrutiny and responsibility. However, this should not be at the expense of one's moral compass whereby internal ambition drives one to make unethical choices.
- It is also important to consider what the underlying 'ambition' is of the political leader. An ambition to serve and improve one's country and global society would be welcome, whereas an ambition to advance one's personal and financial interests would be detrimental to any political leader and wider society.

2) *People injured whilst participating in extreme sports should not be treated by publicly funded health service.*

Explain the reasoning behind this statement. Suggest an argument against this statement. To what extent, if any, does the statement justify a change in public attitudes to personal risk taking?

Explain the reasoning behind this statement.

- This statement is based on the rationale that we have limited health provisions, and as such these should be prioritised for those who have conditions not caused or contributed to by personal actions or choices.

339

Suggest an argument against this statement.

- What is defined as an extreme sport – Football? Rugby? Jet-skiing?
- Where do you draw the line? Should all self-inflicted conditions (arguably obesity) also not be treated on the NHS?
- Encourages inactivity which promotes obesity which adds to in ever-increasing long-term health burden.
- False dichotomy. It is not a case of either permitting or banning the treatment of injuries from extreme sports. Alternative solutions are also possible for example, placing an added tax on extreme sports (similar to smoking) to discourage them and increase NHS contributions from those engaged in extreme sports.

To what extent, if any, does the statement justify a change in public attitudes to personal risk taking?

- People know the dangers before engaging in risky activity and hence should be responsible for the consequences.
- With there being limited resources, we need to prioritise patients, and this notion represents a just way of doing so. Currently, the NHS has to deny patients life-saving cancer drugs (such as, Rituximab – which has limited access), whilst those injured from extreme sports are being treated.
- Nonetheless, a society where legislation limits choices is an inhibited society that may have restricted potential.
- As the statement says, 'personal' risk-taking is very much an individual choice and as such this autonomy should remain independent of government and legislative pressures.

---

3) *A pet belongs to its owner – it is their property. Thus, if a client asks for their healthy cat to be painlessly euthanised, a veterinary clinician should always agree to this request.*

Explain the reasoning behind the statement. Argue to the contrary that a veterinary clinician should never agree to such a request. To what extent should pet owners influence clinicians' decisions?

Explain the reasoning behind the statement

- Pet owners pay their own money to buy and maintain their pet, as they do to other property such as cars/houses; therefore owners have the right to make every decision concerning the fate of their property, including painlessly ending their lives.
- The vet works for and is paid by the owner, not the animal, and therefore the vet must fulfil the wishes of the paying client.

Argue to the contrary

- A pet is not the same as other property because it is a living, sentient being that can feel pain and suffering due to a well-developed central nervous system
- Declaration on admission to the Royal College of Veterinary Surgeons (RCVS) states that: 'above all, my constant endeavour will be to ensure the health and welfare of animals committed to my care'. Therefore the vet has a duty to the patient/animal, not the client primarily, and ending a healthy life would go against this declaration.

To what extent should pet owners influence clinicians' decisions?

- The client's wishes should be followed so long as this does not compromise animal welfare.
- In this case, the difficulty is judging whether painless euthanasia compromises welfare or not.
- Animals are not self-aware, hence have no perception of death, although this is still somewhat debated (The curse of the self, Leary, 2007). Therefore, painless euthanasia is not compromising the RCVS declaration to ensure 'health and welfare'.
- RCVS declaration also states that a vet should 'accept their responsibilities to the public, their clients, the profession, and the RCVS', so the vet has a duty to carry out the wishes of their client.
- In some instances, by not XXXuthanizing the animal, the vet may, in fact, be inadvertently compromising its' welfare, if, for example, the owner does not have enough money to feed/keep their pet healthy.
- Not XXXuthanizing may also compromise the vet's duty to the public, as the unwanted animal might end up as a stray animal, possibly contributing to the spread of disease or traffic accidents.

Conclusion

- It is an apparent ethical dilemma for the vet when the interests of the patient/animal clash with those of the client/owner.
- The vet should do everything in their power to resolve the situation to satisfy both obligations, for example, in this case, helping to find the unwanted pet an alternative home or assessing whether their quality of life can be improved in any other way.
- Overall, such decisions should be judged on a case by case basis, consulting fellow veterinary surgeons were required to maintain 'professional integrity' and act in the best interests of the involved parties.

4) Science only tells us what is possible, not what is right.

Explain what this statement means. Argue to the contrary that science helps us to judge what is right. To what extent can decisions about what is right and wrong be informed by science?

Explain what this statement means.

- This statement suggests that whilst science dictates current knowledge and beliefs, it does not necessarily correlate with the most ethically appropriate approach.

Argue to the contrary that science helps us to judge what is right.

- In some cases, science tells us both. For example, we can use science to select the gender of a child (possible) but also science indirectly prevents the abuse of this, through the requirement of both a male and female to produce an offspring (meaning that it sets boundaries for what is right).
- Depends on the individual – some people do not have a problem with abortion, euthanasia and even nuclear bombs and the like. Therefore, it is inappropriate to generalise 'what is right'.
- In many instances, science is not even able to tell us or explain to us what is possible, for example, the specific mechanism behind the placebo effect, irrespective of its ability to determine whether the use of the placebo effect is 'right'.

To what extent can decisions about what is right and wrong be informed by science?

341

- The fact that science enables us to do many things (such as building nuclear bombs, performing abortion, euthanasia) does not necessarily mean that they are all ethically right, hence supporting this statement.
- Additionally, the boundaries of science (for example, ongoing research) are not always correlated with what is ethically right. For example, there are many (arguably) unethical research projects in existence.
- What is regarded as right or wrong is very much a personal choice, and for many people, this is dictated by religion or an internal moral compass rather than science.

Conclusion

Whilst science does provide boundaries to restrict certain 'wrong' actions; it permits and enables many arguably unethical actions which require policing through alternative measures such as government legislation as well as an inner moral compass.

BMAT Section 3 – 2011

1) Democratic freedom means there should be no restriction on what may be said in public.

Explain what you think democratic freedom means. Argue that there should be restrictions on what is said in public. To what extent do you agree that there should be limitations on what can be said in public?

Explain what you think democratic freedom means.
- Democratic freedom encompasses a broad range of rights ranging from freedom of speech to freedom of the press and the freedom to protest.

Argue that there should be restrictions on what is said in public
- One individual's freedom is another individual's restriction. By allowing individuals to speak as they wish, it is likely that they will make statements that are offensive and oppositional towards the views held by other members of society. As such, to restrict societal conflict, it is important to maintain boundaries regarding what can be said in public.
- With regards to science, many pharmaceutical companies rely on patents to justify scientific investments. Without restrictions, it is likely that these patents will be breached providing a disincentive for companies to invest in research, thus slowing scientific, medical and technological advancements.
- What is said in public (especially in the media) can have significant consequences, including if false and intentionally misleading. Thus, to prevent unnecessary damage to the reputations of innocent individuals or companies, it is essential to ensure that there are restrictions as well as accountability for what is said in public.

To what extent do you agree that there should be limitations on what can be said in public?
- Where do you draw the line? What is offensive to one individual may be acceptable to mainstream society.
- Slippery slope effect – one policy can lead to another. An initial pressure to monitor what can be said in public may develop into restrictions on what can be done in public and thereafter what can be said and done in the privacy of one's home.
- Historically, countries flourish when there is a range of views that challenge each other, thus encouraging one another to improve. With one single, unchallenged uniform voice, a nation's development will be inhibited.

Conclusion
A balance is necessary to ensure that there is freedom of speech and expression, however, that this is not abused at the expense of individuals, corporations or scientific advancements.

2) The art of medicine consists of amusing the patient whilst nature cures the disease.
(Voltaire)

Explain what this statement means. Argue to the contrary that medicine does, in fact, do more than amuse the patient. To what extent do you think Voltaire is correct?

Explain what the statement means

- The medical profession is still limited in its ability to cure many diseases; therefore the doctor's role is to distract the patient with medical tests and treatments that may not necessarily work, to make the patient feel like they are being helped whilst the human body fights the disease.
- Often the best option available is only supportive therapy whilst the disease runs its course, For example:
  - Putting a cast on a broken leg whilst the bone regenerates itself.
  - Symptomatic relief of common cold whilst the immune system clears the rhinovirus.
  - Palliative care and pain management for terminal cancer patients.
- Voltaire also implies that medicine is a form of art, not science, thus emphasising the importance of the human interaction aspect of the profession as opposed to the scientific one.

Argue to the contrary that medicine does, in fact, do more than amuse the patient

- There are a plethora of cases where modern medicine ameliorates or even cures a disease. For example:
  - Gene therapy for cystic fibrosis (CF) – this is not something the human body could do to itself 'naturally'.
  - Bactericidal antibiotics reserved explicitly for immune compromised patients who cannot 'naturally' deal with even small bacterial loads.
  - Surgery to resect/remove tumours or perforated organs (such as a ruptured appendix).
- There are legal requirements for clinical (phases I-III) trials, including randomised control trials (RCTs) to generate large bodies of statistically significant empirical data on the efficacy of medical treatments. Otherwise they cannot be approved for human use (in the UK and USA at least).
  - These usually involve a comparison to a 'placebo' sugar pill or saline to explicitly prove the treatment helps the patient more than simply 'amusing' them
  - This is why homeopathic treatments are not covered by the NHS, whereas Statins(cholesterol lowering drugs) for example, are.
- Furthermore, modern medicine is also necessary for other things like prevention (such as screening campaigns for breast cancer, or anti-smoking campaigns) to stop the disease from developing in the first place.

To what extent do you agree?

Agree to an extent, at least where medicine stands today:

- Empirical data on the Placebo effect definitely supports the power of 'amusing the patient' in healing.
- Many medical interventions still rely on natural healing processes, for example:
  - Even in CF gene therapy, whilst the healthy CFTR gene is artificially introduced via a lipid/viral vector, the methods of integration into host cells and subsequent protein synthesis is left up to 'natural' host cell machinery
  - Even most blood pressure lowering drugs and anti-coagulants for heart disease depend on natural homeostatic and clotting mechanisms to work
- We still do not know enough about how the human body works to be able to cure all diseases, even though we can modify the 'natural' course of many diseases

- However, it is still a doctor's duty to try and help all patients through taking histories, running tests, attempting treatments and so forth, even if they cannot offer the patient a cure in the end.

Conclusion
- Modern medicine endeavours to do more than just amuse the patient.
- However, the importance of 'amusing' the patient should not be disregarded in medicine, as making the patient feel better still has some therapeutic benefit.
- Even though the face of medicine has been transformed drastically in the 300 years since Voltaire made this statement, there may still be some wisdom in his words, from which modern medicine can learn.

3) *A scientific man ought to have no wishes, no affections – a mere heart of stone.*
(Charles Darwin)

Explain what this statement means. Argue that scientific enquiry benefits from personal wishes and affections. To what extent do you think a scientist should have 'a mere heart of stone'?

Explain what this statement means
- The statement suggests that for someone to practice science properly, they should not allow themselves to have personal feeling and emotions, because these feelings are irrational, and will inevitably influence their actions, which may bias their work.
- Instead, scientists should remain entirely emotionless, rational, and objective to ensure what they observe, report, and do in their scientific work remains factual and unbiased.

Argue that scientific enquiry benefits from personal wishes and affections
- Personal wishes and affections are a large part of what motivates us as humans, hence being invested in their work on a personal and emotional level may drive a scientist to spend more hours working in the lab, and employ unconventional methods, or take more significant 'risks', which may accelerate scientific discovery.
    - For example, the discovery of Artemisinin to treat malaria by Youyou Tu was made through a screen of traditional Chinese herbal remedies (Tu, 2001), which may have partly been driven by Tu's respect for the 'ancient wisdom' of her culture. She also volunteered herself to be the first human trial
    - For example, the strong evidence provided by Barry Marshall about the causal link between Helicobacter pylori and peptic ulcers by swallowing a Petri dish of cultured H.pylori to fulfil Koch's postulates (Marshall et al., 1985) may have been motivated by his personal motivations to prove his theory to the scientific community
- Many scientists, including doctors, may choose their field of study based on personal wishes. Hence these personal affections may draw scientific attention to certain diseases for example, due to a family member with cancer or Alzheimer's that they wanted to be able to treat
- Funding and monetary donation for science often come from people with personal affections, such as:
    - the numerous cancer research funds
    - The Nobel Prize was set up under the order of Alfred Nobel's will, as he did not want to be remembered as the inventor of dynamite, a destructive creation.

To what extent do you think scientists should have a 'mere heart of stone'?

- Ultimately, all scientists are people, and it is human nature to have personal wishes and affections.
- It is therefore unrealistic to expect scientists to have 'a mere heart of stone', and indeed, this may discourage students from engaging in STEM subjects if all scientists are viewed as 'emotionless robots'.
- This can be viewed as a good thing, as these personal affections can be used to motivate scientific enquiry.
- It is instrumental, however, that scientists do not let their personal affections bias their experimental design and the interpretation of results. Indeed, it is part of professional integrity for a scientist to be able to recognise when they are no longer able to do so and to distance themselves from the situation.

Conclusion

- Although Darwin's classical view of a scientist is a man with a 'mere heart of stone', there have been countless examples of useful scientific advances made by scientists who may have been influenced by some personal affections.
- However, there are also examples of personal biases hindering science.
- Possibly the hardest part of a career in science is deciding where to draw the line between personal motivations and impartiality.

4) *Veterinary pet care in the UK should be free at the point of delivery, as human care is.*

Explain the argument behind this statement. Argue to the contrary, that if people choose to keep pets, they should pay for all aspects of their care. To what extent do you agree that there should be free pet care?

Introduction

- Currently, there is no NHS equivalent for animals. Therefore all UK veterinary practice is privatised.
- The resulting extortionate price for veterinary treatment means that some pets may be put down instead of receiving life-saving treatment if their owner is unable or unwilling to pay.

Explain the argument behind this statement

- Since access to free medical care is a fundamental human right, this should also be a fundamental animal right because most UK pets are higher vertebrates, like humans, who can experience pain and suffering.
- This would be a more egalitarian system: one animal does not have more right to veterinary treatment just because its owner is able or willing to spend more money, just as a human's quality of medical care should not depend on one's financial status.

Argue to the contrary, that if people choose to keep pets, they should pay for all aspects of their care

- Owning a pet is a personal choice and a luxury and not essential for human life, unlike maintaining one's health, and therefore free pet care should not be considered a fundamental right.
- People should not keep pets in the first place if they cannot afford to pay for all aspects of their care.
- Individuals in society have different values, and some may not value animal health as highly as others. These people should not have to contribute financially to the healthcare of others' pets and should have the option of spending their money on things that are more important to them (such as gardening).
- Logistically, it would also be challenging to set up a veterinary national healthcare service. There would be many issues to resolve for example:

- o   Who has to pay tax/animal social security and how much?
- o   How do you prevent people hiding their pets to avoid paying this tax?
- o   Are large animals and wildlife entitled to this care as well?
- The UK taxpayer is under enough strain to support the NHS, and a veterinary healthcare system, which may be less important for many, maybe even more challenging to sustain. Money and resources could instead be spent on improving human lives, (for example education or reducing homelessness).
- Peoples' pets are essentially their property (legally speaking), and it is therefore solely the owner's responsibility to maintain their health. If we do not offer free car or house maintenance (without insurance), it would be unfair to do so for other forms of optional property like pets.

To what extent do you agree?

Disagree:

- If an individual decides to keep a pet, it should be their responsibility to care for it in all respects, which includes covering the cost of veterinary medical care.
- The high cost of veterinary care may discourage unfit owners, who may not have enough time/money/resources to care for a pet adequately. Expensive pet care may be therefore beneficial for animal welfare in the long run.
- Additionally, privatisation incentivises veterinary practices and pharmaceutical companies to invest in better facilities and research to improve veterinary medicine, which also provides a long-term benefit for animal health. It also benefits human health as several techniques now used in human medicine were pioneered in animal research (for example, prosthetics in sheep, or spinal cord repair in Dachshunds).

Conclusion

- As sentient beings, animals have a right to freedom from pain, suffering and disease.
- However, it should be the owners' financial responsibility to provide these, as pet ownership is a personal choice.
- Though the high cost of veterinary treatment may face individual vets and owners with some ethically and emotionally difficult decisions, a private veterinary industry may be to the long-term benefit of both animals and humans.

BMAT Section 3 – 2012

1) *"Doubt is not a pleasant condition, but certainty is absurd."* (Voltaire)

Explain what this statement means. Argue to the contrary that to be certain about something is not necessarily absurd. To what extent do you agree with Voltaire?

Explain what this statement means
- This statement suggests that having conflicting thoughts is a negative trait, however having unwavering, rigid convictions are far worse.

Argue to the contrary that to be certain about something is not necessarily absurd.
- As a medical professional, you are required to assess and advise patients. Without confidence and certainty in your own judgement, you will not only have difficulty arriving at a diagnosis, but you will also have difficulty convincing the patient of the most appropriate action plan. Without a confident action plan, it is likely that patient compliance will be poor.
- Most research relies on current information to develop new theories and hypotheses. For example, the development of many anti-cancer medications are based on the certainty that excessive cell proliferation causes cancers. Without this underlying certainty, subsequent developments will be restricted
- At the other end of the spectrum, having excessive doubt can be troublesome in all professions especially as a doctor. In particular, during on-call shifts, doctors are required to make rational and decisive decisions which would be far more challenging in a 'doubtful doctor' than a doctor with absolute certainty.

To what extent do you agree with Voltaire?
- On the other hand, science is always changing and what was regarded as a certainty yesterday, today is a 'prior misconception'. For example, previously it has been concluded that daily aspirin was beneficial in preventing cardiovascular disease, many cancers and even Alzheimer's Dementia. However, more recent research has suggested that aspirin should only be used for high-risk patients, especially given the additional risk of gastrointestinal bleeds secondary to aspirin.
- As a medical professional you are working as part of a multidisciplinary team, and as such, need to be open to the views and input of your colleagues. A doctor with absolute certainty will not make a valuable member of the MDT.

Conclusion
This statement accurately reflects the requirements of a suitable medical professional whereby one should have a balance between excessive doubt and absolute certainty when arriving at decisions and acknowledging the views of respected colleagues.

2) *"There is something attractive about people who do not regard their own health and longevity as the most important things in the world."* (Alexander Chancellor)

Explain what this statement means. Argue that nothing is more important than one's own health and longevity. To what extent do you agree with Alexander Chancellor?

Explain what this statement means.

- This statement suggests that individuals, who have selfless motives and in particular prioritise the welfare of others, should be admired.

Argue that nothing is more important than one's own health and longevity

- Whilst it is undoubtedly essential to help others, to do so, one must first look after their own health. A bedbound or deceased doctor is of little/no value, and it would be arguably better to have a selfish but healthy doctor who can still treat others.
- It is important for doctors in particular to set an example for others, and by looking after one's health through a healthy diet and lifestyle choices, this will likely encourage patients to act similarly thus reducing expenditure on health intervention.
- Individuals with a sedentary lifestyle are more likely to require medical intervention as a result of their arguably neglectful behaviour. For example, smoking costs the NHS £5 Billion/year (Oxford University Study, 2009) and similarly obesity costs £5.1 Billion/year (Scarborough et al., 2011).

To what extent do you agree with Alexander Chancellor?

- On the other hand, in order to manage and restrict the spread of conditions like Ebola which have killed in excess of 10,000 people in West Africa (WHO, 2016), we require selfless individuals who are prepared to prioritise the health of others in order to manage affected patients and curb the spread of this high mortality disease.
- With current societal attitudes, life expectancies are longer than ever at 81 in the United Kingdom (World Bank, 2016). If this was to increase further (due to a personal obsession for longevity), this would further stretch the already limited resources of the NHS, and thus will likely reduce the quality of healthcare provision in the United Kingdom.
- Longevity is generally a one-dimensional, numerical term and many would argue that living until 70 with an independent, high quality of life would be preferable to living until 90 with a dependent, reduced quality of life.

Conclusion

Whilst looking after one's health is important, this should not be through selfish means, or at the expense of others. Thus, a balance between a healthy, balanced lifestyle and a drive for longevity should be sought.

3) *The scientist is not someone who gives the right answers but one who asks the right questions.*

Explain what this statement means. Argue to the contrary that the right answers are more important than the right questions. To what extent do you agree that the right questions must be asked before science can progress?

Explain what this statement means.

- This statement suggests that the hallmark of a scientific individual is not the production of results, but instead the initiation of one's thought process by proposing future avenues of research.

Argue to the contrary that the right answers are more important than the right questions.

- A question is only as valuable as its answer. It is more useful to science to have a good answer to an 'average' question than no answer to an excellent question. The unanswered excellent question, whilst being potentially valuable in the future, does not add anything to current scientific practice.
- Similarly, an excellent question with an incorrect answer will mislead society and hinder future research. Thus, providing the right answer is of optimum importance.
- Many vital discoveries have been incidental findings rather than as a result of a well-considered research question. For example, Sir Alexander Fleming accidentally discovered the remarkable antibacterial properties of Penicillin in 1928. Similarly, Viagra was initially researched for treatment of angina (chest pain), however, was later found to be more appropriate for erectile dysfunction. Hence, rather than asking the right question, it could be argued that the scientist is the one who best interprets the answers and the findings produced.

To what extent do you agree that the right questions must be asked before science can progress?

- For science to develop, new avenues and new questions need to be proposed. Without the underlying question, there is no answer and as such, no scientific advancement. For example, without individuals questioning whether cancers can be treated, it would likely not have been possible to develop anti-cancer medication such as Herceptin for breast cancer.
- Furthermore, asking questions in itself is not enough to develop science. An average question to a niche scientific topic of limited importance will produce an answer with limited usefulness. Hence, it is essential to target scientific questions towards topics of vital scientific importance to create answers of equivalent importance and value.

Conclusion

Whilst asking the right questions is important, producing the correct answers as well as correctly interpreting the answers produced is arguably more important, especially with many of science's most important discoveries being unintentional findings without a specific preceding question.

4) *"... Dolphins are very intelligent and so similar to humans that they are worthy of a special ethical status: that of 'non-human persons'."*

Explain what this statement means. Argue to the contrary that dolphins should not be given special ethical status. To what extent do you agree that intelligence and similarity to humans bestows special ethical status?

Explain what this statement means

- This statement suggests that the attributes of dolphins are similar to that of humans and thus they should be treated similarly.
- Based on the work of Marino and Reiss showing dolphins can recognise themselves in mirrors (Marino and Reiss, 2000), they use complex social behaviours and communication similar to humans, and have large and

complex brains that are folded and developed in areas (neocortex) linked to humans intelligence. (Marino et al., 2007; Marino et al., 2009)

- These anatomical and behavioural similarities may imply that dolphins have a similar high-level intelligence and self-awareness to humans. Therefore it is unacceptable to mistreat them by making them do tricks in amusement parks, and killing them accidentally whilst fishing.

Argue to the contrary that dolphin should not be given special ethical status.

- Intelligence is a highly complex, non-linear measure with many components (such as memory, emotional intelligence, spatial awareness, problem-solving, and the like), and studies so far only consider one aspect of intelligence that may not be representative of universal cognitive status.
- Dolphins are still less intelligent than healthy adult humans, as they cannot, for example, write doctoral theses.
- If dolphins are granted special ethical status, we would have to consider other species as well; for example, elephants have an excellent memory, the great apes also show self-recognition in mirrors and tool use, dogs have high emotional intelligence.
- This would force us to change many things in modern life, such as keeping pets, zoos, and the livestock industry, which would have substantial social and economic ramifications.
- We should prioritise human needs for food and entertainment because we have more proof of human intelligence status.

To what extent do you agree that intelligence and similarity to humans bestows special ethical status?

- Intelligence and similarity to humans is a highly complex, non-linear measure. Therefore the line would become very blurred if we started using these criteria to bestow ethical status, which would complicate many things, such as legislation.
- Many resources would be wasted on pointless court cases, for example, PETA suing a wildlife photographer over copyright ownership of a 'selfie' taken by a monkey who stole his camera. (PETA versus Slater, 2011)
- It is much more straightforward ethically and legally (as our knowledge of other animals currently stands), to consider only the *Homo sapiens* species as 'persons' ethically.

Conclusion

This should not prohibit us from campaigning to end the unfair treatment of all animals, not just the intelligent ones, for example, by promoting sustainable fishing.

BMAT Section 3 – 2013

1) *"When you want to know how things really work, study them when they are coming apart." (William Gibson)*

Explain what this statement means. Argue to the contrary. To what extent do you agree with the assertion?

Explain what this statement means.

- This statement suggests that physical and metaphorical dissection of an entity is required to understand its role and functionality truly.

Argue to the contrary.

- From a physical perspective, human behaviour and attributes are better analysed when a human is alive and active rather than when they are being deconstructed during a post-mortem or explored under anaesthetic during a surgical procedure.
- When studying plants and animals, we use a combination of macroscopic and microscopic analysis. Thus there are benefits in both forms of investigation and research.
- In medical practice, assessing the value of a doctor involves much the opposite, and it is more about how a doctor works within a broader multidisciplinary team rather than microscopically evaluating the individual traits of the doctor. The doctor with exceptional individual talent, however who is unwilling to work with other doctors and nurses, would be of less value than the slightly less talented doctor who respects and is respected by their colleagues.

To what extent do you agree with the assertion?

- On the other hand, much of our understanding of human anatomy arises from dissection. As a result of the subsequent anatomical knowledge, we can perform surgeries and procedures which we otherwise would not be able to do.
- Metaphorically, the character and resilience of an individual can only truly be tested when 'things are coming apart', or challenges are faced. During a productive period, it is difficult to differentiate between different characters and their abilities to deal with challenging situations.

Conclusion

There is value to both assessing entities in the broader environment as well as when they are coming apart to assess their holistic value.

2) *Good surgeons should be encouraged to take on tough cases, not just safe, routine ones.*

Publishing an individual surgeon's mortality rates may have the opposite effect. Explain what this statement means. Argue to the contrary. To what extent do you think league tables should change a surgeon's behaviour?

Explain what this statement means.

- This statement suggests that as a result of publishing surgical mortality rates, surgeons are likely to avoid challenging cases which may be detrimental to their mortality figures. The net effect of such behaviour is an overall decline in the quality of surgeons.

Argue to the contrary.

- The publication of such data is a vital patient safeguard to prevent the recurrence of rogue doctors such as Dr Harold Shipman who (although not a surgeon) killed large numbers of patients.
- Transparent mortality rates also empower patients to understand the risks of the respective procedure better as well as allowing patients to compare one surgeon with another. This information along with the NHS' 'Choose, and Book' process increases patient control of their health and healthcare.
- It is likely that by comparing one surgeon to another, this will likely incentivise them to improve the quality of their work to reduce mortality rates which would be to the benefit of patients.

To what extent do you think league tables should change a surgeon's behaviour?

- It would be hoped that league tables would change a surgeon's behaviour for the better through improved care; however, it is likely that it would also have adverse effects as well. Many surgeons would be more reluctant to operate on a ruptured aortic aneurysm due to the significant associated mortality. As a result of this change in behaviour, whilst the surgeon's mortality rates will go down, the overall mortality for patients with this presentation would likely increase due to the limited option for surgical intervention. Thus, the underlying goal of publishing such information (to reduce patient mortality) is defeated.
- In theory, phrases such as acting 'for the good of my patients' as stated in the Hippocratic Oath and GMC guidelines on Good Medical Practice would suggest that surgeons' behaviours should not change in this way as a result of surgical mortality rates publication. However the reality is likely to be very different.

3) *"Ignorance more frequently begets confidence than does knowledge: it is those who know little, and not those who know much, who so positively assert that this or that problem will never be solved by science."* (Charles Darwin)

Explain what you think is meant by this statement. Argue to the contrary. To what extent do you think it is true?

Explain what you think is meant by this statement.

- This statement suggests that the less knowledgeable members of society often with negative views towards science are typically more vocal and projected in their thoughts.

Argue to the contrary.

- History remembers those who have made great discoveries such as Sir Alexander Fleming and Rosalind Franklin who helped humanity understand the potential and attributes of penicillin and DNA respectively. In contrast, the 'ignorant doubters' in society whilst being remembered and heard at the time, their voices fade with history as science disproves their misconceptions.
- This statement very much underestimates the knowledge base of society suggesting that society is more likely to respect ignorant views. However, with widespread media and social media access, society is much

more open to a range of views and perspectives rather than accepting what one source tells them. This is highlighted with attempts to find treatments for many cancers. Rather than accepting that treatments will never be found, mainstream society is open to a wide range of potential management approaches for many different cancers.

To what extent do you think it is true?

- Science often involves changing current beliefs and values which is usually much harder than reinforcing the current beliefs/lack of knowledge. As such, people are more likely to believe the 'ignorant' whose beliefs correlate with what is already known than the scientist who suggests revolutionary and outlandish 'theories'.
- In assessing the credibility of information, humans evaluate as much what is said as how it is said. Thus, if those with ignorant negative views are better spoken than those with well-informed knowledge, it is possible that society will be misled.

4) *In a world where we struggle to feed an ever-expanding human population, owning pets cannot be justified.*

Explain what is meant by this statement. Argue that pet ownership is indefensible. How should moral or ethical concerns influence a decision to own a pet?

Explain what is meant by this statement

- The human population is growing, especially in Africa and SE Asia, and 795 million people or 1 in 9 do not have enough to eat and are malnourished (Food and Agricultural Organisation (FAO), 2015).
- If there are not enough resources to feed and sustain all humans on the planet, people should not be allowed to keep pets because feeding pet animals requires resources that should be allocated to feeding human populations instead.

Argue that pet ownership is indefensible.

- Human needs should take precedence over pet animals, because we have an obligation to prevent suffering/hunger in our own species above all, and because food is essential for life, whilst pets are a 'luxury'.
- Pets also add to a household's carbon footprint, when we are already struggling to secure sustainable energy sources and cut CO_2 emissions to slow climate change.
- Mainly because pets such as cats and dogs, eat meat, which requires a larger area of land to produce, and has a more significant environmental impact than the same mass of grains/rice grown for human consumption, due to losses in the food chain. It is therefore selfish to spend money on pets when people are starving

How should moral and ethical concerns influence a decision to own a pet?

- Pet ownership is a big responsibility and has a significant impact on the owner, the pet, and their community. Ethical and moral viewpoints of all three parties need to be considered
- One must balance the owner's emotional needs with that of the pet and the community:

- o For example, should a lonely old person be allowed to keep a dog in a small apartment for company? What about if the neighbours do not like animals?
- It is difficult to say who should decide, as there are different value systems in various societies.
- Even though under utilitarian ethics (greatest good for the greatest number), pet ownership may be considered unacceptable, pet ownership would be justified under rights-, or duty-based ethics, as individuals have a right to buy a pet.
- Currently, pet ownership is considered to be a personal decision, seen in the same way as owning a car, so individualistic, rights-based ethics are more applicable here.
- Hunger and pet ownership predominate in different parts of the world. For example, a lack of pets does not necessarily mean those resources would go to feeding people in developing countries, and may instead be redirected to other hobbies in developed nations such as cars.

Conclusion
- It is difficult to consider all different ethical frameworks in deciding whether one should be allowed to own a pet.
- Even though reduced pet ownership may lead to a fairer society, current societal moral views in developed countries still consider pet ownership acceptable, as they prioritise the individuals' right to pet ownership

BMAT Section 3 – 2014

1) There is no such thing as dangerous speech; it is up to people to choose how they react.

Explain the reasoning behind this statement. Argue to the contrary that there can be instances of dangerous speech. To what extent should society put limitations on speech or text that it considers threatening?

Explain the reasoning behind this statement.

- This statement suggests that each individual should be responsible for ignoring or disregarding information that they disagree with and everyone should be allowed to express their views freely.
- This statement is based on the principle of freedom of speech. The rationale behind this is that the more views available, the more society will flourish. In contrast, by restricting freedom of speech, members of society could become narrow-minded and oblivious to opposing views.

Argue to the contrary that there can be instances of dangerous speech.

- One individual's freedom is another individual's restriction. By allowing individuals to speak as they wish, it is likely that they will make statements that are offensive and oppositional towards views held by other members of society. As such, to restrict societal conflict, it is important to maintain boundaries regarding what can be said in public.
- With regards to science, many pharmaceutical companies rely on patents to justify scientific investments. Without restrictions, it is likely that these patents will be breached providing a disincentive for companies to invest in research, thus slowing scientific, medical and technological advancements.
- What is said in public (especially in the media) can have significant consequences, including if false and intentionally misleading. Thus, to prevent unnecessary damage to the reputation of innocent individuals or companies, it is necessary to ensure that there are restrictions as well as accountability for what is said in public.

To what extent should society put limitations on speech or text that it considers threatening?

- Where do you draw the line? What is offensive to one individual may be acceptable to mainstream society.
- Slippery slope effect – one policy can lead to another. An initial pressure to monitor what can be said in public may develop into restrictions on what can be done in public and thereafter, what can be said and done in the privacy of one's home.
- Historically, countries flourish when there is a range of views that challenge each other, thus encouraging one another to improve. With one single, unchallenged uniform voice, a nation's development will be inhibited.

Conclusion

One may argue that due to the detrimental impact on tolerance and scientific advancements, speech most deficiently can be dangerous and as such should be moderated and potentially regulated.

2) *Science has been a process of continuous advancement towards objective truth.*

Explain what is meant by this statement. Argue to the contrary. To what extent do you agree that science is a continuous process of advancement towards objective truth?

Explain what is meant by this statement.

- This statement suggests that science involves continually refining what we understand to be the absolute truth rather than one day knowing nothing about a topic, and the following day understanding the topic in full detail.

Argue to the contrary.

- Some scientific discoveries are very much absolute, and despite advances in knowledge and technology, understanding of these areas has remained unchanged. Examples of such developments include the discovery of gravity by Sir Isaac Newton in 1664, our understanding of which has changed very little over the subsequent 350 years.
- Scientific 'advancements' are not always responsible for driving society towards the objective truth and in some cases is responsible for misleading society. For example, flawed research by Dr Andrew Wakefield in The Lancet has misled millions of people worldwide into believing that the MMR vaccine is associated with Autism despite the research being later disproved and retracted (Wakefield et al., 1998).

To what extent do you agree that science is a continuous process of advancement towards objective truth?

- Many of the significant scientific discoveries have represented the beginning of what we presently know. For example, the work of Sir Alexander Fleming on penicillin in 1928 has subsequently been developed by other scientists to generate many variants of penicillin agents to treat a wide range of infections.
- Moreover, many things which we were previously sure about are now being refuted. For example, previously it has been concluded that daily aspirin was beneficial in preventing cardiovascular disease, many cancers and even Alzheimer's Dementia. However, more recent research has suggested that aspirin should only be used for high-risk patients, especially given the additional risk of gastrointestinal bleeds secondary to aspirin. Similarly, smoking was previously thought to be beneficial and social. However it is now widely accepted to be associated with many cancers.

3) *There is money to be made from not curing disease.*

What do you think is meant by this statement? Argue to the contrary. To what extent do you agree that there is money to be made from disease?

What do you think is meant by this statement?

- This statement suggests that resources can be saved by not treating patients.

Argue to the contrary.

- Preventative measures such as vaccination programmes (for example, the HPV vaccine for cervical cancer) cost money in the short term, however, in the long-term are cost saving through prevention of disease and in particular advanced diseases which are detrimental to patients and costly to the NHS.

357

- Not treating infections may lead to an adverse herd effect. With more unwell people in a population, infections such as TB would be more widespread, and thus one would be more likely to catch such an infection. With a greater proportion of the population unwell, the productivity and tax revenues will reduce, thus costing the country money.

To what extent do you agree that there is money to be made from disease?

- With developments in intensive care, it is possible to keep patients alive almost indefinitely (through ventilators and other multi-organ support), finance permitting. By choosing not to prolong life unnecessarily, valuable NHS resources are preserved, allowing them to be spent on other areas of the NHS.
- Many procedures prolong patients' lives and result in them having additional morbidities, which they may not have had if it were not for the initial intervention. For example, by inserting a stent for a patient after a heart attack, you may prevent them from passing away. However, they may develop a pulmonary embolism (lung clot) at a later date, which they may not have developed otherwise.
- Simplistically the NHS charges many patients for prescriptions, and for many generic antibiotics, the cost of the prescription exceeds the cost of the antibiotic and as such money is made from the disease. In other countries, where there is no National Health Service, such as the US, large amounts of money are made by health providers by charging for healthcare.

Conclusion

A productive society requires a healthy population, and as such, whilst in the short term resources can be saved by not treating diseases, the long-term impact of such a policy is likely to be detrimental especially in the UK, where citizens are not required to pay for the majority of health provisions.

4) *Modern veterinary medicine is more for the benefit of humans than the animals under its care.*

Explain what you understand by this statement. Argue to the contrary that veterinary medicine is concerned more with the benefit of non-human animals. How might human and non-human interests diverge within the practice of veterinary medicine?

Explain what you understand by this statement

- In treating animals, the vet's primary objective is to reduce the emotional distress of the owner caused by a suffering/diseased pet, and the actual treatment of the animal is merely secondary to this.
- The whole concept of pet ownership is primarily for the benefit of humans (for example companionship). Therefore all activities arising from it, such as veterinary pet care, are also for human benefit.
- Similarly, veterinary medicine in the livestock industry exists mainly to increase productivity, as sick or dead animals are unproductive and unprofitable. Improving welfare is just a coincidental benefit.
- Moreover, the whole livestock industry exists for the benefit of providing work and food for humans.

Argue to the contrary that veterinary medicine is concerned more with the benefit of non-human animals.

- The declaration for admission to the Royal College of Veterinary Surgeons (RCVS) states that 'above all, my constant endeavour will be to ensure the health and welfare of animals committed to my care' –this explicitly says non-human animal welfare is the primary concern

- Reducing emotional distress in owners by healing their pet is the added benefit
- In some instances where human and non-human interests diverge, veterinary medicine prioritises animal interests, for example:
  - Poorly kept/overcrowded animals may be confiscated under vet advisement from owners, even if they are well-intentioned and this causes the owner emotional distress.
  - Vets advise animal welfare legislation in food animal production, even if this result is more expensive and less desirable products for humans, for example, the UK ban on 'white' veal production by keeping young calves anaemic by feeding them only milk, free-range chicken.

How might human and non-human interests diverge within the practice of veterinary medicine?
- **Hobby/sport animals and pets:** humans may want to attempt complicated treatments with a small chance of success due to economic value, or to avoid the emotional pain of the loss of a pet, for example, chemotherapy and surgery for late-stage cancer, whereas actually, painless euthanasia may minimise suffering for the animal.
- **Livestock:** intensive farming methods designed to increase production and minimise costs may compromise animal welfare, for example, selective breeding and intensive husbandry for high milk producing cattle may cause painful infections such as mastitis. However, access to cheap animal protein helps combat human malnutrition (FAO, 2015).
- **Wildlife:** Some wildlife populations may endanger public health, for example, bovine tuberculosis (TB) being spread by badgers (Defra, 2012). In this case, a vet's job involves advising on the culling (killing) of badgers ultimately to reduce the economic burden on cattle farmers from trade restrictions due to TB positivity.
  - Equally, wildlife conservation may compromise human interests, for example, endangered tigers in India killing the livestock of villagers.

Conclusion
- The RCVS declaration also states that a vet should 'accept their responsibilities to the public, clients, the profession and the Royal College of Veterinary Surgeons' – a big part of the profession is balancing and prioritising duties to these different parties
- Ultimately, this profession aims to serve to the mutual benefit of all humans and non-human animals –in line with the One Health concept (states that human, animal and environmental health are all interconnected).

BMAT Section 3 – 2015

1) *"Computers are useless. They can only give you answers."* (Pablo Picasso)

Explain what is meant by this statement. Argue to the contrary. What are the real limits of technology?

Explain what is meant by this statement.
- This statement suggests that for something to be of value, it needs to be able to ask appropriate questions as well as provide answers.
- This statement is supported by the fact that for science to develop, new avenues and new questions need to be proposed. Without the underlying question, there is no answer and as such, no scientific advancement. For example, without individuals questioning whether cancers can be treated, it would likely not have been possible to develop anti-cancer medication such as Herceptin for breast cancer.

Argue to the contrary.
- Providing answers, especially accurate answers are invaluable. In medicine, a significant proportion of patient harm is due to preventable man-made errors, which could have been prevented through precise calculation. Studies have found a seven-fold reduction in errors following implementation of electronic prescribing, hence supporting the use of computers (Kaushal et al., 2010).
- In comparison to humans, the use of machines is often more efficient, not requiring breaks, holidays or sick days. Furthermore, during worked time, the output of a machine is generally more efficient than that of a human in the same timeframe.
- Technology can help to ensure consistency, whereas there is much higher variability in man-made products. This is particularly important with medicines, where small variations in ingredients can be potentially fatal.

What are the real limits of technology?
- Human knowledge limits technology. One can only train a computer to perform an act, which a human could perform and understand.
- An over-reliance on technology is dangerous, especially in sensitive fields. Technology is prone to malfunction with servers failing as well as other contributing factors. Unfortunately, it is not an option for equipment to fail in an Intensive Care Unit where a matter of seconds without intervention can be fatal. Thus, many technological barriers are implemented to ensure that if one technology fails, a 'backup mechanism' is in place.

2) *"That which can be asserted without evidence can be dismissed without evidence."* (Christopher Hitchens)

Explain what you think Christopher Hitchens means. Argue to the contrary that some assertions do not require evidence. To what extent do you agree with the statement?

Explain what you think Christopher Hitchens means.

- This statement suggests that any comments or conclusions made without accompanying proof can be disregarded without further investigation or attention.

Argue to the contrary that some assertions do not require evidence.

- It is not possible to have specific evidence for everything. For example, we may have general evidence that a Type 1 Diabetic may respond to insulin, however in a newly diagnosed diabetic, this is no prior evidence that this particular insulin-naïve patient will respond to insulin, and in this case, a clinician will be relying on their clinical judgement to treat the patient.
- In acute outbreaks, such as Ebola and H5N1 there is often insufficient time to obtain sufficient evidence. In cases such as this, where the alternative is usually certain death, the use of trial medications which may not have adequate supporting evidence may be considered.
- The evidence is also a subjective matter; what one individual may regard as adequate evidence, another individual may consider disputed. For example, Dr Andrew Wakefield believed that his research showed a significant correlation between the MMR vaccine and autism, whereas the majority of clinicians believed the research to be flawed due to the small sample size and lack of reproducibility (Wakefield et al., 1998).

To what extent do you agree with the statement?

- On the other hand, there are frequent mentions of wonder drugs in sensationalist media headlines, many of which have little scientific backing. As such, it would be more appropriate to disregard these headlines rather than allowing them to mislead mainstream society.
- In the NHS, we use NICE guidelines (for example, hypertension, asthma and the like) which are based on evidence-based medicine; thus, highlighting the importance of evidence in clinical practice.
- This statement is likely to promote research which can only be a positive thing. Those with strong views are encouraged to research the evidence behind their them, with the net effect being better societal understanding.

Conclusion

Whilst assertions without evidence cannot be disregarded altogether, proposals with evidence should be prioritised in encouraging further research as well as the implementation of the evidence-based clinical practice.

3) *When treating an individual patient, a physician must also think of the wider society.*

Explain the reasoning behind this statement. Argue that a doctor should only consider the individual that he or she is treating at the time. With respect to medical treatment, to what extent can a patient's interests differ from those of the wider population?

Explain the reasoning behind this statement.

- This statement is based on the medical ethics principle of 'justice'. A physician has a duty to all of his patients, including how to share and allocate limited resources to an increasing population of patients.

Argue that a doctor should only consider the individual that he or she is treating at the time.

- 'Considering wider society' may be used as an excuse for providing suboptimal care. For example, an unethical doctor such as Dr Harold Shipman may try to justify killing approximately 200 patients by suggesting that he was thinking of broader society and reducing the strain on limited NHS resources.
- Each patient is unique, and in another sense, considering how other patients in society may have responded to treatment following a similar presentation, may be of some use. However, patients often present atypically and respond very differently. Thus, whilst general societal guidelines can be useful, a bespoke approach should be taken into account for each patient, considering their respective co-morbidities and associated factors.

With respect to medical treatment, to what extent can a patient's interests differ from those of the wider population?

- For a patient with advanced cancer, it may be in their interests to receive the latest treatment, which may not be necessarily licensed by NICE due to unjustifiable cost. For example, Provenge which can be used for metastatic prostate cancer costs between £250,000 and £500,000/QALY and as such is not funded by the NHS (NICE, 2015). It would likely be in the individual's interest to have the medication, whereas wider society cannot justify the expense when correlated with the additional life expectancy.
- Many procedures have substantial waiting lists, for example, current NHS waiting lists for knee replacements are approximately 18 weeks (The Guardian, 2017), whereas it is likely that the patient would prefer to have the procedure as soon as possible.
- On the other hand, it is generally in society's interests to provide the best available medical care in the shortest time frame to preserve workforce productivity. For every day that a patient goes without a knee replacement, it may represent an additional day of income tax revenue lost by society. Similarly, not providing the cancer patient with the best chemotherapy agent would similarly shorten their life expectancy and reduce their positive societal contribution.

Conclusion

Whilst it is important for doctors to consider wider society, this should not compromise the care of the patient in front of them. Furthermore, although the broader aims of society and an individual are unified, the limited nature of resources means that in many cases, the NHS is unable to provide the complete scope of healthcare provision for individuals, especially within their desired timescale.

4) *Just because behaviour occurs amongst animals in the wild does not mean it should be allowed within domesticated populations of the same species.*

Explain what you think is meant by this statement. Argue to the contrary. To what extent should humans interfere with the natural behaviours of animals?

Explain what is meant by this statement

- Many behaviours evolved in the wild ancestors of domesticated animals to help them survive in their often harsh environments.
- However, these behaviours may lose their purpose and even become a nuisance or danger to the owner and the animal when that animal is moved from its wild environment to a domesticated environment

- Therefore part of a vets job is prescribing treatments and procedures to eliminate such undesirable behaviours, for example:
  - Spraying in tomcats to mark territory makes the owner's house smell bad. A vet may prescribe an anti-anxiety medication or a calming pheromone infuser.
  - Male dogs may fight for females for the right to reproduce and exhibit aggressive behaviour or run away. This is why vets castrate most male dogs to limit aggressive and dangerous behaviour (and control the stray population size).

Argue to the contrary

- These behaviours evolved with a very important purpose: to increase the animals' chance of survival and to propagate its genes, and are therefore driven by a powerful evolutionary drive.
- There is often specific neural circuitry 'hardwired' in the animals' brain for these behaviours, and this is an intense area of research
- Depriving the animal of the opportunity to perform these actions may lead to behavioural abnormalities, called stereotypies, which are recognised as signs of poor welfare (Mason, 1991) for example:
  - Box walking for horses who do not get enough exercise
  - Tail biting for pigs who are frustrated, bored, and overcrowded

To what extent should humans interfere with the natural behaviour of animals?

- Modern society has deemed it acceptable to keep domesticated animals out of their natural environments (often for human benefit, for example keeping a pet for companionship; horses for sport; livestock for food).
- These animals are unable to seek out most resources for themselves (food, water, shelter, and finding mates) and the owner/keeper, therefore, must provide for all of these needs.
- Maintaining health, welfare, and freedom from suffering and disease is also the owner's duty, and it is the vet's role to support the owner in fulfilling this obligation.
- Often, behaviours that have lost their purpose will compromise welfare, and it follows that it is the owner's and vet's duty to reduce the animal's desire to perform these destructive behaviours (such as through medication or castration).
- One must balance the animal's right to perform a behaviour with its right to freedom from suffering/ behavioural frustration, and often the only solution is further behavioural modification if we want to keep the animal in a domesticated environment.

Conclusion

- Ultimately, we have already changed the lives and behaviours, and even physiologies of many species by domesticating them.
- We should, therefore, employ all tools known to us as vets and as owners, to maximise the welfare and well-being of these animals under our care, even if this involves further behaviour modification.

BMAT Section 3 – 2016

1) 'You can resist an invading army; you cannot resist an idea whose time has come.'
(Victor Hugo)

Explain the reasoning behind this statement. Argue that, on the contrary, any idea can be suppressed with sufficient force. What do you think gives power to an idea?

Explain the reasoning behind this statement.

- This statement suggests that ideological revolutions are more powerful than physical or military interventions. This statement is based on the rationale that whilst physical strength and power may have its time, the ideological will of wider society will ultimately prevail and cannot be suppressed indefinitely.

Argue that, on the contrary, any idea can be suppressed with sufficient force.

- There are many countries worldwide where freedom of speech and expression is significantly restricted and military powers predominate. Furthermore, in such countries when there have been attempts to overthrow military dictatorships, the ideological democracies have in many cases been subsequently exiled and overthrown by further military rulers. Without naming specific countries, these territories are evidence that physical power supersedes ideological revolutions.
- In many cases, the force required to quash an idea is financial as opposed to physical. For example, there have been notable cases where economic powers have threatened to 'suspend funding' for those who oppose their ideologies. Hence, financial corruption also impacts the strength of ideologies.

What do you think gives power to an idea?

- The weight of any idea (especially in science) is proportionate to its supporting evidence. For example, a new cancer drug which is evidenced by ten large studies is likely to be more powerful than an alternative cancer drug supported by a single small study.
- Additionally, publicity and recognition are essential for any breakthrough; in particular media publicity and NICE recognition for medical breakthroughs in the United Kingdom. Without adequate 'exposure', ideas irrespective of their value to society are unlikely to fulfil their potential benefit.

2) Science is not a follower of fashion nor of other social or cultural trends.

Explain what you think the statement means. Argue to the contrary. To what extent do you agree with the statement?

Explain what you think the statement means.

- This statement suggests that scientific advancements are independent of external pressures such as media and societal interests.

Argue to the contrary.

- Scientific research, as with many aspects of life, relies on funding to develop. Furthermore, funding is dependent mainly on societal trends and interests. For example, at present, there is significant global publicity regarding the impact of many cancers as well as strokes on life expectancy and quality of life. The medical consequence of which is increased research in these areas as well as more significant NHS funding for Stroke Care as well as the 2 Week NHS Cancer Referral Pathway, which assists in the early identification of cancers.

To what extent do you agree with the statement?

- On the other hand, irrespective of financial backing and media coverage, scientific developments are primarily dependent on internal will (within the researching population) as well as natural factors outside of one's control. Treatment for any condition can only be established if nature allows there to be a treatment. For example, despite the billions of pounds invested worldwide in establishing a treatment for Alzheimer's Dementia, science has been limited in its developments. Whilst cholinesterase inhibitors such as Donepezil can slow progression for many with Alzheimer's Dementia, ultimately we have not been able to find a treatment for this progressive condition.
- In many ways, social trends follow science. For example, there are many television shows, films and theatre productions based on science and medical practice. Many children's' toys are also based on the equipment used by doctors and laboratory professionals.

Conclusion

Whilst societal interests contribute to areas of scientific focus and investment, ultimately scientific advancements are independent of this and are often restricted by natural and knowledge-based limitations.

3) The option of taking strike action should not be available to doctors as they have a special duty of care to their patients.

Explain what is meant by this statement. Argue that it should be possible for doctors to go on strike as other workers do. To what extent should doctors' duty of care to patients affect the conditions of their employment?

Explain what is meant by this statement.

This statement suggests that the action of striking is in contrary to a doctor's duty of care.

Argue that it should be possible for doctors to go on strike as other workers do.

- It can be argued that by striking, doctors are protecting the long-term interests of their patients. Whilst in the short term, procedures and appointments may be cancelled; in the long term, doctors will have the appropriate working conditions and resources to manage their patients optimally.
- A restriction preventing doctors from striking may result in working conditions that do not allow doctors to appropriately manage patients, which not only will impact immediate patient care but in the long term will deter future aspiring professionals from joining the medical profession.

To what extent should doctors' duty of care to patients affect the conditions of their employment?

- Doctors' conditions of employment should be optimised towards patient care. On the one hand, there should not be an overworking requirement, where doctors are overworked resulting in the provision of dangerous medical care and on the other hand, doctors should not be allowed to strike indefinitely to obtain employment conditions that may not be favourable to societal health.

- It is vital also to accept other factors which should also be taken into consideration in doctors' conditions of employment. These include the welfare of a doctor as well as the impact of contracts encouraging and discouraging future generations of medical professionals.

4) If we truly care about the welfare of animals, we must recognise them as fellow members of our communities with their own political rights and status.

Explain the thinking behind this statement. Argue that it is not necessary to confer political rights or status upon animals in order to ensure their welfare. To what extent is it possible to incorporate the interests of animals into political institutions?

Explain the thinking behind this statement

- Since we, as a society, truly care about the welfare of humans, and all humans are generally considered full members of our communities with their own political rights and status, then animals must also be community members with political rights and status, just like humans, in order to enjoy the same level of welfare as other humans.

- It assumes that real welfare depends on political status, thus politically-speaking, animal welfare will only be truly protected and prioritised in legislation if animals are considered to have their own rights, such as the right to freedom from abuse, disease and suffering.

Argue that it is not necessary to confer political rights or status upon animals to ensure their welfare

- As it is humans who shape welfare legislation rather than animals (given that no animal would be capable of being elected into or voting/speaking in office to represent fellow animals), the political rights of animals are almost immaterial, and instead what is important is how highly we as humans value their welfare.

- One may think it necessary to have good welfare without thinking they have political rights.

- The animal welfare legislation in place today provides the best case for this: animals are generally considered to have quite limited rights and status, yet there is a good standard of protection of many aspects of welfare for a wide range of species in the UK Animal Welfare Act (2006).

- There may be other reasons to care about welfare that are unrelated to animal rights. For example, good welfare ensures good productivity for food production animals; hence a farmer may genuinely care about the welfare of his animals without believing in their political rights to ensure his own business is profitable.

To what extent is it possible to incorporate the interests of animals into political institutions?

- It is possible to incorporate animal interests into political institutions, as we have done so already to a moderate extent in the UK.

- However, animals do not currently have political rights equivalent to that of humans and are unable to represent their own interests in government. Therefore they rely on humans to assess and represent their interests in government.

366

- There is an entire branch of UK government called Defra (Department of Environment, Food, and Rural Affairs) set up to deal mainly with animal-related issues, including animal welfare
    - They have been involved in gathering evidence for and passing many welfare acts, for example, Animal Welfare act (2006), Hunting Act (2004).
    - Animal (Scientific Procedures) Act 1986 was also passed before Defra was set up, so there was clearly some representation of animal interest before them as well
- There are many official advisory bodies, such as the Farm Animal Welfare Committee (FAWC), which advises Defra, and promotes the agenda that 'animals should have a life worth living' through the Five Freedoms (such as the freedom from fear, hunger and thirst, freedom to express normal behaviour, and so on).
    - These freedoms are a form of animal right and are underpinned by scientific research.
- There are also numerous independent public driven lobby groups, most famously People for the Ethical Treatment of Animals (PETA), or charities such as the Royal Society for the Prevention of Cruelty in Animals (RSPCA) which put public opinion pressure on the government to pass specific laws.

Conclusion

- Animals are unable to represent themselves in political institutions, so they ultimately rely on humans to represent their interests and advocate for good welfare. Although, for this reason, human welfare will probably always be prioritised.
- From a practical perspective, the human motivation for representing animal interests in government is immaterial if it achieves good welfare, be it selfish to improve animal productivity, or due to the belief that animals have rights.
- We should continue along the right track to putting comprehensive animal welfare legislation in place in all countries.

BMAT Section 3 – 2017

1) 'He who has never learned to obey cannot be a good commander' (Aristotle)

Explain what you understand by this statement. Argue to the contrary. To what extent do you agree that someone cannot be a good leader without learning how to follow?

Explain what you understand by this statement.
This statement suggests that successful leadership requires a willingness and experience of obedience.

Argue to the contrary
It may be argued that other qualities such as being a powerful orator and being trustworthy are more important to successful leadership. This is evidenced by historical leaders such as Martin Luther King and Gandhi who effectively demonstrated the aforementioned qualities.
Additionally, it may be argued that learning to obey is not a pre-requisite to becoming a good commander, and instead one may become a commander and acquire such skills. Thus, whilst obedience is of value, it should not limit one's ability to lead or command.

To what extent do you agree that someone cannot be a good leader without learning how to follow?
Almost all commanders have a superior, to whom they are accountable and as such must be receptive to their requests. For example, a hospital consultant is accountable to the hospital medical director, who in turn is accountable to local commissioning groups and the Department of Health, who are accountable to the minister for health, prime minister and electoral population respectively. Failure to obey the requests of superiors will likely result in a short-lived and ineffective leadership.

Many may argue that consultants are leaders in the acute hospital settings. Effective management of the MDT workforce involves being receptive to the input of nurses, junior doctors and auxiliary health professionals.

In conclusion, obeying and being receptive to the requests, input and demands of others is essential for all, especially those in positions of command. Nonetheless, it would be unnecessarily restrictive to suggest that obeying must be learned prior to assuming a position of leadership, and instead I believe that obeying can equally be learned by good commanders who share equally important additional qualities such as trust, respect and compassion.

2. The only moral obligation a scientist has is to reveal the truth.

What is the reasoning behind this statement? Present an argument to the contrary. To what extent do you agree that the only moral duty a scientist has is to reveal the truth?

What is the reasoning behind this statement?

This statement is based on the rational that research should be driven by one's moral compass rather than any financial, personal or cultural motivation.

Present an argument to the contrary.
With many aspects of science, the truth is disputed and hence what one scientist may regard as 'the truth' may be disputed by another professional. Complete acceptance of the current status quo will inhibit scientific development and critical analysis of possible inaccuracies.

It may also be argued that scientist and researchers should be driven by the requirements of society, which do not always correlate with the truth. For example, during the Ebola outbreak which started in 2014, scientists were intent on finding a cure for this dangerous virus. Whilst a treatment would be ideal, society equally required hope and motivation from researchers in order to mobilise people and volunteers to fight against this fast spreading virus. Whilst a definitive cure has not been found, supportive measures and on-going research has been welcomed by the international community.

The concept of placebo effects demonstrates how the 'scientific truth' is not always required to obtain a positive outcome. With some conditions, by simply suggesting to a patient that they are being given a treatment, this can improve their symptoms significantly. This has been seen in the management of a range of conditions varying from depression to epilepsy. Thus, the truth is not always required in medical management.

To what extent do you agree that the only moral duty a scientist has is to reveal the truth?
Inaccurate scientific research can have profound implications. This can be seen in the case of the MMR Autism study published in The Lancet (Wakefield et al, 1998) which has resulted in reduced vaccination uptake worldwide and increased prevalence of previously near eradicated conditions such as measles. Hence, no research is better than potentially inaccurate research.

Furthermore, research motivated by sponsors, funding and political interests not only misleads the general public, but it also misleads fellow scientists resulting in inappropriate follow-up research with associated wastage of resources and valuable researchers' time.

In conclusion, whilst in most cases the truth provides the optimum outcome, it is not always required as seen in the case of placebo effects. As such, scientists should aim to preserve the truth alongside ensuring the most beneficial societal outcome.

3. The health care profession is wrong to treat ageing as if it were a disease.

What do you understand by this statement? Argue that it is not wrong to treat the effects of ageing as if they were a disease. To what extent do you agree with the statement?

What do you understand by this statement?
Diseases are generally regarded as conditions that cause a decline in health with associated symptoms and similarly ageing causes a health decline. Furthermore, ageing causes generally characteristic changes including atrophy of cerebral cells with the resultant effect on memory, cognition and decreased mobility.

Argue that it is not wrong to treat the effects of ageing as if they were a disease.

- By labelling ageing as a disease, it allows more funding to be targeted towards reducing its effects and finding new management approaches; thus helping to prevent unnecessary hospital admissions with its associated costs and implications.

- Diseases are often defined as conditions with characteristic symptoms and similarly ageing has characteristic features, hence it would be appropriate to classify ageing as a disease.

To what extent do you agree with the statement?

- On the other hand, whilst the NHS provides healthcare for all, the elderly wishing to have private healthcare would be further deterred by the likely increased premiums from this 'additional disease'.

- Furthermore, it would be unfair to characterise all elderly people in the same way, with some 90 year olds driving, working and self-caring far more independently than their younger counterparts. Additionally, diseases have almost exclusively negative associations and symptoms whereas there are many benefits to ageing such as generally increased experience and knowledge base.

- We're would one draw the line? Is elderly defined as over 60, 80 or even over 45. Additionally, with the increasing life expectancy globally, would this definition need to be reviewed regularly.

- Such policies may also lead to a slippery slope effect. Being newborn or very young is also a risk factor for medical conditions and hence some may argue that these patients should also be labelled as having a 'disease' due to their generally decreased mobility, independence and often increased susceptibility to infections.

In conclusion, whilst ageing generally has characteristic features, due to the varying speed at which people age and the likely negative impact on one's ability to obtain health insurance and a possible slippery slope effect for other health risk factors, I do not believe that it would be beneficial to label ageing as a disease.

Printed in Poland
by Amazon Fulfillment
Poland Sp. z o.o., Wrocław